普通高等教育规划教材

# International Accounting

# 国际会计学

主编　吴泽福

机 械 工 业 出 版 社

本书以国际会计准则（IASB 准则）与美国会计准则（FASB 准则）为蓝本，情景式地解释了重要会计术语的基本定义，灵活地运用准则解决案例中的问题，细致地剖析了国际会计准则中存在的优缺点，详尽地介绍了国际会计的发展状况和热点问题。本书正是基于这一宗旨安排的各章节内容，并确保文字简练、易学、易懂，同时在每一章的结尾附有讨论问题、练习题及其答案，使学生在学习新内容之前复习并应用该章的重点内容。

本书适合中高年级本科生及研究生水平的国际会计课程，对于全世界的执业会计师、财务管理人员、投资管理人员、大学教师和行业监管者也大有裨益，还可作为国际会计、财务管理人员、法律工作者等各界人士解决国际财务会计实际问题的参考用书。

**图书在版编目（CIP）数据**

国际会计学：英文/吴泽福主编. —北京：机械工业出版社，2015.5（2023.1 重印）
普通高等教育规划教材
ISBN 978-7-111-49175-0

Ⅰ.①国… Ⅱ.①吴… Ⅲ.①国际会计—高等学校—教材—英文
Ⅳ.①F811.2

中国版本图书馆 CIP 数据核字（2015）第 005551 号

机械工业出版社（北京市百万庄大街 22 号 邮政编码 100037）
策划编辑：商红云 责任编辑：商红云 马碧娟 李书全
版式设计：霍永明 责任校对：赵 蕊
封面设计：张 静 责任印制：郜 敏
北京盛通商印快线网络科技有限公司印刷
2023 年 1 月第 1 版第 2 次印刷
184mm×260mm · 21 印张 · 515 千字
标准书号：ISBN 978-7-111-49175-0
定价：59.90 元

电话服务
客服电话：010-88361066
010-88379833
010-68326294

网络服务
机 工 官 网：www.cmpbook.com
机 工 官 博：weibo.com/cmp1952
金 书 网：www.golden-book.com
机工教育服务网：www.cmpedu.com

# 前　言

21世纪，世界经济日益走向全球化，在新世纪、新经济、新环境中，为了适应全球贸易经济和全球资本市场发展的需要，1973年创立的国际会计准则委员会（IASC）改组为国际会计准则理事会（IASB），促使全球的会计准则不断走向高质量，进一步提高了企业财务会计报告的透明度、可比性和充分披露。在我国蓬勃发展的会计学事业中，掌握国际财务会计报告标准和技巧成为迫切的任务，主要体现在以下两个方面：

第一，随着改革开放的不断深入，中国在国际市场上的地位不断提高，国家综合实力也不断增强，而会计制度作为经济活动的重要保障，需要与时俱进，与国际会计准则进一步接轨。自2006年2月15日财政部颁布新的《企业会计准则——基本准则》和38项具体会计准则以来，我国的会计准则和规章迅速地向国际标准趋同。

第二，随着我国引进外资的进一步深入，越来越多的企业倾向于开拓其全球化的国际市场，因而，国际会计在企业的实际运用变得越来越重要，会计从业人员掌握一门国际会计学成为其从事会计工作的一种基本的必备素质。同时，只有具有国际化视角和能力的会计从业人员，才能更好地帮助企业实现全球化发展，实现企业的全球发展战略。

基于以上原因，编写出一本适合中国经济发展的参考教材就显得任重而道远。

本书以国际会计准则（IASB准则）与美国会计准则（FASB准则）为蓝本，情景式地解释了重要会计术语的基本定义，灵活地运用准则解决案例中的问题，细致地剖析了国际会计准则中存在的优缺点，详尽地介绍了国际会计的发展状况和热点问题。本书正是基于这一宗旨安排各章节内容，并确保文字简练、易学、易懂，同时在每一章的结尾附有讨论问题、练习题及其答案，使学生在学习新内容之前复习并应用该章的重点内容。

本书主要围绕国际会计准则、国际会计假设、国际会计原则、国际会计的实务处理和会计相关问题进行内容安排。全书包括三个部分。第一部分主要介绍会计核算的基本概念和方法，共六章。第一章主要介绍会计行业在国家经济生活中的重要性；第二章分析了经济生活中的交易行为；第三章介绍了会计记录经济业务的流程；第四章主要阐述了会计循环中各要素之间的比较；第五章介绍了会计系统的组成和流程；第六章具体指出了会计实践在经济生活中是如何发挥作用的。第二部分介绍了日常经济生活中会计实践在科目上的具体操作，共八章，这八章的内容囊括了存货、内控、应收科目、流动资产、负债、股票交易以及税务等方面的知识。第三部分介绍了现金流量表等方面的基本内容。本书内所有涉及税法的内容均指的美国税务法律规定。

本书适合中高年级本科生及研究生水平的国际会计课程，对于全世界的执业会计师、财务管理人员、投资管理人员、大学教师和行业监管者也大有裨益，还可作为国际会计、财务管理人员、法律工作者等各界人士解决国际财务会计实际问题的参考用书。

本书由国际注册会计师、华侨大学教授吴泽福主编，负责提纲拟定、内容审定及定稿前的修改、补充和总纂。参加本书编写的人员还有华侨大学工商管理学院的王莹、邓浩、朱丽华、李培、徐波，王莹负责第一～三章的编写，邓浩负责第四～六章的编写，朱丽华负责第七～九章的编写，李培负责第十～十二章的编写，徐波负责第十三～十五章的编写。

编写一部好的教材是一项艰巨的工程，凝聚着众多编写者的心血和经验积累。由于编写时间仓促，加上编者水平有限，书中难免有不妥之处，真诚希望广大读者不断地对本书提出好的意见和建议，以使将来再版时能够满足读者更高的要求。

# Contents

前言
Chapter 1 **Introduction to Accounting and Business** ······ 1
1. Nature of Business and Accounting ······ 2
2. Generally Accepted Accounting Principles ······ 7
3. The Accounting Equation ······ 9
4. Business Transactions and the Accounting Equation ······ 9
5. Financial Statements ······ 13

Chapter 2 **Analyzing Transactions** ······ 20
1. Using Accounts to Record Transactions ······ 21
2. Posting of Journal Entries to Accounts ······ 28
3. Trial Balance ······ 42
4. Discovery and Correction of Errors ······ 43

Chapter 3 **The Adjusting Process** ······ 50
1. Nature of the Adjusting Process ······ 51
2. Recording Adjusting Entries ······ 52
3. Summary of the Adjustment Process ······ 61
4. Adjusted Trial Balance ······ 67

Chapter 4 **Completing the Accounting Cycle** ······ 74
1. Flow of Accounting Information ······ 75
2. Financial Statements ······ 78
3. Closing Entries ······ 81
4. The Accounting Cycle ······ 84
5. Fiscal Year ······ 84

Chapter 5 **Accounting Systems** ······ 88
1. Basic Accounting Systems ······ 89
2. Manual Accounting Systems ······ 89
3. Adapting Manual Accounting Systems ······ 100
4. Computerized Accounting Systems ······ 101

Chapter 6 **Accounting for Merchandising Businesses** …… 106
1. Nature of Merchandising Businesses …… 107
2. Financial Statement of Merchandising Businesses …… 107
3. Merchandising Transactions …… 112
4. The Adjusting and Closing Process …… 124

Chapter 7 **Inventory** …… 131
1. Control of Inventory …… 132
2. Inventory Cost Flow Assumptions …… 135
3. Cost of Inventory on Perpetual Inventory System …… 140
4. Inventory Costing Methods under a Periodic Inventory System …… 142
5. Reporting Merchandise Inventory in the Financial Statements …… 143

Chapter 8 **Internal Control and Cash** …… 150
1. Internal Control …… 151
2. The Limitations of Internal Control—Costs and Benefits …… 152
3. Elements of Internal Control …… 152
4. Cash Controls over Receipts and Payments …… 157
5. Bank Accounts …… 161
6. Bank Reconciliation …… 163
7. Special – Purpose Cash Funds …… 167
8. Financial Statements Reporting of Cash …… 168

Chapter 9 **Receivables** …… 173
1. Classification of Receivables …… 174
2. Uncollectible Receivables …… 175
3. Direct Write-Off Method for Uncollectible Accounts …… 176
4. Allowance Method for Uncollectible Accounts …… 177
5. Comparing Direct Write – Off and Allowance Methods …… 183
6. Notes Receivable …… 184
7. Reporting Receivables on the Balance Sheet …… 187

Chapter 10 **Fixed Assets and Intangible Assets** …… 196
1. Nature of Fixed Assets …… 197
2. Accounting for Depreciation …… 201
3. Disposal of Fixed Assets …… 206
4. Natural Resources …… 212
5. Intangible Assets …… 212
6. Financial Reporting for Fixed Assets and Intangible Assets …… 215

Chapter 11 **Current Liabilities and Payroll** ······ 220
1. Current Liabilities ······ 221
2. Payroll and Payroll Taxes ······ 223
3. Accounting for Payroll and Payroll Taxes ······ 227
4. Employees' Fringe Benefits ······ 232
5. Contingent Liabilities ······ 235

Chapter 12 **Stock Transactions, and Dividends** ······ 239
1. Nature of a Corporation ······ 240
2. Stockholders' Equity ······ 242
3. Paid – In Capital from Issuing Stock ······ 242
4. Accounting for Dividends ······ 246
5. Treasury Stock Transactions ······ 248
6. Reporting Stockholders' Equity ······ 249
7. Stock Splits ······ 252

Chapter 13 **Bonds Payable and Investments in Bonds** ······ 256
1. Financing Corporations ······ 257
2. Characteristics and Pricing of Bonds Payable ······ 258
3. Accounting for Bonds Payable ······ 262
4. Payment and Redemption of Bonds Payable ······ 266
5. Investment in Bonds ······ 268
6. Corporation Balance Sheet ······ 271
7. Effective Interest Rate Method of Amortization ······ 273

Chapter 14 **Income Taxes, Unusual Income Items, and Investments in Stocks** ······ 279
1. Corporations Income Taxes ······ 280
2. Reporting Unusual Items on the Income Statement ······ 283
3. Earnings per Common Share ······ 287
4. Comprehensive Income ······ 289
5. Accounting for Investment in Stocks ······ 290

Chapter 15 **Statement of Cash Flows** ······ 300
1. Reporting Cash Flows ······ 301
2. Statement of Cash Flows—The Indirect Method ······ 305
3. Statement of Cash Flows—The Direct Method ······ 314

References ······ 325

# Chapter 1

# Introduction to Accounting and Business

**Objectives**

1. Describe the nature of a business and the role of ethics and accounting in business.
2. Summarize the development of accounting principles and relate them to practice.
3. State the accounting equation and define each element of the equation.
4. Illustrate how to record business transactions in the accounting equation.
5. Describe the financial statements of proprietor and explain how they interrelate.

# 1. Nature of Business and Accounting

You can probably list some examples of companies like Google with which you have recently done business. Your examples might be large companies, such as The Coca- Cola Company, Dell Inc. , or Amazon. com. They might be local companies, such as gas stations or grocery stores, or perhaps employers. They might be restaurants, law firms, or medical offices. What do all these examples have in common that identify them as businesses?

In general, a business is an organization in which basic resources (inputs), such as materials and labor, are assembled and processed to provide goods or services (outputs) to customers. Businesses come in all sizes, from a local coffee house to a Daimler Chrysler, which sells several billion dollars worth of cars and trucks each year. A business's customers are individuals or other businesses who purchase goods or services in exchange for money or other items of value. In contrast, a church is not a business, because those who receive its services are not legally obligated to pay for them.

The objective of most businesses is to maximize profits. Profit is the difference between the amounts received from customers for goods or services provided and the amounts paid for the inputs used to provide the goods or services. Some businesses operate with an objective other than to maximize profits. The objective of such not-for-profit businesses is to provide some benefit to society, such as medical research or conservation of natural resources. In other cases, governmental units such as cities operate water works or sewage treatment plants on a nonprofit basis. We will focus in this text on businesses operating to earn a profit. Keep in mind, though, that many of the same concepts and principles apply to not-for-profit businesses as well.

## TYPES OF BUSINESSES

There are three different types of businesses that are operated for profit: service, merchandising, and manufacturing businesses. Each type of business has unique characteristics.

**Service businesses** provide services rather than products to customers. **Merchandising businesses** sell products they purchase from other businesses to customers. In this sense, merchandisers bring products and customers together. **Manufacturing businesses** transfer materials into products and sell to merchandisers. Examples of merchandising (manufacturing or service) businesses and some of the products (or services) they sell are shown in Exhibit 1-1.

**Exhibit 1-1 Types of businesses**

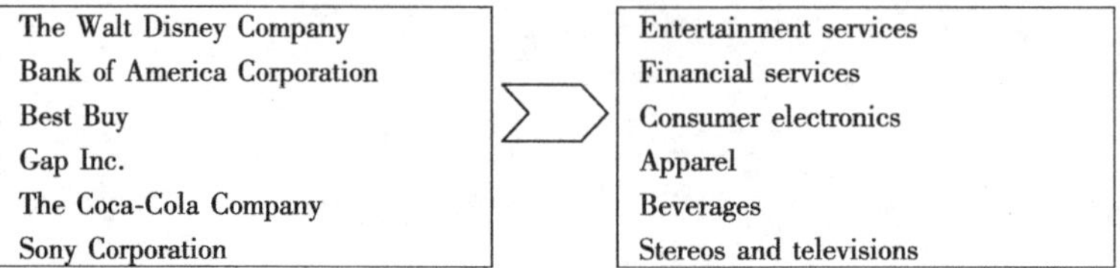

## TYPES OF BUSINESS ORGANIZATIONS

The common forms of business organization are proprietorship, partnership, corporation, or limited liability company. Each of these forms and their major characteristics are listed below.

A **proprietorship** is owned by one individual, of which cost of organizing is low and is limited to financial resources of the owner and is used by small businesses.

A **partnership** is similar to a proprietorship except that it is owned by two or more individuals and combines the skills and resources of more than one person.

A **corporation** is organized under state or federal statutes as a separate legal taxable entity and generates 90% of the total dollars of business receipts received, includes ownership divided into shares of stock, sold to shareholders (stockholders) and is able to obtain large amounts of resources by issuing stock and is used by large businesses.

A **limited liability company** (**LLC**) combines attributes of a partnership and a corporation in that it is organized as a corporation. However, an LLC can elect to be taxed as a partnership and is a popular alternative to a partnership, which has tax and liability advantages to the owners.

The three types of businesses we discussed earlier—service, merchandising, and manufacturing—may be organized as proprietorship, partnership, corporation, or LLC. Because of the large amount of resources required to operate a manufacturing business, most manufacturing businesses are corporations. Likewise, most large retailers such as Wal-Mart, Home Depot, and JC Penney are corporations.

## BUSINESS STAKEHOLDERS

A **business stakeholder** is a person or entity that has an interest in the economic performance and well-being of a business. For example, owners, suppliers, customers, and employees are all stakeholders in a business. Business stakeholders can be classified into one of the four categories illustrated in Exhibit 1-2.

**Exhibit 1-2 Business stakeholders**

| Business Stakeholder | Interest in the Business | Examples |
|---|---|---|
| Capital market stakeholders | Providers of major financing for the business | Banks and owners |
| Product or service market stakeholders | Buyers of products or services and vendors to the business | Customers and suppliers |
| Government stakeholders | Collect taxes and fees from the business and its employees | Federal, state, and local governments |
| Internal stakeholders | Individuals employed by the business | Employees and managers |

**Capital market stakeholders** provide the major financing for the business in order for the business to begin and continue its operations. Banks and other long-term creditors have an economic interest in recovering the amount they loaned the business plus interest. Owners want to maximize the economic value of their investments and thus also have an economic interest in the business.

**Product or service market stakeholders** include customers who purchase the business's products or services as well as the vendors who supply inputs to the business. Customers have an economic interest in the continued success of the business. For example, customers who purchase advance tickets from Southwest Airlines Co. have an economic interest in whether Southwest Airlines Co. will stay in business. Similarly, suppliers are stakeholders in the continued success of their customers as a source of business.

**Government stakeholders** have an interest in the economic performance of businesses. As a result, city and state governments often provide incentives for businesses to locate in their jurisdictions. City, county, state, and federal governments collect taxes from businesses within their jurisdictions. In addition, workers are taxed on their wages. The better a business does, the more taxes the government can collect.

**Internal stakeholders** include individuals employed by the business. The managers are those individuals whom the owners have authorized to operate the business. Managers are primarily evaluated on the economic performance of the business. Thus, managers have an incentive to maximize the economic value of the business. Owners may offer managers salary contracts that are tied directly to how well the business performs. For example, a manager might receive a percentage of the profits or a percentage of the increase in profits. Employees provide services to the company they work for in exchange for pay. Thus, employees have an interest in the economic performance of the business, because their jobs depend upon it.

## ROLE OF ETHICS IN BUSINESS

The moral principles that guide the conduct of individuals are called ethics. Unfortunately, business managers can be pressured to violate personal ethics. Such was the case for a number of companies listed in Exhibit 1-3, that engaged in fraudulent business practices and accounting cover-ups in the early 2000s.

**Exhibit 1-3 Accounting and business fraud in the 2000s**

| Company | Nature of scandal | Results |
|---|---|---|
| American International Group Inc. (AIG) | Used sham accounting transactions to inflate performance | CEO resigned. Executives indicted. AIG paid $ 126 million in fines |
| Computer Associates International Inc. | Fraudulently inflated its financial results | CEO and senior executives indicted. Five executives plead guilty. $ 225 million fine |
| Enron | Fraudulently inflated its financial results | Bankruptcy. Criminal charges against senior executives, $ 60 billion in stock market losses |
| HealthSouth | Overstated performance by $ 4 billion in false entries | Senior executives criminally indicted |
| Tyco International, Ltd. | Failed to disclose secret loans to executives that were subsequently forgiven | CEO forced to resign and subjected to frozen asset order and criminal proceedings |
| WorldCom | Misstated financial results by nearly $ 9 billion | Bankruptcy. Criminal conviction of CEO and CFO. Over $ 100 billion in stock market losses. Directors forced to pay $ 18 million |

The companies listed in Exhibit 1-3 were caught in the midst of ethical lapses that led to fines, firings, and criminal and/or civil prosecution. The second column of Exhibit 1-3 identifies the nature of scandal. The third column of the table identifies some of the results of these events. In most cases, senior and mid-level executives lost their jobs and were sued by upset investors. In some cases, the executives were also criminally prosecuted and are serving prison terms.

What went wrong for these companies and executives? The answer to this question involves the following three factors.

(1) Individual character.

(2) Firm culture.

(3) Laws and enforcement.

**Individual Character**

An ethical businessperson displays character by embracing honesty, integrity, and fairness in the face of pressure to hide the truth. Executives often face pressures from senior managers to meet company and analysts' expectations. In many of the cases in Exhibit 1-3, executives initially justified small violations to avoid such pressures. However, these small lies became big lies as the company's financial problems became worse. By the time the abuses were discovered, the misstatements became sufficient to ruin businesses and wreck lives.

**Firm Culture**

By their behavior and attitude, senior managers of a company set the firm culture. As explained by one author, when the leader of a company is put on a pedestal, "they begin to believe they and their organizations are one-of-a-kind, that they're changing the face of the industry. They desire rewards and benefits beyond any other CEOs (chief executive officers)." In most of the firms shown in Exhibit 1-3, the senior managers created a culture of greed and indifference to the truth. This culture flowed down to lower-level managers, creating an environment of short cuts, greed, and lies that ultimately resulted in financial fraud.

**Laws and Enforcement**

As a result of the accounting and business frauds shown in Exhibit 1-3, US Congress passed Sarbanes-Oxley Act of 2002 (SOX) to monitor the behavior of accounting and business. SOX established a new oversight body for the accounting profession called the Public Company Accounting Oversight Board (PCAOB), and standards for independence, corporate responsibility, and disclosure.

## THE ROLE OF ACCOUNTING IN BUSINESS

What is the role of accounting in business? The simplest answer to this question is that accounting provides information for managers to use in operating the business. In addition, accounting provides information to other stakeholders to use in assessing the economic performance and condition of the business.

In a general sense, accounting can be defined as an information system that provides reports to stakeholders about the economic activities and condition of a business. As we indicated earlier in this chapter, we will focus our discussions on accounting and its role in business. However, many of the concepts in this text apply also to individuals, governments, and other types of organizations.

You may think of accounting as the "language of business". This is because accounting is the means by which business information is communicated to the stakeholders. For example, accounting reports summarizing the profitability of a new product help The Coca-Cola Company's management decide whether to continue selling the product. Likewise, financial analysts use accounting reports in deciding whether to recommend the purchase of Coca-Cola's stock. Banks use accounting reports in determining the amount of credit to extend to Coca-Cola. Suppliers use accounting reports in deciding whether to offer credit for Coca-Cola's purchases of supplies and raw materials. State and federal governments use accounting reports as a basis for assessing taxes on Coca-Cola.

The process by which accounting provides information to business stakeholders is as follows.

(1) Identify stakeholders.

(2) Assess stakeholders' informational needs.

(3) Design the accounting information system to meet stakeholders' needs.

(4) Record economic data about business activities and events.

(5) Prepare accounting reports for stakeholders.

As illustrated in Exhibit 1-4, stakeholders use accounting reports as a primary, although not the only, source of information on which they base their decisions. Stakeholders use other information as well. For example, in deciding whether to extend credit to a local retail store, a banker would not only use the store's accounting reports, but might also visit the store and inquire about the owner's reputation in the business community.

**Exhibit 1-4 Accounting information and stakeholders of business**

**Providing Information to Users**

1. Identify stakeholders — Internal: Owners, Managers, Employees | Stakeholders | External: Customers, Creditors, Government

2. Assess stakeholders' informational needs

3. Design the accounting information system to meet stakeholders' needs

4. Record economic data about business activities and events

Accounting Information System

5. Prepare accounting reports for stakeholders

## PROFESSION OF ACCOUNTING

You may think that all accounting is the same. However, you will find several specialized fields of accounting in practice. The two most common are financial accounting and managerial accounting. Other fields include cost accounting, environmental accounting, tax accounting, accounting systems, international accounting, not-for-profit accounting, and social accounting.

**Financial accounting** is primarily concerned with the recording and reporting of economic data and activities for a business. Although such reports provide useful information for managers, they are the primary reports for owners, creditors, governmental agencies, and the public. For example, if you wanted to buy some stock in PepsiCo Inc., American Airlines, or McDonald's, how would you know in which company to invest? One way is to review financial reports and compare the financial performance and condition of each company. The purpose of financial accounting is to provide such reports.

**Managerial accounting**, or **management accounting**, uses both financial accounting and estimated data to aid management in running day-to-day operations and in planning future operations. Management accountants gather and report information that is relevant and timely to the decision-making needs of management. For example, management might need information on alternative ways to finance the construction of a new building. Alternatively, management might need information on whether to expand its operations into a new product line. Thus, reports to management can differ widely in form and content.

## 2. Generally Accepted Accounting Principles

Financial accountants follow generally accepted accounting principles (GAAP) in preparing reports. These reports allow investors and other stakeholders to compare one company to another. To illustrate the importance of generally accepted accounting principles, assume that each sports conference in college football used different rules for counting touchdowns. For example, assume that the Pacific Athletic Conference (PAC 10) counted a touchdown as six points and the Atlantic Coast Conference (ACC) counted a touchdown as two points. It would be difficult to evaluate the teams under such different scoring systems. A standard set of rules and a standard scoring system help fans compare teams across conferences. Likewise, a standard set of generally accepted accounting principles allows for the comparison of financial performance and condition across companies.

Accounting principles and concepts develop from research, accepted accounting practices, and pronouncements of authoritative bodies. Currently, the Financial Accounting Standards Board (FASB) is the authoritative body having the primary responsibility for developing accounting principles. The FASB publishes Statements of Financial Accounting Standards as well as interpretations of these standards.

Because generally accepted accounting principles impact how companies report and what they report, all stakeholders are interested in the setting of these principles. Thus, standards are established according to a process that seeks and considers input from all affected parties. The standard-setting activities of the FASB are published and made available at http://www.fasb.org.

In this chapter and throughout this text, we emphasize accounting principles and concepts. It is through this emphasis on the "why" of accounting as well as the "how" that you will gain an understanding of the full significance of accounting. In the following paragraphs, we discuss the business entity concept and the cost concept.

## THE BUSINESS ENTITY CONCEPT

The individual business unit is the business entity for which economic data are needed. This entity could be an automobile dealer, a department store, or a grocery store. The business entity must be identified, so that the accountant can determine which economic data should be analyzed, recorded, and summarized in reports.

The business entity concept is important because it limits the economic data in the accounting system to data related directly to the activities of the business. In other words, the business is viewed as an entity separate from its owners, creditors, or other stakeholders. For example, the accountant for a business with one owner (a proprietorship) would record the activities of the business only, not the personal activities, property, or debts of the owner.

## THE COST CONCEPT

If a building is bought for $150,000, that amount should be entered into the buyer's accounting records. The seller may have been asking $170,000 for the building up to the time of the sale. The buyer may have initially offered $130,000 for the building. The building may have been assessed at $125,000 for property tax purposes. The buyer may have received an offer of $175,000 for the building the day after it was acquired. These latter amounts have no effect on the accounting records because they did not result in an exchange of the building from the seller to the buyer. The cost concept is the basis for entering the exchange price, or cost, of $150,000 into the accounting records for the building.

Continuing the illustration, the $175,000 offer received by the buyer the day after the building was acquired indicates that it was a bargain purchase at $150,000. To use $175,000 in the accounting records, however, would record an illusory or unrealized profit. If, after buying the building, the buyer accepts the offer and sells the building for $175,000, a profit of $25,000 is then realized and recorded. The new owner would record $175,000 as the cost of the building.

Using the cost concept involves two other important accounting concepts—objectivity and the unit of measure.

**The objectivity concept** requires that the accounting records and reports be based upon objective evidence. In exchanges between a buyer and a seller, both try to get the best price. Only the final agreed-upon amount is objective enough for accounting purposes. If the amounts at which properties were recorded were constantly being revised upward and downward based on offers, appraisals, and opinions, accounting reports could soon become unstable and unreliable.

**The unit of measure concept** requires that economic data be recorded in dollars. Money is a common unit of measurement for reporting uniform financial data and reports.

# 3. The Accounting Equation

The resources owned by a business are its assets, including cash, land, buildings, and equipment. The rights or claims to the properties are normally divided into two principal types: the rights of creditors and the rights of owners. The rights of creditors represent debts of the business and are called **liabilities**. The rights of the owners are called **owner's equity**. The relationship between the two may be stated in the form of an equation, as follows.

Assets = Liabilities + Owner's Equity

This equation is known as the **accounting equation**. Liabilities usually are shown before owner's equity in the accounting equation because creditors have first rights to the assets. The claim of the owners is sometimes given greater emphasis by transposing liabilities to the other side of the equation, which yields:

Assets − Liabilities = Owner's Equity

To illustrate, if the assets owned by a business amount to \$1,000,000 and the liabilities amount to \$400,000, the owner's equity is equal to \$600,000, as shown below.

| Assets − Liabilities | = | Owner's Equity |
|---|---|---|
| \$1,000,000 − \$400,000 | = | \$600,000 |

# 4. Business Transactions and the Accounting Equation

An economic event or condition that directly changes an entity's financial condition or directly affects its results of operations is a business transaction. For example, purchasing land for \$50,000 is a **business transaction**. In contrast, a change in a business's credit rating does not directly affect cash or any other element of its financial condition. All business transactions can be stated in terms of changes in the elements of the accounting equation.

Assume that on November 1, 2007, John begins a business that will be known as Darming. The first phase of John's business plan is to operate Darming as a service business that provides assistance to individuals and small businesses in developing Web pages and in configuring and installing application software. John expects this initial phase of the business to last one to two years. During this period, John will gather information on the software and hardware needs of customers. During the second phase of the business plan, John plans to expand Darming into a personalized retailer of software and hardware for individuals and small businesses.

**Transaction a**. John deposits \$200,000 in a bank account in the name of Darming. The effect of this transaction is to increase the asset cash by \$200,000. To balance the equation, the owner's equity is increased by the same amount, as shown in Exhibit 1-5. The equity of the owner is referred to by using the owner's name and "Capital", such as "John, Capital".

**Exhibit 1-5 Transaction a**[⊖]

| | Assets | = | Owner's Equity |
|---|---|---|---|
| | Cash | = | John, Capital |
| a. | 200,000 | | 200,000 |

Note that since John is the sole owner, Darming is a proprietorship. The accounting equation shown above relates only to the business, Darming. Under the business entity concept, John's personal assets, such as personal bank account, and liabilities are excluded from the equation.

**Transaction b.** Darming exchanged $100,000 cash for land. The land is located in a new business park with convenient access to transportation facilities. John plans to rent office space and equipment during the first phase of the business plan. During the second phase, John plans to build an office and a warehouse on the land. The purchase of the land changes the makeup of the assets, as shown in Exhibit 1-6.

**Exhibit 1-6 Transaction b**

| | Assets | | = | Owner's Equity |
|---|---|---|---|---|
| | Cash | + Land | = | John, Capital |
| Bal. | 200,000 | | | 200,000 |
| b. | −100,000 | + 100,000 | | |
| Bal. | 100,000 | 100,000 | | 200,000 |

**Transaction c.** During the month, Darming entered into a similar transaction, buying supplies for $4,000 and agreeing to pay the supplier in the near future. This type of transaction is called a purchase on account. The liability created is called an **account payable**. Items such as supplies that will be used in the business in the future are called **prepaid expenses**, which are assets. The effect of this transaction is to increase asset and liabilities by $4,000, as shown in Exhibit 1-7.

**Exhibit 1-7 Transaction c**

| | Assets | | | = | Liabilities + | Owner's Equity |
|---|---|---|---|---|---|---|
| | Cash + | Supplies + | Land | = | Accounts Payable + | John, Capital |
| Bal. | 100,000 | | 100,000 | | | 200,000 |
| c. | | +4,000 | | | +4,000 | |
| Bal. | 100,000 | 4,000 | 100,000 | | 4,000 | 200,000 |

**Transaction d.** During its first month of operations, Darming provided services to customers, earning fees of $10,000 and receiving the amount in cash. The receipt of cash increases Darming's assets and also increases John's equity in the business. In order to aid in the preparation of financial statements, the revenues of $10,000 are recorded in a separate column to the right of "John, Cap-

⊖ 本书所有图、表、会计分录中的数据单位均为美元。

ital". This is done so that the effects on owner's capital can be separately identified and summarized. Thus, this transaction is recorded as an increase in Cash and Service Income of $10,000 as shown in Exhibit 1-8.

**Exhibit 1-8 Transaction d**

| | Assets | | | = | Liabilities + Owner's Equity | | |
|---|---|---|---|---|---|---|---|
| | Cash | + Supplies | + Land | = | Accounts Payable | + John, Capital | + Service Income |
| Bal. | 100,000 | 4,000 | 100,000 | | 4,000 | 200,000 | |
| d. | +10,000 | | | | | | +10,000 |
| Bal. | 110,000 | 4,000 | 100,000 | | 4,000 | 200,000 | 10,000 |

Special terms may be used to describe certain kinds of revenue, such as sales for the sale of merchandise. Revenue from providing services is called fees earned. For example, a physician would record fees earned for services to patients. Other examples include rent revenue (money received for rent) and interest revenue (money received for interest).

Instead of requiring the payment of cash at the time services are provided or goods are sold, a business may accepts payment at a later date. Such revenues are called fees on account or sales on account. In such cases, the firm has an account receivable, which is a claim against the customer. An account receivable is an asset, and the revenue is earned as if cash had been received. When customers pay their accounts, there is an exchange of one asset for another. Cash increases, while accounts receivable decreases.

**Transaction e.** Darming also spent cash or used up other assets in earning revenue. The amounts used in this process of earning revenue are called expenses. Expenses include supplies used, wages of employees, and other assets and services used in operating the business. Darming paid the following expenses during the month: wages, $2,000; rent, $800; utilities, $400; and miscellaneous, $200. Miscellaneous expenses include small amounts paid for such items as postage, coffee, and magazine subscriptions. The effect of this group of transactions is the opposite of the effect of revenues. These transactions reduce cash and owner's equity. Like service income, the expenses are recorded in separate columns to the right of John, Capital. However, since expenses reduce owner's equity, the expenses are entered as negative amounts, as shown in Exhibit 1-9. Businesses usually record each revenue and expense transaction separately as it occurs.

**Exhibit 1-9 Transaction e**

| | Assets | | | = | Liabilities + Owner's Equity | | | | | | |
|---|---|---|---|---|---|---|---|---|---|---|---|
| | Cash | + Supplies | + Land | = | Accounts Payable | + John, Capital | + Service Income | − Wages Expense | − Rent Expense | − Utilities Expense | − Misc. Expense |
| Bal. | 110,000 | 4,000 | 100,000 | | 4,000 | 200,000 | 10,000 | | | | |
| e. | 3,400 | | | | | | | −2,000 | −800 | −400 | −200 |
| Bal. | 106,600 | 4,000 | 100,000 | | 4,000 | 200,000 | 10,000 | −2,000 | −800 | −400 | −200 |

**Transaction f.** Darming pays $1,000 to creditors during the month, and it reduces both assets and liabilities, as shown in Exhibit 1-10. The payment of an expense reduces owner's equity, as illustrated in transaction e. Paying an amount on account reduces the amount owed on a liability.

**Exhibit 1-10 Transaction f**

| | Assets | | | = | Liabilities + Owner's Equity | | | | | | |
|---|---|---|---|---|---|---|---|---|---|---|---|
| | Cash | + Supplies | + Land | = | Accounts Payable | + John, Capital | + Service Income | − Wages Expense | − Rent Expense | − Utilities Expense | − Misc. Expense |
| Bal. | 106,600 | 4,000 | 100,000 | | 4,000 | 200,000 | 10,000 | −2,000 | −800 | −400 | −200 |
| f. | −1,000 | | | | −1,000 | | | | | | |
| Bal. | 105,600 | 4,000 | 100,000 | | 3,000 | 200,000 | 10,000 | −2,000 | −800 | −400 | −200 |

**Transaction g.** At the end of the month, the cost of the supplies on hand (not yet used) is \$3,000. The remainder of the supplies (\$4,000 − \$3,000) was used in the operations of the business and is treated as an expense. This decrease of \$1,000 in supplies and owner's equity is shown in Exhibit 1-11.

**Exhibit 1-11 Transaction g**

| | Assets | | | = | Liabilities + Owner's Equity | | | | | | | |
|---|---|---|---|---|---|---|---|---|---|---|---|---|
| | Cash | + Supplies | + Land | = | Accounts Payable | + John, Capital | + Service Income | − Wages Exp. | − Rent Exp. | − Supplies Exp. | − Utilities Exp. | − Misc. Exp. |
| Bal. | 105,600 | 4,000 | 100,000 | | 3,000 | 200,000 | 10,000 | −2,000 | −800 | | −400 | −200 |
| g. | | −1,000 | | | | | | | | −1,000 | | |
| Bal. | 105,600 | 3,000 | 100,000 | | 3,000 | 200,000 | 10,000 | −2,000 | −800 | −1,000 | −400 | −200 |

**Transaction h.** At the end of the month, John withdraws \$1,000 in cash from the business for personal use. This transaction is the exact opposite of an investment in the business by the owner. Withdrawals do not represent assets or services used in the process of earning revenues. Instead, withdrawals are considered a distribution of capital to the owner. Owner withdrawals are identified by the owner's name followed by Drawing, as shown in Exhibit 1-12.

**Exhibit 1-12 Transaction h**

| | Assets | | | = | Liabilities + Owner's Equity | | | | | | | | |
|---|---|---|---|---|---|---|---|---|---|---|---|---|---|
| | Cash | + Supp. | + Land | = | Accounts Payable | + John, Capital | − John, Drawing | + Service Income | − Wages Exp. | − Rent Exp. | − Supplies Exp. | − Utilities Exp. | − Misc. Exp. |
| Bal. | 105,600 | 3,000 | 100,000 | | 3,000 | 200,000 | | 10,000 | −2,000 | −800 | −1000 | −400 | −200 |
| h. | −1,000 | | | | | | −1,000 | | | | | | |
| Bal. | 104,600 | 3,000 | 100,000 | | 3,000 | 200,000 | −1,000 | 10,000 | −2,000 | −800 | −1000 | −400 | −200 |

In summary, there are three points which apply to all types of businesses: ① The effect of every transaction is an increase or a decrease in one or more of the accounting equation elements. ② The two sides of the accounting equation are always equal. ③ The owner's equity is increased by amounts invested by the owner and is decreased by withdrawals by the owner. In addition, the owner's equity is increased by revenues and is decreased by expenses.

# 5. Financial Statements

Reports are prepared for users after transactions have been recorded and summarized. The accounting reports that provide this information are called financial statements. The principal financial statements of a proprietorship are the income statement, the statement of owner's equity, the balance sheet, and the statement of cash flows. The order in which the statements are normally prepared and the nature of the data presented in each statement are as follows.

(1) Income statement—A summary of the revenues and expenses for a specific period of time, such as a month or a year.

(2) Statement of owner's equity—A summary of the changes in the owner's equity that have occurred during a specific period of time, such as a month or a year.

(3) Balance sheet—A list of the assets, liabilities, and owner's equity as of a specific date, usually at the close of the last day of a month or a year.

(4) Statement of cash flows—A summary of the cash receipts and cash payments for a specific period of time, such as a month or a year.

The basic features of the four statements and their interrelationships are illustrated in Exhibit 1-13. The data for the statements were taken from the summary of transactions of Darming.

All financial statements should be identified by the name of the business, the title of the statement, and the date or period of time. The data presented in the income statement, the statement of owner's equity, and the statement of cash flows are for a period of time. The data presented in the balance sheet are for a specific date.

## INCOME STATEMENT

The income statement reports the revenues and expenses for a period of time, based on the **matching concept**, which is applied by matching the expenses with the revenues generated during a period by those expenses. This excess of the revenues over the expenses is called **net income** or **net profit**. If the expenses exceed the revenues, the excess is a **net loss.**

The revenue, expenses, and the net income for Darming are reported in the income statement in Exhibit 1-13. The order in which the expenses are listed in the income statement varies among businesses. One method is to list them in order of size, beginning with the larger items. Miscellaneous expense is usually shown as the last item, regardless of the amount.

The effects of revenue earned and expenses incurred during the month for Darming were shown in the equation as separate increases and decreases in each item. Net income for a period has the effect of increasing owner's equity (capital) for the period, whereas a net loss has the effect of decreasing owner's equity (capital) for the period.

**Exhibit 1-13 Financial statements for Darming**

Darming
Income Statement
For the Month Ended November 30, 2007

| | | |
|---|---|---|
| Service Income | | 10,000 |
| Expenses: | | |
| Wages expense | 2,000 | |
| Rent expense | 800 | |
| Supplies expense | 1,000 | |
| Utilities expense | 400 | |
| Miscellaneous expense | 200 | |
| Total expenses | | 4,400 |
| Net income | | 5,600 |

Darming
Statement of Owner's Equity
For the Month Ended November 30, 2007

| | | |
|---|---|---|
| John, capital, November 1, 2007 | | 0 |
| Add: Investment on November 1, 2007 | 200,000 | |
| Net income for November | 5,600 | |
| Less: Withdrawals | 1,000 | |
| Increase in owner's equity | | 204,600 |
| John, capital, November 30, 2007 | | 204,600 |

Adds net income (or subtracts net loss). Net income comes directly from the income statement

Darming
Balance Sheet
November 30, 2007

| Assets | | Liabilities | |
|---|---|---|---|
| Cash | 104,600 | Accounts payable | 3,000 |
| Supplies | 3,000 | **Owner's Equity** | |
| Land | 100,000 | John, capital | 204,600 |
| **Total assets** | **207,600** | **Total liabilities and owner's equity** | **207,600** |

The ending capital of the balance sheet comes from the statement of owner's equity

The ending of net cash flows of the statement of cash flows equals with cash balance in the balance sheet

Darming
Statement of Cash Flows
For the Month Ended November 30, 2007

| | | |
|---|---|---|
| Cash flows from operating activities: | | |
| Cash received from customers | | 10,000 |
| Deduct cash payments for expenses and payments to creditors | 4,400 | |
| **Net cash flows from operating activities** | | **5,600** |
| Cash flows from investing activities: | | |
| Cash payments for purchase of land | 100,000 | |
| **Net Cash flows from investing activities** | | **−100,000** |
| Cash flows from financing activities: | | |
| Cash received as owner's investment | | 200,000 |
| Deduct cash withdrawal by owner | 1,000 | |
| **Net cash flows from financing activities** | | **199,000** |
| **Net cash flows and November 30, 2007, cash balance** | | **104,600** |

## STATEMENT OF OWNER'S EQUITY

The statement of owner's equity reports the changes in the owner's equity for a period of time. The net income or net loss for the period must be reported in this statement. Similarly, it is prepared before the balance sheet because the amount of owner's equity at the end of the period must be reported on the balance sheet. Because of this, the statement of owner's equity is often viewed as the connecting link between the income statement and balance sheet.

Three types of transactions affected owner's equity for Darming during November: ① The original investment of $200,000, ② The revenue and expenses that resulted in net income of $5,600 for the month. ③ A withdrawal of $1,000 by the owner. This information is summarized in the statement of owner's equity in Exhibit 1-13.

## BALANCE SHEET

The balance sheet in Exhibit 1-13 reports the amounts of Darming's assets, liabilities, and owner's equity at the end of November. John's capital as of November 30, 2007, is taken from the statement of owner's equity. The form of balance sheet shown in Exhibit 1 – 13 is called the account form because it resembles the basic format of the accounting equation, with assets on the left side and the liabilities and owner's equity sections on the right side.

Cash is presented first, followed by accounts receivable, supplies, prepaid insurance, and other assets. The assets of a more permanent nature are shown next, such as land, buildings, and equipment. The assets section of the balance sheet presents assets in the sequence that they will be converted into cash or used in operations.

In the liabilities section of the balance sheet in Exhibit 1 – 13, accounts payable is the only liability. When there are two or more categories of liabilities, each should be listed and the total amount of liabilities presented in sequence.

## STATEMENT OF CASH FLOWS

The statement of cash flows comprises of three sections: operating activities, investing activities, and financing activities. Each of these sections is briefly described below.

### Cash Flows from Operating Activities

The net cash flows from operating activities will normally differ from the amount of net income for the period. In Exhibit 1-13, Darming reported net cash flows from operating activities and net income of $5,600. Sometimes the difference occurs because revenues and expenses may not be recorded at the same time that cash is received from customers or paid to creditors.

### Cash Flows from Investing Activities

This section discloses the cash transactions for the acquisition and sale of relatively permanent assets. Exhibit 1-13 reports that Darming paid $100,000 for the purchase of land during November.

### Cash Flows from Financing Activities

This section descripts the cash transactions related to cash investments by the owner, borrowings, and cash withdrawals by the owner. Exhibit 1-13 shows that John invested $200,000 in the business and withdrew $1,000 during November.

Since November is Darming's first period of operations, the net cash flows for November and the November 30, 2007, cash balance are the same amount, $104,600, as shown in Exhibit 1-13. In subsequent periods, Darming will report in its statement of cash flows a beginning cash balance, an increase or a decrease in cash for the period, and an ending cash balance. For example, assume that for December Darming has a decrease in cash of $10,500. The last three lines of Darming's statement of cash flows for December appear as follows.

| | |
|---|---|
| Decrease in cash | $10,500 |
| Cash as of December 1, 2007 | $104,600 |
| Cash as of December 31, 2007 | $94,100 |

## INTERRELATIONSHIPS AMONG FINANCIAL STATEMENTS

As we mentioned earlier, financial statements are prepared in the order of the income statement, statement of owner's equity, balance sheet, and statement of cash flows. Preparing them in this order is important because the financial statements are interrelated. Using the financial statements of Darming as an example, these interrelationships are shown in Exhibit 1-13 as follows. The preceding interrelationships shown in Exhibit 1-13 are important in analyzing financial statements and checking on whether the financial statements have been prepared correctly.

(1) The income statement and the statement of owner's equity are interrelated. The net income or net loss appears on the income statement and also on the statement of owner's equity as either an addition (net income) to or deduction (net loss) from the beginning owner's equity and any additional investments by the owner during the period. To illustrate, Darming's net income of $5,600 for November is added to John's investment of $200,000 in the statement of owner's equity as shown in Exhibit 1-13.

(2) The statement of owner's equity and the balance sheet are interrelated. The owner's capital at the end of the period on the statement of owner's equity also appears on the balance sheet as owner's capital. To illustrate, John's Capital of $204,600 as of November 30, 2007, on the statement of owner's equity also appears on the November 30, 2007, balance sheet as shown in Exhibit 1-13.

(3) The balance sheet and the statement of cash flows are interrelated. The cash on the balance sheet also appears as the end-of-period cash on the statement of cash flows. To illustrate, the cash of $104,600 reported on Darming's balance sheet as of November 30, 2007, is also reported on Darming's November statement of cash flows as the end-of-period cash as shown in Exhibit 1-13.

## TERMINOLOGY:

Accounting: 会计学

Accounting Equation: 会计恒等式

Asset: 资产

Balance Sheet: 资产负债表

Capital：资本
Corporation：公司
Entity：主体
Expense：费用
Financial Accounting：财务会计
Financial Statements：财务报表
Income Statement：利润表
Liability：负债
Management Accounting：管理会计
Owner's Equity：所有者权益
Partnership：合伙
Proprietorship：个体户
Shareholder：股东
Statement of Cash Flows：现金流量表
Statement of Owner's Equity：所有者权益变动表
Stakeholder：利益相关者
Transaction：交易

**QUESTIONS：**

**1. Describe the nature of a business and the role of accounting in business.**

A business is an organization in which basic resources (inputs), such as materials and labor, are assembled and processed to provide goods or services (outputs) to customers. The objective of most businesses is to maximize profits. There are three different types of businesses that are operated for profit: manufacturing, merchandising, and service businesses. A business is normally organized in one of the following forms: proprietorship, partnership, corporation, or limited liability corporation. A business stakeholder is a person or entity (such as an owner, manager, employee, customer, creditor, or the government) who has an interest in the economic performance of the business.

Accounting is an information system that provides reports to stakeholders about the economic activities and condition of a business. Accounting is the "language of business".

**2. Summarize the accounting principles and relate them to practice.**

The business entity concept views the business as an entity separate from its owners, creditors, or other stakeholders. The business entity limits the economic data in the accounting system to that related directly to the activities of the business. The cost concept requires that properties and services bought by a business be recorded in terms of actual cost. The objectivity concept requires that the accounting records and reports be based upon objective evidence. The unit of measure concept requires that economic data be recorded in dollars.

**3. State the accounting equation and explain how business transactions can be stated in terms of the resulting changes in the basic elements of the accounting equation.**

The resources owned by a business and the rights or claims to these resources may be stated in the form of an equation, as follows.

Assets = Liabilities + Owner's Equity

All business transactions can be stated in terms of the change in one or more of the three elements of the accounting equation. That is, the effect of every transaction can be stated in terms of increases or decreases in one or more of these elements, while maintaining the equality between the two sides of the equation.

**4. Describe the financial statements of a corporation and explain how they interrelate.**

The principal financial statements of a corporation are the income statement, the statement of owner's equity, the balance sheet, and the statement of cash flows. The income statement reports a period's net income or net loss, which also appears on the statement of owner's equity. The ending capital is reported on the statement of owner's equity and which is also reported on the balance sheet. The ending cash balance is reported on the balance sheet and the statement of cash flows.

**PROBLEM:**

On March 1, 2008, David Richardson opened a painting business near a historical housing district. David was the sole owner of the proprietorship, which he named DR Painting. During March 2008, David engaged in the following transactions.

a. David invested $40,000 of personal cash to start the business.

b. The business paid $20,000 cash to acquire a truck.

c. The business purchased supplies costing $1,800 on account.

d. The business painted a house for a customer and received $3,000 cash.

e. The business painted a house for a customer for $4,000. The customer agreed to pay next week.

f. The business paid $800 cash toward the supplies purchased in transaction c.

g. The business paid employee salaries of $1,000 cash.

h. David withdrew $1,500 cash from the business for personal use.

i. The business collected $2,600 from the customer in transaction e.

j. David paid $100 cash for personal groceries.

**Requirements**

1. Analyze the preceding transactions based on the accounting equation of DR Painting.

2. Prepare the income statement, statement of owner's equity, and balance sheet of the business.

**Solution**

Requirement 1. All of the recorded transactions are summarized in Exhibit 1-14.

Requirement 2. Financial statements are shown in Exhibit 1-15.

**Exhibit 1-14 Transactions of DR Painting**

| | ASSETS | | | | | LIABILITIES | OWNER'S EQUITY | TYPE OF OWNER'S EQUITY TRANSATION |
|---|---|---|---|---|---|---|---|---|
| Transac-tions | Cash | Accounts Receivable | Supplies | Truck | = | Accounts Payable | David Richardson, Capital | |
| a | +40,000 | | | | | | +40,000 | Owner investment |
| b | -20,000 | | | +20,000 | | | | |
| c | | | +1,800 | | | +1,800 | | |
| d | +3,000 | | | | | | +3,000 | Service revenue |
| e | | +4,000 | | | | | +4,000 | Service revenue |
| f | -800 | | | | | -800 | | |
| g | -1,000 | | | | | | -1,000 | Salary expense |
| h | -1,500 | | | | | | -1,500 | Owner withdrawal |
| i | +2,600 | -2,600 | | | | | | |
| j | | | | | | Not a transaction of the business | | |
| Total | 22,300 | 1,400 | 1,800 | 20,000 | | 1,000 | 44,500 | |

**Exhibit 1-15 Financial statements for DR Painting**

DR Painting

Income Statement

For the Month Ended March 31,2008

| | | |
|---|---|---|
| Service Income | | 7,000 |
| Expenses: | | |
| Wages expense | 1,000 | |
| Total expenses | | 1,000 |
| Net income | | 6,000 |

DR Painting

Statement of Owner's Equity

For the Month Ended March 31, 2008

| | | |
|---|---|---|
| D. Richardson, capital, March 1, 2008 | | 0 |
| Add: Investment on March 1,2008 | 40,000 | |
| Net income for March | 6,000 | |
| Less: Withdrawals | 1,500 | |
| Increase in owner's equity | | 44,500 |
| D. Richardson, capital, March 31,2008 | | 44,500 |

DR Painting Balance Sheet

March 31, 2008

| Assets | | Liabilities | |
|---|---|---|---|
| Cash | 22,300 | Accounts payable | 1,000 |
| Accounts receivable | 1,400 | Owner's Equity | |
| Supplies | 1,800 | D. Richardson, capital | 44,500 |
| Truck | 20,000 | | |
| Total assets | 45,500 | Total liabilities and owner's equity | 45,500 |

# Chapter 2

## Analyzing Transactions

**Objectives**

1. Record transactions using accounts and journal.
2. Describe the posting of journal entries to accounts.
3. Prepare an unadjusted trial balance and explain how to use it to discover errors.
4. Discover and correct errors in recording transactions.

# 1. Using Accounts to Record Transactions

Recorded the November transactions for Darming using the accounting equation format, is not efficient or practical for companies that have to record and summarize thousands or millions of transactions daily. As a result, accounting systems are designed to show the increases and decreases in each financial statement item as a separate record. This record is called an account. As we illustrate next, each of these columns can be organized into a separate account that more efficiently records and summarizes transactions.

An account, in its simplest form, has three parts. First, each account has a title, which is the name of the item recorded in the account. Second, each account has a space for recording increases in the amount of the item. Third, each account has a space for recording decreases in the amount of the item. The account form presented below is called a T account because it resembles the letter T. The left side of the account is called the debit side, and the right side is called the credit side.

| Title | |
|---|---|
| Left side | Right side |
| Debit | Credit |

Amounts entered on the left side of an account, regardless of the account title, are called debits to the account. When debits are entered in an account, the account is said to be debited. Amounts entered on the right side of an account are called credits, and the account is said to be credited. Debits and credits are sometimes abbreviated as Dr. and Cr.

The cash account shown below illustrates how Darming's November cash transactions shown in the first column of Exhibit 2-1 would be recorded in an account. Transactions involving receipts of cash are listed on the debit side of the account. For example, the receipt of $ 200,000 from John in transaction a is entered on the debit side of the account. The letter or date of the transaction is also entered into the account. This is done so that if any questions later arise related to the entry, the entry can be traced back to the underlying transaction data. The transactions involving cash payments are listed on the credit side. For example, the payment of $ 100,000 to purchase land in transaction b is entered on the credit side of the account.

| | Cash | | |
|---|---|---|---|
| Debit side of account | a. $ 200,000 | b. $ 100,000 | Credit side of account |
| | $ 10,000 | $ 3,400 | |
| | | $ 1,000 | |
| | | $ 1,000 | |
| | Bal $ 104,600 | | |

**Exhibit 2-1 Darming November transactions**

| | Assets | | | = Liabilities + | | Owner's Equity | | | | | | |
|---|---|---|---|---|---|---|---|---|---|---|---|---|
| | Cash + | Supp. + | Land = | Accounts Payable | + John, Capital | − John, Drawing | + Service Income | − Wages Exp | − Rent Exp | − Supplies Exp | − Utilities Exp | − Misc Exp |
| a. | +200,000 | | | | +200,000 | | | | | | | |
| b. | −100,000 | | +100,000 | | | | | | | | | |
| | | | 0 | | | | | | | | | |
| Bal. | 100,000 | | 100,000 | | 200,000 | | | | | | | |
| c. | | +4,000 | | +4,000 | | | | | | | | |
| Bal. | 100,000 | 4,000 | 100,000 | 4,000 | 200,000 | | | | | | | |
| d. | +10,000 | | | | | | +10,000 | | | | | |
| Bal | 110,000 | 4,000 | 100,000 | 4,000 | 200,000 | | 10,000 | | | | | |
| e. | −3,400 | | | | | | | −2,000 | −800 | | −400 | −200 |
| Bal | 106,600 | 4,000 | 100,000 | 4,000 | 200,000 | | 10,000 | −2,000 | −800 | | −400 | −200 |
| f. | −1,000 | | | −1,000 | | | | | | | | |
| Bal. | 105,600 | 4,000 | 100,000 | 3,000 | 200,000 | | 10,000 | −2,000 | −800 | | −400 | −200 |
| g. | | −1,000 | | | | | | | | −1,000 | | |
| Bal. | 105,600 | 3,000 | 100,000 | 3,000 | 200,000 | | 10,000 | −2,000 | −800 | −1,000 | −400 | −200 |
| h. | −1,000 | | | | | −1,000 | | | | | | |
| Bal. | 104,600 | 3,000 | 100,000 | 3,000 | 200,000 | −1,000 | 10,000 | −2,000 | −800 | −1,000 | −400 | −200 |

If at any time the total of the cash receipts is needed, the entries on the debit side of the account may be added. For Darming, the total receipts is \$210,000 (\$200,000 + \$10,000). Likewise, the total cash payments of \$105,400 (\$100,000 + \$3,400 + \$1,000 + \$1,000) may be determined by adding the entries on the credit side of the account. Subtracting the smaller sum from the larger, \$210,000 − \$105,400, identifies the amount of cash on hand, \$104,600. This amount is called the balance of the account and is inserted in the account, in the debit column. In this way, the balance is identified as a debit balance. This balance is reported on the balance sheet for Darming as of November 30, 2007, shown in Exhibit 1-13. Each of the columns in Exhibit 2-1 can be converted into an account form in a similar manner as was done for the cash column of Exhibit 2-1. We illustrate each of these accounts later in this chapter.

## CHART OF ACCOUNTS

Ledger indicates a group of accounts for a business entity. A list of the accounts in the ledger is called a chart of accounts. The accounts are normally listed in the order in which they appear in the financial statements. The income statement accounts are listed in the order of revenues and expenses. The balance sheet accounts are usually listed in the order of assets, liabilities, and owner's equity. Each of these major account classifications is briefly described below.

**Assets** are resources owned by the business entity. These resources can be physical items, such as cash and supplies, or intangibles that have value, such as patent rights, including other assets as accounts receivable, prepaid expenses, buildings, equipment, and land.

**Liabilities** are debts owed to outsiders (creditors). Examples of liabilities include accounts payable, notes payable, and wages payable. Cash received before services are delivered creates a liability to perform the services, called as unearned revenues.

**Owner's equity** is the owner's right to the assets of the business. A proprietorship's owner's equity on the balance sheet is represented by the balance of the owner's capital account and the balance of a drawing account on amount of withdrawals made by the owner.

**Revenues** are increases in owner's equity as a result of selling services or products to customers, including fees earned, fares earned, commissions revenue, and rent revenue.

**Expenses** result from using up assets or consuming services in the process of generating revenues, including wages expense, rent expense, utilities expense, supplies expense, and miscellaneous expense.

A chart of accounts is designed to meet the information needs of a company's managers and other users of its financial statements. A flexible numbering system is normally used, so that new accounts can be added without affecting other account numbers.

Exhibit 2-2 is Darming's chart of accounts that we will be using in this chapter. In Exhibit 2-2, each account number has two digits. The first digit indicates the major classification of the ledger in which the account is located. Accounts beginning with 1 represent assets; 2, liabilities; 3, owner's equity; 4, revenue; and 5, expenses. The second digit indicates the location of the account within its class.

**Exhibit 2-2 Analysis and recording of transactions using accounts**

| Balance Sheet Accounts | | Income Statement Accounts | |
|---|---|---|---|
| | 1. Assets | | 4. Revenue |
| 11 | Cash | 41 | Service Income |
| 12 | Accounts Receivable | | 5. Expenses |
| 14 | Supplies | 51 | Wages Expense |
| 15 | Prepaid Insurance | 52 | Rent Expense |
| 17 | Land | 54 | Utilities Expense |
| 18 | Office Equipment | 55 | Supplies Expense |
| | 2. Liabilities | 59 | Miscellaneous Expense |
| 21 | Accounts Payable | | |
| 23 | Unearned Rent | | |
| | 3. Owner's Equity | | |
| 31 | John, Capital | | |
| 32 | John, Drawing | | |

## ANALYZING AND SUMMARIZING TRANSACTIONS IN ACCOUNTS

Every business transaction affects at least two accounts. To illustrate how transactions are analyzed and summarized in accounts, we will use the Darming transactions from Chapter 1, with dates added. First, we illustrate how transactions a, b, c, and f are analyzed and summarized in balance sheet accounts (assets, liabilities, and owner's equity). Next, we illustrate how transactions d, e, and g are analyzed and summarized in income statement accounts (revenues and expenses). Finally, we illustrate how the withdrawal of cash by John, transaction h, is analyzed and summarized in the accounts.

**Balance Sheet Accounts**

**Transaction a.** John deposited $200,000 in a bank account in the name of Darming. The effect of this November 1 transaction on the balance sheet is to increase assets and owner's equity, as shown in Exhibit 2-3.

**Exhibit 2-3 November 1 transaction on the balance sheet**

Darming
Balance Sheet
November 1, 2007

| Assets | | Owner's Equity | |
|---|---|---|---|
| Cash | 200,000 | John, capital | 200,000 |

This transaction is initially entered in a record called a journal. The title of the account to be debited is listed first, followed by the amount to be debited. The title of the account to be credited is listed below and to the right of the debit, followed by the amount to be credited. This process of recording a transaction in the journal is called journalizing. This form of recording a transaction is called a journal entry.

The journal entry for transaction a is shown in Exhibit 2-4.

**Exhibit 2-4 Journal entry for transaction a**

| Date | | Description | Post. Ref. | Debit | Credit |
|---|---|---|---|---|---|
| 2007 Nov. | 1 | Cash | 11 | 200,000 | |
| | | John, Capital | 31 | | 200,000 |
| | | Invested cash in Darming | | | |

The increase in the asset (Cash), which is reported on the left side of the balance sheet, is debited to the cash account. The increase in owner's equity, which is reported on the right side of the balance sheet, is credited to the John, capital account. As other assets are acquired, the increases are also recorded as debits to asset accounts. Likewise, other increases in owner's equity will be recorded as credits to owner's equity accounts.

The effects of this transaction are shown in the accounts by transferring the amount and date of the journal entry to the left (debit) side of Cash and to the right (credit) side of John, Capital as follows.

| Cash | |
|---|---|
| Nov. 1 $200,000 | |

| John, Capital | |
|---|---|
| | Nov. 1 $200,000 |

**Transaction b.** On November 5, Darming bought land for $100,000, paying cash. This transaction increases one asset account and decreases another. It is entered in the journal as a $100,000 increase (debit) to Land and a $100,000 decrease (credit) to Cash, as shown in Exhibit 2-5.

**Exhibit 2-5 Journal entry for transaction b**

| Date | | Description | Post. Ref. | Debit | Credit |
|---|---|---|---|---|---|
| 2007 Nov. | 5 | Land | 17 | 100,000 | |
| | | Cash | 11 | | 100,000 |
| | | Purchased land for building site | | | |

The rules of debit and credit may also be stated in relationship to the accounting equation, as shown in Exhibit 2-6.

**Exhibit 2-6 Balance sheet accounts**

| ASSETS | | | LIABILITIES | | | OWNER'S EQUITY | |
|---|---|---|---|---|---|---|---|
| Asset Accounts | | – | Liability Accounts | | = | Owner's Equity Accounts | |
| Debit for increases(+) | Credit for decreases(−) | | Debit for decreases(−) | Credit for increases(+) | | Debit for decreases(−) | Credit for increases(+) |

**Transaction c.** On November 11, Darming purchased supplies on account for $4,000. The journal entry for transaction c is shown in Exhibit 2-7.

**Exhibit 2-7 Journal entry for transaction c**

| Date | | Description | Post. Ref. | Debit | Credit |
|---|---|---|---|---|---|
| 2007 Nov. | 11 | Supplies | 14 | 4,000 | |
| | | Accounts Payable | 21 | | 4,000 |
| | | Purchased supplies on account | | | |

**Transaction d.** On November 30, Darming paid creditors on account, $1,000, as shown in Exhibit 2-8.

**Exhibit 2-8 Journal entry for transaction d**

| Date | | Description | Post. Ref. | Debit | Credit |
|---|---|---|---|---|---|
| 2007 Nov. | 30 | Accounts Payable | 21 | 1,000 | |
| | | Cash | 11 | | 1,000 |
| | | Paid creditors on account | | | |

### Income statement accounts

The analysis of revenue and expense transactions focuses on how each transaction affects owner's equity. Transactions that increase revenue will increase owner's equity. Just as increases in owner's equity are recorded as credits, so, too, are increases in revenue accounts. Transactions that increase expense will decrease owner's equity. Just as decreases in owner's equity are recorded as debits, increases in expense accounts are recorded as debits.

We will use Darming's transactions d, e, and g to illustrate the analysis of transactions and the rules of debit and credit for revenue and expense accounts.

**Transaction e.** On November 18, Darming received fees of $ 10,000 from customers for services provided. This transaction increases an asset account and increases a revenue account. It is entered in the journal as a $ 10,000 increase (debit) to Cash and a $ 10,000 increase (credit) to Service Income, as shown in Exhibit 2-9.

**Exhibit 2-9 Journal entry for transaction e**

| Date | | Description | Post. Ref. | Debit | Credit |
|---|---|---|---|---|---|
| 2007 Nov. | 18 | Cash | 11 | 10,000 | |
| | | Service Income | 41 | | 10,000 |
| | | Received fees from customers | | | |

**Transaction f.** Throughout the month, Darming incurred the following expenses: wages, $2,000; rent, $800; utilities, $400; and miscellaneous, $200. To simplify the illustration, the entry to journalize the payment of these expenses is recorded on November 30, as shown in Exhibit 2-10. This transaction increases various expense accounts and decreases an asset account.

**Exhibit 2-10 Journal entry for transaction f**

| Date | | Description | Post. Ref. | Debit | Credit |
|---|---|---|---|---|---|
| 2007 Nov. | 30 | Wages Expense | 51 | 2,000 | |
| | | Rent Expense | 52 | 800 | |
| | | Utilities Expense | 54 | 400 | |
| | | Miscellaneous Expense | 59 | 200 | |
| | | Cash | 11 | | 3,400 |
| | | Paid expenses | | | |

You should note that regardless of the number of accounts, the sum of the debits is always equal to the sum of the credits in a journal entry.

**Transaction g.** On November 30, Darming recorded the amount of supplies used in the operations during the month. This transaction increases an expense account and decreases an asset account, as shown in Exhibit 2-11.

**Exhibit 2-11 Journal entry for transaction g**

| Date | | Description | Post. Ref. | Debit | Credit |
|---|---|---|---|---|---|
| 2007 Nov | 30 | Supplies Expense | 55 | 1,000 | |
| | | Supplies | 14 | | 1,000 |
| | | Supplies used during November | | | |

The rules of debit and credit for income statement accounts may also be summarized in relationship to the accounting equation, owner's equity accounts, and net income or net loss as shown in Exhibit 2-12.

**Exhibit 2-12 Income statement accounts**

**Owner's Equity Accounts**

| Debit for | Credit for |
|---|---|
| decreases(−) | increases(+) |

**Income Statement Accounts**

**Revenue Accounts**

| Debit for | Credit for |
|---|---|
| decreases(−) | increases(+) |

**Less**

**Expense Accounts**

| Debit for | Credit for |
|---|---|
| increases(+) | decreases(−) |

**Equals**

**Net Income**
**Revenues exceed expenses**
**Increases owner's equity (capital)**
**or**
**Net Loss**
**Expenses exceed revenues Decreases owner's equity (capital)**

### Drawing Account

The owner of a proprietorship may withdraw cash from the business for personal use. This is common practice for owners devoting full time to the business, since the business may be the owner's main source of income. Such withdrawals have the effect of decreasing owner's equity. Just as decreases in owner's equity are recorded as debits, increases in withdrawals are recorded as debits. Withdrawals are debited to an account with the owner's name followed by Drawing or Personal.

**Transaction h.** John withdrew $1,000 in cash from Darming for personal use. The effect of this transaction is to increase the John, Drawing account and decrease the Cash account. The journal entry for transaction h is shown in Exhibit 2-13.

**Exhibit 2-13 Journal entry for transaction h**

| Date | | Description | Post. Ref. | Debit | Credit |
|---|---|---|---|---|---|
| 2007 Nov. | 30 | John, Drawing | 32 | 1,000 | |
| | | Cash | 11 | | 1,000 |
| | | John withdrew cash for personal use | | | |

## NORMAL BALANCES OF ACCOUNTS

The sum of the increases recorded in an account is usually equal to or greater than the sum of the decreases recorded in the account. For this reason, the normal balances of all accounts are positive rather than negative. For example, the total debits (increases) in an asset account will ordinarily be greater than the total credits (decreases). Thus, asset accounts normally have debit balances.

When an account normally having a debit balance actually has a credit balance, or vice versa, an error may have occurred or an unusual situation may exist. For example, a credit balance in the office equipment account could result only from an error. On the other hand, a debit balance in an accounts payable account could result from an overpayment.

### DOUBLE-ENTRY ACCOUNTING SYSTEM

In the preceding paragraphs, we illustrated the rules of debit and credit for recording transactions in accounts using journal entries. In doing so, the sum of the debits is always equal to the sum of the credits for each journal entry. This equality of debits and credits for each transaction is built into the accounting equation: Assets = Liabilities + Owner's Equity. Because of this double equality, this system of recording transactions is called the double-entry accounting system.

As we illustrate in the remainder of this text, the double-entry accounting system is a very powerful tool in analyzing the effects of transactions. Using this system to analyze transactions is summarized below.

(1) Determine whether asset, liability, equity, revenue, expense account is affected.

(2) Determine whether the account affected by transaction increases or decreases.

(3) Determine whether each increase or decrease should be recorded as a debit or a credit.

(4) Record the transaction using a journal entry.

(5) Periodically post journal entries to the accounts in the ledger.

(6) Prepare an unadjusted trial balance at the end of the period.

## 2. Posting of Journal Entries to Accounts

As we discussed in the preceding section, a transaction is first recorded in a journal. Periodically, the journal entries are transferred to the accounts in the ledger. The ledger is a history of transactions by account. The process of transferring the debits and credits from the journal entries to the accounts is called posting.

In practice, businesses use a variety of formats for recording journal entries. A business may use one all-purpose journal, sometimes called a two-column journal, or it may use several journals. In the latter case, each journal is used to record different types of transactions, such as cash receipts or cash payments. The journals may be part of either a manual accounting system or a computerized accounting system.

As a review of the analysis and recording of transactions and to illustrate posting in a manual accounting system, we will use the December transactions of Darming. The first transaction in December occurred on December 1.

**Transaction 1.** On December 1, Darming paid a premium of $1,200 for a comprehensive insurance policy covering liability, theft, and fire. The policy covers a one-year period.

**Analysis** When you purchase insurance for your automobile, you may be required to pay the insurance premium in advance. In this case, your transaction is similar to Darming. Advance payments of expenses such as insurance are prepaid expenses, which are assets. For Darming, the asset acquired for the cash payment is insurance protection for 12 months. The asset Prepaid Insurance increases and is debited for $1,200. The asset Cash decreases and is credited for $1,200.

The debits and credits for each journal entry are posted to the accounts in the order in which they occur in the journal. To illustrate, the debit portion of the December 1 journal entry is posted to the prepaid account in Exhibit 2-14 using the following four steps.

Step 1: The date (Dec. 1) is entered in the Date column of Prepaid Insurance.

Step 2: The amount ($1,200) is entered into the Debit column of Prepaid Insurance.

Step 3: The journal page number (2) is entered in the Posting Reference (Post. Ref.) column of Prepaid Insurance.

Step 4: The account number (15) is entered in the Posting Reference (Post. Ref.) column in the journal.

**Exhibit 2-14 Diagram of posting of a debit and a credit**

JOURNAL

| Date | Description | Post. Ref. | Debit | Credit |
|---|---|---|---|---|
| 2007 Dec. 1 | Prepaid Insurance | 15 | 1,200 | |
| | Cash | 11 | | 1,200 |
| | Paid premium on one-year Policy | | | |

ACCOUNT Prepaid Insurance

| Date | Item | Post. Ref. | Debit | Credit | Balance Debit | Balance Credit |
|---|---|---|---|---|---|---|
| 2007 Dec. 1 | | 2 | 1,200 | | 1,200 | |

ACCOUNT Cash

| Date | Item | Post. Ref. | Debit | Credit | Balance Debit | Balance Credit |
|---|---|---|---|---|---|---|
| 30 | | 2 | | 1,000 | 104,600 | |
| 2007 Dec. 1 | | 2 | | 1,200 | 103,400 | |

As shown in Exhibit 2-14, the credit portion of the December 1 journal entry is posted to the Cash account in a similar manner. The remaining December transactions for Darming are analyzed in the following paragraphs. These transactions are posted to the ledger in Exhibit 2-32, shown later. To simplify and reduce repetition, some of the December transactions are stated in summary form. For example, cash received for services is normally recorded on a daily basis.

**Transaction 2.** On December 1, Darming paid rent for December, $1,000. The company from which Darming is renting its store space now requires the payment of rent on the first of each month, rather than at the end of the month.

**Analysis** The advance payment of rent is an asset. Unlike the insurance premium, this prepaid rent will expire in one month. When an asset that is purchased will be used up in a short period of time, such as a month, it is normal to debit an expense account initially. This avoids having to transfer the balance from an asset account (Prepaid Rent) to an expense account (Rent Expense) at the end of the month. Thus, when the rent for December is prepaid at the beginning of the month, Rent Expense is debited for $1,000, and Cash is credited for $1,000, as shown in Exhibit 2-15.

**Exhibit 2-15 Journal entry for transaction 2**

| Date | | Description | Post. Ref. | Debit | Credit |
|---|---|---|---|---|---|
| 2007 Dec. | 1 | Rent Expense | 52 | 1,000 | |
| | | Cash | 11 | | 1,000 |
| | | Paid rent for December | | | |

**Transaction 3.** On December 1, Darming received an offer from a local retailer to rent the land purchased on November 5. The retailer plans to use the land as a parking lot for its employees and customers. Darming agreed to rent the land to the retailer for three months, with the rent payable in advance. Darming received $3,000 for three months' rent beginning on December 1.

**Analysis.** Darming has incurred an obligation (liability) to the retailer by agreeing to rent the land and accepting the $3,000. The liability created by receiving the cash in advance of providing the service is called unearned revenue. Thus, the $3,000 received is an increase in an asset and is debited to Cash. The liability account Unearned Rent increases and is credited for $3,000, as shown in Exhibit 2-16. As time passes, the unearned rent liability will decrease and will become revenue.

**Exhibit 2-16 Journal entry for transaction 3**

| Date | | Description | Post. Ref. | Debit | Credit |
|---|---|---|---|---|---|
| 2007 Dec. | 1 | Cash | 11 | 3,000 | |
| | | Unearned Rent | 23 | | 3,000 |
| | | Received advance payment for three months' rent on | | | |

**Transaction 4.** On December 4, Darming purchased office equipment on account from Jeffery Supply Co. for $1,000.

**Analysis.** The asset account Office Equipment increases and is therefore debited for $1,000. The liability account Accounts Payable increases and is credited for $1,000, as shown in Exhibit 2-17.

**Transaction 5.** On December 6, Darming paid $100 for a newspaper advertisement.

**Analysis.** An expense increases and is debited for $100. The asset Cash decreases and is credited for $100. Expense items that are expected to be minor in amount are normally included as part of the miscellaneous expense. Thus, Miscellaneous Expense is debited for $100, as shown in Exhibit 2-18.

**Exhibit 2-17 Journal entry for transaction 4**

| Date | | Description | Post. Ref. | Debit | Credit |
|---|---|---|---|---|---|
| 2007 Dec. | 4 | Office Equipment | 18 | 1,000 | |
| | | Accounts Payable | 21 | | 1,000 |
| | | Purchased office equipment on account | | | |

**Exhibit 2-18 Journal entry for transaction 5**

| Date | | Description | Post. Ref. | Debit | Credit |
|---|---|---|---|---|---|
| 2007 Dec. | 6 | Miscellaneous Expense | 59 | 100 | |
| | | Cash | 11 | | 100 |
| | | Paid for newspaper advertisement | | | |

**Transaction 6.** On December 11, Darming paid creditors $3,000.

**Analysis.** This payment decreases the liability account Accounts Payable, which is debited for $3,000. Cash also decreases and is credited for $3,000, as shown in Exhibit 2-19.

**Exhibit 2-19 Journal entry for transaction 6**

| Date | | Description | Post. Ref. | Debit | Credit |
|---|---|---|---|---|---|
| 2007 Dec. | 11 | Accounts Payable | 21 | 3,000 | |
| | | Cash | 11 | | 3,000 |
| | | Paid creditors on account | | | |

**Transaction 7.** On December 13, Darming paid a receptionist and a part-time assistant $1,000 for two weeks' wages.

**Analysis.** This transaction is similar to the transaction 5, where an expense account is increased and Cash is decreased. Thus, Wages Expense is debited for $1,000, and Cash is credited for $1,000, as shown in Exhibit 2-20.

**Exhibit 2-20 Journal entry for transaction 7**

| Date | | Description | Post. Ref. | Debit | Credit |
|---|---|---|---|---|---|
| 2007 Dec. | 13 | Wages Expense | 51 | 1,000 | |
| | | Cash | 11 | | 1,000 |
| | | Paid two weeks' wages | | | |

**Transaction 8.** On December 16, Darming received $3,000 from fees earned for the first half of December.

**Analysis.** Cash increases and is debited for $3,000. The revenue account Service Income increases and is credited for $3,000, as shown in Exhibit 2-21.

**Exhibit 2-21 Journal entry for transaction 8**

| Date | | Description | Post. Ref. | Debit | Credit |
|---|---|---|---|---|---|
| 2007 Dec. | 16 | Cash | 11 | 3,000 | |
| | | Service Income | 41 | | 3,000 |
| | | Received fees from customers | | | |

**Transaction 9.** On December 16, Fees earned on account totaled $2,000 for the first half of December.

**Analysis.** Assume that you have agreed to take care of a neighbor's dog for a week for $2,000. At the end of the week, you agree to wait until the first of the next month to receive the $2,000. The account receivable is an asset, and the revenue is earned even though no cash has been received. Thus, Accounts Receivable increases and is debited for $2,000. The revenue account Service Income increases and is credited for $2,000, as shown in Exhibit 2-22.

**Exhibit 2-22 Journal entry for transaction 9**

| Date | | Description | Post. Ref. | Debit | Credit |
|---|---|---|---|---|---|
| 2007 Dec. | 16 | Accounts Receivable | 12 | 2,000 | |
| | | Service Income | 41 | | 2,000 |
| | | Recorded fees earned on account | | | |

**Transaction 10.** On December 20, Darming paid $1,000 to Jeffery Supply Co. on the $1,000 debt owed from the transaction 4, as shown in Exhibit 2-23.

**Exhibit 2-23 Journal entry for transaction 10**

| Date | | Description | Post. Ref. | Debit | Credit |
|---|---|---|---|---|---|
| 2007 Dec. | 20 | Accounts Payable | 21 | 1,000 | |
| | | Cash | 11 | | 1,000 |
| | | Paid part of amount owed to Jeffery Supply Co. | | | |

**Transaction 11.** On December 21, Darming received $600 from customers in payment of their accounts.

**Analysis.** When customers pay amounts owed for services they have previously received, one asset increases and another asset decreases. This transaction is recorded as a $600 increase (debit) to Cash and a $600 decrease (credit) to Accounts Receivable, as shown in Exhibit 2-24.

**Transaction 12.** On December 23, Darming paid $1,000 for supplies, as shown in Exhibit 2-25.

**Transaction 13.** On December 27, Darming paid the receptionist and the part – time assistant $1,000 for two weeks' wages, as shown in Exhibit 2-26.

**Exhibit 2-24 Journal entry for transaction 11**

| Date | | Description | Post. Ref. | Debit | Credit |
|---|---|---|---|---|---|
| 2007 Dec. | 21 | Cash | 11 | 600 | |
| | | Accounts Receivable | 12 | | 600 |
| | | Received cash from customers on account | | | |

**Exhibit 2-25 Journal entry for transaction 12**

| Date | | Description | Post. Ref. | Debit | Credit |
|---|---|---|---|---|---|
| 2007 Dec. | 23 | Supplies | 14 | 1,000 | |
| | | Cash | 11 | | 1,000 |
| | | Purchased supplies | | | |

**Exhibit 2-26 Journal entry for transaction 13**

| Date | | Description | Post. Ref. | Debit | Credit |
|---|---|---|---|---|---|
| 2007 Dec. | 27 | Wages Expense | 51 | 1,000 | |
| | | Cash | 11 | | 1,000 |
| | | Paid two weeks' wages | | | |

**Transaction 14.** On December 31, Darming paid its $100 telephone bill for the month.

**Analysis.** You pay a telephone bill each month. Businesses, such as Darming, also must pay monthly utility bills. Such transactions are similar to the transaction of December 6. The expense account Utilities Expense is debited for $100, and Cash is credited for $100, as shown in Exhibit 2-27.

**Exhibit 2-27 Journal entry for transaction 14**

| Date | | Description | Post. Ref. | Debit | Credit |
|---|---|---|---|---|---|
| 2007 Dec. | 31 | Utilities Expense | 54 | 100 | |
| | | Cash | 11 | | 100 |
| | | Paid telephone bill | | | |

**Transaction 15.** On December 31, Darming paid its $500 electric bill for the month, as shown in Exhibit 2-28.

**Exhibit 2-28 Journal entry for transaction 15**

| Date | | Description | Post. Ref. | Debit | Credit |
|---|---|---|---|---|---|
| 2007 Dec. | 31 | Utilities Expense | 54 | 500 | |
| | | Cash | 11 | | 500 |
| | | Paid electric bill | | | |

**Transaction 16.** On December 31, Darming received $2,000 from fees earned for the second half of December, as shown in Exhibit 2-29.

**Exhibit 2-29 Journal entry for transaction 16**

| Date | | Description | Post. Ref. | Debit | Credit |
|---|---|---|---|---|---|
| 2007 Dec. | 31 | Cash | 11 | 2,000 | |
| | | Service Income | 41 | | 2,000 |
| | | Received fees from customers | | | |

**Transaction 17.** On December 31, Fees earned on account totaled $1,000 for the second half of December, as shown in Exhibit 2-30.

**Exhibit 2-30 Journal entry for transaction 17**

| Date | | Description | Post. Ref. | Debit | Credit |
|---|---|---|---|---|---|
| 2007 Dec. | 31 | Accounts Receivable | 12 | 1,000 | |
| | | Service Income | 41 | | 1,000 |
| | | Recorded fees earned on account | | | |

**Transaction 18.** On December 31, John withdrew $1,000 for personal use.

**Analysis.** This transaction resulted in an increase in the amount of withdrawals and is recorded by a $1,000 debit to John, Drawing. The decrease in business cash is recorded by a $1,000 credit to Cash, as shown in Exhibit 2-31.

**Exhibit 2-31 Journal entry for transaction 18**

| Date | | Description | Post. Ref. | Debit | Credit |
|---|---|---|---|---|---|
| 2007 Dec. | 31 | John, Drawing | 32 | 1,000 | |
| | | Cash | 11 | | 1,000 |
| | | John withdrew cash for personal use | | | |

The journal for Darming since it was organized on November 1 is shown in Exhibit 2-32. Exhibit 2-32 also shows the ledger after the transactions for both November and December have been posted.

**Exhibit 2-32 Journal and ledger—Darming**

JOURNAL Page 1

| Date | | Description | Post. Ref. | Debit | Credit |
|---|---|---|---|---|---|
| 2007 Nov. | 1 | Cash | 11 | 200,000 | |
| | | John, Capital | 31 | | 200,000 |
| | | Invested cash in Darming | | | |
| | | | | | |
| | 5 | Land | 17 | 100,000 | |
| | | Cash | 11 | | 100,000 |
| | | Purchased land for building site | | | |
| | | | | | |
| | 11 | Supplies | 14 | 4,000 | |
| | | Accounts Payable | 21 | | 4,000 |
| | | Purchased supplies on account | | | |
| | | | | | |
| | 18 | Cash | 11 | 10,000 | |
| | | Service Income | 41 | | 10,000 |
| | | Received fees from customers | | | |
| | | | | | |
| | 30 | Wages Expense | 51 | 2,000 | |
| | | Rent Expense | 52 | 800 | |
| | | Utilities Expense | 54 | 400 | |
| | | Miscellaneous Expense | 59 | 200 | |
| | | Cash | 11 | | 3,400 |
| | | Paid expenses | | | |
| | | | | | |
| | 30 | Accounts Payable | 21 | 1,000 | |
| | | Cash | 11 | | 1,000 |
| | | Paid creditors on account | | | |
| | | | | | |
| | 30 | Supplies Expense | 55 | 1,000 | |
| | | Supplies | 14 | | 1,000 |
| | | Supplies used during November | | | |
| | | | | | |

JOURNAL Page 2

| Date | | Description | Post. Ref. | Debit | Credit |
|---|---|---|---|---|---|
| 2007Nov. | 30 | John, Drawing | 32 | 1,000 | |
| | | Cash | 11 | | 1,000 |
| | | John withdrew cash for personal use | | | |
| | | | | | |
| Dec. | 1 | Prepaid Insurance | 15 | 1,200 | |
| | | Cash | 11 | | 1,200 |
| | | Paid premium on one – year policy | | | |
| | | | | | |
| | 1 | Rent Expense | 52 | 1,000 | |
| | | Cash | 11 | | 1,000 |
| | | Paid rent for December | | | |
| | | | | | |
| | 1 | Cash | 11 | 3,000 | |
| | | Unearned Rent | 23 | | 3,000 |
| | | Received advance payment for three months' rent on. | | | |
| | | | | | |
| | 4 | Office Equipment | 18 | 1,000 | |
| | | Accounts Payable | 21 | | 1,000 |
| | | Purchased office equipment on account | | | |
| | | | | | |
| | 6 | Miscellaneous Expense | 59 | 100 | |
| | | Cash | 11 | | 100 |
| | | Paid for newspaper advertisement | | | |
| | | | | | |
| | 11 | Accounts Payable | 21 | 3,000 | |
| | | Cash | 11 | | 3,000 |
| | | Paid creditors on account | | | |
| | | | | | |
| | 13 | Wages Expense | 51 | 1,000 | |
| | | Cash | 11 | | 1,000 |
| | | Paid two weeks' wages | | | |
| | | | | | |

JOURNAL Page 3

| Date | | Description | Post. Ref. | Debit | Credit |
|---|---|---|---|---|---|
| 2007 Dec. | 16 | Cash | 11 | 3,000 | |
| | | Service Income | 41 | | 3,000 |
| | | Received fees from customers | | | |
| | | | | | |
| | 16 | Accounts Receivable | 12 | 2,000 | |
| | | Service Income | 41 | | 2,000 |
| | | Recorded fees earned on account | | | |
| | | | | | |
| | 20 | Accounts Payable | 21 | 1,000 | |
| | | Cash | 11 | | 1,000 |
| | | Paid part of amount owed to Jeffery Supply Co. | | | |
| | | | | | |
| | 21 | Cash | 11 | 600 | |
| | | Accounts Receivable | 12 | | 600 |
| | | Received cash from customers on account | | | |
| | | | | | |
| | 23 | Supplies | 14 | 1,000 | |
| | | Cash | 11 | | 1,000 |
| | | Purchased supplies | | | |
| | | | | | |
| | 27 | Wages Expense | 51 | 1,000 | |
| | | Cash | 11 | | 1,000 |
| | | Paid two weeks' wages | | | |
| | | | | | |
| | 31 | Utilities Expense | 54 | 100 | |
| | | Cash | 11 | | 100 |
| | | Paid telephone bill | | | |

JOURNAL

Page 4

| Date | | Description | Post. Ref. | Debit | Credit |
|---|---|---|---|---|---|
| 2007 Dec. | 31 | Utilities Expense | 54 | 500 | |
| | | Cash | 11 | | 500 |
| | | Paid electric bill | | | |
| | | | | | |
| | 31 | Cash | 11 | 2,000 | |
| | | Service Income | 41 | | 2,000 |
| | | Received fees from customers | | | |
| | | | | | |
| | 31 | Accounts Receivable | 12 | 1,000 | |
| | | Service Income | 41 | | 1,000 |
| | | Recorded fees earned on account | | | |
| | | | | | |
| | 31 | John, Drawing | 32 | 1,000 | |
| | | Cash | 11 | | 1,000 |
| | | John withdrew cash for personal use | | | |
| | | | | | |

**LEDGER**

ACCOUNT Cash

ACCOUNT NO. 11

| Date | | Item | Post. Ref. | Debit | Credit | Balance | |
|---|---|---|---|---|---|---|---|
| | | | | | | Debit | Credit |
| 2007 Nov. | 1 | | 1 | 200,000 | | 200,000 | |
| | 5 | | 1 | | 100,000 | 100,000 | |
| | 18 | | 1 | 10,000 | | 110,000 | |
| | 30 | | 1 | | 3,400 | 106,600 | |
| | 30 | | 1 | | 1,000 | 105,600 | |
| | 30 | | 2 | | 1,000 | 104,600 | |
| Dec. | 1 | | 2 | | 1,200 | 103,400 | |
| | 1 | | 2 | | 1,000 | 102,400 | |
| | 1 | | 2 | 3,000 | | 105,400 | |
| | 6 | | 2 | | 100 | 105,300 | |
| | 11 | | 2 | | 3,000 | 102,300 | |
| | 13 | | 2 | | 1,000 | 101,300 | |
| | 16 | | 3 | 3,000 | | 104,300 | |
| | 20 | | 3 | | 1,000 | 103,300 | |
| | 21 | | 3 | 600 | | 103,900 | |
| | 23 | | 3 | | 1,000 | 102,900 | |
| | 27 | | 3 | | 1,000 | 101,900 | |
| | 31 | | 3 | | 100 | 101,800 | |
| | 31 | | 4 | | 500 | 101,300 | |
| | 31 | | 4 | 2,000 | | 103,300 | |
| | 31 | | 4 | | 1,000 | 102,300 | |

ACCOUNT Accounts Receivable ACCOUNT NO. 12

| Date | | Item | Post. Ref. | Debit | Credit | Balance | |
|---|---|---|---|---|---|---|---|
| | | | | | | Debit | Credit |
| 2007 Dec. | 16 | | 3 | 2,000 | | 2,000 | |
| | 21 | | 3 | | 600 | 1,400 | |
| | 31 | | 4 | 1,000 | | 2,400 | |

ACCOUNT Supplies ACCOUNT NO. 14

| Date | | Item | Post. Ref. | Debit | Credit | Balance | |
|---|---|---|---|---|---|---|---|
| | | | | | | Debit | Credit |
| 2007 Nov. | 11 | | 1 | 4,000 | | 4,000 | |
| | 30 | | 1 | | 1,000 | 3,000 | |
| Dec. | 23 | | 3 | 1,000 | | 4,000 | |

ACCOUNT Prepaid Insurance ACCOUNT NO. 15

| Date | | Item | Post. Ref. | Debit | Credit | Balance | |
|---|---|---|---|---|---|---|---|
| | | | | | | Debit | Credit |
| 2007 Dec. | 1 | | 2 | 1,200 | | 1,200 | |

ACCOUNT Land ACCOUNT NO. 17

| Date | | Item | Post. Ref. | Debit | Credit | Balance | |
|---|---|---|---|---|---|---|---|
| | | | | | | Debit | Credit |
| 2007 Nov. | 5 | | 1 | 100,000 | | 100,000 | |

ACCOUNT Office Equipment ACCOUNT NO. 18

| Date | | Item | Post. Ref. | Debit | Credit | Balance | |
|---|---|---|---|---|---|---|---|
| | | | | | | Debit | Credit |
| 2007 Dec. | 4 | | 2 | 1,000 | | 1,000 | |

ACCOUNT Accounts Payable ACCOUNT NO. 21

| Date | | Item | Post. Ref. | Debit | Credit | Balance | |
|---|---|---|---|---|---|---|---|
| | | | | | | Debit | Credit |
| 2007 Nov. | 11 | | 1 | | 4,000 | | 4,000 |
| | 30 | | 1 | 1,000 | | | 3,000 |
| Dec. | 4 | | 2 | | 1,000 | | 4,000 |
| | 11 | | 2 | 3,000 | | | 1,000 |
| | 20 | | 3 | 1,000 | | | 0 |

ACCOUNT Unearned Rent ACCOUNT NO. 23

| Date | | Item | Post. Ref. | Debit | Credit | Balance | |
|---|---|---|---|---|---|---|---|
| | | | | | | Debit | Credit |
| 2007 Dec. | 1 | | 2 | | 3,000 | | 3,000 |

ACCOUNT John, Capital ACCOUNT NO. 31

| Date | | Item | Post. Ref. | Debit | Credit | Balance | |
|---|---|---|---|---|---|---|---|
| | | | | | | Debit | Credit |
| 2007 Nov. | 1 | | 1 | | 200,000 | | 200,000 |

ACCOUNT John, Drawing ACCOUNT NO. 32

| Date | | Item | Post. Ref. | Debit | Credit | Balance | |
|---|---|---|---|---|---|---|---|
| | | | | | | Debit | Credit |
| 2007 Nov. | 30 | | 2 | 1,000 | | 1,000 | |
| Dec. | 31 | | 4 | 1,000 | | 2,000 | |

ACCOUNT Service Income ACCOUNT NO. 41

| Date | | Item | Post. Ref. | Debit | Credit | Balance | |
|---|---|---|---|---|---|---|---|
| | | | | | | Debit | Credit |
| 2007 Nov. | 18 | | 1 | | 10,000 | | 10,000 |
| Dec. | 16 | | 3 | | 3,000 | | 13,000 |
| | 16 | | 3 | | 2,000 | | 15,000 |
| | 31 | | 4 | | 2,000 | | 17,000 |
| | 31 | | 4 | | 1,000 | | 18,000 |

ACCOUNT Wages Expense ACCOUNT NO. 51

| Date | | Item | Post. Ref. | Debit | Credit | Balance | |
|---|---|---|---|---|---|---|---|
| | | | | | | Debit | Credit |
| 2007 Nov. | 30 | | 1 | 2,000 | | 2,000 | |
| Dec. | 13 | | 2 | 1,000 | | 3,000 | |
| | 27 | | 3 | 1,000 | | 4,000 | |

ACCOUNT Rent Expense ACCOUNT NO. 52

| Date | | Item | Post. Ref. | Debit | Credit | Balance | |
|---|---|---|---|---|---|---|---|
| | | | | | | Debit | Credit |
| 2007 Nov. | 30 | | 1 | 800 | | 800 | |
| Dec. | 1 | | 2 | 1,000 | | 1,800 | |

ACCOUNT Utilities Expense ACCOUNT NO. 54

| Date | | Item | Post. Ref. | Debit | Credit | Balance | |
|---|---|---|---|---|---|---|---|
| | | | | | | Debit | Credit |
| 2007 Nov. | 30 | | 1 | 400 | | 400 | |
| Dec. | 31 | | 3 | 100 | | 500 | |
| | 31 | | 4 | 500 | | 1,000 | |

ACCOUNT Supplies Expense ACCOUNT NO. 55

| Date | | Item | Post. Ref. | Debit | Credit | Balance | |
|---|---|---|---|---|---|---|---|
| | | | | | | Debit | Credit |
| 2007 Nov. | 30 | | 1 | 1,000 | | 1,000 | |

ACCOUNT Miscellaneous Expense ACCOUNT NO. 59

| Date | | Item | Post. Ref. | Debit | Credit | Balance | |
|---|---|---|---|---|---|---|---|
| | | | | | | Debit | Credit |
| 2007 Nov. | 30 | | 1 | 200 | | 200 | |
| Dec. | 6 | | 2 | 100 | | 300 | |

## 3. Trial Balance

How can you be sure that you have not made an error in posting the debits and credits to the ledger? One way is to determine the equality of the debits and credits in the ledger. This equality should be proved at the end of each accounting period, if not more often. Such a proof, called a trial balance, may be in the form of a computer printout or in the form shown in Exhibit 2-33.

**Exhibit 2-33 Trial balance**

Darming
Unadjusted Trial Balance
December 31,2007

| Accounts | Debit Balances | Credit Balances |
|---|---|---|
| Cash | 102,300 | |
| Accounts Receivable | 2,400 | |
| Supplies | 4,000 | |
| Prepaid Insurance | 1,200 | |
| Land | 100,000 | |
| Office Equipment | 1,000 | |
| Accounts Payable | | 0 |
| Unearned Rent | | 3,000 |
| John, Capital | | 200,000 |
| John, Drawing | 2,000 | |
| Service Income | | 18,000 |
| Wages Expense | 4,000 | |
| Rent Expense | 1,800 | |
| Utilities Expense | 1,000 | |
| Supplies Expense | 1,000 | |
| Miscellaneous Expense | 300 | |
| Total | 221,000 | 221,000 |

The trial balance shown in Exhibit 2-33 is prepared by first listing the name of the company (Darming), its title (Unadjusted Trial Balance), and the date it is prepared (December 31, 2007). The trial balance shown in Exhibit 2-33 is titled an unadjusted trial balance. This is to distinguish it from other trial balances that we will be preparing in later chapters. These other trial balances include an adjusted trial balance and a postclosing trial balance.

The account balances in Exhibit 2-33 are taken from the ledger shown in Exhibit 2-32. Thus, before the trial balance can be prepared, each account balance in the ledger must be determined. When the standard account form is used, the balance of each account appears in the balance column on the same line as the last posting to the account.

The trial balance does not provide complete proof of the accuracy of the ledger. It indicates only that the debits and the credits are equal. This proof is of value, however, because errors often affect the equality of debits and credits. If the two totals of a trial balance are not equal, an error has occurred. In the next section of this chapter, we will discuss procedures for discovering and correcting errors.

## 4. Discovery and Correction of Errors

Errors will sometimes occur in journalizing and posting transactions. In some cases, however, an error might not be significant enough to affect the decisions of management or others. In such cases, the materiality concept implies that the error may be treated in the easiest possible way. For example, an error of a few dollars in recording an asset as an expense for a business with millions of dollars in assets would be considered immaterial, and a correction would not be necessary. In the remaining paragraphs, we assume that errors discovered are material and should be corrected.

### DISCOVERY OF ERRORS

As mentioned previously, preparing the trial balance is one of the primary ways to discover errors in the ledger. However, it indicates only that the debits and credits are equal. If the two totals of the trial balance are not equal, it is probably due to one or more of the errors.

Among the types of errors that will not cause the trial balance totals to be unequal are the following.

(1) Failure to record a transaction or to post a transaction.

(2) Recording the same erroneous amount for both debit and credit parts of a transaction.

(3) Recording the same transaction more than once.

(4) Posting a part of a transaction correctly as a debit or credit but to the wrong account.

It is obvious that care should be used in recording transactions in the journal and in posting to the accounts. The need for accuracy in determining account balances and reporting them on the trial balance is also evident.

Errors in the accounts may be discovered in various ways: through audit procedures, by looking at the trial balance, or by chance. If the two trial balance totals are not equal, the amount of the difference between the totals should be determined before searching for the error.

The amount of the difference between the two totals of a trial balance sometimes gives a clue as to the nature of the error or where it occurred. For example, a difference of \$10, 100, or \$1,000 between two totals is often the result of an error in addition. A difference between totals can also be due to omitting a debit or a credit posting. If the difference can be evenly divided by 2, the error may be due to the posting of a debit as a credit, or vice versa. For example, if the debit total is

$20,640 and the credit total is $20,236, the difference of $404 may indicate that a credit posting of $404 was omitted or that a credit of $202 was incorrectly posted as a debit.

Two other common types of errors are known as transpositions and slides. A transposition occurs when the order of the digits is changed mistakenly, such as writing $542 as $452 or $524. In a slide, the entire number is mistakenly moved one or more spaces to the right or the left, such as writing $542.00 as $54.20 or $5,420.00. If an error of either type has occurred and there are no other errors, the difference between the two trial balance totals can be evenly divided by 9.

If an error is not revealed by the trial balance, the steps in the accounting process must be retraced, beginning with the last step and working back to the entries in the journal. Usually, errors causing the trial balance totals to be unequal will be discovered before all of the steps are retraced.

### CORRECTION OF ERRORS

The procedures used to correct an error vary according to the nature of the error, when the error is discovered, and whether a manual or computerized accounting system is used. Oftentimes, an error is discovered as it is being journalized or posted. In such cases, the error is simply corrected. For example, computerized accounting systems automatically verify for each journal entry whether the total debits equal the total credits. If the totals are not equal, an error report is created and the computer program will not proceed until the journal entry is corrected.

Occasionally, however, an error is not discovered until after a journal entry has been recorded and posted to the accounts. Correcting this type of error is more complex. To illustrate, assume that on May 5 a $12,500 purchase of office equipment on account was incorrectly journalized and posted as a debit to Supplies and a credit to Accounts Payable for $12,500. This posting of the incorrect entry is shown in the following T accounts.

| | Supplies | | Accounts Payable | |
|---|---|---|---|---|
| Incorrect | $12,500 | | | $12,500 |

Before making a correcting entry, it is best to determine the debit(s) and credit(s) that should have been recorded. These are shown in the following T accounts.

| | Office Equipment | | Accounts Payable | |
|---|---|---|---|---|
| Correct | $12,500 | | | $12,500 |

Comparing the two sets of T accounts shows that the incorrect debit to Supplies may be corrected by debiting Office Equipment for $12,500 and crediting Supplies for $12,500. The correcting entry is then journalized and posted as shown in Exhibit 2-34.

**Exhibit 2-34 Entry to correct error**

| Date | | Description | Post. Ref. | Debit | Credit |
|---|---|---|---|---|---|
| May | 31 | Office Equipment | 18 | 12,500 | |
| | | Supplies | 14 | | 12,500 |
| | | To correct erroneous debit to Supplies on May 5 | | | |

**TERMINOLOGY:**

Account：账户

Chart of Accounts：会计科目表

Credit：贷方

Debit：借方

Journal：分录

Ledger：账簿

Posting：过账

Trial Balance：试算平衡表

**QUESTIONS:**

**1. Describe the characteristics of an account.**

The simplest form of an account, a T account, has three parts: ① a title, which is the name of the item recorded in the account. ② a left side, called the debit side. ③ a right side, called the credit side. Amounts entered on the left side of an account, regardless of the account title, are called debits to the account. Amounts entered on the right side of an account are called credits. Periodically, the debits in an account are added, the credits in the account are added, and the balance of the account is determined.

**2. List the rules of debit and credit and the normal balances of accounts.**

General rules of debit and credit have been established for recording increases or decreases in asset, liability, revenue, expense, and capital accounts. Each transaction is recorded so that the sum of the debits is always equal to the sum of credits. Transactions are initially entered in a record called a journal.

The sum of the increases recorded in an account is usually equal to or greater than the sum of the decreases recorded in the account. For this reason, the normal balance of an account is indicated by the side of the account (debit or credit) that receives the increases. Rules of debit and credit and normal account balances are summarized in Exhibit 2-35.

**Exhibit 2-35 Rules of debit and credit and normal account balances**

| Accounts Title | Increase | Decrease |
|---|---|---|
| Balance Sheet accounts: | | |
| Asset | Debit | Credit |
| Liability | Credit | Debit |
| Owner's (Stockholders') Equity accounts: | | |
| Capital | Credit | Debit |
| Income Statement accounts: | | |
| Revenue | Credit | Debit |
| Expense | Debit | Credit |

**3. Analyze and summarize the financial statement effects of transactions.**

Transactions are analyzed by determining whether: an asset, liability, revenue, expense, or capital account is affected, each account affected increases or decreases, and each increase or decrease is recorded as a debit or a credit. A journal is used for recording the transaction initially. The journal entries are periodically posted to the accounts.

**4. What is a trial balance and explain how it can be used to discover errors?**

A trial balance is prepared by listing the accounts from the ledger and their balances. If the two totals of the trial balance are not equal, an error has occurred.

Errors may be discovered by audit procedures, by looking at the trial balance or by chance. The procedures for correcting errors are summarized in Exhibit 2-36.

**Exhibit 2-36 Procedures for correcting errors**

| Error | Correction Procedure |
|---|---|
| Journal entry is incorrect but not posted | Draw a line through the error and insert correct title or amount |
| Journal entry is correct but posted incorrectly | Draw a line through the error and post correctly |
| Journal entry is incorrect and posted | Journalize and post a correcting entry |

**PROBLEM:**

The trial balance of Reitmeier Service Center on March 1, 2007, lists the entity's assets, liabilities, and owner's equity on that date, as shown in Exhibit 2-37.

**Exhibit 2-37 Trial balance**

| Account Title | Balance | |
|---|---|---|
| | Debit | Credit |
| Cash | 26,000 | |
| Accounts Receivable | 4,500 | |
| Accounts Payable | | 2,000 |
| Mike Reitmeier, Capital | | 28,500 |
| Total | 30,500 | 30,500 |

During March, the business engaged in the following transactions.

a. Borrowed $45,000 from bank and signed a note payable in the name of business.

b. Paid cash of $40,000 to acquire land.

c. Performed service for a customer and received cash of $5,000.

d. Purchased supplies on account, $300.

e. Performed customer service and earned revenue on account, $2,600.

f. Paid $1,200 on account.

g. Paid the following cash expenses: wages $3,000; rent $1,500; and interest $400.

h. Received $3,100 on account.

i. Received a $200 utility bill that be paid next week.

j. Withdrew $1,800 for personal use.

**Requirements**

**1. Open the following accounts, with the balances indicated, in the ledger of Reitmeier Service Center. Use the T-account format.**

(1) Assets: Cash, $26,000; Accounts Receivable, $4,500; Supplies, no balance; Land, no balance.

(2) Liabilities: Accounts Payable, $2,000; Note Payable, no balance.

(3) Owner's Equity: Mike Reitmeier, Capital, $28,500; Mike Reitmeier, Drawing, no balance.

(4) Revenues: Service Income, no balance.

(5) Expenses: Wages Expense, no balance; Rent Expense, no balance; Utilities Expense, no balance; Interest Expense, no balance.

**2. Journalize each transaction. Key journal entries by transaction letter.**

**3. Post to the ledger.**

**4. Prepare the trial balance of Reitmeier Service Center at March 31, 2007.**

**Solution**

**Requirement 1 and 3.**

| Cash | |
|---|---|
| Bal. $26,000 | $40,000 |
| $45,000 | $1,200 |
| $5,000 | $4,900 |
| $3,100 | $1,800 |
| Bal. $31,200 | |

| Accounts Payable | |
|---|---|
| $1,200 | Bal. $2,000 |
| | $300 |
| | $200 |
| | Bal. $1,300 |

| Mike Reitmeier, Capital | |
|---|---|
| | Bal. $28,500 |

| Accounts Receivable | |
|---|---|
| Bal. $4,500 | $3,100 |
| $2,600 | |
| Bal. $4,000 | |

| Note Payable | |
|---|---|
| | $45,000 |
| | Bal. $45,000 |

| Mike Reitmeier, Drawing | |
|---|---|
| $1,800 | |
| Bal. $1,800 | |

| Supplies | |
|---|---|
| $300 | |
| Bal. $300 | |

| Service Income | |
|---|---|
| | $5,000 |
| | $2,600 |
| | Bal. $7,600 |

| Land | |
|---|---|
| $40,000 | |
| Bal. $40,000 | |

| Interest Expense | |
|---|---|
| $400 | |
| Bal. $400 | |

| Utilities Expense | |
|---|---|
| $200 | |
| Bal. $200 | |

| Wages Expense | |
|---|---|
| $3,000 | |
| Bal. $3,000 | |

| Rent Expense | |
|---|---|
| $1,500 | |
| Bal. $1,500 | |

**Requirement 2.**

a. Dr. Cash 45,000
Cr. Note Payable 45,000
Borrowed cash on note payable.

b. Dr. Land 40,000
Cr. Cash 40,000
Purchased land.

c. Dr. Cash 5,000
Cr. Service Income 5,000
Preformed service and received cash.

d. Dr. Supplies 300
Cr. Accounts Payable 300
Purchased supplies on account.

e. Dr. Accounts Receivable 2,600
Cr. Service Income 2,600
Performed service on account.

f. Dr. Accounts Payable 1,200
Cr. Cash 1,200
Paid on account.

g. Dr. Wages Expense 3,000
Rent Expense 1,500
Interest Expense 400
Cr. Cash 4,900
Paid expenses.

h. Dr. Cash 3,100
Cr. Accounts Receivable 3,100
Received cash on account.

i. Dr. Utilities Expense 200
Cr. Accounts Payable 200
Received utility bill.

j. Dr. Mike Reitmeier, Drawing 1,800
Cr. Cash 1,800
Owner withdrawal.

**Requirement 4.**

The trial balance of Reitmeier Service Center is shown in Exhibit 2-38.

**Exhibit 2-38 Traial balance**

Reitmeier Service Center
Trial Balance
March 31, 2007

| Account Title | Balance | |
|---|---|---|
| | Debit | Credit |
| Cash | 31,200 | |
| Accounts Receivable | 4,000 | |
| Supplies | 300 | |
| Land | 40,000 | |
| Accounts Payable | | 1,300 |
| Note Payable | | 45,000 |
| Mike Reitmeier, Capital | | 28,500 |
| Mike Reitmeier, Drawing | 1,800 | |
| Service Income | | 7,600 |
| Wages Expense | 3,000 | |
| Rent Expense | 1,500 | |
| Interest Expense | 400 | |
| Utilities Expense | 200 | |
| Total | 82,400 | 82,400 |

# Chapter 3

## The Adjusting Process

**Objectives**

1. Describe the nature of the adjusting process.
2. Journalize entries for accounts requiring adjustment.
3. Summarize the adjustment process.
4. Prepare an adjusted trial balance.

# 1. Nature of the Adjusting Process

To determine the proper period, accountants use generally accepted accounting principles, which require the use of the accrual basis of accounting.

Under the accrual basis of accounting, revenues are reported in the income statement in the period in which they are earned, expenses are reported in the same period as the revenues to which they relate. For example, revenue is reported when the services are provided to customers. Employee wages are reported as an expense in the period in which the employees provided services to customers, and not necessarily when the wages are paid. The accounting concept that supports reporting revenues and related expenses in the same period is called the matching concept.

Under the cash basis of accounting, revenues and expenses are reported in the income statement in the period in which cash is received or paid. For example, fees are recorded when cash is received from clients, and wages are recorded when cash is paid to employees. For most large businesses, the cash basis will not provide accurate financial statements for user needs. For this reason, we will emphasize the accrual basis in this text.

## THE ADJUSTING PROCESS

Under the accrual basis, however, some accounts in the ledger require updating.

For example, the balances listed for prepaid expenses are normally overstated because the use of these assets is not recorded on a day-to-day basis. The balance of the supplies account usually represents the cost of supplies at the beginning of the period plus the cost of supplies acquired during the period. To record the daily use of supplies would require many entries with small amounts. In addition, the total amount of supplies is small relative to other assets, and managers usually do not require day-to-day information about supplies.

The analysis and updating of accounts at the end of the period before the financial statements are prepared is called the adjusting process. The journal entries that bring the accounts up to date at the end of the accounting period are called adjusting entries. All adjusting entries affect at least one income statement account and one balance sheet account. Thus, an adjusting entry will always involve a revenue or an expense account and an asset or a liability account. In the next section, we describe how to determine if an account needs adjusting.

## TYPES OF ACCOUNTS REQUIRING ADJUSTMENT

Is there an easy way to know when an adjusting entry is needed? Yes, four basic types of accounts require adjusting entries. These accounts are prepaid expenses, unearned revenues, accrued revenues, and accrued expenses.

Prepaid expenses, sometimes referred to as deferred expenses, are items that have been initially recorded as assets but are expected to become expenses over time or through the normal operations of the business. Supplies and prepaid insurance are two examples of prepaid expenses that may require adjustment at the end of an accounting period. Other examples include prepaid advertising and prepaid interest.

Unearned revenues, sometimes referred to as deferred revenues, are items that have been initially recorded as liabilities but are expected to become revenues over time or through the normal operations of the business. An example of unearned revenue is unearned rent. Other examples include tuition received in advance by a school, an annual retainer fee received by an attorney, premiums received in advance by an insurance company, and magazine subscriptions received in advance by a publisher.

Prepaid expenses and unearned revenues are created from transactions that involve the receipt or payment of cash. In both cases, the recording of the related expense or revenue is delayed until the end of the period or to a future period. For example, Darming paid $1,200 as a premium on a one-year insurance policy on December 1. The payment was recorded as a debit to Prepaid Insurance and credit to Cash for $1,200. At the end of December, only $100 ($1,200 divided by 12 months) of the insurance premium will have expired as insurance expense, and the recording of the remaining $1,100 of insurance expense will be delayed to future periods. As we will see in the next section, the $100 insurance premium expiring in December will be recorded as insurance expense at the end of December, using an adjusting entry.

Accrued revenues, sometimes referred to as accrued assets, are revenues that have been earned but have not been recorded in the accounts. An example of an accrued revenue is fees for services that an attorney has provided but hasn't billed to the client at the end of the period. Other examples include unbilled commissions by a travel agent, accrued interest on notes receivable, and accrued rent on property rented to others.

Accrued expenses, sometimes referred to as accrued liabilities, are expenses that have been incurred but have not been recorded in the accounts. An example of an accrued expense is accrued wages owed to employees at the end of a period. Other examples include accrued interest on notes payable and accrued taxes.

Accrued revenues and expenses are created by an unrecorded revenue that has been earned or an unrecorded expense that has been incurred. For example, in the next section, we will record accrued revenues and accrued wages expense for Darming at the end of December by using adjusting entries. Prior to recording the adjusting entries, neither accrued revenues nor accrued wages have been recorded.

## 2. Recording Adjusting Entries

The examples of adjusting entries in the following paragraphs are based on the ledger of Darming as reported in the December 31, 2007, unadjusted trial balance in Exhibit 3-1. An expanded chart of accounts for Darming is shown in Exhibit 3-2. The additional accounts that will be used in this chapter are shown in bold.

**Exhibit 3-1 Unadjusted trial balance for Darming**

Darming

Unadjusted Trial Balance

December 31, 2007

| Accounts | Debit Balances | Credit Balances |
|---|---|---|
| Cash | 102,300 | |
| Accounts Receivable | 2,400 | |
| Supplies | 4,000 | |
| Prepaid Insurance | 1,200 | |
| Land | 100, 000 | |
| Office Equipment | 1,000 | |
| Accounts Payable | | 0 |
| Unearned Rent | | 3,000 |
| John, Capital | | 200,000 |
| John, Drawing | 2,000 | |
| Service Income | | 18,000 |
| Wages Expense | 4,000 | |
| Rent Expense | 1,800 | |
| Utilities Expense | 1,000 | |
| Supplies Expense | 1,000 | |
| Miscellaneous Expense | 300 | |
| Total | 221,000 | 221,000 |

**Exhibit 3-2 Expanded chart of accounts for Darming**

| Balance Sheet Accounts | Income Statement Accounts |
|---|---|
| 1. Assets | 4. Revenue |
| 11 Cash | 41 Service Income |
| 12 Accounts Receivable | **42 Rent Revenue** |
| 14 Supplies | 5. Expenses |
| 15 Prepaid Insurance | 51 Wages Expense |
| 17 Land | 52 Rent Expense |
| 18 Office Equipment | **53 Depreciation Expense** |
| **19 Accumulated Depreciation— office Equipment** | 54 Utilities Expense |
| 2. Liabilities | 55 Supplies Expense |
| 21 Accounts Payable | **56 Insurance Expense** |
| **22 Wages Payable** | 59 Miscellaneous Expense |
| 23 Unearned Rent | |
| 3. Owner's Equity | |
| 31 John, Capital | |
| 32 John, Drawing | |

## PREPAID EXPENSES

The concept of adjusting accounting records was introduced in Chapters 1 and 2 in the illustration for Darming. In that illustration, supplies were purchased on November 11 (transaction c). The supplies used during November were recorded on November 30 (transaction g).

The balance in Darming's supplies account on December 31 is $4,000. Some of these supplies (CDs, paper, envelopes, etc) were used during December, and some are still on hand (not used). If either amount is known, the other can be determined. It is normally easier to determine the cost of the supplies on hand at the end of the month than it is to keep a daily record of those used. Assuming that on December 31 the amount of supplies on hand is $760, the amount to be transferred from the asset account to the expense account is $1,240, computed as follows.

| | |
|---|---|
| Supplies available during December (balance of account): | $4,000 |
| Supplies on hand, December 31: | $760 |
| Supplies used (amount of adjustment): | $3,240 |

As we discussed in Chapter 2, increases in expense accounts are recorded as debits and decreases in asset accounts are recorded as credits. At the end of December, the Supplies Expense account should be debited for $3,240, and the Supplies account should be credited for $3,240 to record the supplies used during December. The adjusting journal entry and T accounts for Supplies and Supplies Expense are shown in Exhibit 3-3.

**Exhibit 3-3 The adjusting journal entry and T accounts**

| Date | | Description | Post. Ref. | Debt | Credit |
|---|---|---|---|---|---|
| 2007 Dec. | 31 | Supplies Expense | 55 | 3,240 | |
| | | Supplies | 14 | | 3,240 |
| | | Supplies used ($4,000 − $760) | | | |

Supplies

| | | | |
|---|---|---|---|
| Bal. | $4,000 | Dec.31 | $3,240 |
| Adj. Bal. | $760 | | |

Supplies Expense

| | | |
|---|---|---|
| Bal. | $1,000 | |
| Dec.31 | $3,240 | |
| Adj. Bal. | $4,240 | |

After the adjustment has been recorded and posted, the Supplies account has a debit balance of $760. This balance represents an asset that will become an expense in a future period.

The debit balance of $1,200 in Darming's Prepaid Insurance account represents a December 1 prepayment of insurance for 12 months. At the end of December, the Insurance Expense account should be increased (debited), and the Prepaid Insurance account should be decreased (credited) by $100, the insurance for one month. The adjusting journal entry and T accounts for Prepaid Insurance and Insurance Expense are shown in Exhibit 3-4.

**Exhibit 3-4 The adjusting journal entry and T accounts**

| Date | | Description | Post. Ref. | Debit | Credit |
|---|---|---|---|---|---|
| 2007 Dec. | 31 | Insurance Expense | 56 | 100 | |
| | | Prepaid Insurance | 15 | | 100 |
| | | Insurance expired ( $1,200/12months) | | | |

| Prepaid Insurance | | | |
|---|---|---|---|
| Bal. | $1,200 | Dec.31 | $100 |
| Adj. Bal. | $1,100 | | |

| Insurance Expense | |
|---|---|
| Dec.31 | $100 |
| Adj. Bal. | $100 |

After the adjustment has been recorded and posted, the Prepaid Insurance account has a debit balance of $1,100. This balance represents an asset that will become an expense in future periods. The Insurance Expense account has a debit balance of $100, which is an expense of the current period.

What is the effect of omitting adjusting entries? If the preceding adjustments for supplies ($3,240) and insurance ($100) are not recorded, the financial statements prepared as of December 31 will be misstated. On the income statement, Supplies Expense and Insurance Expense will be understated by a total of $3,340, and net income will be overstated by $3,340. On the balance sheet, Supplies and Prepaid Insurance will be overstated by a total of $3,340. Since net income increases owner's equity, John, Capital will also be overstated by $3,340 on the balance sheet. The effects of omitting these adjusting entries on the income statement and balance sheet are shown in Exhibit 3-5.

**Exhibit 3-5 Amount of misstatement**

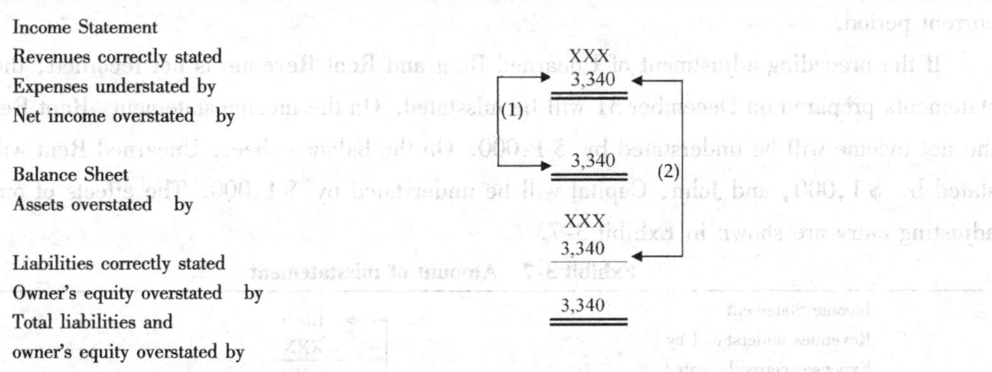


Arrow (1) indicates the effect of the understated expenses on assets. Arrow (2) indicates the effect of the overstated net income on owner's equity.

Prepayments of expenses are sometimes made at the beginning of the period in which they will be entirely consumed. On December 1, for example, Darming paid rent of $1,000 for the month. On December 1, the rent payment represents the asset prepaid rent. The prepaid rent expires daily, and at the end of December, the entire amount has become an expense (rent expense). In cases such as this, the initial payment is recorded as an expense rather than as an asset. Thus, if the payment is recorded as a debit to Rent Expense, no adjusting entry is needed at the end of the period.

## UNEARNED REVENUES

According to Darming's trial balance on December 31, the balance in the Unearned Rent account is $3,000. This balance represents the receipt of three months' rent on December 1 for December, January, and February. At the end of December, the Unearned Rent account should be decreased (debited) by $1,000, and the Rent Revenue account should be increased (credited) by $1,000. The $1,000 represents the rental revenue for one month ($3,000/3 months). The adjusting journal entry and T accounts are shown in Exhibit 3-6.

**Exhibit 3-6 The adjusting journal entry and T accounts**

| Date | | Description | Post. Ref. | Debit | Credit |
|---|---|---|---|---|---|
| 2007<br>Dec. | 31 | Unearned Rent | 23 | 1,000 | |
| | | Rent Revenue | 42 | | 1,000 |
| | | Rent earned ($3,000/3 months) | | | |

| Unearned Rent | | Rent Revenue | |
|---|---|---|---|
| Dec. 31 $1,000 | Bal. $3,000 | | Dec.31 $1,000 |
| | Adj. Bal. $2,000 | | Adj. Bal. $1,000 |

After the adjustment has been recorded and posted, the Unearned Rent account, which is a liability, has a credit balance of $2,000. This amount represents a deferral that will become revenue in a future period. The Rent Revenue account has a balance of $1,000, which is revenue of the current period.

If the preceding adjustment of Unearned Rent and Rent Revenue is not recorded, the financial statements prepared on December 31 will be misstated. On the income statement, Rent Revenue and the net income will be understated by $1,000. On the balance sheet, Unearned Rent will be overstated by $1,000, and John, Capital will be understated by $1,000. The effects of omitting this adjusting entry are shown in Exhibit 3-7.

**Exhibit 3-7 Amount of misstatement**

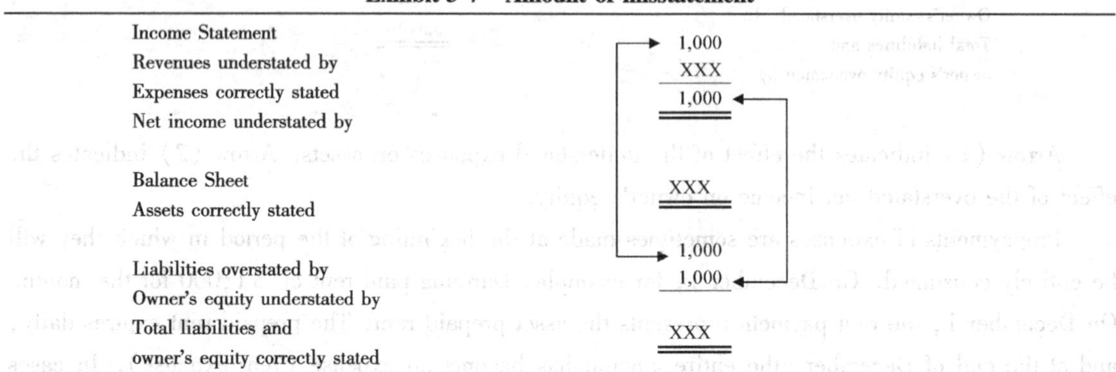

## ACCRUED REVENUES

During an accounting period, some revenues are recorded only when cash is received. Thus, at the end of an accounting period, there may be items of revenue that have been earned but have not been recorded. In such cases, the amount of the revenue should be recorded by debiting an asset account and crediting a revenue account.

To illustrate, assume that Darming signed an agreement with Dankner Co. on December 15. The agreement provides that Darming will be on call to answer computer questions and render assistance to Dankner Co.'s employees. The services provided will be billed to Dankner Co. on the fifteenth of each month at a rate of $20 per hour. As of December 31, Darming had provided 25 hours of assistance to Dankner Co. Although the revenue of $500 (25 hours × $20) will be billed and collected in January, Darming earned the revenue in December. The adjusting journal entry to record the claim against the customer (an account receivable) and the fees earned in December are shown in Exhibit 3-8.

**Exhibit 3-8 The adjusting journal entry**

| Date | Description | Post. Ref. | Debit | Credit |
|---|---|---|---|---|
| 31 | Accounts Receivable | 12 | 500 | |
| | Servie Income | 41 | | 500 |
| | Accrued fees (25 hours. × $20). | | | |

If the adjustment for the accrued asset ($500) is not recorded, Service Income and the net income will be understated by $500 on the income statement. On the balance sheet, Accounts Receivable and John, Capital will be understated by $500. The effects of omitting this adjusting entry are shown in Exhibit 3-9.

**Exhibit 3-9 Amount of misstatement**

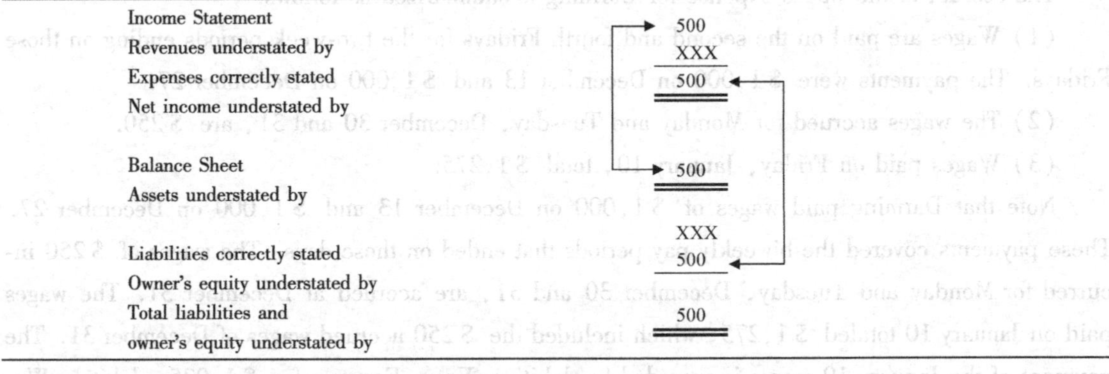

| | |
|---|---|
| Income Statement | |
| Revenues understated by | 500 |
| Expenses correctly stated | XXX |
| Net income understated by | 500 |
| Balance Sheet | |
| Assets understated by | 500 |
| Liabilities correctly stated | XXX |
| Owner's equity understated by | 500 |
| Total liabilities and owner's equity understated by | 500 |

## ACCRUED EXPENSES

Some types of services, such as insurance, are normally paid for before they are used. These prepayments are deferrals. Other types of services are paid for after the service has been performed. For example, wages expense accumulates or accrues hour by hour and day by day, but payment may be made only weekly, biweekly, or monthly. The amount of such an accrued but unpaid item at the end of the accounting period is both an expense and a liability. In the case of wages expense, if the last day of a pay period is not the last day of the accounting period, the accrued wages expense and the related liability must be recorded in the accounts by an adjusting entry. This adjusting entry is necessary so that expenses are properly matched to the period in which they were incurred.

At the end of December, accrued wages for Darming were $250. This amount is an additional expense of December and is debited to the Wages Expense account. It is also a liability as of December 31 and is credited to Wages Payable. The adjusting journal entry and T accounts are shown in Exhibit 3-10.

**Exhibit 3-10 The adjusting journal entry and T accounts**

| Date | | Description | Post. Ref. | Debit | Credit |
|---|---|---|---|---|---|
| 2007 Dec. | 31 | Wages Expense | 51 | 250 | |
| | | Wages Payable | 22 | | 250 |
| | | Accrued wages | | | |

Wages Expense

| | | |
|---|---|---|
| Bal. | $4,000 | |
| Dec.31 | $250 | |
| Adj. Bal. | $4,250 | |

Wages Payable

| | | |
|---|---|---|
| | Dec.31 | $250 |
| | Adj. Bal. | $250 |

After the adjustment has been recorded and posted, the debit balance of the Wages Expense account is $4,250, which is the wages expense for the two months, November and December. The credit balance of $250 in Wages Payable is the amount of the liability for wages owed as of December 31.

The accrual of the wages expense for Darming is summarized as follows.

(1) Wages are paid on the second and fourth Fridays for the two-week periods ending on those Fridays. The payments were $1,000 on December 13 and $1,000 on December 27.

(2) The wages accrued for Monday and Tuesday, December 30 and 31, are $250.

(3) Wages paid on Friday, January 10, total $1,275.

Note that Darming paid wages of $1,000 on December 13 and $1,000 on December 27. These payments covered the biweekly pay periods that ended on those days. The wages of $250 incurred for Monday and Tuesday, December 30 and 31, are accrued at December 31. The wages paid on January 10 totaled $1,275, which included the $250 accrued wages of December 31. The payment of the January 10 wages is recorded by debiting Wages Expense for $1,025, debiting Wages Payable for $250, and crediting Cash for $1,275, as shown in Exhibit 3-11.

What would be the effect on the financial statements if the adjustment for wages ($250) is not recorded? On the income statement, Wages Expense will be understated by $250, and the net income will be overstated by $250. On the balance sheet, Wages Payable will be understated by $250, and John, Capital will be overstated by $250. The effects of omitting this adjusting entry are shown in Exhibit 3-12.

**Exhibit 3-11 Journal entry**

| Date | | Description | Post. Ref. | Debit | Credit |
|---|---|---|---|---|---|
| 2008 Jan. | 10 | Wages Expense | 51 | 1,025 | |
| | | Wages Payable | 22 | 250 | |
| | | Cash | 11 | | 1,275 |
| | | Paid wages | | | |

**Exhibit 3-12 Amount of misstatement**

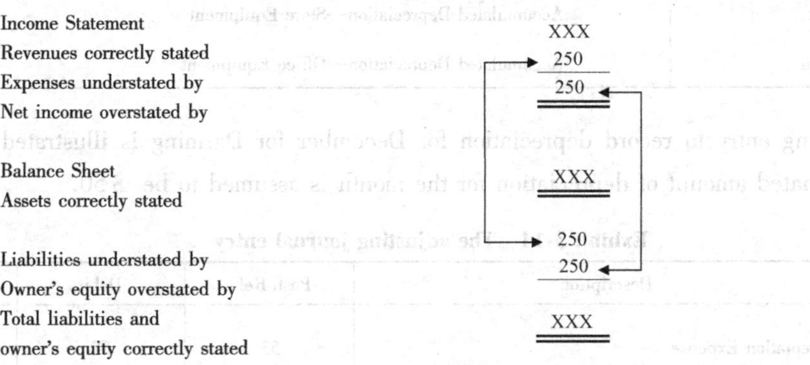

| | |
|---|---|
| Income Statement | XXX |
| Revenues correctly stated | 250 |
| Expenses understated by | 250 |
| Net income overstated by | |
| Balance Sheet | XXX |
| Assets correctly stated | |
| | 250 |
| Liabilities understated by | 250 |
| Owner's equity overstated by | |
| Total liabilities and owner's equity correctly stated | XXX |

## DEPRECIATION EXPENSES

Physical resources that are owned and used by a business and are permanent or have a long life are called fixed assets, or plant assets. In a sense, fixed assets are a type of long – term prepaid expense. Because of their nature and long life, they are discussed separately from other prepaid expenses, such as supplies and prepaid insurance.

Darming's fixed assets include office equipment, which is used much like supplies are used to generate revenue. Unlike supplies, however, there is no visible reduction in the quantity of the equipment. Instead, as time passes, the equipment loses its ability to provide useful services. This decrease in usefulness is called depreciation.

All fixed assets, except land, lose their usefulness. Decreases in the usefulness of assets that are used in generating revenue are recorded as expenses. However, such decreases for fixed assets are difficult to measure. For this reason, a portion of the cost of a fixed asset is recorded as an expense each year of its useful life. This periodic expense is called depreciation expense. Methods of computing depreciation expense are discussed and illustrated in a later chapter.

The adjusting entry to record depreciation is similar to the adjusting entry for supplies used. The account debited is a depreciation expense account. However, the asset account Office Equipment is not credited because both the original cost of a fixed asset and the amount of depreciation recorded since its purchase are normally reported on the balance sheet. The account credited is an accumulated depreciation account. Accumulated depreciation accounts are called contra accounts, or contra asset accounts, because they are deducted from the related asset accounts on the balance sheet. The normal balance of a contra account is opposite to the account from which it is deducted. Thus, the normal balance for Accumulated Depreciation is a credit.

Normal titles for fixed asset accounts and their related contra asset accounts are shown in Exhibit 3-13.

**Exhibit 3-13 Fixed asset accounts and their related contra asset accounts**

| Fixed Asset | Contra Asset |
|---|---|
| Land | None—Land is not depreciated |
| Buildings | Accumulated Depreciation—Buildings |
| Store Equipment | Accumulated Depreciation—Store Equipment |
| Office Equipment | Accumulated Depreciation—Office Equipment |

The adjusting entry to record depreciation for December for Darming is illustrated in Exhibit 3-14. The estimated amount of depreciation for the month is assumed to be $50.

**Exhibit 3-14 The adjusting journal entry**

| Date | | Description | Post. Ref. | Debit | Credit |
|---|---|---|---|---|---|
| 2007<br>Dec. | 31 | Depreciation Expense | 53 | 50 | |
| | | Accumulated Depreciation—Office Equipment | 19 | | 50 |
| | | Depreciation on office equipment | | | |

The $50 increase in the Accumulated Depreciation account is subtracted from the $1,000 cost recorded in the related fixed asset account. The difference between the two balances is the $950 cost that has not yet been depreciated. This amount ( $950) is called the book value of the asset (or net book value), which may be presented on the balance sheet in the following manner.

| | | |
|---|---|---|
| Office equipment | $1,000 | |
| Less: accumulated depreciation | $50 | $950 |

You should note that the market value of a fixed asset usually differs from its book value. This is because depreciation is an allocation method, not a valuation method. That is, depreciation allocates the cost of a fixed asset to expense over its estimated life. Depreciation does not attempt to measure changes in market values, which may vary significantly from year to year.

If the previous adjustment for depreciation ( $50) is not recorded, Depreciation Expense on the income statement will be understated by $50, and the net income will be overstated by $50. On the balance sheet, the book value of Office Equipment and John, Capital will be overstated by $50. The effects of omitting the adjustment for depreciation are shown in Exhibit 3-15.

**Exhibit 3-15 Amount of misstatement**

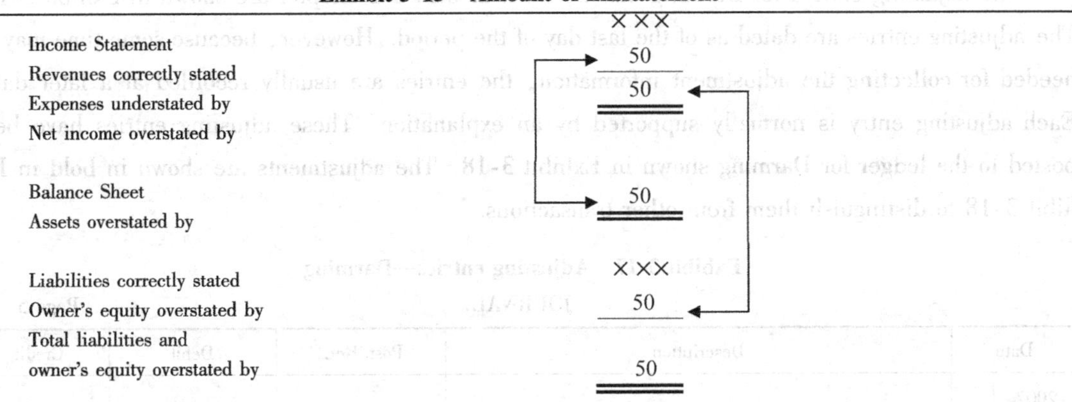

| | |
|---|---|
| Income Statement | |
| Revenues correctly stated | ××× |
| Expenses understated by | 50 |
| Net income overstated by | 50 |
| Balance Sheet | |
| Assets overstated by | 50 |
| Liabilities correctly stated | ××× |
| Owner's equity overstated by | 50 |
| Total liabilities and owner's equity overstated by | 50 |

## 3. Summary of the Adjustment Process

We have described and illustrated the basic types of adjusting entries in the preceding section. A summary of these basic adjustments, including the type of adjustment, the adjusting entry, and the effect of the adjustment on the financial statements, is shown in Exhibit 3-16. As Exhibit 3-16 illustrates, each adjustment affects the income statement and balance sheet.

**Exhibit 3-16 Summary of adjustments**

| | | | | Financial Statement Effect of Adjustment Increase (Decrease) | | | | | |
|---|---|---|---|---|---|---|---|---|---|
| | | | | Income Statement | | | Balance Sheet | | |
| Type of Adjustment | Adjusting Entry | | | Revenues | −Expenses | =Net Income | Assets | =Liabilities | +Owner's Equity |
| Prepaid Expenses | | | | | | | | | |
| Supplies | Supplies Exp. | 3,240 | | | 3,240 | (3,240) | | | |
| | Supplies | | 3,240 | | | | (3,240) | | (3,240) |
| Prepaid Insurance | Insurance Exp. | 100 | | | 100 | (100) | | | |
| | Prepaid Ins. | | 100 | | | | (100) | | (100) |
| Unearned Revenue | | | | | | | | | |
| Unearned Rent | Unearned Rent | 1,000 | | | | | | (1,000) | 1,000 |
| | Rent Revenue | | 1,000 | 1,000 | | 1,000 | | | |
| Accrued Revenue | | | | | | | | | |
| Accrued Fees | Accts.Receivable | 500 | | | | | 500 | | 500 |
| | Service Income | | 500 | 500 | | 500 | | | |
| Accrued Expenses | | | | | | | | | |
| Accrued Wages | Wages Expense | 250 | | | 250 | (250) | | | |
| | Wages Payable | | 250 | | | | | 250 | (250) |
| Depreciation Expenses | | | | | | | | | |
| Office Equipment | Depreciation Exp. | 50 | | | 50 | (50) | | | |
| | Acc. Dep. — Office Equip. | | 50 | | | | (50) | | (50) |

The adjusting entries for Darming that we illustrated in this chapter are shown in Exhibit 3-17. The adjusting entries are dated as of the last day of the period. However, because some time may be needed for collecting the adjustment information, the entries are usually recorded at a later date. Each adjusting entry is normally supported by an explanation. These adjusting entries have been posted to the ledger for Darming shown in Exhibit 3-18. The adjustments are shown in bold in Exhibit 3-18 to distinguish them from other transactions.

**Exhibit 3-17 Adjusting entries—Darming**

JOURNAL Page 5

| Date | | Description | Post. Ref. | Debit | Credit |
|---|---|---|---|---|---|
| 2007 Dec. | | Adjusting Entries | | | |
| | 31 | Supplies Expense | 55 | 3,240 | |
| | | Supplies | 14 | | 3,240 |
| | | Supplies used ( $4,000 - $760) | | | |
| | | | | | |
| | 31 | Insurance Expense | 56 | 100 | |
| | | Prepaid Insurance | 15 | | 100 |
| | | Insurance expired ( $1,200/12 months) | | | |
| | | | | | |
| | 31 | Unearned Rent | 23 | 1,000 | |
| | | Rent Revenue | 42 | | 1,000 |
| | | Rent earned ( $3,000/3 months) | | | |
| | | | | | |
| | 31 | Accounts Receivable | 12 | 500 | |
| | | Service Income | 41 | | 500 |
| | | Accrued fees (25 hours. × $20) | | | |
| | | | | | |
| | 31 | Wages Expense | 51 | 250 | |
| | | Wages Payable | 22 | | 250 |
| | | Accrued wages | | | |
| | | | | | |
| | 31 | Depreciation Expense | 53 | 50 | |
| | | Accum. Depr. —Office Equip. | 19 | | 50 |
| | | Depreciation on office Equipment | | | |
| | | | | | |

**Exhibit 3-18 Leger with adjusting entries—Darming**

ACCOUNT Cash ACCOUNT NO. 11

| Date | | Item | Post. Ref. | Debit | Credit | Balance | |
|---|---|---|---|---|---|---|---|
| | | | | | | Debit | Credit |
| 2007 Nov. | 1 | | 1 | 200,000 | | 200,000 | |
| | 5 | | 1 | | 100,000 | 100,000 | |
| | 18 | | 1 | 10,000 | | 110,000 | |
| | 30 | | 1 | | 3,400 | 106,600 | |
| | 30 | | 1 | | 1,000 | 105,600 | |
| | 30 | | 2 | | 1,000 | 104,600 | |
| | 1 | | 2 | | 1,200 | 103,400 | |
| | 1 | | 2 | | 1,000 | 102,400 | |
| | 1 | | 2 | 3,000 | | 105,400 | |
| | 6 | | 2 | | 100 | 105,300 | |
| | 11 | | 2 | | 3,000 | 102,300 | |
| | 13 | | 2 | | 1,000 | 101,300 | |
| | 16 | | 3 | 3,000 | | 104,300 | |
| | 20 | | 3 | | 1,000 | 103,300 | |
| | 21 | | 3 | 600 | | 103,900 | |
| | 23 | | 3 | | 1,000 | 102,900 | |
| | 27 | | 3 | | 1,000 | 101,900 | |
| | 31 | | 3 | | 100 | 101,800 | |
| | 31 | | 4 | | 500 | 101,300 | |
| | 31 | | 4 | 2,000 | | 103,300 | |
| | 31 | | 4 | | 1,000 | 102,300 | |

ACCOUNT Accounts Receivable ACCOUNT NO. 12

| Date | | Item | Post. Ref. | Debit | Credit | Balance | |
|---|---|---|---|---|---|---|---|
| | | | | | | Debit | Credit |
| 2007 Dec. | 16 | | 3 | 2,000 | | 2,000 | |
| | 21 | | 3 | | 600 | 1,400 | |
| | 31 | | 4 | 1,000 | | 2,400 | |
| | 31 | Adjusting | 5 | 500 | | 2,900 | |

ACCOUNT Supplies ACCOUNT NO. 14

| Date | | Item | Post. Ref. | Debit | Credit | Balance | |
|---|---|---|---|---|---|---|---|
| | | | | | | Debit | Credit |
| 2007 Nov. | 11 | | 1 | 4,000 | | 4,000 | |
| | 30 | | 1 | | 1,000 | 3,000 | |
| Dec. | 23 | | 3 | 1,000 | | 4,000 | |
| | 31 | Adjusting | 5 | | 3,240 | 760 | |

ACCOUNT Prepaid Insurance ACCOUNT NO. 15

| Date | | Item | Post. Ref. | Debit | Credit | Balance | |
|---|---|---|---|---|---|---|---|
| | | | | | | Debit | Credit |
| 2007 Dec. | 1 | | 2 | 1,200 | | 1,200 | |
| | 31 | Adjusting | 5 | | 100 | 1,100 | |

ACCOUNT Land ACCOUNT NO. 17

| Date | | Item | Post. Ref. | Debit | Credit | Balance | |
|---|---|---|---|---|---|---|---|
| | | | | | | Debit | Credit |
| 2007 Nov. | 5 | | 1 | 100,000 | | 100,000 | |

ACCOUNT Office Equipment ACCOUNT NO. 18

| Date | | Item | Post. Ref. | Debit | Credit | Balance | |
|---|---|---|---|---|---|---|---|
| | | | | | | Debit | Credit |
| 2007 Dec. | 4 | | 2 | 1,000 | | 1,000 | |

ACCOUNT Acc. Depr. —Office Equip. ACCOUNT NO. 19

| Date | | Item | Post. Ref. | Debit | Credit | Balance | |
|---|---|---|---|---|---|---|---|
| | | | | | | Debit | Credit |
| 2007 Dec. | 31 | Adjusting | 5 | | 50 | | 50 |

ACCOUNT Accounts Payable ACCOUNT NO. 21

| Date | | Item | Post. Ref. | Debit | Credit | Balance | |
|---|---|---|---|---|---|---|---|
| | | | | | | Debit | Credit |
| 2007 Nov. | 10 | | 1 | | 4,000 | | 4,000 |
| | 30 | | 1 | 1,000 | | | 3,000 |
| Dec. | 4 | | 2 | | 1,000 | | 4,000 |
| | 11 | | 2 | 3,000 | | | 1,000 |
| | 20 | | 3 | 1,000 | | | 0 |

ACCOUNT Wages Payable ACCOUNT NO. 22

| Date | | Item | Post. Ref. | Debit | Credit | Balance | |
|---|---|---|---|---|---|---|---|
| | | | | | | Debit | Credit |
| 2007 Dec. | 31 | Adjusting | 5 | | 250 | | 250 |

ACCOUNT Unearned Rent ACCOUNT NO. 23

| Date | | Item | Post. Ref. | Debit | Credit | Balance | |
|---|---|---|---|---|---|---|---|
| | | | | | | Debit | Credit |
| 2007 Dec. | 1 | | 2 | | 3,000 | | 3,000 |
| | 31 | Adjusting | 5 | 1,000 | | | 2,000 |

ACCOUNT John, Capital ACCOUNT NO. 31

| Date | | Item | Post. Ref. | Debit | Credit | Balance | |
|---|---|---|---|---|---|---|---|
| | | | | | | Debit | Credit |
| 2007 Nov. | 1 | | 1 | | 200,000 | | 200,000 |

ACCOUNT John, Drawing ACCOUNT NO. 32

| Date | | Item | Post. Ref. | Debit | Credit | Balance | |
|---|---|---|---|---|---|---|---|
| | | | | | | Debit | Credit |
| 2007 Nov. | 30 | | 2 | 1,000 | | 1,000 | |
| Dec. | 31 | | 4 | 1,000 | | 2,000 | |

ACCOUNT Service Income ACCOUNT NO. 41

| Date | | Item | Post. Ref. | Debit | Credit | Balance | |
|---|---|---|---|---|---|---|---|
| | | | | | | Debit | Credit |
| 2007 Nov. | 18 | | 1 | | 10,000 | | 10,000 |
| Dec. | 16 | | 3 | | 3,000 | | 13,000 |
| | 16 | | 3 | | 2,000 | | 15,000 |
| | 31 | | 4 | | 2,000 | | 17,000 |
| | 31 | | 4 | | 1,000 | | 18,000 |
| | **31** | **Adjusting** | **5** | | **500** | | **18,500** |

ACCOUNT Rent Revenue ACCOUNT NO. 42

| Date | | Item | Post. Ref. | Debit | Credit | Balance | |
|---|---|---|---|---|---|---|---|
| | | | | | | Debit | Credit |
| 2007 Dec. | 31 | Adjusting | 5 | | 1,000 | | 1,000 |

ACCOUNT Wages Expense ACCOUNT NO. 51

| Date | | Item | Post. Ref. | Debit | Credit | Balance | |
|---|---|---|---|---|---|---|---|
| | | | | | | Debit | Credit |
| 2007 Nov. | 30 | | 1 | 2,000 | | 2,000 | |
| Dec. | 13 | | 2 | 1,000 | | 3,000 | |
| | 27 | | 3 | 1,000 | | 4,000 | |
| | 31 | Adjusting | 5 | 250 | | 4,250 | |

ACCOUNT Rent Expense ACCOUNT NO. 52

| Date | | Item | Post. Ref. | Debit | Credit | Balance | |
|---|---|---|---|---|---|---|---|
| | | | | | | Debit | Credit |
| 2007 Nov. | 30 | | 1 | 800 | | 800 | |
| Dec. | 1 | | 2 | 1,000 | | 1,800 | |

ACCOUNT Depreciation Expense ACCOUNT NO. 53

| Date | | Item | Post. Ref. | Debit | Credit | Balance | |
|---|---|---|---|---|---|---|---|
| | | | | | | Debit | Credit |
| 2007 Dec. | 31 | Adjusting | 5 | 50 | | 50 | |

ACCOUNT Utilities Expense ACCOUNT NO. 54

| Date | | Item | Post. Ref. | Debit | Credit | Balance | |
|---|---|---|---|---|---|---|---|
| | | | | | | Debit | Credit |
| 2007 Nov. | 30 | | 1 | 400 | | 400 | |
| Dec. | 31 | | 3 | 100 | | 500 | |
| | 31 | | 4 | 500 | | 1,000 | |

ACCOUNT Supplies Expense ACCOUNT NO. 55

| Date | | Item | Post. Ref. | Debit | Credit | Balance | |
|---|---|---|---|---|---|---|---|
| | | | | | | Debit | Credit |
| 2007 Nov. | 30 | | 1 | 1,000 | | 1,000 | |
| Dec. | 31 | Adjusting | 5 | 3,240 | | 4,240 | |

ACCOUNT Insurance Expense ACCOUNT NO. 56

| Date | | Item | Post. Ref. | Debit | Credit | Balance | |
|---|---|---|---|---|---|---|---|
| | | | | | | Debit | Credit |
| 2007 Dec. | 31 | Adjusting | 5 | 100 | | 100 | |

ACCOUNT Miscellaneous Expense ACCOUNT NO. 59

| Date | | Item | Post. Ref. | Debit | Credit | Balance | |
|---|---|---|---|---|---|---|---|
| | | | | | | Debit | Credit |
| 2007 Nov. | 30 | | 1 | 200 | | 200 | |
| Dec. | 6 | | 2 | 100 | | 300 | |

# 4. Adjusted Trial Balance

After all the adjusting entries have been posted, another trial balance, called the adjusted trial balance, is prepared. The purpose of the adjusted trial balance is to verify the equality of the total debit balances and total credit balances before we prepare the financial statements. If the adjusted trial balance does not balance, an error has occurred. However, as we discussed in Chapter 2, errors may have occurred even though the adjusted trial balance totals agree. For example, the adjusted trial balance totals would agree if an adjusting entry has been omitted.

Exhibit 3-19 shows the adjusted trial balance for Darming as of December 31, 2007. In Chapter 4, we discuss how financial statements, including a classified balance sheet, can be prepared from an adjusted trial balance. We also discuss the use of an end-of-period spreadsheet (work sheet) as an aid in summarizing the data for preparing adjusting entries and financial statements.

**Exhibit 3-19 Adjusted trial balance**

Darming

Adjusted Trial Balance

December 31, 2007

| Accounts | Debit | Credit |
|---|---|---|
| Cash | 102,300 | |
| Accounts Receivable | 2,900 | |
| Supplies | 760 | |
| Prepaid Insurance | 1,100 | |
| Land | 100,000 | |
| Office Equipment | 1,000 | |
| Accumulated Depreciation—Office Equipment | | 50 |
| Accounts Payable | | 0 |
| Wages Payable | | 250 |
| Unearned Rent | | 2,000 |
| John, Capital | | 200,000 |
| John, Drawing | 2,000 | |

(Continued)

| Accounts | Debit | Credit |
|---|---|---|
| Service Income | | 18,500 |
| Rent Revenue | | 1,000 |
| Wages Expense | 4,250 | |
| Rent Expense | 1,800 | |
| Depreciation Expense | 50 | |
| Utilities Expense | 1,000 | |
| Supplies Expense | 4,240 | |
| Insurance Expense | 100 | |
| Miscellaneous Expense | 300 | |
| Total | 221,800 | 221,800 |

**TERMINOLOGY:**

Accounting Period Concept：会计分期
Accrual Basis of Accounting：权责发生制
Accrued Expenses：应计费用
Accrued Revenues：应计收入
Accumulated Depreciation：累计折旧
Adjusted Trial Balance：调整试算平衡
Adjusting Entries：调整分录
Adjusting Process：调整过程
Net Book Value of the Asset：资产账面价值
Cash Basis of Accounting：收付实现制
Contra Account：备抵账户
Depreciation：折旧
Depreciation Expense：折旧费用
Fixed Assets：固定资产
Matching Principle：配比原则
Prepaid Expenses：预付费用
Unearned Revenue：预收收入

**QUESTIONS:**

**1. Explain how the matching concept relates to the accrual basis of accounting.**

The accrual basis of accounting requires the use of an adjusting process at the end of the accounting period to match revenues and expenses properly. Revenues are reported in the period in which they are earned, and expenses are matched with the revenues they generate.

**2. Explain why adjustments are necessary and list the characteristics of adjusting entries.**

At the end of an accounting period, some of the amounts listed on the trial balance are not necessarily current balances. For example, amounts listed for prepaid expenses are normally overstated because the use of these assets has not been recorded on a daily basis. A delay in recognizing an expense already paid or revenue already received is called a deferral.

Some revenues and expenses related to a period may not be recorded at the end of the period, since these items are normally recorded only when cash has been received or paid. A revenue or expense that has not been paid or recorded is called an accrual.

The entries required at the end of an accounting period to being accounts up to date and to ensure the proper matching of revenues and expenses are called adjusting entries. Adjusting entries require a debit or a credit to a revenue or an expense account and an offsetting debit or credit to an asset or a liability account.

Adjusting entries affect amounts reported in the income amounts reported in the income statement and the balance sheet. Thus, if an adjusting entry is not recorded, these financial statements will be incorrect (misstated).

**3. Journalize entries for accounts requiring adjustment.**

Adjusting entries illustrated in this accounting include deferred (prepaid) expenses, deferred (unearned) revenues, accrued expenses (accrued liabilities), and accrued revenues (accrued assets). In addition, the adjusting entry necessary to record depreciation on fixed assets was illustrated.

**4. Use vertical analysis to compare financial statement items with each other and with industry averages.**

Comparing each item in a current statement with a total amount within the same statement is called vertical analysis. In vertical analysis of a balance sheet, each asset item is stated as a percent of the total assets. Each liability and owner's equity item is stated as a percent of the total liabilities and owner's equity. In vertical analysis of an income statement, each item is stated as a percent of revenues of fees earned.

**PROBLEM:**

The trial balance of Clay Employment Services in Exhibit 3-20 pertains to December 31, 2009, which is the end of Clay's annual accounting period. Date needed for the adjusting entries include:

a. Supplies on hand at year-end, $200.

b. Depreciation on furniture, $2,000.

c. Depreciation on building, $1,000.

d. Salaries owed but not yet paid, $500.

e. Accrued service revenue, $1,300.

f. $3,000 of the unearned service revenue has been earned.

**Exhibit 3-20 The trial balance of Clay Employment Services**

Clay Employment Services
Trial Balance
December 31,2009

| Account Title | Balance | |
|---|---|---|
| | Debit | Credit |
| Cash | 6,000 | |
| Accounts Receivable | 5,000 | |
| Supplies | 1,000 | |
| Furniture | 10,000 | |
| Accumulated Depreciation—Furniture | | 4,000 |
| Building | 50,000 | |
| Accumulated Depreciation—Building | | 30,000 |
| Accounts Payable | | 2,000 |
| Unearned Service Revenue | | 8,000 |
| Jay Clay, Capital | | 12,000 |
| Jay Clay, Drawing | 25,000 | |
| Service Income | | 60,000 |
| Wages Expense | 16,000 | |
| Supplies Expense | | |
| Depreciation Expense—Furniture | | |
| Depreciation Expense—Building | | |
| Miscellaneous Expense | 3,000 | |
| Total | 116,000 | 116,000 |

## Requirements

1. Open the ledger accounts with their unadjusted balances as for Accounts Receivable.

| Accounts Receivable | |
|---|---|
| $5,000 | |

2. Journalize Clay's adjusting entries at December 31,2009.

3. Post the adjusting entries.

4. Write the trial balance on a work sheet ,enter the adjusting entries, and prepare an adjusted trial balance.

5. Prepare the income statement, the statement of owner's equity, and the balance sheet. Draw arrows linking the three financial statements.

**Solution**

**Requirement 1 and 3.**

| Cash | |
|---|---|
| Bal. $6,000 | |

| Building | |
|---|---|
| Bal. $50,000 | |

| Accounts Receivable | |
|---|---|
| Bal. $5,000 | |
| e. $1,300 | |
| Bal. $6,300 | |

| Accumulated Depreciation — Building | |
|---|---|
| | Bal. $30,000 |
| | c. $1,000 |
| | Bal. $31,000 |

| Supplies | |
|---|---|
| Bal. $1,000 | a. $800 |
| Bal. $200 | |

| Accounts Payable | |
|---|---|
| | Bal. $2,000 |

| Furniture | |
|---|---|
| Bal. $10,000 | |

| Wages Payable | |
|---|---|
| | d. $500 |
| | Bal. $500 |

| Accumulated Depreciation—Furniture | |
|---|---|
| | Bal. $4,000 |
| | b. $2,000 |
| | Bal. $6,000 |

| Unearned Service Revenue | |
|---|---|
| f. $3,000 | Bal. $8,000 |
| | Bal. $5,000 |

| Wages Expense | |
|---|---|
| Bal. $16,000 | |
| d. $500 | |
| Bal. $16,500 | |

| Jay Clay, Capital | |
|---|---|
| | Bal. $12,000 |

| Supplies Expense | |
|---|---|
| a. $800 | |
| Bal. $800 | |

| Jay Clay, Drawing | |
|---|---|
| Bal. $25,000 | |

| Depreciation Expense—Furniture | |
|---|---|
| b. $2,000 | |
| Bal. $2,000 | |

| Service Income | |
|---|---|
| | Bal. $60,000 |
| | e. $1,300 |
| | f. $3,000 |
| | Bal. $64,300 |

| Depreciation Expense—Building | |
|---|---|
| c. $1,000 | |
| Bal. $1,000 | |

| Miscellaneous Expense | |
|---|---|
| Bal. $3,000 | |

**Requirement 2.** The adjusting entries for Clay Employment Services are shown in Exhibit 3-21.

**Requirement 4.** The preparation of adjusted trial balance for Clay Employment Services are Shown in Exhibit 3-22.

**Exhibit 3-21 Adjusting entries**

| Transaction | Date | | Description | Debit | Credit |
|---|---|---|---|---|---|
| a | 2009 Dec. | 31 | Supplies Expense ( $1,000 - $200) | 800 | |
| | | | Supplies | | 800 |
| | | | To record supplies used | | |
| b | | 31 | Depreciation Expense—Furniture | 2,000 | |
| | | | Accumulated Depreciation—Furniture | | 2,000 |
| | | | To record depreciation expense on furniture | | |
| c | | 31 | Depreciation Expense—Building | 1,000 | |
| | | | Accumulated Depreciation—Building | | 1,000 |
| | | | To record depreciation expense on building | | |
| d | | 31 | Wages Expense | 500 | |
| | | | Wages Payable | | 500 |
| | | | To accrue salary expense | | |
| e | | 31 | Accounts Receivable | 1,300 | |
| | | | Service Income | | 1,300 |
| | | | To accrue service revenue | | |
| f | | 31 | Unearned Service Revenue | 3,000 | |
| | | | Service Income | | 3,000 |
| | | | To record service revenue that was collected in advance | | |

**Exhibit 3-22 Preparation of adjusted trial balance**

Clay Employment Services
Preparation of Adjusted Trial Balance
December 31,2009

| Account Title | Trial Balance | | Adjustments | | Adjusted Trial Balance | |
|---|---|---|---|---|---|---|
| | Debit | Credit | Debit | Credit | Debit | Credit |
| Cash | 6,000 | | | | 6,000 | |
| Accounts Receivable | 5,000 | | e. 1,300 | | 6,300 | |
| Supplies | 1,000 | | | a. 800 | 200 | |
| Furniture | 10,000 | | | | 10,000 | |
| Accumulated Depreciation—Furniture | | 4,000 | | b. 2,000 | | 6,000 |
| Building | 50,000 | | | | 50,000 | |
| Accumulated Depreciation—Building | | 30,000 | | c. 1,000 | | 31,000 |
| Accounts Payable | | 2,000 | | | | 2,000 |
| Wages Payable | | | | d. 500 | | 500 |
| Unearned Service Revenue | | 8,000 | f. 3,000 | | | 5,000 |
| Jay Clay, Capital | | 12,000 | | | | 12,000 |
| Jay Clay, Drawing | 25,000 | | | | 25,000 | |
| Service Income | | 60,000 | | e. 1,300<br>f. 3,000 | | 64,300 |
| Wages Expense | 16,000 | | d.500 | | 16,500 | |
| Supplies Expense | | | a. 800 | | 800 | |
| Depreciation Expense—Furniture | | | b.2,000 | | 2,000 | |
| Depreciation Expense—Building | | | c. 1,000 | | 1,000 | |
| Miscellaneous Expense | 3,000 | | | | 3,000 | |
| Total | 116,000 | 116,000 | 8,600 | 8,600 | 120,800 | 120,800 |

**Requirement 5.** The financial statements of Clay Employment Services are in Exhibit 3-23.

**Exhibit 3-23 Financial statements**

Clay Employment Services
Income Statement
Year Ended December 31,2009

| | | |
|---|---|---|
| Revenue: | | |
| Service Income | | 64,300 |
| Expenses: | | |
| Wages expense | 16,500 | |
| Depreciation expense—furniture | 2,000 | |
| Depreciation expense—building | 1,000 | |
| Supplies expense | 800 | |
| Miscellaneous expense | 3,000 | |
| Total expenses | | 23,300 |
| Net income | | 41,000 |

Clay Employment Services
Statement of Owner's Equity
Year Ended December 31,2009

| | | |
|---|---|---|
| Jay Clay, capital, January 1, 2009 | | 12,000 |
| Add: Net income | 41,000 | |
| Less. Withdrawals | 25,000 | |
| Increase in owner's equity | | 16,000 |
| Jay Clay, capital, December 31, 2009 | | 28,000 |

Clay Employment Services
Balance Sheet
December 31,2009

| Assets | | | Liabilities | |
|---|---|---|---|---|
| Cash | | 6,000 | Accounts payable | 2,000 |
| Accounts receivable | | 6,300 | Wages payable | 500 |
| Supplies | | 200 | Unearned service revenue | 5,000 |
| Furniture | 10,000 | | Total liabilities | 7,500 |
| Less: Accumulated depreciation | 6,000 | 4,000 | | |
| Building | 50,000 | | Owner's Equity | |
| Less: Accumulated depreciation | 31,000 | 19,000 | Jay Clay, capital | 28,000 |
| Total assets | | 35,500 | Total liabilities and owner's equity | 35,500 |

# Chapter 4

# Completing the Accounting Cycle

**Objectives**

1. Describe how to transfer from unadjusted trial balance into adjusted trial balance.
2. Prepare financial statements from adjusted account balances.
3. Prepare closing entries.
4. Describe the accounting cycle.
5. Illustrate the accounting cycle for one period.
6. Explain the fiscal year and the natural business year.

# 1. Flow of Accounting Information

The end-of-period process by which accounts are adjusted is one of the most important in accounting. Using our illustration of Darming from Chapters 13, this process is summarized in spreadsheet form in Exhibit 4-1. Exhibit 4-1 begins with the unadjusted trial balance as of the end of the period. The unadjusted trial balance serves as a control to verify that the total of the debit balances equals the total of the credit balances. If the trial balance totals are unequal, an error has occurred, which must be found and corrected before the end-of-period process can continue.

**Exhibit 4-1 End-of-period work sheet**

Darming

End-of-Period Spreadsheet (Work Sheet)

For the Two Months Ended December 31, 2007

| Account Title | Unadjusted Trial Balance | | Adjustments | | Adjusted Trial Balance | | Income Statement | | Balance Sheet | |
|---|---|---|---|---|---|---|---|---|---|---|
| | Dr. | Cr. | Dr. | Cr. | Dr. | Cr. | Dr. | Cr. | Dr. | Cr. |
| Cash | 102,300 | | | | 102,300 | | | | 102,300 | |
| Accounts Receivable | 2,400 | | (4)500 | | 2,900 | | | | 2,900 | |
| Supplies | 4,000 | | | (1)3,240 | 760 | | | | 760 | |
| Prepaid Insurance | 1,200 | | | (2)100 | 1,100 | | | | 1,100 | |
| Land | 100,000 | | | | 100,000 | | | | 100,000 | |
| Office Equipment | 1,000 | | | | 1,000 | | | | 1,000 | |
| Accounts Payable | | 0 | | | | 0 | | | | 0 |
| Unearned Rent | | 3,000 | (3)1,000 | | | 2,000 | | | | 2,000 |
| John, Capital | | 200,000 | | | | 200,000 | | | | 200,000 |
| John, Drawing | 2,000 | | | | 2,000 | | | | 2,000 | |
| Service Income | | 18,000 | | (4)500 | | 18,500 | | 18,500 | | |
| Wages Expense | 4,000 | | (5)250 | | 4, 250 | | 4, 250 | | | |
| Rent Expense | 1,800 | | | | 1,800 | | 1,800 | | | |
| Utilities Expense | 1,000 | | | | 1,000 | | 1,000 | | | |
| Supplies Expense | 1,000 | | (1)3,240 | | 4,240 | | 4,240 | | | |
| Miscellaneous Expense | 300 | | | | 300 | | 300 | | | |
| Insurance Expense | | | (2)100 | | 100 | | 100 | | | |
| Rent Revenue | | | | (3)1,000 | | 1,000 | | 1,000 | | |
| Wages Payable | | | | (5)250 | | 250 | | | | 250 |
| Depreciation Expense | | | (6)50 | | 50 | | 50 | | | |
| Accumulated Depreciation—Office Equipment | | | | (6)50 | | 50 | | | | 50 |
| Total | 221,000 | 221,000 | 5,140 | 5,140 | 221,800 | 221,800 | 11,740 | 19,500 | 210,060 | 202,300 |

The adjustments that we explained and illustrated for Darming in Chapter 3 are shown in the Adjustments columns of Exhibit 4-1. Cross-referencing (by letters) the debit and credit of each adjustment is useful in reviewing the impact of the adjustments on the unadjusted account balances. The order of the adjustments on the spreadsheet is not important, and the adjustments are normally entered in the order in which the data are assembled. When the titles of the accounts to be adjusted do not appear in the unadjusted trial balance, the accounts are inserted in the Account Title column, below the unadjusted trial balance accounts The total of the Adjustments columns is a control to verify the mathematical accuracy of the adjustment data and adjusting entries. The total of the Debit column must equal the total of the Credit column.

The end-of-period spreadsheet (work sheet) shown in Exhibit 4-1 is a working paper that accountants can use to summarize adjusting entries and the account balances for the financial statements. In small companies with few accounts and adjustments, an end-of-period spreadsheet (work sheet) may not be necessary. For example, the financial statements for Darming can be prepared directly from the adjusted trial balance in Exhibit 4-1. However, many accountants prefer to use an end-of-period spreadsheet (work sheet) as an aid to analyzing adjustment data and preparing the financial statements.

## UNADJUSTED TRIAL BALANCE COLUMNS

To begin the spreadsheet (work sheet), enter at the top the name of the business, the type of working paper, and the period of time. Next, enter the unadjusted trial balance directly on the spreadsheet. The first two columns of spreadsheet show the unadjusted trial balance for Darming at December 31,2007.

## ADJUSTMENTS COLUMNS

To review, the entries in the Adjustments columns of the work sheet are:

(1) Supplies. The Supplies account has a debit balance of $4,000. The cost of the supplies on hand at the end of the period is $760. Therefore, the supplies expense for December is the difference between the two amounts, or $3,240. The adjustment is entered as (1) $3,240 in the Adjustments Debit column on the same line as Supplies Expense and (1) $3,240 in the Adjustments Credit column on the same line as Supplies.

(2) Prepaid Insurance. The Prepaid Insurance account has a debit balance of $1,200, which represents the prepayment of insurance for 12 months beginning at December 1. Thus, the insurance expense for December is $100 ($1,200/12months). The adjustment is entered as (2) $100 in the Adjustments Debit column on the same line as Insurance Expense and (2) $100 in the Adjustments Credit column on the same line as Prepaid Insurance.

(3) Unearned Rent. The Unearned Rent account has a credit balance of $3,000, which represents the receipt of three months' rent, beginning with December. Thus, the rent revenue for December is $1,000. The adjustment is entered as (3) $1,000 in the Ad justments Debit column on the same line as Unearned Rent and (3) $1,000 in the Adjustments Credit column on the same

line as Rent Revenue.

(4) Accrued Fees. Fees accrued at the end of December but not recorded total $500. This amount is an increase in an asset and an increase in revenue. The adjustment is entered as (4) $500 in the Adjustments Debit column on the same line as Accounts Receivable and (4) $500 in the Adjustments Credit column on the same line as Service Income.

(5) Wages. Wages accrued but not paid at the end of December total $250. This amount is an increase in expenses and an increase in liabilities. The adjustment is entered as (5) $250 in the Adjustments Debit column on the same line as Wages Expense and (5) $250 in the Adjustments Credit column on the same line as Wages Payable.

(6) Depreciation. Depreciation of the office equipment is $50 for December. The adjustment is entered as (6) $50 in the Adjustments Debit column on the same line as Depreciation Expense and (6) $50 in the Adjustments Credit column on the same line as Accumulated Depreciation—Office Equipment.

Total the Adjustments columns to verify the mathematical accuracy of the adjustment data. The total of the Debit column must equal the total of the Credit column.

## ADJUSTED TRIAL BALANCE COLUMNS

The Adjusted Trial Balance columns of Exhibit 4-1 illustrate the impact of the adjusting entries on the unadjusted accounts. The adjustment data are added to or subtracted from the amounts in the Unadjusted Trial Balance columns to arrive at the Adjusted Trial Balance columns. The totals of the Adjusted Trial Balance columns prove the equality of the totals of the debit and credit balances after adjustment.

For example, the cash amount of $102,300 is extended to the Adjusted Trial Balance Debit column, since no adjustments affected Cash. Accounts Receivable has an initial balance of $2,400 and a debit adjustment (increase) of $500. The amount entered in the Adjusted Trial Balance Debit column is the debit balance of $2,900. The same procedure continues until all account balances are extended to the Adjusted Trial Balance columns. Total the columns of the Adjusted Trial Balance to verify the equality of debits and credits.

## INCOME STATEMENT AND BALANCE SHEET COLUMNS

The spreadsheet (work sheet) is completed by extending the adjusted trial balance amounts to the Income Statement and Balance Sheet columns. The amounts for revenues and expenses are extended to the Income Statement columns. The amounts for assets, liabilities, owner's capital, and drawing are extended to the Balance Sheet columns.

In the Darming spreadsheet (work sheet), the first account listed is Cash, and the balance appearing in the Adjusted Trial Balance Debit column is $102,300. Cash is an asset, is listed on the balance sheet, and has a debit balance. Therefore, $102,300 is extended to the Balance Sheet Debit column. The Service Income balance of $18,500 is extended to the Income Statement Credit column. The same procedure continues until all account balances have been extended to the proper columns.

As we will describe and illustrate in the next section, the financial statements can be prepared directly from Exhibit 4-1.

To summarize, Exhibit 4-1 illustrates the end-of-period process by which accounts are adjusted and how the adjusted accounts flow into the financial statements. The spreadsheet shown in Exhibit 4-1 is not a required part of the accounting process. However, many accountants prepare such a spreadsheet, often called a work sheet, in manual or electronic form, as part of their normal end-of-period process. The primary advantage in doing so is that it allows managers and accountants to see the impact of the adjustments on the financial statements. This is especially useful for adjustments that depend upon estimates.

## 2. Financial Statements

Accounting is an information system. It measures business activities, processes data into reports, and communicates results to people. Accounting is "the language of business". The better you understand the language, the better you can manage your finances.

Accounting produces financial statements, which report information about a business entity. The financial statements measure performance and tell where a business stands in financial terms.

### INCOME STATEMENT

The income statement lists all the revenues together under a heading such as Revenues, or Revenues and Gains. The expenses are listed together in a single category titled Expenses, or Expenses and Losses. There is only one step, the subtraction of Expenses and Losses from the sum of Revenues and Gains, in arriving at net income.

### STATEMENT OF OWNER'S EQUITY

The first item presented on the statement of owner's equity is the balance of the owner's capital account at the beginning of the period. In Exhibit 4-1, however, the amount listed as owner's capital is not always the account balance at the beginning of the period. The owner may have invested additional assets in the business during the period. Thus, for the beginning balance and any additional investments, it is necessary to refer to the owner's capital account in the ledger. These amounts, along with the net income (or net loss) and the drawing account balance shown on the adjusted trial balance, are used to determine the ending owner's capital account balance.

The basic form of the statement of owner's equity is shown in Exhibit 4-2. For Darming, the amount of drawings by the owner was less than the net income. If the owner's withdrawals had exceeded the net income, the order of the net income and the withdrawals would have been reversed. The difference between the two items would then be deducted from the beginning capital account balance.

**Exhibit 4-2 Financial statements for Darming**

Darming
Income Statement
For the Two Months Ended December 31, 2007

| | | |
|---|---|---|
| Service Income | 18,500 | |
| Rent revenue | 1,000 | |
| Total revenues | | 19,500 |
| Expenses: | | |
| Wages expense | 4,250 | |
| Supplies expense | 4,240 | |
| Rent expense | 1,800 | |
| Utilities expense | 1,000 | |
| Insurance expense | 100 | |
| Depreciation expense | 50 | |
| Miscellaneous expense | 300 | |
| Total expenses | | 11,740 |
| Net income | | 7,760 |

Darming
Statement of Owner's Equity
For the Two Months Ended December 31, 2007

| | | |
|---|---|---|
| John, capital, November 1, 2007 | | 0 |
| Add: Investment on November 1, 2007 | 200,000 | |
| Net income for November and December | 7,760 | |
| Less,Withdrawals | 2,000 | |
| Increase in owner's equity | | 205,760 |
| John, capital, December 31, 2007 | | 205,760 |

Darming
Balance Sheet
December 31, 2007

| Assets | | | | Liabilities | | |
|---|---|---|---|---|---|---|
| Current assets: | | | | Current liabilities: | | |
| Cash | | 102,300 | | Accounts payable | 0 | |
| Accounts receivable | | 2,900 | | Wages payable | 250 | |
| Supplies | | 760 | | Unearned rent | 2,000 | |
| Prepaid insurance | | 1,100 | | Total liabilities | | 2,250 |
| Total current assets | | | 107060 | | | |
| Property, plant, and equipment: | | | | | | |
| Land | | 100,000 | | | | |
| Office equipment | 1,000 | | | | | |
| Less: accum. depr. | 50 | 950 | | **Owner's Equity** | | |
| Total property, plant, and equipment | | | 100,950 | John, capital | | 205,760 |
| Total assets | | | 208,010 | Total liabilities and owber's equity | | 208,010 |

Other factors, such as additional investments or a net loss, also require some change in the form, as shown in the following examplein Exhibit 4-3.

**Exhibit 4-3 Statement of owner's equity**

| | | |
|---|---|---|
| Allan Johnson, capital, January 1,2007 | 38,000 | |
| Additional investment during the year | 8,000 | |
| Total | | 46,000 |
| Less: Net loss for the year | 5,700 | |
| Withdrawals | 8,400 | |
| Decrease in owner's equity | | 14,100 |
| Allan Johnson, capital, December 31,2007 | | 31,900 |

## BALANCE SHEET

A classified balance sheet separates current assets from long-term assets and current liabilities from long-term liabilities.

### Assets

Assets are economic resources that provide a future benefit for a business. Most firms use the following asset accounts: ① Current assets. ② Property, plant, and equipment.

### Current Assets

Cash and other assets that will be converted to cash or sold or used up usually during the next 12 months or within the business's normal operating cycle if longer than a year. The operating cycle is the time span during which cash is paid for goods and services and these goods and services are sold to bring in cash. For most businesses, the operating cycle is a few months. Cash, Short-Term Investments, Accounts Receivable, Merchandise Inventory, and Prepaid Expenses are the current assets.

### Property, Plant, and Equipment

The property, plant, and equipment section may also be described as fixed assets or plant assets. These assets include equipment, machinery, buildings, and land. With the exception of land, fixed assets depreciate over a period of time. The cost, accumulated depreciation, and book value of each major type of fixed asset are normally reported on the balance sheet or in accompanying notes.

### Liabilities

Liabilities are something which are owed to somebody else. Liabilities is the accounting term for the debts of a business. The two most common classes of liabilities are current liabilities and long-term liabilities.

### Current Liabilities

Current liabilities must be paid with cash or with goods and services within one year or within the entity's operating cycle if the cycle is longer than a year. Other current liability accounts commonly found in the ledger are Wages Payable, Interest Payable, Taxes Payable, and Unearned Service Revenue.

**Long-Term Liabilities**

All liabilities that are not current are classified as long-term liabilities. Many notes payable are long term. Some notes payable are paid in installments, with the first installment due within 1 year, the second installment due the second year, and so on. The first installment is a current liability and the remainder is long term.

**Owner's Equity**

The owner's right to the assets of the business is called owner's equity. A proprietorship or a partnership has a separate capital account and a separate withdrawal account for each owner.

# 3. Closing Entries

The closing process reduces the balance of nominal (temporary) accounts to zero in order to prepare the accounts for the next period's transactions. In the closing process Darming transfers all of the revenue and expense account balances (income statement items) to a clearing or suspense account called Income Summary. The Income Summary account matches revenues and expenses.

Darming uses this clearing account only at the end of each accounting period. The account represents the net income or net loss for the period. It then transfers this amount (the net income or net loss) to an owner's equity account. For a corporation, the owner's equity account is Retained Earnings; for proprietorships and partnerships, it is a capital account. Companies post all such closing entries to the appropriate general ledger accounts.

In practice, companies generally prepare closing entries only at the end of a company's annual accounting period. However, to illustrate the journalizing and posting of closing entries, we will assume that Darming Inc. closes its books monthly. Exhibit 4-4 shows the closing entries at October 31, 2012.

A couple of cautions about preparing closing entries: ① Avoid unintentionally doubling the revenue and expense balances rather than zeroing them. ② Do not close Dividends through Income Summary account. Dividends are not expenses, and they are not a factor in determining net income similarly with Drawing or Withdrawal account. Dividends are transferred into Retained Earnings account but Drawing or Withdrawal contra with Capital.

## POSTING CLOSING ENTRIES

Exhibit 4-5 shows the posting of closing entries and the ruling of accounts. All temporary accounts have zero balances after posting the closing entries. In addition, note that the balance in Retained Earnings represents the accumulated undistributed earnings of Darming at the end of the accounting period. Darming reports this amount in the balance sheet as the ending amount reported on the retained earnings statement. As noted above, Darming uses the Income Summary account only in closing.

**Exhibit 4-4 Closing entries for Darming Inc.**

GENERAL JOURNAL

| Date | Account Titles and Explanation | Debit | Credit |
|---|---|---|---|
| | Closing Entries | | |
| | (1) | | |
| 2012 Oct. 31 | Service Income | 106,000 | |
| | Income Summary | | 106,000 |
| | To close revenue account | | |
| | (2) | | |
| 31 | Income Summary | 73,000 | |
| | Supplies Expense | | 15,000 |
| | Depreciation Expense | | 400 |
| | Insurance Expense | | 500 |
| | Wages Expense | | 46,000 |
| | Rent Expense | | 9,000 |
| | Interest Expense | | 500 |
| | Bad Debt Expense | | 1,600 |
| | To close expense accounts | | |
| | (3) | | |
| 31 | Income Summary | 33,000 | |
| | Retained Earnings | | 33,000 |
| | To close net income to retained earnings | | |
| | (4) | | |
| 31 | Retained Earnings | 5,000 | |
| | Dividends | | 5,000 |
| | To close dividends to retained earnings | | |

It does not journalize and post entries to this account during the year. As part of the closing process, Darming totals, balances, and double-rules the temporary accounts—revenues, expenses, and dividends—as shown in T-account form in Exhibit 4-5. It does not close the permanent accounts—assets, liabilities, and stockholders' equity (Common Stock and Retained Earnings). Instead, the preparer draws a single rule beneath the current-period entries, and enters beneath the single rules the account balance to be carried forward to the next period (for example, see Retained Earnings). After the closing process, each income statement account and the dividend account are balanced out to zero and are ready for use in the next accounting period.

## POST-CLOSING TRIAL BALANCE

Recall that a trial balance is prepared after entering the regular transactions of the period, and that a second trial balance (the adjusted trial balance) occurs after posting the adjusting entries. A company may take a third trial balance after posting the closing entries. The trial balance after closing, called the post-closing trial balance, consists only of asset, liability, and owners' equity accounts—the real accounts. Exhibit 4-6 shows the post-closing trial balance of Darming Inc.

**Exhibit 4-5 Flowchart of closing entries for Darming Inc.**

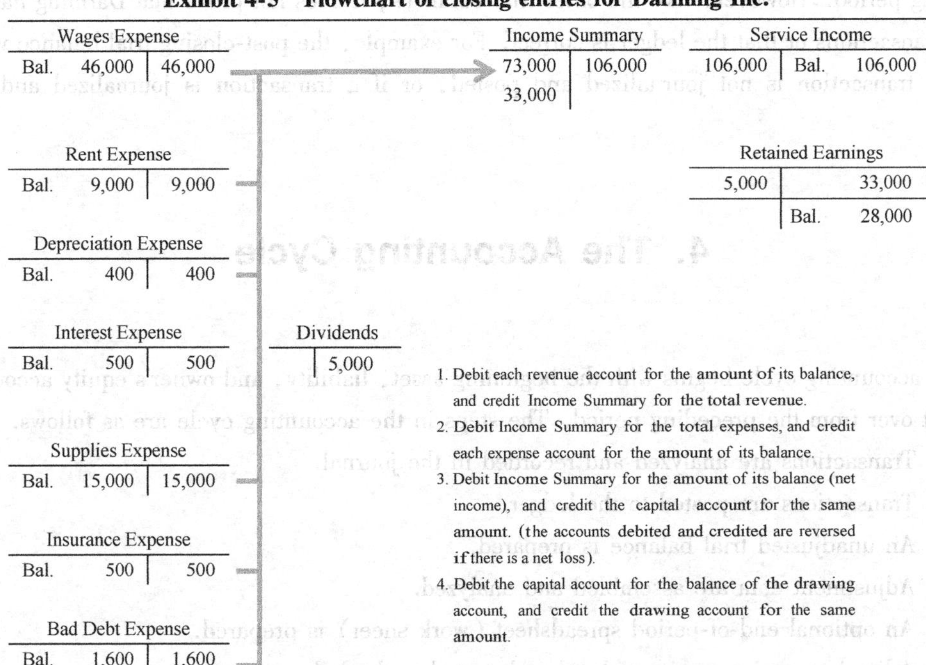


**Exhibit 4-6 Post-closing trial balance**

Darming, Inc.
Post-Closing Trial Balance
October 31, 2012

| Account | Debit | Credit |
|---|---|---|
| Cash | 80,000 | |
| Accounts Receivable | 74,000 | |
| Allowance for Doubtful Accounts | | 1,600 |
| Supplies | 10,000 | |
| Prepaid Insurance | 5,500 | |
| Office Equipment | 50,000 | |
| Accumulated Depreciation—Office Equipment | | 400 |
| Note Payable | | 50,000 |
| Accounts Payable | | 25,000 |
| Unearned Service Revenue | | 8,000 |
| Wages Payable | | 6,000 |
| Interest Payable | | 500 |
| Common Stock | | 100,000 |
| Retained Earnings | | 28,000 |
| | 219,500 | 219,500 |

A post-closing trial balance provides evidence that the company has properly journalized and posted the closing entries. It also shows that the accounting equation is in balance at the end of the accounting period. However, like the other trial balances, it does not prove that Darming has recorded all transactions or that the ledger is correct. For example, the post-closing trial balance will balance if a transaction is not journalized and posted, or if a transaction is journalized and posted twice.

## 4. The Accounting Cycle

The accounting cycle begins with the beginning asset, liability, and owner's equity account balances left over from the preceding period. The steps in the accounting cycle are as follows.

(1) Transactions are analyzed and recorded in the journal.
(2) Transactions are posted to the ledger.
(3) An unadjusted trial balance is prepared.
(4) Adjustment data are assembled and analyzed.
(5) An optional end-of-period spreadsheet (work sheet) is prepared.
(6) Adjusting entries are journalized and posted to the ledger.
(7) An adjusted trial balance is prepared.
(8) Financial statements are prepared.
(9) Closing entries are journalized and posted to the ledger.
(10) A post-closing trial balance is prepared.

## 5. Fiscal Year

You may think of the income statements, balance sheets, and financial history of a business as similar to the record of a college football team. The final score of each football game is similar to the net income reported on the income statement of a business. The team's season record after each game is similar to the balance sheet. At the end of the season, the final record of the team measures its success or failure. Likewise, at the end of a life of a business, its final balance sheet is a measure of its financial success or failure.

Fiscal years begin with the first day of the month selected and end on the last day of the following twelfth month. The period most commonly used is the calendar year. Other periods are not unusual, especially for businesses organized as corporations. Because companies with fiscal years often have highly seasonal operations, investors and others should be careful in interpreting partial-year reports for such companies. That is, you should expect the results of operations for these companies to vary significantly throughout the fiscal year.

The financial history of a business may be shown by a series of balance sheets and income statements for several fiscal years. If the life of a business is expressed by a line moving from left to right, the series of balance sheets and income statements may be graphed in Exhibit 4-7.

**Exhibit 4-7 Financial history of a business**

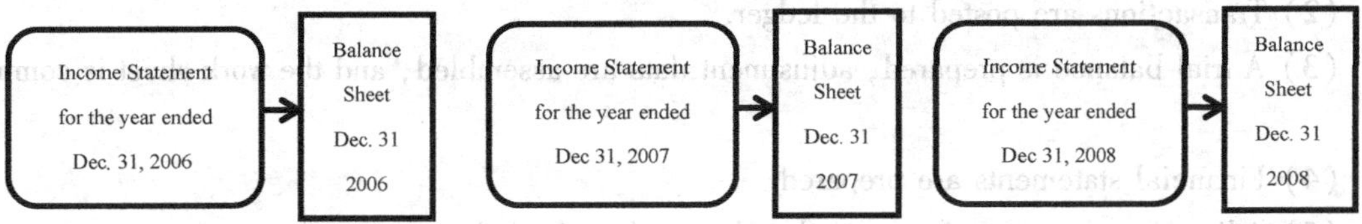


**TERMINOLOGY:**

Accounting Cycle：会计循环
Clearing Account：清算账户
Closing Entries：结账分录
Closing Process：结账过程
Current Assets：流动资产
Current Liabilities：流动负债
Fiscal Year：会计年度
Income Summary：本年利润
Long-term Liabilities：长期负债
Natural Business Year：营业周期
Temporary (Nominal) Accounts：过渡账户

**QUESTIONS:**

**1. How to prepare the adjusting and closing entries from a work sheet?**

The data for journalizing the adjusting entries are in the Adjustments columns of the work sheet. The four entries required in closing the temporary accounts are:

(1) Debit each revenue account for the amount of its balance, and credit Income Summary for the total revenue.

(2) Debit Income Summary for the total expenses, and credit each expense account for the amount of its balance.

(3) Debit Income Summary for the amount of its balance (net income), and credit the capital account for the same amount. Debit and credit are reversed if there is a net loss.

(4) Debit the capital account for the balance of the drawing account, and credit the drawing account for the same amount.

After the closing entries have been posted to the ledger, the balance in the capital account will agree with the amount reported on the statement of owner's equity and balance sheet. In addition, the revenue, expense, and drawing accounts will have zero balances.

The last step of the accounting cycle is to prepare a post-closing trial balance. The purpose of the post-closing trial balance is to make sure that the ledger is in balance at the beginning of the next period.

**2. What is the seven basic steps of the accounting cycle?**

The basic steps of the accounting cycle are:

(1) Transactions are analyzed and recorded in a journal.

(2) Transactions are posted to the ledger.

(3) A trial balance is prepared, adjustment data are assembled, and the work sheet is completed.

(4) Financial statements are prepared.

(5) Adjusting entries are journalized and posted to the ledger.

(6) Closing entries are journalized and posted to the ledger.

(7) A post-closing trial balance is prepared.

## PROBLEM:

The adjusted trial balance of Clay Employment Services at December 31, 2009, is in Exhibit 4-8.

**Exhibit 4-8 Adjusted trial balance**

Clay Employment Services

Adjusted Trial Balance

December 31, 2009

| Account Title | Debit Bal. | Credit Bal. |
|---|---|---|
| Cash | 6,000 | |
| Accounts Receivable | 6,300 | |
| Supplies | 200 | |
| Furniture | 10,000 | |
| Accumulated Depreciation—Furniture | | 6,000 |
| Building | 50,000 | |
| Accumulated Depreciation—Building | | 31,000 |
| Accounts Payable | | 2,000 |
| Wages Payable | | 500 |
| Unearned Service Revenue | | 5,000 |
| Jay Clay, Capital | | 12,000 |
| Jay Clay, Drawing | 25,000 | |
| Service Income | | 64,300 |
| Wages Expense | 16,500 | |
| Supplies Expense | 800 | |
| Depreciation Expense—Furniture | 2,000 | |
| Depreciation Expense—Building | 1,000 | |
| Miscellaneous Expense | 3,000 | |
| Total | 120,800 | 120,800 |

**Requirement**

Journalize and post the closing entries.

**Solution**

Journalize and post the closing entries in Exhibit 4-9.

**Exhibit 4-9 Journalize and post the closing entries**

| Date | Closing Entries | Debit | Credit |
|---|---|---|---|
| 2009<br>Dec. 31 | Service Income | 64,300 | |
| | Income Summary | | 64,300 |
| 31 | Income Summary | 23,300 | |
| | Wages Expense | | 16,500 |
| | Supplies Expense | | 800 |
| | Depreciation Expense—Furniture | | 2,000 |
| | Depreciation Expense—Building | | 1,000 |
| | Miscellaneous Expense | | 3,000 |
| 31 | Income Summary | 41,000 | |
| | Jay, Clay, Capital | | 41,000 |
| 31 | Jay Clay, Capital | 25,000 | |
| | Jay Clay, Drawing | | 25,000 |

# Chapter 5

## Accounting Systems

**Objectives**

1. Define an accounting system and describe its implementation.
2. Journalize transactions using subsidiary ledgers and special journals.
3. Describe additional subsidiary ledgers and modified special journals.
4. Apply computerized accounting to the revenue and collection cycle.
5. Describe the basic features of e-commerce.

# 1. Basic Accounting Systems

In the four previous chapters, we developed an accounting system for Darming. An accounting system is the methods and procedures for collecting, classifying, summarizing, and reporting a business's financial and operating information. The accounting system for most businesses, however, is more complex than Darming. Accounting systems for large businesses must be able to collect, accumulate, and report many types of transactions. For example, American Airlines' accounting system collects and maintains information on ticket reservations, credit card collections, aircraft maintenance, employee hours, frequent-flier mileage balances, fuel consumption, and travel agent commissions, just to name a few. As you might expect, American Airlines' accounting system has evolved as the company has grown.

Accounting systems evolve through a three-step process as a business grows and changes. The first step in this process is analysis, which consists of identifying the needs of those who use the business's financial information and determining how the system should provide this information. For Darming, we determined that John would need financial statements for the new business. In the second step, the system is designed so that it will meet the users' needs. For Darming, a very basic manual system was designed. This system included a chart of accounts, a two-column journal, and a general ledger. Finally, the system is implemented and used. For Darming, the system was used to record transactions and prepare financial statements.

Once a system has been implemented, feedback, or input, from the users of the information can be used to analyze and improve the system. For example, in later chapters we will see that Darming will expand its chart of accounts as it becomes a more complex business.

# 2. Manual Accounting Systems

Accounting systems may be either manual or computerized. Understanding a manual accounting system assists in recognizing the relationships between accounting data and accounting reports. In addition, most computerized systems use principles used in a manual system. Therefore, we illustrate the manual system first.

In preceding chapters, all transactions for Darming were manually recorded in an all-purpose (two-column) journal. The journal entries were then posted individually to the accounts in the ledger. Such manual accounting systems are simple to use and easy to understand. Manually kept records may serve a business reasonably well when the amount of data collected, stored, and used is relatively small. For a large business, such manual processing is too costly and time consuming;

thus, a computerized system is preferred. For example, a large company such as Verizon Communications has millions of telephone fees earned on account with millions of customers daily. Each telephone fee on account requires an entry debiting Accounts Receivable and crediting Service Income. In addition, a record of each customer's receivable must be kept. Clearly, a simple manual system would not serve the business needs of Verizon Communications.

When a business has a large number of similar transactions, using an all-purpose journal is inefficient and impractical. In such cases, subsidiary ledgers and special journals are useful. As a business becomes more complex, the manual system can be supplemented or replaced by a computerized system. Although we will illustrate the manual use of subsidiary ledgers and special journals, the basic principles described in the following paragraphs also apply to a computerized accounting system.

**SUBSIDIARY LEDGERS**

You must create an account for each customer in a subsidiary ledger called the Accounts Receivable ledger. A subsidiary ledger holds individual accounts that support a general ledger account. The customer accounts in the subsidiary ledger are arranged in alphabetical order.

Amounts in the sales journal are posted to the subsidiary ledger daily to keep a current record of the amount receivable from each customer.

A large number of individual accounts with a common characteristic can be grouped together in a separate ledger called a subsidiary ledger. The primary ledger, which contains all of the balance sheet and income statement accounts, is then called the general ledger. Each subsidiary ledger is represented in the general ledger by a summarizing account, called a controlling account. The sum of the balances of the accounts in a subsidiary ledger must equal the balance of the related controlling account. Thus, you may think of a subsidiary ledger as a secondary ledger that supports a controlling account in the general ledger.

The individual accounts with customers are arranged in alphabetical order in a subsidiary ledger called the accounts receivable subsidiary ledger, or customer ledger. The controlling account in the general ledger that summarizes the debits and credits to the individual customer accounts is Accounts Receivable. The individual accounts with creditors are arranged in alphabetical order in a subsidiary ledger called the accounts payable subsidiary ledger, or creditors ledger. The related controlling account in the general ledger is Accounts Payable. The relationship between the general ledger and these subsidiary ledgers is illustrated in Exhibit 5-1.

**SPECIAL JOURNALS**

The journal is the record of prime entry for transactions which are not recorded in any of the other books of prime entry.

You should remember that one of the books of prime entry was the journal.

The journal keeps a record of unusual movement between accounts. It is used to record any double entries made which do not arise from the other books of prime entry. For example, journal entries are made when errors are discovered and need to be corrected.

**Exhibit 5-1 General ledger and subsidiary ledgers**

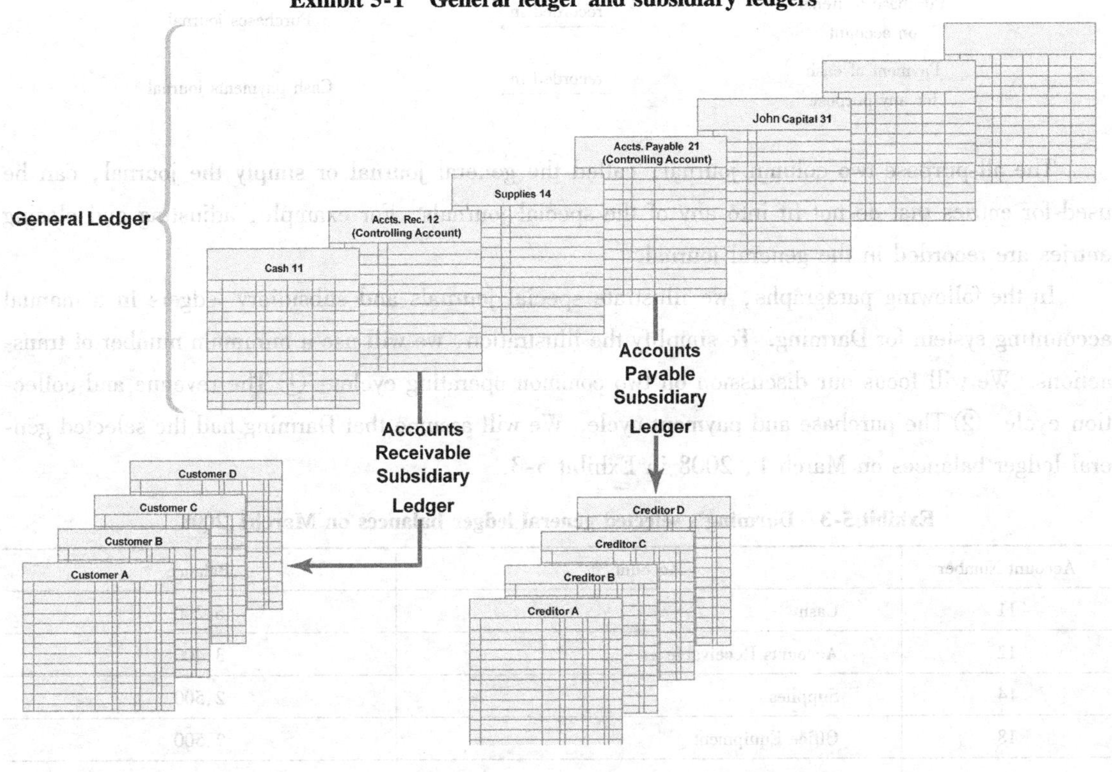


Systems designers can create a special screen for each accounting module—credit sales, cash receipts, purchases on account, and cash payments.

The next logical extension of the accounting system is to replace the single multi-column journal with several special journals. Each special journal is designed to be used for recording a single kind of transaction that occurs frequently. For example, since most businesses have many transactions in which cash is paid out, they will likely use a special journal for recording cash payments. Likewise, they will use another special journal for recording cash receipts. Special journals are a method of summarizing transactions, which is a basic feature of any accounting system.

The format and number of special journals that a business uses depends upon the nature of the business. A business that gives credit might use a special journal designed for recording only revenue from services provided on credit. On the other hand, a business that does not give credit would have no need for such a journal. In other cases, record-keeping costs may be reduced by using supporting documents as special journals.

The transactions that occur most often in a small to medium-sized service business and the special journals in which they are recorded are shown in Exhibit 5-2.

**Exhibit 5-2 The transactions recorded in special journal**

| | | |
|---|---|---|
| Providing services on account | recorded in → | Revenues journal |
| Receipt of cash from any source | recorded in → | Cash receipts journal |

| | | |
|---|---|---|
| Purchase of items on account | recorded in → | Purchases journal |
| Payment of cash for any purpose | recorded in → | Cash payments journal |

The all-purpose two-column journal, called the general journal or simply the journal, can be used for entries that do not fit into any of the special journals. For example, adjusting and closing entries are recorded in the general journal.

In the following paragraphs, we illustrate special journals and subsidiary ledgers in a manual accounting system for Darming. To simplify the illustration, we will use a minimum number of transactions. We will focus our discussion on two common operating cycles: ① The revenue and collection cycle. ② The purchase and payment cycle. We will assume that Darming had the selected general ledger balances on March 1, 2008 in Exhibit 5-3.

**Exhibit 5-3 Darming's selected general ledger balances on March1,2008**

| Account Number | Account | Balance |
|---|---|---|
| 11 | Cash | 6,200 |
| 12 | Accounts Receivable | 3,400 |
| 14 | Supplies | 2,500 |
| 18 | Office Equipment | 2,500 |
| 21 | Accounts Payable | 1,230 |

## MANUAL ACCOUNTING SYSTEM: THE REVENUE AND COLLECTION CYCLE

The revenue and collection cycle for Darming consists of providing services on account and collecting cash from customers. Revenues earned on account create a customer receivable and will be recorded in a revenue journal. Customers' accounts receivable are collected and will be recorded in a cash receipts journal.

Internal control is enhanced by separating the function of recording revenue transactions in the revenue journal from recording cash collections in the cash receipts journal. For example, if these duties are separated, it is more difficult for one person to embezzle cash collections and manipulate the accounting records.

### Revenue Journal

The revenue journal is used only for recording fees earned on account. Cash fees earned would be recorded in the cash receipts journal. The sale of products is recorded in a sales journal, which is similar to a revenue journal. We will compare the efficiency of using a revenue journal with a general journal by assuming that Darming recorded the following revenue transactions in a general journal, as shown in Exhibit 5-4.

For these four transactions, Darming recorded eight account titles and eight amounts. In addition, Darming made 12 postings to the ledgers—four to Accounts Receivable in the general ledger, four to the accounts receivable subsidiary ledger (indicated by each check mark), and four to

Service Income in the general ledger. These transactions could be recorded more efficiently in a revenue journal, as shown in Exhibit 5-5. In each revenue transaction, the amount of the debit to Accounts Receivable is the same as the amount of the credit to Service Income. Therefore, only a single amount column is necessary. The date, invoice number, customer name, and amount are entered separately for each transaction.

**Exhibit 5-4 Darming's revenue transaction in a general journal**

| Date | | Description | Post. Ref. | Debit | Credit |
|---|---|---|---|---|---|
| 2008 Mar. | 2 | Accounts Receivable—Accessories By Claire | 12/√ | 2,200 | |
| | | Service Income | 41 | | 2,200 |
| | | | | | |
| | 6 | Accounts Receivable—RapZone | 12/√ | 1,750 | |
| | | Service Income | 41 | | 1,750 |
| | | | | | |
| | 18 | Accounts Receivable—Web Cantina | 12/√ | 2,650 | |
| | | Service Income | 41 | | 2,650 |
| | | | | | |
| | 27 | Accounts Receivable—Accessories By Claire | 12/√ | 3,000 | |
| | | Service Income | 41 | | 3,000 |

**Exhibit 5-5 Revenue journal**

Page 35

| | Date | | Invoice No. | Account Debited | Post. Ref. | Accts. Rec. Dr. Service Income Cr. | |
|---|---|---|---|---|---|---|---|
| 1 | 2008 Mar. | 2 | 615 | Accessories By Claire | | 2,200 | 1 |
| 2 | | 6 | 616 | RapZone | | 1,750 | 2 |
| 3 | | 18 | 617 | Web Cantina | | 2,650 | 3 |
| 4 | | 27 | 618 | Accessories By Claire | | 3,000 | 4 |
| 5 | | 31 | | | | 9600 | 5 |

The basic procedure of posting from a revenue journal is shown in Exhibit 5-6. A single monthly total is posted to Accounts Receivable and Service Income in the general ledger. Each transaction, such as the $2,200 debit to Accessories By Claire, must also be posted individually to a customer account in the accounts receivable subsidiary ledger. These postings to customer accounts should be made frequently. In this way, management has information on the current balance of each customer's account. Since the balances in the customer accounts are usually debit balances, the three-column account form shown in the exhibit is often used.

To provide a trail of the entries posted to the subsidiary ledger, the source of these entries is indicated in the Posting Reference column of each account by inserting the letter R (for revenue journal) and the page number of the revenue journal. A check mark (√) instead of a number is then inserted in the Posting Reference column of the revenue journal, as shown in Exhibit 5-6.

**Exhibit 5-6 Revenue journal postings to ledgers**

REVENUE JOURNAL

| Data | Invoice No. | Account Debited | Post. Ref. | Service Income Cr. |
|---|---|---|---|---|
| 2008 | | | | |
| Mar. 2 | 615 | Accessories By Claire | ✔ | 2,200 |
| 6 | 616 | RapZone | ✔ | 1,750 |
| 18 | 617 | Web Cantina | ✔ | 2,650 |
| 27 | 618 | Accessories By Claire | ✔ | 3,000 |
| 31 | | | | 9,600 |
| | | | | (12) (41) |

GENERAL LEDGER

ACCOUNT Accounts Receivable — Account No. 12

| Data | Item | Post. Ref. | Dr. | Cr. | Balance Dr. | Balance Cr. |
|---|---|---|---|---|---|---|
| 2008 | | | | | | |
| Mar. 1 | Balance | ✔ | | | 3,400 | |
| 31 | | R35 | 9,600 | | 13,000 | |

ACCOUNT Service Income — Account No. 41

| Data | Item | Post Ref | Dr. | Cr. | Balance Dr. | Balance Cr. |
|---|---|---|---|---|---|---|
| 2008 | | | | | | |
| Mar. 31 | | ✔ | | 9,600 | | 9,600 |

ACCOUNTS RECEIVABLE SUBSIDIARY LEDGER

NAME: Accessories By Claire

| Data | Item | Post. Ref. | Dr. | Cr. | Balance |
|---|---|---|---|---|---|
| 2008 | | | | | |
| Mar.2 | | R35 | 2,200 | | 2,200 |
| 27 | | R35 | 3,000 | | 5,200 |

NAME: RapZone

| Data | Item | Post. Ref. | Dr. | Cr. | Balance |
|---|---|---|---|---|---|
| 2008 | | | | | |
| Mar.6 | | R35 | 1,750 | | 1,750 |

NAME: Web Cantina

| Data | Item | Post. Ref. | Dr. | Cr. | Balance |
|---|---|---|---|---|---|
| 2008 | | | | | |
| Mar.1 | Balance | ✔ | | | 3,400 |
| 18 | | R35 | 2,650 | | 6,050 |

If a customer's account has a credit balance, that fact should be indicated by an asterisk or parentheses in the Balance column. When an account's balance is zero, a line may be drawn in the Balance column.

At the end of each month, the amount column of the revenue journal is totaled. This total is equal to the sum of the month's debits to the individual accounts in the subsidiary ledger. It is posted in the general ledger as a debit to Accounts Receivable and a credit to Service Income, as shown in Exhibit 5-6. The accounts receivable account number (12) and the service income account number (41) are then inserted below the total in the revenue journal to indicate that the posting is completed, as shown in Exhibit 5-6. In this way, all of the transactions for fees earned during the month are posted to the general ledger only once—at the end of the month—greatly simplifying the posting process.

**Cash Receipts Journal**

All transactions that involve the receipt of cash are recorded in a cash receipts journal. Thus, the cash receipts journal has a column entitled Cash Dr., as shown in Exhibit 5-7. All transactions recorded in the cash receipts journal will involve an entry in the Cash Dr. column. For example, on March 28 Darming received cash of $2,200 from Accessories By Claire and entered that amount in the Cash Dr. column.

**Exhibit 5-7 Cash receipts journal and postings**

CASH RECEIPTS JOURNAL

Page14

| Data | Account Debited | Post. Ref. | Other Accounts Cr. | Accounts Receivable Cr. | Cash Dr. |
|---|---|---|---|---|---|
| 2008 | | | | | |
| Mar. 1 | Rent Revenue | 42 | 400 | | 400 |
| 19 | Web Cantina | ✓ | | 3,400 | 3,400 |
| 28 | Accessories By Claire | ✓ | | 2,200 | 2,200 |
| 30 | RapZone | ✓ | | 1,750 | 1,750 |
| 31 | | | 400 | 7,350 | 7,750 |
| | | | | (12) | (11) |

GENERAL LEDGER

ACCOUNT Rent Revenue — Account No. 42

| Data | Item | Post. Ref. | Dr. | Cr. | Balance Dr. | Balance Cr. |
|---|---|---|---|---|---|---|
| 2008 | | | | | | |
| Mar. 1 | | CR14 | | 400 | | 400 |

ACCOUNT Accounts Receivable — Account No. 12

| Data | Item | Post. Ref. | Dr. | Cr. | Balance Dr. | Balance Cr. |
|---|---|---|---|---|---|---|
| 2008 | | | | | | |
| Mar. 1 | Balance | ✓ | | | 3,400 | |
| 31 | | R35 | 9,600 | | 13,000 | |
| 31 | | CR14 | | 7,350 | 5,650 | |

ACCOUNT Cash — Account No. 11

| Data | Item | Post. Ref. | Dr. | Cr. | Balance Dr. | Balance Cr. |
|---|---|---|---|---|---|---|
| 2008 | | | | | | |
| Mar. 1 | Balance | ✓ | | | 6,200 | |
| 31 | | CR14 | 7,750 | | 13,950 | |

ACCOUNTS RECEIVABLE SUBSIDIARY LEDGER

NAME: Accessories By Claire

| Data | Item | Post. Ref. | Dr. | Cr. | Balance |
|---|---|---|---|---|---|
| 2008 | | | | | |
| Mar.2 | | R35 | 2,200 | | 2,200 |
| 27 | | R35 | 3,000 | | 5,200 |
| 28 | | CR14 | | 2,200 | 3,000 |

NAME: RapZone

| Data | Item | Post. Ref. | Dr. | Cr. | Balance |
|---|---|---|---|---|---|
| 2008 | | | | | |
| Mar.6 | | R35 | 1,750 | | 1,750 |
| 30 | | CR14 | | 1,750 | — |

NAME: Web Cantina

| Data | Item | Post. Ref. | Dr. | Cr. | Balance |
|---|---|---|---|---|---|
| 2008 | | | | | |
| Mar.1 | Balance | ✓ | | | 3,400 |
| 18 | | R35 | 2,650 | | 6,050 |
| 19 | | CR14 | | 3,400 | 2,650 |

The kinds of transactions in which cash is received and how often they occur determine the titles of the other columns. For Darming, the most frequent source of cash is collections from customers. Thus, the cash receipts journal in Exhibit 5-7 has an Accounts Receivable Cr. column. On March 28, when Accessories By Claire made a payment on its account, Darming entered Accessories By Claire in the Account Credited column and entered $2,200 in the Accounts Receivable Cr. column.

The Other Accounts Cr. column in Exhibit 5-7 is used for recording credits to any account for which there is no special credit column. For example, Darming received cash on March 1 for rent. Since no special column exists for Rent Revenue, Darming entered Rent Revenue in the Account

Credited column and entered $400 in the Other Accounts Cr. column.

Postings from the cash receipts journal to the ledgers of Darming are also shown in Exhibit 5-7. This posting process is similar to that of the revenue journal. At regular intervals, each amount in the Other Accounts Cr. column is posted to the proper account in the general ledger. The posting is indicated by inserting the account number in the Posting Reference column of the cash receipts journal. The posting reference CR (for cash receipts journal) and the proper page number are inserted in the Posting Reference columns of the accounts.

The amounts in the Accounts Receivable Cr. column are posted individually to the customer accounts in the accounts receivable subsidiary ledger. These postings should be made frequently. The posting reference CR and the proper page number are inserted in the Posting Reference column of each customer's account. A check mark is placed in the Posting Reference column of the cash receipts journal to show that each amount has been posted. None of the individual amounts in the Cash Dr. column is posted separately.

At the end of the month, all of the amount columns are totaled. The debits should equal the credits. Because each amount in the Other Accounts Cr. column has been posted individually to a general ledger account, a check mark is inserted below the column total to indicate that no further action is needed. The totals of the Accounts Receivable Cr. and Cash Dr. columns are posted to the proper accounts in the general ledger, and their account numbers are inserted below the totals to show that the postings have been completed.

### Accounts Receivable Control and Subsidiary Ledger

After all posting has been completed for the month, the sum of the balances in the accounts receivable subsidiary ledger should be compared with the balance of the accounts receivable controlling account in the general ledger. If the controlling account and the subsidiary ledger do not agree, the error or errors must be located and corrected. The balances of the individual customer accounts may be summarized in a customer balance summary report. The total of Darming's customer balance summary report, $5,650, agrees with the balance of its accounts receivable control account on March 31, 2008, as shown in Exhibit 5-8.

**Exhibit 5-8 Darming's customer balance summary and accounts receivable**

| Accounts Receivable (Control) | | Darming Customer Balance Summary March 31, 2008 | |
|---|---|---|---|
| Balance, March 1, 2008 | 3,400 | Accessories By Claire | 3,000 |
| Total debits (from revenue journal) | 9,600 | RapZone | 0 |
| Total credits (from cash receipts journal) | (7,350) | Web Cantina | 2,650 |
| Balance, March 31, 2008 | 5,650 | Total accounts receivable | 5,650 |

## MANUAL ACCOUNTING SYSTEM: THE PURCHASE AND PAYMENT CYCLE

The purchase and payment cycle for Darming consists of purchases on account and payments of cash to suppliers. To make purchases of supplies and other items on account requires establishing a supplier account payable. These transactions will be recorded in a purchases journal. The payments of suppliers' accounts payable will be recorded in the cash payments journal.

Internal control is enhanced by separating the function of recording purchases in the purchases journal from recording cash payments in the cash payments journal. Separating duties in this way prevents an individual from establishing a fictitious supplier and then collecting payments for fictitious purchases from this supplier.

**Purchases Journal**

The purchases journal is designed for recording all purchases on account. Cash purchases would be recorded in the cash payments journal. The purchases journal has a column entitled Accounts Payable Cr. The purchases journal also has special columns for recording debits to the accounts most often affected. Since Darming makes frequent debits to its supplies account, a Supplies Dr. column is included for these transactions. For example, as shown in Exhibit 5-9, Darming recorded the purchase of supplies on March 3y entering $600 in the Supplies Dr. column, $600 in the Accounts Payable Cr. column, and Howard Supplies in the Account Credited column.

**Exhibit 5-9 Purchases journal and postings**

PURCHASES JOURNAL — Page11

| Data | Account Credited | Post. Ref. | Accounts Payable Cr. | Supplies Dr. | Other Accounts Dr. | Post. Ref. | Amount |
|---|---|---|---|---|---|---|---|
| 2008 | | | | | | | |
| Mar. 3 | Howard Supplies | ✔ | 600 | 600 | | | |
| 7 | Donnelly Supplies | ✔ | 420 | 420 | | | |
| 12 | Jewett Business Systems | ✔ | 2,800 | | Office Equipment | 18 | 2,800 |
| 19 | Donnelly Supplies | ✔ | 1,450 | 1,450 | | | |
| 27 | Howard Supplies | ✔ | 960 | 960 | | | |
| 31 | | | 6,230 | 3,430 | | | 2,800 |
| | | | (21) | (14) | | | (✔) |

GENERAL LEDGER

ACCOUNT Accounts Payable — Account No. 21

| Data | Item | Post. Ref. | Dr. | Cr. | Balance |
|---|---|---|---|---|---|
| 2008 | | | | | |
| Mar. 1 | Balance | ✔ | | | 1,230 |
| 31 | | P11 | | 6,230 | 7,460 |

ACCOUNT Supplies — Account No. 14

| Data | Item | Post. Ref. | Dr. | Cr. | Balance |
|---|---|---|---|---|---|
| 2008 | | | | | |
| Mar. 1 | Balance | ✔ | | | 2,500 |
| 31 | | P11 | 3,430 | | 5,930 |

ACCOUNT Office Equipment — Account No. 18

| Data | Item | Post. Ref. | Dr. | Cr. | Balance |
|---|---|---|---|---|---|
| 2008 | | | | | |
| Mar. 1 | Balance | ✔ | | | 2,500 |
| 12 | | P11 | 2,800 | | 5,300 |

ACCOUNTS PAYABLE SUBSIDIARY LEDGER

NAME: Donnelly Supplies

| Data | Item | Post. Ref. | Dr. | Cr. | Balance |
|---|---|---|---|---|---|
| 2008 | | | | | |
| Mar.7 | | P11 | | 420 | 420 |
| 19 | | P11 | | 1,450 | 1,870 |

NAME: Grayco Supplies

| Data | Item | Post. Ref. | Dr. | Cr. | Balance |
|---|---|---|---|---|---|
| 2008 | | | | | |
| Mar.1 | Balance | ✔ | | | 1,230 |

NAME: Howard Supplies

| Data | Item | Post. Ref. | Dr. | Cr. | Balance |
|---|---|---|---|---|---|
| 2008 | | | | | |
| Mar.3 | | | | 600 | 600 |
| 27 | | P11 | | 960 | 1,560 |

NAME: Jewett Business Systems

| Data | Item | Post. Ref. | Dr. | Cr. | Balance |
|---|---|---|---|---|---|
| 2008 | | | | | |
| Mar.12 | | | | 2,800 | 2,800 |

The Other Accounts Dr. column in Exhibit 5-9 is used to record purchases, on account, of any item for which there is no special debit column. The title of the account to be debited is entered in the Other Accounts Dr. column, and the amount is entered in the Amount column. For example, Darming recorded the purchase of office equipment on account on March 12 by entering Office Equipment in the Other Accounts Dr. column, \$2,800 in the Amount column, \$2,800 in the Accounts Payable Cr. column, and Jewett Business Systems in the Account Credited column.

Postings from the purchases journal to the ledgers of Darming are also shown in Exhibit 5-9. The principles used in posting the purchases journal are similar to those used in posting the revenue and cash receipts journals. The source of the entries posted to the subsidiary and general ledgers is indicated in the Posting Reference column of each account by inserting the letter P (for purchases journal) and the page number of the purchases journal. A check mark (√) is inserted in the Posting Reference column of the purchases journal after each credit is posted to a creditor's account in the accounts payable subsidiary ledger.

At regular intervals, the amounts in the Other Accounts Dr. column are posted to the accounts in the general ledger. As each amount is posted, the related general ledger account number is inserted in the Posting Reference column of the Other Accounts section.

At the end of each month, the amount columns in the purchases journal are totaled. The sum of the two debit column totals should equal the sum of the credit column.

The totals of the Accounts Payable Cr. and Supplies Dr. columns are posted to the appropriate general ledger accounts in the usual manner, with the related account numbers inserted below the column totals. Because each amount in the Other Accounts Dr. column was posted individually, a check mark is placed below the \$2,800 total to show that no further action is needed.

**Cash Payments Journal**

The special columns for the cash payments journal are determined in the same manner as for the revenue, cash receipts, and purchases journals. The determining factors are the kinds of transactions to be recorded and how often they occur.

The cash payments journal has a Cash Cr. column, as shown in Exhibit 5-10. All transactions recorded in the cash payments journal will involve an entry in this column. Payments to creditors on account happen often enough to require an Accounts Payable Dr. column. Debits to creditor accounts for invoices paid, often called bills, are recorded in the Accounts Payable Dr. column. For example, on March 15 Darming paid \$1,230 on its account with Grayco Supplies. Darming recorded this transaction by entering \$1,230 in the Accounts Payable Dr. column, \$1,230 in the Cash Cr. column, and Grayco Supplies in the Account Debited column.

Darming makes all payments by check. As each transaction is recorded in the cash payments journal, the related check number is entered in the column at the right of the Date column. The check numbers are helpful in controlling cash payments, and they provide a useful cross-reference.

The Other Accounts Dr. column is used for recording debits to any account for which there is no special column. For example, Darming paid \$1,600 on March 2 for rent. The transaction was recorded by entering Rent Expense in the space provided and \$1,600 in the Other Accounts Dr.

and Cash Cr. columns.

**Exhibit 5-10 Cash payments journal and postings**

CASH PAYMENTS JOURNAL Page7

| Data | Ck. No. | Account Debited | Post. Ref. | Other Accounts Dr. | Accounts Payable Dr. | Cash Cr. |
|---|---|---|---|---|---|---|
| 2008 | | | | | | |
| Mar. 2 | 150 | Rent Expense | 52 | 1,600 | | 1,600 |
| 15 | 151 | Grayco Supplies | ✓ | | 1,230 | 1,230 |
| 21 | 152 | Jewett Business System | ✓ | | 2,800 | 2,800 |
| 22 | 153 | Donnelly Supplies | ✓ | | 420 | 420 |
| 30 | 154 | Utilities Expense | 54 | 1,050 | | 1,050 |
| 31 | 155 | Howard Supplies | ✓ | | 600 | 600 |
| 31 | | | | 2,650 | 5,050 | 7,700 |
| | | | | (✓) | (21) | (11) |

GENERAL LEDGER

ACCOUNT Accounts Payable Account No. 21

| Data | Item | Post. Ref. | Dr. | Cr. | Balance |
|---|---|---|---|---|---|
| 2008 | | | | | |
| Mar. 1 | Balance | ✓ | | | 1,230 |
| 31 | | P11 | | 6,230 | 7,460 |
| 31 | | CP7 | 5,050 | | 2,410 |

ACCOUNT Cash Account No. 11

| Data | Item | Post. Ref. | Dr. | Cr. | Balance |
|---|---|---|---|---|---|
| 2008 | | | | | |
| Mar. 1 | Balance | ✓ | | | 6,200 |
| 31 | | CR14 | 7,750 | | 13,950 |
| 31 | | CP7 | | 7,700 | 6,250 |

ACCOUNT Rent Expense Account No. 52

| Data | Item | Post. Ref. | Dr. | Cr. | Balance |
|---|---|---|---|---|---|
| 2008 | | | | | |
| Mar. 2 | | CP7 | 1,600 | | 1,600 |

ACCOUNT Utilities Expense Account No. 54

| Data | Item | Post. Ref. | Dr. | Cr. | Balance |
|---|---|---|---|---|---|
| 2008 | | | | | |
| Mar. 30 | | CP7 | 1,050 | | 1,050 |

ACCOUNTS PAYABLE SUBSIDIARY LEDGER

NAME: Donnelly Supplies

| Data | Item | Post Ref | Dr. | Cr. | Balance |
|---|---|---|---|---|---|
| 2008 | | | | | |
| Mar.7 | | P11 | | 420 | 420 |
| 19 | | P11 | | 1,450 | 1,870 |
| 22 | | CP7 | 420 | | 1,450 |

NAME: Grayco Supplies

| Data | Item | Post Ref | Dr. | Cr. | Balance |
|---|---|---|---|---|---|
| 2008 | | | | | |
| Mar.1 | Balance | ✓ | | | 1,230 |
| 15 | | CP7 | 1,230 | | — |

NAME: Howard Supplies

| Data | Item | Post Ref | Dr. | Cr. | Balance |
|---|---|---|---|---|---|
| 2008 | | | | | |
| Mar.3 | | P11 | | 600 | 600 |
| 27 | | P11 | | 960 | 1,560 |
| 31 | | CP7 | 600 | | 960 |

NAME: Jewett Business Systems

| Data | Item | Post Ref | Dr. | Cr. | Balance |
|---|---|---|---|---|---|
| 2008 | | | | | |
| Mar.12 | | P11 | | 2,800 | 2,800 |
| 21 | | CP7 | 2,800 | | — |

Postings from the cash payments journal to the ledgers of Darming are also shown in Exhibit 5-10. The amounts entered in the Accounts Payable Dr. column are posted to the individual creditor accounts in the accounts payable subsidiary ledger. These postings should be made frequently. After each posting, CP (for cash payments journal) and the page number of the journal are inserted in the Posting Reference column of the account. A check mark is placed in the Posting Reference column of the cash payments journal to indicate that each amount has been posted.

At regular intervals, each item in the Other Accounts Dr. column is also posted individually to an account in the general ledger. The posting is indicated by writing the account number in the Posting Reference column of the cash payments journal.

At the end of the month, each of the amount columns in the cash payments journal is totaled. The sum of the two debit totals is compared with the credit total to determine their equality. A check mark is placed below the total of the Other Accounts Dr. column to indicate that no further action is needed. When each of the totals of the other two columns is posted to the general ledger, an account number is inserted below each column total.

**Accounts Payable Control and Subsidiary Ledger**

After all posting has been completed for the month, the sum of the balances in the accounts payable subsidiary ledger should be compared with the balance of the accounts payable control account in the general ledger. If the controlling account and the subsidiary ledger do not agree, the error or errors must be located and corrected. The balances of the individual creditor (supplier) accounts may be summarized in a supplier balance summary report. The total of Darming's supplier balance summary report, $2,410, agrees with the balance of the accounts payable control account on March 31, 2008, as shown in Exhibit 5-11.

**Exhibit 5-11 Darming's supplier balance summary and accounts payable**

| Accounts Payable (Control) | | Darming Supplier Balance Summary March 31, 2008 | |
|---|---|---|---|
| Balance, March 1, 2008 | 1,230 | Donnelly Supplies | 1,450 |
| Total credits (from purchases journal) | 6,230 | Grayco Supplies | 0 |
| Total debits | | Howard Supplies | 960 |
| (from cash payments journal) | (5,050) | Jewett Business Systems | 0 |
| Balance, March 31, 2008 | 2,410 | Total | 2,410 |

## 3. Adapting Manual Accounting Systems

The preceding sections of this chapter illustrate subsidiary ledgers and special journals that are common for a medium-sized business. Many businesses use subsidiary ledgers for other accounts, in addition to Accounts Receivable and Accounts Payable. Also, special journals are often adapted or modified in practice to meet the specific needs of a business. In the following paragraphs, we describe other subsidiary ledgers and modified special journals.

### ADDITIONAL SUBSIDIARY LEDGERS

Generally, subsidiary ledgers are used for accounts that consist of a large number of individual items, each of which has unique characteristics. For example, businesses may use a subsidiary equipment ledger to keep track of each item of equipment purchased, its cost, location, and other data. Such ledgers are similar to the accounts receivable and accounts payable subsidiary ledgers that we illustrated in this chapter.

## MODIFIED SPECIAL JOURNALS

A business may modify its special journals by adding one or more columns for recording transactions that occur frequently. For example, a business may collect sales taxes that must be remitted periodically to the taxing authorities. Thus, the business may add a special column for Sales Taxes Payable Cr. in its revenue journal, as shown in Exhibit 5-12.

**Exhibit 5-12 Revenue journal** Page 40

| | Date | | Invoice No. | Account Debited | Post. Ref. | Accts. Rec. Dr. | Service Income Cr. | Sales Taxes Payable Cr. | |
|---|---|---|---|---|---|---|---|---|---|
| 1 | 2008 Nov. | 2 | 842 | Litten Co. | √ | 47,700 | 45,000 | 2,700 | 1 |
| 2 | | 3 | 843 | Kauffman Supply Co. | √ | 11,606 | 11,000 | 606 | 2 |

Some other examples of how special journals may be modified for a variety of different types of businesses are:

➢ **Automobile Repair Shop**—The revenue journal may be modified to include columns for each major type of repair service. In addition, columns for warranty repairs, credit card charges, and sales taxes may be added.

➢ **Movie Theater**—The cash receipts journal may be modified to include columns for revenues from admissions, gift certificates, and concession sales.

➢ **Restaurant**—The purchases journal may be modified to include columns for food, linen, silverware and glassware, and kitchen supplies.

Regardless of how a special journal is modified, the basic principles and procedures discussed in this chapter apply. For example, the columns in special journals are normally totaled at periodic intervals. The totals of the debit and credit columns are then compared to verify their equality before the totals are posted to the general ledger accounts.

# 4. Computerized Accounting Systems

Computerized accounting systems have become more widely used as the cost of hardware and software has declined. In addition, computerized accounting systems have three main advantages over manual systems. First, computerized systems simplify the record-keeping process. Transactions are recorded in electronic forms and, at the same time, posted electronically to general and subsidiary ledger accounts. Second, computerized systems are generally more accurate than manual systems. Third, computerized systems provide management current account balance information to support decision making, since account balances are posted as the transactions occur.

How do computerized accounting systems work? Exhibit 5-13 provides a general overview. Many transactions must first be authorized. This means that the transaction is approved by management before it is permitted. For example, most sales and purchase transactions must first be authorized before they are permitted. Without this step, sales may be made to customers that have insufficient credit, or purchases may be made for items that are not needed. Most computerized accounting systems include authorization steps in the software. Once authorized, the transaction can be completed. The completed transaction must be recorded in the accounting system. In computerized accounting systems, details of the specific transaction are input on a computer screen. The computer screen is often tailored to the specific transaction, much the way a special journal is tailored to a specific transaction. Once the computer screen is compl'eted, the transaction is submitted into the computer system, often by the click of a button. The submitted transaction updates information in a database. A database collects, stores, and organizes information so it can be quickly retrieved. Once transaction details have been submitted to the database, managers are able to create reports from the database to answer questions about the business. Examples would include reports identifying the revenues of a customer, the cash receipts of a customer, or the account summary of a customer.

**Exhibit 5-13 Elements of a computerized accounting system**

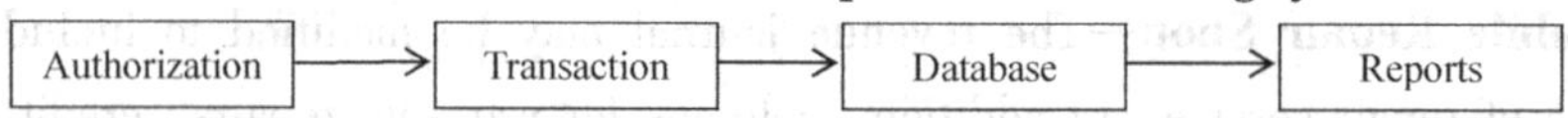


While all accounting systems have these general features, the specific details can vary across accounting software solutions.

## TERMINOLOGY:

Accounting System: 会计系统
Subsidiary Ledger: 明细账
Accounts Payable Subsidiary Ledger: 应付账款明细分类账
Accounts Receivable Subsidiary Ledger: 应收账款明细分类账
Cash Payments Journal: 现金支出日记账
Cash Receipts Journal: 现金收入日记账
Controlling Account: 控制账户
General Journal: 普通日记账
General Ledger: 总分类账
Internal Controls: 内部控制
Invoice: 商业发票
Purchases Journal: 购货日记账
Revenue Journal: 收入日记账
Special Journal: 特种日记账

## QUESTIONS:

**1. Define an accounting system and describe the three steps for designing an accounting system.**

An accounting system is the methods and procedures for collecting, classifying, summarizing, and reporting a business's financial information. The three steps through which an accounting system evolves are: ① Analysis of information needs. ② Design of the system. ③ Implementation of the system design.

**2. Define subsidiary ledger accounts for customers and creditors.**

Subsidiary ledgers may be used to maintain separate records for customers and creditors (vendors). A controlling account summarizes the subsidiary ledger accounts. The sum of the subsidiary ledger must agree with the balance in the related controlling account. Subsidiary ledgers may be maintained for a variety of accounts, such as fixed assets, accounts receivable, and accounts payable.

**3. Describe the special journals.**

Special journals efficiently summarize a large number of similar transactions as follows: The revenue journal is used to record the sale of services on account. The cash receipts journal is used to record the collection of accounts and other cash receipts. The purchases journal is used to record purchases on account. The cash payments journal is used to record the payments of creditor accounts and other cash payments. Special journals may be modified by adding columns for frequently occurring transactions.

**4. Differentiate between a manual and a computerized accounting system.**

Computerized accounting systems are similar to manual systems. The main advantages of a computerized accounting system are the simultaneous recording and posting of transactions, high degree of accuracy, and timeliness of reporting.

## PROBLEM:

Selected transactions of Darming for the month of May are as follows:

a. May 1: Issued Check No. 1001 in payment of rent for May, $1,200.

b. May 2: Purchased office supplies on account from McMillan Co., $3,600.

c. May 4: Issued Check No. 1003 in payment of freight charges on the supplies purchased on May 2, $320.

d. May 8: Provided services on account to Waller Co., Invoice No. 51, $4,500.

e. May 9: Issued Check No. 1005 for office supplies purchased, $450.

f. May 10: Received cash for office supplies sold to employees at cost, $120.

g. May 11: Purchased office equipment on account from Fender Office Products, $15,000.

h. May 12: Issued Check No. 1010 in payment of the supplies purchased from McMillan Co. on May 2, $3,600.

i. May 16: Provided services on account to Riese Co., Invoice No. 58, $8,000.

j. May 18: Received $4,500 from Waller Co. in payment of May 8 invoice.

k. May 20: Invested additional cash in the business, $10,000.

l. May25: Provided services for cash, $15,900.

m. May 30: Issued Check No. 1040 for withdrawal of cash for personal use, $1,000.

n. May 30: Issued Check No. 1041 in payment of electricity and water invoices, $690.

o. May 30: Issued Check No. 1042 in payment of office and sales salaries for May, $15,800.

p. May 31: Journalized adjusting entries from the work sheet prepared for the fiscal year ended May 31.

Darming maintains a revenue journal, a cash receipts journal, a purchases journal, a cash payments journal, and a general journal. In addition, accounts receivable and accounts payable subsidiary ledgers are used.

**Requirements**

1. Indicate the journal in which each of the preceding transactions, a through p, would be recorded.

2. Indicate whether an account in the accounts receivable or accounts payable subsidiary ledgers would be affected for each of the preceding transactions.

3. Journalize transactions b, c, d, h, and j in the appropriate journals.

**Solution**

Requirement 1 and 2. Transaction and journal, subsidiary ledger are shown in Exhibit 5-14.

**Exhibit 5-14 Transaction and journal, subsidiary ledger**

| 1. Journal | 2. Subsidiary Ledger |
|---|---|
| a. Cash payments journal | |
| b. Purchases journal | Accounts payable ledger |
| c. Cash payments journal | |
| d. Revenue journal | Accounts receivable ledger |
| e. Cash payments journal | |
| f. Cash receipts journal | |
| g. Purchases journal | Accounts payable ledger |
| h. Cash payments journal | Accounts payable ledger |
| i. Revenue journal | Accounts receivable ledger |
| j. Cash receipts journal | Accounts receivable ledger |
| k. Cash receipts journal | |
| l. Cash receipts journal | |
| m. Cash payments journal | |
| n. Cash payments journal | |
| o. Cash payments journal | |
| p. General journal | |

Requirement 3. Journalize thansactions in Exhibit 5-15 ~ Exhibit 5-18.

**Exhibit 5-15 Transaction b**

PURCHASES JOURNAL

| Date | Account Credited | Post. Ref. | Accounts Payable Cr. | Supplies Dr. | Other Accounts Dr. | Post. Ref. | Amount |
|---|---|---|---|---|---|---|---|
| May 2 | McMillan Co. | | 3,600 | 3,600 | | | |

**Exhibit 5-16 Transaction c and h**

CASH PAYMENTS JOURNAL

| Date | Ck. No. | Account Debited | Post. Ref. | Other Accounts Dr. | Accounts Payable Dr. | Cash Cr. |
|---|---|---|---|---|---|---|
| May 4 | 1003 | Freight Expense | | 320 | | 320 |
| 12 | 1010 | McMillan Co. | | | 3,600 | 3,600 |

**Exhibit 5-17 Transaction d**

REVENUE JOURNAL

| Date | Invoice No. | Account Debited | Post. Ref. | Accts. Rec. Dr. Service Income Cr. |
|---|---|---|---|---|
| May 8 | 51 | Waller Co. | | 4,500 |

**Exhibit 5-18 Transaction j**

CASH RECEIPTS JOURNAL

| Date | Account Credited | Post. Ref. | Other Accounts Cr. | Accounts Payable Cr. | Cash Dr. |
|---|---|---|---|---|---|
| May 18 | Waller Co. | | | 4,500 | 4,500 |

# Chapter 6

# Accounting for Merchandising Businesses

**Objectives**

1. Distinguish between activities of service and merchandising businesses.
2. Describe the financial statements of a merchandising business.
3. Accounting for sale, purchase, transportation costs, sales taxes, and trade discounts.
4. Describe the adjusting and closing process for a merchandising business.

# 1. Nature of Merchandising Businesses

How do the activities of Darming, an attorney, and an architect, which are service businesses, differ from those of Wal – Mart or Best Buy, which are merchandising businesses? These differences are best illustrated by focusing on the revenues and expenses in the condensed income statements shown in Exhibit 6-1.

**Exhibit 6-1 The differences between service and merchandising business in income statement**

| Service Business | | Merchandising Business | |
|---|---|---|---|
| Fees earned | XXX | Sales | XXX |
| Operating expenses | – XXX | Cost of merchandise sold | – XXX |
| Net income | XXX | Gross profit | XXX |
| | | Operating expenses | – XXX |
| | | Net income | XXX |

The revenue activities of a service business involve providing services to customers. The revenues from services are reported as fees earned on the income statement for a service business. The operating expenses incurred in providing the services are subtracted from the fees earned to arrive at net income.

In contrast, the revenue activities of a merchandising business involve the buying and selling of merchandise. A merchandising business must first purchase merchandise to sell to its customers. When this merchandise is sold, the revenue is reported as sales, and its cost is recognized as an expense called the cost of merchandise sold. Merchandise on hand (not sold) at the end of an accounting period is called merchandise inventory. Merchandise inventory is reported as a current asset on the balance sheet.

In the remainder of this chapter, we illustrate merchandiser financial statements and transactions that affect the income statement (sales, cost of merchandise sold, and gross profit) and the balance sheet (merchandise inventory).

# 2. Financial Statement of Merchandising Businesses

Merchandise inventory is the heart of a merchandising business, and cost of goods sold is the most important expense for a company that sells goods rather than services. This chapter covers the accounting for inventory and cost of merchandise sold. It also shows you how to analyze financial statements. Here we focus on inventory, cost of merchandise sold, and gross profit.

## MULTI-STEP INCOME STATEMENT

A multi-step income statement reports a number of subtotals to highlight important relationships between revenues and expenses. Exhibit 6-2 shows Darming's income statement in multi-step format. Gross profit, income from operations, and net income are highlighted for emphasis.

**Exhibit 6-2 Multi-step income statement**

Darming

Income Statement

For the Year Ended December 31, 2009

| | | |
|---|---|---|
| Net operating revenues | | 708,255 |
| Cost of sales (Cost of merchandise sold) | | 525,305 |
| Gross profit | | 182,950 |
| Total selling expenses | 70,820 | |
| General and administrative expense | 34,890 | |
| Total operating expenses | | 105,710 |
| Income from operations | | 77,240 |
| Other income and expense | | -1,840 |
| Net income | | 75,400 |

To continue the illustration, assume that during 2009 Darming purchased additional merchandise of $521,980. It received credit for purchases returns and allowances of $9,100, took purchases discounts of $2,525, and paid transportation costs of $17,400. The purchases returns and allowances and the purchases discounts are deducted from the total purchases to yield the net purchases. The transportation costs, termed transportation in, are added to the net purchases to yield the cost of merchandise purchased of $527,755, as shown below.

| | | |
|---|---|---|
| Purchases | | $521,980 |
| Less: Purchases returns and allowances | $9,100 | |
| Purchases discounts | $2,525 | $11,625 |
| Net purchases | | $510,355 |
| Add transportation in | | $17,400 |
| Cost of merchandise purchased | | $527,755 |

The ending inventory of Darming on December 31, 2008, $59,700, becomes the beginning inventory for 2009. This beginning inventory is added to the cost of merchandise purchased to yield merchandise available for sale. The ending inventory, which is assumed to be $62,150, is then subtracted from the merchandise available for sale to yield the cost of merchandise sold of $525,305, as shown in Exhibit 6-3.

The cost of merchandise sold was determined by deducting the merchandise on hand at the end of the period from the merchandise available for sale during the period. The merchandise on hand at the end of the period is determined by taking a physical count of inventory on hand. This method of determining the cost of merchandise sold and the amount of merchandise on hand is called the periodic system of accounting for merchandise inventory. Under the periodic system, the inventory records do not show the amount available for sale or the amount sold during the period. In contrast, under the perpetual system of accounting for merchandise inventory, each purchase and sale of merchandise is recorded in the inventory and the cost of merchandise sold accounts. As a result, the amount of merchandise available for sale and the amount sold are continuously (perpetually) disclosed in the inventory records.

**Exhibit 6-3 Cost of merchandise sold**

| | | |
|---|---|---|
| Merchandise inventory, January 1, 2009 | | 59,700 |
| Purchases | | 521,980 |
| Less: Purchases returns and allowances | 9,100 | |
| Purchases discounts | 2,525 | 11,625 |
| Net purchases | | 510,355 |
| Add transportation in | | 17,400 |
| Cost of merchandise purchased | | 527,755 |
| Merchandise available for sale | | 587,455 |
| Less merchandise inventory, December 31, 2009 | | 62,150 |
| Cost of merchandise sold | | 525,305 |

Most large retailers and many small merchandising businesses use computerized perpetual inventory systems. Such systems normally use bar codes, such as the one on the back of this textbook. An optical scanner reads the bar code to record merchandise purchased and sold. Merchandise businesses using a perpetual inventory system report the cost of merchandise sold as a single line on the income statement, as shown in Exhibit 6-2 for Darming. Merchandise businesses using the periodic inventory system report the cost of merchandise sold by using the format shown in Exhibit 6-3. Because of its wide use, we will use the perpetual inventory system throughout the remainder of this chapter.

Gross profit is determined by subtracting the cost of merchandise sold from net sales. Exhibit 6-2 shows that Darming reported gross profit of $ 182,950 in 2009. Operating income, sometimes called income from operations, is determined by subtracting operating expenses from gross profit. Most merchandising businesses classify operating expenses as either selling expenses or administrative expenses. Expenses that are incurred directly in the selling of merchandise are selling expenses. They include such expenses as salespersons' salaries, store supplies used, depreciation of store equipment, delivery expense, and advertising. Expenses incurred in the administration or general operations of the business are administrative expenses or general expenses. Examples of these expenses are office salaries, depreciation of office equipment, and office supplies used. Credit card expense is also normally classified as an administrative expense. Although selling and administrative expenses may be reported separately, many companies report operating expenses as a single item.

Other income and expense is reported on Darming's income statement in Exhibit 6-2. Revenue from sources other than the primary operating activity of a business is classified as other income. In a merchandising business, these items include income from interest, rent, and gains resulting from the sale of fixed assets.

Expenses that cannot be traced directly to operations are identified as other expense. Interest expense that results from financing activities and losses incurred in the disposal of fixed assets are examples of these items.

## SINGLE-STEP INCOME STATEMENT

A single-step income statement lists all the revenues together under a heading such as Revenues, or Revenues and Gains. The expenses are listed together in a single category titled Expenses, or Expenses and Losses. There is only one step, the subtraction of Expenses and Losses from the sum of Revenues and Gains, in arriving at net income. Exhibit 6-4 shows the Darming's income statement appears in single-step format.

**Exhibit 6-4 Single-step income statement**

Darming

Income Statement For the Year Ended December 31, 2009

| | | |
|---|---|---|
| Revenues: | | |
| Net sales | | 708,255 |
| Rent revenue | | 600 |
| Total revenues | | 708,855 |
| Expenses: | | |
| Cost of merchandise sold | 525,305 | |
| Selling expenses | 70,820 | |
| Administrative expenses | 34,890 | |
| Interest expense | 2,440 | |
| Total expenses | | 633,455 |
| Net income | | 75,400 |

## STATEMENT OF OWNER'S EQUITY

Owner's equity is defined as stockholders' equity, shareholders' equity, or corporate capital. Exhibit 6-5 shows the Darming's statement of owner's equity.

**Exhibit 6-5 Statement of owner's equity for merchandising business**

Darming

Statement of Owner's Equity For the Year Ended December 31, 2009

| | | |
|---|---|---|
| John, capital, January 1, 2009 | | 153,800 |
| Net income for year | 75,400 | |
| Less withdrawals | 18,000 | |
| Increase in owner's equity | | 57,400 |
| John, capital, December 31, 2009 | | 211,200 |

## BALANCE SHEET

The balance sheet for Darming is a classified balance sheet. Accounts receivable, merchandise inventory, prepaid insurance, and office supplies are included as current assets. Darming considers these assets current because they will be converted into cash or used by the business within a relatively short period of time. Darming deducts the amount of Allowance for Doubtful Accounts from the total of accounts, notes, and interest receivable because it estimates that only $91,080 will be collected in cash. The balance sheet is shown in Exhibit 6-6.

**Exhibit 6-6 Balance sheet for a merchandising company**

Darming

Balance Sheet December 31, 2009

| Assets | | | |
|---|---|---|---|
| Current assets | | | |
| Cash | 52,950 | | |
| Accounts receivable | 91,080 | | |
| Merchandise inventory | 62,150 | | |
| Office supplies | 480 | | |
| Prepaid insurance | 2,650 | | |
| Total current assets | | | 209,310 |
| Property, plant, and equipment | | | |
| Land | | 20,000 | |
| Store equipment | 27,100 | | |
| Less: Accumulated depreciation | 5,700 | 21,400 | |
| Furniture and equipment | 15,570 | | |
| Less: Accumulated depreciation | 4,720 | 10,850 | |
| Total property, plant and equipment | | | 52,250 |
| Total assets | | | 261,560 |
| **Liabilities and Stockholders' Equity** | | | |
| Current liabilities | | | |
| Accounts payable | | 22,420 | |
| Note payable | | 5,000 | |
| Salaries payable | | 1,140 | |
| Unearned rent | | 1,800 | |
| Total current liabilities | | | 30,360 |
| Long-term liabilities | | | |
| Bonds payable, due June 30, 2018 | | | 20,000 |
| Total liabilities | | | 50,360 |
| Stockholder's equity | | | |
| Common stock, $5.00 par value, issued and outstanding, 10,000 shares | | 153,800 | |
| Retained earnings | | 57,400 | |
| Total stockholders' equity | | | 211,200 |
| Total liabilities and stockholders' equity | | | 261,560 |

In the property, plant, and equipment section, Uptown deducts the accumulated depreciation from the cost of the furniture and equipment. The difference represents the book or carrying value of the furniture and equipment.

The balance sheet shows salaries payable as a current liability because it is an obligation that is payable within a year. The balance sheet also shows other short-term liabilities such as accounts payable.

The bonds payable, due in 2018, are long-term liabilities. As a result, the balance sheet shows the account in a separate section. Because Darming is a corporation, the capital section of the balance sheet, called the stockholders' equity section in the illustration, differs somewhat from the capital section for a proprietorship. Total stockholders' equity consists of the common stock, which is the original investment by stockholders, and the earnings retained in the business.

# 3. Merchandising Transactions

In the preceding section, we described and illustrated the financial statements of a merchandising business, Darming. In this section, we describe and illustrate the recording of merchandise transactions including sales, purchases, transportation costs, and sales taxes. We also discuss trade discounts and the dual nature of merchandising transactions. As a basis for recording merchandise transactions, we begin by describing the chart of accounts for a merchandising business.

## CHART OF ACCOUNTS FOR A MERCHANDISING BUSINESS

The chart of accounts for a merchandising business should reflect the elements of the financial statements we described and illustrated in the preceding section. The chart of accounts for Darming is shown in Exhibit 6-7.

**Exhibit 6-7 Chart of accounts for Darming merchandising business**

| Balance Sheet Accounts | | Income Statement Accounts | |
|---|---|---|---|
| 100 | Assets | 400 | Revenues |
| 110 | Cash | 410 | Sales |
| 112 | Accounts Receivable | 411 | Sales Returns and Allowances |
| 115 | Merchandise Inventory | 412 | Sales Discounts |
| 116 | Office Supplies | 500 | Costs and Expenses |
| 117 | Prepaid Insurance | 510 | Cost of Merchandise Sold |
| 120 | Land | 520 | Sales Salaries Expense |
| 123 | Store Equipment | 521 | Advertising Expense |
| 124 | Accumulated Depreciation—Store Equipment | 522 | Depreciation Expense—Store Equipment |
| 125 | Office Equipment | 523 | Delivery Expense |

(Continued)

| Balance Sheet Accounts | | Income Statement Accounts | |
|---|---|---|---|
| 126 | Accumulated Depreciation—Office Equipment | 529 | Miscellaneous Selling Expense |
| | | 530 | Office Salaries Expense |
| 200 | Liabilities | 531 | Rent Expense |
| 210 | Accounts Payable | 532 | Depreciation Expense—Office Equipment |
| 211 | Salaries Payable | | |
| 212 | Unearned Rent | 533 | Insurance Expense |
| 215 | Notes Payable | 534 | Office Supplies Expense |
| 300 | Owner's Equity | 539 | Misc. Administrative Expense |
| 310 | John, Capital | 540 | Other Income |
| 311 | John, Drawing | 550 | Other Expense |
| 312 | Income Summary | 560 | Interest Expense |

Darming is using a more complex numbering system because it has a greater variety of transactions. In addition, its growth creates a need for more detailed information for use in managing it. For example, a wages expense account was adequate for Darming when it was a small service business with few employees. However, as a merchandising business, Darming now uses two payroll accounts, one for Sales Salaries Expense and one for Office Salaries Expense. In the following paragraphs, we use the accounts appearing in Exhibit 6-7 to record various merchandising transactions of Darming.

## SALES TRANSACTIONS

Merchandise transactions are recorded in the accounts, using the rules of debit and credit that we described and illustrated in earlier chapters. Special journals may be used, or transactions may be entered, recorded, and posted to the accounts electronically. Although journal entries may not be manually prepared, we will use a two column general journal format in this chapter in order to simplify the discussion.

### Cash Sales

A business may sell merchandise for cash. Cash sales are normally rung up (entered) on a cash register and recorded in the accounts. To illustrate, assume that on January 3, Darming sells merchandise for $1,800. These cash sales can be recorded as shown in Exhibit 6-8.

**Exhibit 6-8 Journal entry**

| Date | | Description | Post. Ref. | Debit | Credit |
|---|---|---|---|---|---|
| 2009 Jan. | 3 | Cash | | 1,800 | |
| | | Sales | | | 1,800 |
| | | To record cash sales | | | |

Under the perpetual inventory system, the cost of merchandise sold and the reduction in merchandise inventory should also be recorded. In this way, the merchandise inventory account will indicate the amount of merchandise on hand (not sold). To illustrate, assume that the cost of merchandise sold on January 3 was $1,200. The entry to record the cost of merchandise sold and the reduction in the merchandise inventory is shown in Exhibit 6-9.

**Exhibit 6-9 Journal entry**

| Date | | Description | Post. Ref. | Debit | Credit |
|---|---|---|---|---|---|
| 2009 Jan. | 3 | Cost of Merchandise Sold | | 1,200 | |
| | | Merchandise Inventory | | | 1,200 |
| | | To record the cost of merch sold | | | |

In recent years, a large percentage of retail sales have been made to customers who use credit cards such as MasterCard or VISA. How do retailers record sales made with the use of credit cards? Such sales are recorded as cash sales. This is because the retailer normally receives payment within a few days of making the sale. Specifically, such sales are normally processed by a clearing-house that contacts the bank that issued the card. The issuing bank then electronically transfers cash directly to the retailer's bank account. Thus, if the customers in the preceding sales had used MasterCards to pay for their purchases, the sales would be recorded exactly as shown above. Any processing fees charged by the clearing-house or issuing bank are periodically recorded as an expense as shown in Exhibit 6-10.

**Exhibit 6-10 Journal entry**

| Date | | Description | Post. Ref. | Debit | Credit |
|---|---|---|---|---|---|
| Jan. | 31 | Credit Card Expense | | 48 | |
| | | Cash | | | 48 |
| | | To record service charges on credit card sales for the month | | | |

Instead of using MasterCard or VISA, a customer may use a credit card that is not issued by a bank, such as American Express or Discover. If the seller uses a clearing house, the clearing-house will collect the receivable and transfer the cash to the retailer's bank account similar to the way it would have if the customer had used MasterCard or VISA.

**Sales on Account**

A business may sell merchandise on account. The seller records such sales as a debit to Accounts Receivable and a credit to Sales. An example of an entry for a Darming sale on account of $510 is shown in Exhibit 6-11. The cost of merchandise sold was $280.

**Sales Discounts**

The terms of a sale are normally indicated on the invoice or bill that the seller sends to the buyer, as shown in Exhibit 6-12.

**Exhibit 6-11 Journal entry**

| Date | | Description | Post. Ref. | Debit | Credit |
|---|---|---|---|---|---|
| Jan. | 12 | Accounts Receivable—Sims Co. | | 510 | |
| | | Sales | | | 510 |
| | | Invoice No. 7172 | | | |
| | | | | | |
| | 12 | Cost of Merchandise Sold | | 280 | |
| | | Merchandise Inventory | | | 280 |
| | | Cost of merch. sold on Invoice No. 7172 | | | |

**Exhibit 6-12 The terms of a sale**

| Sold to APS | Darming Invoice | Terms | Shipping |
|---|---|---|---|
| 2 digital cameras | 1,500 | 2/10, *n*/30 | FOB |

The credit terms of 2/10, *n*/30 are summarized in Exhibit 6-13.

**Exhibit 6-13 Credit terms**

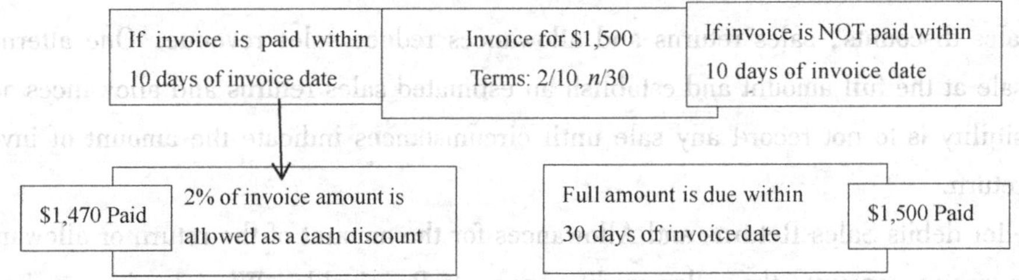


**Discounts taken by the buyer for early payment are recorded as sales discounts by the seller. Since managers may want to know the amount of the sales discounts for a period, the seller normally records the sales discounts in a separate account. The sales discounts account is a contra (or offsetting) account to Sales. To illustrate, assume that cash is received within the discount period (10 days) from the credit sale of $1,500, shown on the invoice in Exhibit 6-12. Darming would record the receipt of the cash as shown in Exhibit 6-14.**

**Exhibit 6-14 Journal entry**

| Date | | Description | Post. Ref. | Debit | Credit |
|---|---|---|---|---|---|
| Jan. | 22 | Cash | | 1,470 | |
| | | Sales Discounts | | 30 | |
| | | Accounts Receivable—APS | | | 1,500 |
| | | Collection on Invoice No. 106-8, less 2% discount | | | |

## Sales Returns and Allowances

Merchandise sold may be returned to the seller (sales return). In addition, because of defects or for other reasons, the seller may reduce the initial price at which the goods were sold (sales allowance). If the return or allowance is for a sale on account, the seller usually issues the buyer a credit memorandum. This memorandum shows the amount of and the reason for the seller's credit to an account receivable. A credit memorandum issued by Darming is illustrated in Exhibit 6-15.

**Exhibit 6-15 Credit memorandum**

No. 32

3942 Washington Ave.
Los Angeles, CA 90025 - 3942

**CREDIT MEMORANDUM**

| **TO** | **DATE** |
|---|---|
| Maxim Systems | January 13, 2009 |
| 7519 East Willson Ave. | |
| Seattle, WA 98101 - 7519 | |

**WE CREDIT YOUR ACCOUNT AS FOLLOWS**

| | | |
|---|---|---|
| 1 | Controller Kit | 225 |

Like sales discounts, sales returns and allowances reduce sales revenue. One alternative is to record the sale at the full amount and establish an estimated sales returns and allowances account. A second possibility is to not record any sale until circumstances indicate the amount of inventory the buyer will return.

The seller debits Sales Returns and Allowances for the amount of the return or allowance. If the original sale was on account, the seller credits Accounts Receivable. When buying receivables without recourse, the purchaser assumes the risk of collectability and absorbs any credit losses. The transfer of accounts receivable in a non-recourse transaction is an outright sale of the receivables both in form (transfer of title) and substance (transfer of control). In non-recourse transactions, as in any sale of assets, the seller debits Cash for the proceeds and credits Accounts Receivable for the face value of the receivables. The seller recognizes the difference, reduced by any provision for probable adjustments (discounts, returns, allowances, etc.), as a Loss on the Sale of Receivables. The seller uses a Due from Factor account (reported as a receivable) to account for the proceeds retained by the factor to cover probable sales discounts, sales returns, and sales allowances. Darming records the credit memo as shown in Exhibit 6-16.

What if the buyer pays for the merchandise and the merchandise is later returned? In this case, the seller may issue a credit and apply it against other accounts receivable owed by the buyer, or the cash may be refunded. If the credit is applied against the buyer's other receivables, the seller records entries similar to those preceding. If cash is refunded for merchandise returned or for an allowance, the seller debits Sales Returns and Allowances and credits Cash.

**Exhibit 6-16 Journal entry**

| Date | | Description | Post. Ref. | Debit | Credit |
|---|---|---|---|---|---|
| Jan. | 13 | Sales Returns and Allowances | | 225 | |
| | | Accounts Receivable—Maxim Systems | | | 225 |
| | | Credit Memo No. 32 | | | |
| | 13 | Merchandise Inventory | | 140 | |
| | | Cost of Merchandise Sold | | | 140 |
| | | Cost of merchandise returned, Credit Memo No. 32 | | | |

## PURCHASE TRANSACTIONS

As we indicated earlier in this chapter, most large retailers and many small merchandising businesses use computerized perpetual inventory systems. Under the perpetual inventory system, cash purchases of merchandise are recorded as shown in Exhibit 6-17.

**Exhibit 6-17 Journal entry**

| Date | | Description | Post. Ref. | Debit | Credit |
|---|---|---|---|---|---|
| 2009 Jan. | 3 | Merchandise Inventory | | 2,510 | |
| | | Cash | | | 2,510 |
| | | Purchased inventory from Bowen Co | | | |

Purchases of merchandise on account are recorded as shown in Exhibit 6-18.

**Exhibit 6-18 Journal entry**

| Date | | Description | Post. Ref. | Debit | Credit |
|---|---|---|---|---|---|
| Jan. | 4 | Merchandise Inventory | | 9,250 | |
| | | Accounts Payable—Thomas Corporation | | | 9,250 |
| | | Purchased inventory on account. | | | |

### Purchases Discounts

Purchases discounts taken by the buyer for early payment of an invoice reduce the cost of the merchandise purchased. Most businesses design their accounting systems so that all available discounts are taken. Even if the buyer has to borrow to make the payment within a discount period, it is normally to the buyer's advantage to do so. To illustrate, assume that Alpha Technologies issues an invoice for $3,000 to Darming, dated March 12, with terms 2/10, *n*/30. The last day of the discount period in which the $60 discount can be taken is March 22. Assume that in order to pay the invoice on March 22, Darming borrows the money for the remaining 20 days of the credit period. If we assume an annual interest rate of 6% and a 360-day year, the interest on the loan of $2,940 ($3,000 − $60) is $9.8 ($2,940 × 6% × 20days/360days). The net savings to Darming is $502, computed as follows.

Discount of 2% on $3,000 $60.00

| | |
|---|---|
| Interest for 20 days at rate of 6% on $2,940 | – $9.80 |
| Savings from borrowing | $50.20 |

The savings can also be seen by comparing the interest rate on the money saved by taking the discount and the interest rate on the money borrowed to take the discount. For Darming, the interest rate on the money saved in this example is estimated by converting 2% for 20 days to a yearly rate, as follows.

$$2\% \times \frac{360 \text{ days}}{20 \text{ days}} = 2\% \times 18 = 36\%$$

If Darming borrows the money to take the discount, it pays interest of 6%. If Darming does not take the discount, it pays estimated interest of 36% for using the $2,940 for an additional 20 days.

Under the perpetual inventory system, the buyer initially debits the merchandise inventory account for the amount of the invoice. When paying the invoice, the buyer credits the merchandise inventory account for the amount of the discount. In this way, the merchandise inventory shows the net cost to the buyer. For example, Darming would record the Alpha Technologies invoice and its payment at the end of the discount period as shown in Exhibit 6-19.

**Exhibit 6-19 Journal entry**

| Date | | Description | Post. Ref. | Debit | Credit |
|---|---|---|---|---|---|
| Mar. | 12 | Merchandise Inventory | | 3,000 | |
| | | Accounts Payable—Alpha Technologies | | | 3,000 |
| | | Purchased inventory on account | | | |
| | | | | | |
| | 22 | Accounts Payable—Alpha Technologies | | 3,000 | |
| | | Cash | | | 2,940 |
| | | Merchandise Inventory | | | 60 |
| | | Make the payment at the end of the discount period | | | |

If Darming does not take the discount because it does not pay the invoice until April 11, it would record the payment as shown in Exhibit 6-20.

**Exhibit 6-20 Journal entry**

| Date | | Description | Post. Ref. | Debit | Credit |
|---|---|---|---|---|---|
| Apr. | 11 | Accounts Payable—Alpha Technologies | | 3,000 | |
| | | Cash | | | 3,000 |
| | | Pay the invoice until April 11 | | | |

### Purchases Returns and Allowances

When merchandise is returned (purchases return) or a price adjustment is requested (purchases allowance), the buyer (debtor) usually sends the seller a letter or a debit memorandum. A debit memorandum, shown in Exhibit 6-21, informs the seller of the amount the buyer proposes to debit to the account payable due the seller. It also states the reasons for the return or the request for a price reduction.

**Exhibit 6-21 Debit memorandum**

No. 18

5101 Washington Ave.

Cincinnati, OH 45227 -5101

**CREDIT MEMORANDUM**

| **TO** | **DATE** | |
|---|---|---|
| Krier Company | March 7, 2009 | |
| 7608 Melton Avenue | | |
| Los Angeles, CA 90025 -3942 | | |

**WE DEBIT YOUR ACCOUNT AS FOLLOWS**

| | | |
|---|---|---|
| 10 Server Network Interface Cards, your Invoice No. 8281, are being returned via parcel post. Our order specified No. 725X. | 10 units@ 90.00 | 900.00 |

The buyer may use a copy of the debit memorandum as the basis for recording the return or allowance or wait for approval from the seller (creditor). In either case, the buyer must debit Accounts Payable and credit Merchandise Inventory. To illustrate, Darming records the return of the merchandise indicated in the debit memo as shown in Exhibit 6-22.

**Exhibit 6-22 Journal entry**

| Date | | Description | Post. Ref. | Debit | Credit |
|---|---|---|---|---|---|
| Mar. | 7 | Accounts Payable—Krier Company | | 900 | |
| | | Merchandise Inventory | | | 900 |
| | | Debit Memo No. 18. | | | |

When a buyer returns merchandise or has been granted an allowance prior to paying the invoice, the amount of the debit memorandum is deducted from the invoice amount. The amount is deducted before the purchase discount is computed. For example, assume that on May 2, Darming purchases $5,000 of merchandise from Delta Data Link, subject to terms 2/10, *n*/30. On May 4, Darming returns $3,000 of the merchandise, and on May 12, Darming pays the original invoice less the return. Darming would record these transactions as shown in Exhibit 6-23.

**Exhibit 6-23 Journal entry**

| Date | | Description | Post. Ref. | Debit | Credit |
|---|---|---|---|---|---|
| May | 2 | Merchandise Inventory | | 5,000 | |
| | | Accounts Payable—Delta Data Link | | | 5,000 |
| | | Purchased merchandise | | | |
| | | | | | |
| | 4 | Accounts Payable—Delta Data Link | | 3,000 | |
| | | Merchandise Inventory | | | 3,000 |
| | | Returned portion of merch. purchased | | | |
| | | | | | |
| | 12 | Accounts Payable—Delta Data Link | | 2,000 | |
| | | Cash | | | 1,960 |
| | | Merchandise Inventory | | | 40 |
| | | Paid invoice (( \$5,000 − \$3,000) × (1 − 2%) = \$1,960) | | | |

## TRANSPORTATION COSTS, SALES TAXES, AND TRADE DISCOUNTS

In the preceding two sections, we described and illustrated merchandise transactions involving sales and purchases. In this section, we discuss merchandise transactions involving transportation costs, sales taxes, and trade discounts.

### Transportation Costs

The terms of a sale should indicate when the ownership (title) of the merchandise passes to the buyer. This point determines which party, the buyer or the seller, must pay the transportation costs.

The ownership of the merchandise may pass to the buyer when the seller delivers the merchandise to the transportation company or freight carrier. For example, DaimlerChrysler records the sale and the transfer of ownership of its vehicles to dealers when the vehicles are shipped from the factory. In this case, the terms are said to be FOB (free on board) shipping point. This term means that the dealer pays the transportation costs from the shipping point (factory) to the final destination. Such costs are part of the dealer's total cost of purchasing inventory and should be added to the cost of the inventory by debiting Merchandise Inventory.

To illustrate, assume that on June 10, Darming buys merchandise from Magna Data on account, \$900, terms FOB shipping point, and pays the transportation cost of \$50. Darming records these two transactions as shown in Exhibit 6-24.

The ownership of the merchandise may pass to the buyer when the buyer receives the merchandise. In this case, the terms are said to be FOB (free on board) destination. This term means that the seller delivers the merchandise to the buyer's final destination, free of transportation charges to the buyer. The seller thus pays the transportation costs to the final destination. The seller debits Delivery Expense or Transportation Out, which is reported on the seller's income statement as an expense.

**Exhibit 6-24 Journal entry**

| Date | | Description | Post. Ref. | Debit | Credit |
|---|---|---|---|---|---|
| June | 10 | Merchandise Inventory | | 900 | |
| | | Accounts Payable—Magna Data | | | 900 |
| | | Purchased merchandise, terms FOB shipping point | | | |
| | 10 | Merchandise Inventory | | 50 | |
| | | Cash | | | 50 |
| | | Paid shipping cost on merchandise purchased | | | |

To illustrate, assume that on June 15, Darming sells merchandise to Kranz Company on account, $700, terms FOB destination. The cost of the merchandise sold is $480, and Darming pays the transportation cost of $40. Darming records the sale, the cost of the sale, and the transportation cost as shown in Exhibit 6-25.

**Exhibit 6-25 Journal entry**

| Date | | Description | Post. Ref. | Debit | Credit |
|---|---|---|---|---|---|
| June | 15 | Accounts Receivable—Kranz Company | | 700 | |
| | | Sales | | | 700 |
| | | Sold merchandise, terms FOB destination | | | |
| | | | | | |
| | 15 | Cost of Merchandise Sold | | 480 | |
| | | Merchandise Inventory | | | 480 |
| | | Recorded cost of merchandise sold to Kranz Company | | | |
| | | | | | |
| | 15 | Delivery Expense | | 40 | |
| | | Cash | | | 40 |
| | | Paid shipping cost on merch. sold | | | |

As a convenience to the buyer, the seller may prepay the transportation costs, even though the terms are FOB shipping point. The seller will then add the transportation costs to the invoice. The buyer will debit Merchandise Inventory for the total amount of the invoice, including the transportation costs. Any discount terms would not apply to the prepaid transportation costs.

To illustrate, assume that on June 20, Darming sells merchandise to Planter Company on account, $800 terms FOB shipping point. Darming pays the transportation cost of $45 and adds it to the invoice. The cost of the merchandise sold is $360. Darming records these transactions as shown in Exhibit 6-26.

Shipping terms, the passage of title, and whether the buyer or seller is to pay the transportation costs are classified into FOB destination, and FOB shipping point.

**Exhibit 6-26 Journal entry**

| Date | | Description | Post. Ref. | Debit | Credit |
|---|---|---|---|---|---|
| June | 20 | Accounts Receivable—Planter Company | | 800 | |
| | | Sales | | | 800 |
| | | Sold merch. terms FOB shipping point | | | |
| | 20 | Cost of Merchandise Sold | | 360 | |
| | | Merchandise Inventory | | | 360 |
| | | Recorded cost of merchandise sold to Planter Company | | | |
| | 20 | Accounts Receivable—Planter Company | | 45 | |
| | | Cash | | | 45 |
| | | Prepaid shipping cost on merch. sold | | | |

## Sales Taxes

The liability for the sales tax is incurred when the sale is made. At the time of a cash sale, the seller collects the sales tax. When a sale is made on account, the seller charges the tax to the buyer by debiting Accounts Receivable. The seller credits the sales account for the amount of the sale and credits the tax to Sales Tax Payable. For example, the seller would record a sale of $100 on account, subject to a tax of 6%, as shown in Exhibit 6-27.

**Exhibit 6-27 Journal entry**

| Date | | Description | Post. Ref. | Debit | Credit |
|---|---|---|---|---|---|
| Aug. | 12 | Accounts Receivable—Lemon Co. | | 106 | |
| | | Sales | | | 100 |
| | | Sales Tax Payable | | | 6 |
| | | Invoice No. 339 | | | |

Normally on a regular basis, the seller pays to the taxing unit the amount of the sales tax collected. The seller records such a payment as shown in Exhibit 6-28.

**Exhibit 6-28 Journal entry**

| Date | | Description | Post. Ref. | Debit | Credit |
|---|---|---|---|---|---|
| Sept. | 15 | Sales Tax Payable | | 2,900 | |
| | | Cash | | | 2,900 |
| | | Payment for sales taxes collected during August | | | |

## Trade Discounts

Wholesalers' prices may be subject to a trade or quantity discount. Companies use such trade discounts to avoid frequent changes in catalogs, to alter prices for different quantities purchased, or to hide the true invoice price from competitors.

Trade discounts are commonly quoted in percentages. For example, say your text-book has a list price of $90, and the publisher sells it to college bookstores for list less a 30 percent trade discount. The publisher then records the receivable at $63 per text-book. The publisher, per normal practice, simply deducts the trade discount from the list price and bills the customer net.

## DUAL NATURE OF MERCHANDISE TRANSACTIONS

Each merchandising transaction affects a buyer and a seller. In the illustration, we show how the same transactions would be recorded by both the seller and the buyer. In this example, the seller is Oksana Company and the buyer is Thomason, as shown in Exhibit 6-29.

**Exhibit 6-29 The same transaction recorded by both the seller and the buyer**

| Transaction | Oksana Company (Seller) | | | Thomason (Buyer) | | |
|---|---|---|---|---|---|---|
| April 1. Oksana Co. sold merchandise on account to Thomason, $7,500, terms FOB shipping point, n/45. The cost of the merchandise sold was $4,500 | Accounts Receivable—Thomason | 7,500 | | Merchandise Inventory | 7,500 | |
| | Sales | | 7,500 | Accounts Payable—Oksana Co. | | 7,500 |
| | Cost of Merchandise Sold | 4,500 | | | | |
| | Merchandise Inventory | | 4,500 | | | |
| April 2. Thomason paid transportation charges of $150 on April 1 purchase from Oksana Company | No entry | | | Merchandise Inventory | 150 | |
| | | | | Cash | | 150 |
| April 5. Oksana Co. sold merchandise on account to Thomason, $5,000, terms FOB destination, n/30. The cost of the merchandise sold was $3,500 | Accounts Receivable—Thomason | 5,000 | | Merchandise Inventory | 5,000 | |
| | Sales | | 5,000 | Accounts Payable—Oksana Co. | | 5,000 |
| | Cost of Merchandise Sold | 3,500 | | | | |
| | Merchandise Inventory | | 3,500 | | | |
| April 7. Oksana Co. paid transportation costs of $250 for delivery of merchandise sold to Thomason on April 5 | Delivery Expense | 250 | | No entry | | |
| | Cash | | 250 | | | |
| April 13. Oksana Co. issued Thomason a credit memorandum for merchandise returned, $1,000. The merchandise had been purchased by Thomason on account on April 5. The cost of the merchandise returned was $700 | Sales Returns and Allowances | 1,000 | | Accounts Payable—Oksana Co. | 1,000 | |
| | Accounts Receivable—Thomason | | 1,000 | Merchandise Inventory | | 1,000 |
| | Merchandise Inventory | 700 | | | | |
| | Cost of Merchandise Sold | | 700 | | | |
| April 15. Oksana Company received payment from Thomason for purchase of April 5 | Cash | 4,000 | | Accounts Payable—Oksana Co. | 4,000 | |
| | Accounts Receivable—Thomason | | 4,000 | Cash | | 4,000 |

(Continued)

| Transaction | Oksana Company (Seller) | | | Thomason (Buyer) | | |
|---|---|---|---|---|---|---|
| July 18. Oksana Company sold merchandise on account to Thomason $12,000, terms FOB shipping point, 2/10, n/30. Oksana Company prepaid transportation costs of $500, which were added to the invoice. The cost of the merchandise sold was $7,200 | Accounts Receivable—Thomason | 12,000 | | Merchandise Inventory | 12,500 | |
| | Sales | | 12,000 | Accounts Payable—Oksana Co. | | 12,500 |
| | Accounts Receivable—Thomason | 500 | | | | |
| | Cash | | 500 | | | |
| | Cost of Merchandise Sold | 7,200 | | | | |
| | Merchandise Inventory | | 7,200 | | | |
| July 28. Oksana Company received payment from Thomason for purchase of July 18, less discount (2% × $12,000) | Cash | 12,260 | | Accounts Payable—Oksana Co. | 12,500 | |
| | Sales Discounts | 240 | | Merchandise Inventory | | 240 |
| | Accounts Receivable—Thomason | | 12,500 | Cash | | 12,260 |

# 4. The Adjusting and Closing Process

We have illustrated the chart of accounts and the analysis and recording of transactions for a merchandising business. The closing process reduces the balance of nominal (temporary) accounts to zero in order to prepare the accounts for the next period's transactions. In the closing process Darming transfers all of the revenue and expense account balances (income statement items) to a clearing or suspense account called Income Summary. The Income Summary account matches revenues and expenses.

## ADJUSTING ENTRY FOR INVENTORY SHRINKAGE

Under the perpetual inventory system, a separate merchandise inventory account is maintained in the ledger. During the accounting period, this account shows the amount of merchandise for sale at any time. However, merchandising businesses may experience some loss of inventory due to shoplifting, employee theft, or errors in recording or counting inventory. As a result, the physical inventory taken at the end of the accounting period may differ from the amount of inventory shown in the inventory records. Normally, the amount of merchandise for sale, as indicated by the balance of the merchandise inventory account, is larger than the total amount of merchandise counted during the physical inventory. For this reason, the difference is often called inventory shrinkage or inventory shortage.

To illustrate, Darming's inventory records indicate that $63,950 of merchandise should be available for sale on December 31, 2009. The physical inventory taken on December 31, 2009, however, indicates that only $62,150 of merchandise is actually available. Thus, the inventory shrinkage for the year ending December 31, 2009, is $1,800 ($63,950 − $62,150). This amount is recorded by the adjusting entry shown in Exhibit 6-30.

**Exhibit 6-30 Adjusting entry**

| Date | | Description | Post. Ref. | Debit | Credit |
|---|---|---|---|---|---|
| Dec. | 31 | Cost of Merchandise Sold | | 1,800 | |
| | | Merchandise Inventory | | | 1,800 |
| | | Adjusting Entry, Inv. shrinkage ( $63,950 - $62,150) | | | |

After this entry has been recorded, the accounting records agree with the actual physical inventory at the end of the period. Since no system of procedures and safeguards can totally eliminate it, inventory shrinkage is often considered a normal cost of operations. If the amount of the shrinkage is abnormally large, it may be disclosed separately on the income statement. In such cases, the shrinkage may be recorded in a separate account, such as Loss from Merchandise Inventory Shrinkage.

## CLOSING ENTRIES

The closing entries for a merchandising business are similar to those for a service business. The closing process reduces the balance of nominal (temporary) accounts to zero in order to prepare the accounts for the next period's transactions. In the closing process, Darming transfers all of the revenue and expense account balances (income statement items) to a clearing or suspense account called Income Summary. The Income Summary account matches revenues and expenses. Darming uses this clearing account only at the end of each accounting period.

The account represents the net income or net loss for the period. It then transfers this amount (the net income or net loss) to an owner's equity account (for a corporation, the owner's equity account is retained earnings; for proprietorships and partnerships, it is a capital account). Companies post all such closing entries to the appropriate general ledger accounts. The closing entries for Darming are shown in Exhibit 6-31.

**Exhibit 6-31 The closing entries for Darming**

JOURNAL Page 29

| | Date | | Item | Post. Ref. | Debit | Credit |
|---|---|---|---|---|---|---|
| 1 | 2009 | | Closing Entries | | | |
| 2 | Dec. | 31 | Sales | 410 | 720,185 | |
| 3 | | | Rent Revenue | 610 | 600 | |
| 4 | | | Income Summary | 312 | | 720,785 |
| 5 | | | | | | |
| 6 | | 31 | Income Summary | 312 | 645,385 | |
| 7 | | | Sales Returns and Allowances | 411 | | 6,140 |
| 8 | | | Sales Discounts | 412 | | 5,790 |
| 9 | | | Cost of Merchandise Sold | 510 | | 525,305 |
| 10 | | | Sales Salaries Expense | 520 | | 53,430 |
| 11 | | | Advertising Expense | 521 | | 10,860 |

(Continued)

| | Date | | Item | Post. Ref. | Debit | Credit |
|---|---|---|---|---|---|---|
| 12 | | | Depr. Expense—Store Equipment | 522 | | 3,100 |
| 13 | | | Delivery Expense | 523 | | 2,800 |
| 14 | | | Miscellaneous Selling Expense | 529 | | 630 |
| 15 | | | Office Salaries Expense | 530 | | 21,020 |
| 16 | | | Rent Expense | 531 | | 8,100 |
| 17 | | | Depr. Expense—Office Equipment | 532 | | 2,490 |
| 18 | | | Insurance Expense | 533 | | 1,910 |
| 19 | | | Office Supplies Expense | 534 | | 610 |
| 20 | | | Misc. Administrative Expense | 539 | | 760 |
| 21 | | | Interest Expense | 560 | | 2,440 |
| 22 | | | | | | |
| 23 | | 31 | Income Summary | 312 | 75,400 | |
| 24 | | | John, Capital | 310 | | 75,400 |
| 25 | | | | | | |
| 26 | | 31 | John, Capital | 310 | 18,000 | |
| 27 | | | John, Drawing | 311 | | 18,000 |

The balance of Income Summary, after the first two closing entries have been posted, is the net income or net loss for the period. The third closing entry transfers this balance to the owner's capital account. Darming's income summary account after the closing entries have been posted as shown in Exhibit 6-32.

**Exhibit 6-32 Income summary of Darming**

ACCOUNT Income Summary　　　　ACCOUNT NO. 312

| Date | | Item | Post. Ref. | Debit | Credit | Balance | |
|---|---|---|---|---|---|---|---|
| | | | | | | Debit | Credit |
| 2009 Dec. | 31 | Revenues | 29 | | 720,785 | | 720,785 |
| | 31 | Expenses | 29 | 645,385 | | | 75,400 |
| | 31 | Net income | 29 | 75,400 | | — | — |

After the closing entries have been prepared and posted to the accounts, a post-closing trial balance may be prepared to verify the debit-credit equality. The only accounts that should appear on the post-closing trial balance are the asset, contra asset, liability, and owner's capital accounts with balances. These are the same accounts that appear on the end-of-period balance sheet.

## TERMINOLOGY:

Accounting System: 会计系统

Accounts Payable Subsidiary Ledger：应付账款明细分类账
Accounts Receivable Subsidiary Ledger：应收账款明细分类账
Cash Payment Journal：现金支出日记账
Cash Receipts Journal：现金收入日记账
Controlling Account：控制账户
Database：数据库
E-commerce：电子商务
General Journal：普通日记账
General Ledger：总分类账
Internal Controls：内部控制
Purchases Journal：购货日记账
Revenue Journal：收入日记账
Special Journals：特种日记账
Subsidiary Ledger：明细分类账

**QUESTIONS：**

**1. Distinguish the activities of a service business from those of a merchandising business.**

The primary differences between a service business and a merchandising business relate to revenue activities. Merchandising businesses purchase merchandise for selling to customers. On a merchandising business's income statement, revenue from selling merchandise is reported as sales. The cost of the merchandise sold is subtracted from sales to arrive at gross profit. The operating expenses are subtracted from gross profit to arrive at net income. Merchandise inventory, which is merchandise not sold, is reported as a current asset on the balance sheet.

**2. Describe the accounting cycle for a merchandising business.**

The accounting cycle for a merchandising business is similar to that of a service business. However, a merchandiser is likely to experience inventory shrinkage, which must be recorded. The normal adjusting entry is to debit Cost of Merchandise Sold and credit Merchandise Inventory for the amount of the shrinkage.

**3. Compute the rate of net sales to assets as a measure of how effectively a business is using its assets.**

The assets used in computing the ratio of net sales to assets may be total assets at the end of the year, the average of the total assets at the beginning and end of the year, or the average of the monthly assets. A high ratio of net sales to assets indicates an effective use of assets.

**PROBLEM：**

Jan King Distributing Co.'s Adjusted Trial Balance as at December 31, 2007 is as shown in Exhibit 6-33.

**Exhibit 6-33 Jan King Distributing Co.'s adjusted trial balance**

Jan King Distributing Company
Adjusted Trial Balance
December 31, 2007

| | | |
|---|---|---|
| Cash | 5,600 | |
| Accounts receivable | 37,100 | |
| Merchandise Inventory | 25,800 | |
| Supplies | 1,300 | |
| Prepaid rent | 1,000 | |
| Furniture | 26,500 | |
| Accumulated depreciation | | 23,800 |
| Accounts payable | | 6,300 |
| Salaries payable | | 2,000 |
| Interest payable | | 600 |
| Unearned sales revenue | | 2,400 |
| Note payable (long-term) | | 35,000 |
| Jan King, capital | | 22,200 |
| Jan King, drawing | 48,000 | |
| Sales | | 244,000 |
| Interest revenue | | 2,000 |
| Sales discounts | 10,000 | |
| Sales returns and allowances | 8,000 | |
| Cost of merchandise sold | 81,000 | |
| Salaries expense | 72,700 | |
| Rent expense | 7,700 | |
| Depreciation expense | 2,700 | |
| Utilities expense | 5,800 | |
| Supplies expense | 2,200 | |
| Interest expense | 2,900 | |
| Total | 338,300 | 338,300 |

**Requirements**

1. Journalize the closing entries at December 31. Post to the Income summary account as an accuracy check on net income. The credit balance closed out of Income Summary should equal net income computed on the income statement. Also post to Jan King, Capital. The ending capital balance should agree with the amount reported on the balance sheet.

2. Prepare the company's single-step income statement, statement of owner's equity, and balance sheet in account form.

**Solution**

Requirement 1. The closing entries for Jan King Distributing Co. are shown in Exhibit 6-34.

**Exhibit 6-34 The closing entries for Jan King Distributing Co.**

| 2007 | | | |
|---|---|---|---|
| Dec. 31 | Sales | 244,000 | |
| | Interest Revenue | 2,000 | |
| | Income Summary | | 246,000 |
| 31 | Income Summary | 193,000 | |
| | Sales Discounts | | 10,000 |
| | Sales Returns and Allowances | | 8,000 |
| | Cost of Merchandise Sold | | 81,000 |
| | Salaries Expense | | 72,700 |
| | Rent Expense | | 7,700 |
| | Depreciation Expense | | 2,700 |
| | Utilities Expense | | 5,800 |
| | Supplies Expense | | 2,200 |
| | Interest Expense | | 2,900 |
| 31 | Income Summary ( $246,000 – $193,000) | 53,000 | |
| | Jan King, Capital | | 53,000 |
| 31 | Jan King, Capital | 48,000 | |
| | Jan King, Drawing | | 48,000 |

**Income Summary**

| Debit | Credit |
|---|---|
| Clo. $193,000 | Clo. $246,000 |
| Clo. $53,000 | |
| | Bal. $53,000 |

**Jan King, Capital**

| Debit | Credit |
|---|---|
| Withdrawals $48,000 | $22,200 |
| | Net inc. $53,000 |
| | Bal. $27,200 |

Requirement 2. Financial statements are shown in Exhibit 6-35 ~ Exhibit 6-37.

**Exhibit 6-35 The income statement for Jan King Distributing Co.**

| | | |
|---|---|---|
| Revenues: | | |
| Sales | 244,000 | |
| Less: Sales discounts | 10,000 | |
| Sales returns and allowances | 8,000 | |
| Net sales | | 226,000 |
| Interest revenue | | 2,000 |
| Total revenue | | 228,000 |
| Expenses: | | |
| Cost of merchandise sold | 81,000 | |
| Salaries expense | 72,700 | |
| Rent expense | 7,700 | |
| Utilities expense | 5,800 | |
| Interest expense | 2,900 | |
| Depreciation expense | 2,700 | |
| Supplies expense | 2,200 | |
| Total expenses | | 175,000 |
| Net income | | 53,000 |

**Exhibit 6-36 The statement of owner's equity for Jan King Distributing Co.**

Jan King Distributing Company
Statement of Owner's Equity
For the Year Ended December 31, 2007

| | |
|---|---|
| Jan King, capital, Dec. 31, 2006 | 22,200 |
| Add: Net income | 53,000 |
| | 75,200 |
| Less: Withdrawals | 48,000 |
| Jan King, capital, Dec. 31, 2007 | 27,200 |

**Exhibit 6-37 The balance sheet for Jan King Distributing Co.**

Jan King Distributing Company
Balance Sheet
December 31, 2007

| Assets | | | Liabilities | |
|---|---|---|---|---|
| Current assets: | | | Current liabilities: | |
| Cash | | 5,600 | Accounts payable | 6,300 |
| Accounts receivable | | 37,100 | Salaries payable | 2,000 |
| Merchandise inventory | | 25,800 | Interest payable | 600 |
| Supplies | | 1,300 | Unearned sales revenue | 2,400 |
| Prepaid rent | | 1,000 | Total current liabilities | 11,300 |
| Total current assets | | 70,800 | Long-term liabilities: | |
| Plant: | | | Note payable | 35,000 |
| Furniture | 26,500 | | Total liabilities | 46,300 |
| Less: Accumulated depreciation | 23,800 | 2,700 | Owner's Equity | |
| | | | Jan King, capital | 27,200 |
| Total assets | | 73,500 | Total liabilities and owner's equity | 73,500 |

# Chapter 7

# Inventory

**Objectives**

1. Describe the importance of control over inventory.
2. Describe three inventory cost flow assumptions and impact on financial statement.
3. Determine the cost of inventory under the perpetual inventory system.
4. Determine the cost of inventory under the periodic inventory system.
5. Compare and contrast the use of the three inventory costing methods.
6. Describe the reporting of merchandise inventory in financial statements.

# 1. Control of Inventory

## CLASSIFICATION

Inventories are asset items that a company holds for sale in the ordinary course of business, or goods that it will use or consume in the production of goods to be sold. The description and measurement of inventory require careful attention. The investment in inventories is frequently the largest current asset of merchandising (retail) and manufacturing businesses.

A merchandising concern, such as Wal-Mart, usually purchases its merchandise in a form ready for sale. It reports the cost assigned to unsold units left on hand as merchandise inventory. Only one inventory account, Merchandise Inventory, appears in the financial statements.

Manufacturing concerns, on the other hand, produce goods to sell to merchandising firms. Many of the largest U. S. businesses are manufacturers, such as Boeing, IBM, Exxon Mobil, Procter & Gamble, Ford, and Motorola. Although the products they produce may differ, manufacturers normally have three inventory accounts—Raw Materials, Work in Process, and Finished Goods.

A company reports the cost assigned to goods and materials on hand but not yet placed into production as raw materials inventory. Raw materials include the wood to make a baseball bat or the steel to make a car. These materials can be traced directly to the end product.

At any point in a continuous production process some units are only partially processed. The cost of the raw material for these unfinished units, plus the direct labor cost applied specifically to this material and a ratable share of manufacturing overhead costs, constitutes the work in process inventory.

Companies report the costs identified with the completed but unsold units on hand at the end of the fiscal period as finished goods inventory. Exhibit 7-1 contrasts the financial statement presentation of inventories of Wal- Mart (a merchandising company) with those of Caterpillar (a manufacturing company.) The remainder of the balance sheet is essentially similar for the two types of companies.

As indicated above, a manufacturing company, like Caterpillar, also might include a Manufacturing or Factory Supplies Inventory account. In it, Caterpillar would include such items as machine oils, nails, cleaning material, and the like—supplies that are used in production but are not the primary materials being processed.

Exhibit 7-2 shows the differences in the flow of costs through a merchandising company and a manufacturing company.

## CONTROL

For companies such as Best Buy, good control over inventory must be maintained. Two primary objectives of control over inventory are safeguarding the inventory and properly reporting it in the financial statements.

**Exhibit 7-1 Comparison of presentation of current assets for merchandising and manufacturing companies**

| Merchandising Company | | Manufacturing Company | | |
|---|---|---|---|---|
| Wal-Mart | | Caterpillar | | |
| Balance sheet | | Balance sheet | | |
| January 31, 2008 | | December 31, 2007 | | |
| Current assets (amounts in millions) | | Current assets (amounts in millions) | | |
| Cash and equivalents | 5,569 | Cash | | 1,122 |
| Accounts receivables | 3,654 | Accounts receivables | | 15,752 |
| Inventories | 35,180 | Inventories | | |
| Prepaid expenses and other | 3,183 | Raw materials | 2,474 | |
| Total current assets | 47,585 | Work in process | 1,215 | |
| | | Finished goods | 3,230 | |
| | | Supplies | 285 | |
| | | Total inventories | | 7,204 |
| | | Other current assets | | 1,399 |
| | | Total current assets | | 25,477 |

**Exhibit 7-2 Flow of costs—manufacturing and merchandising companies**

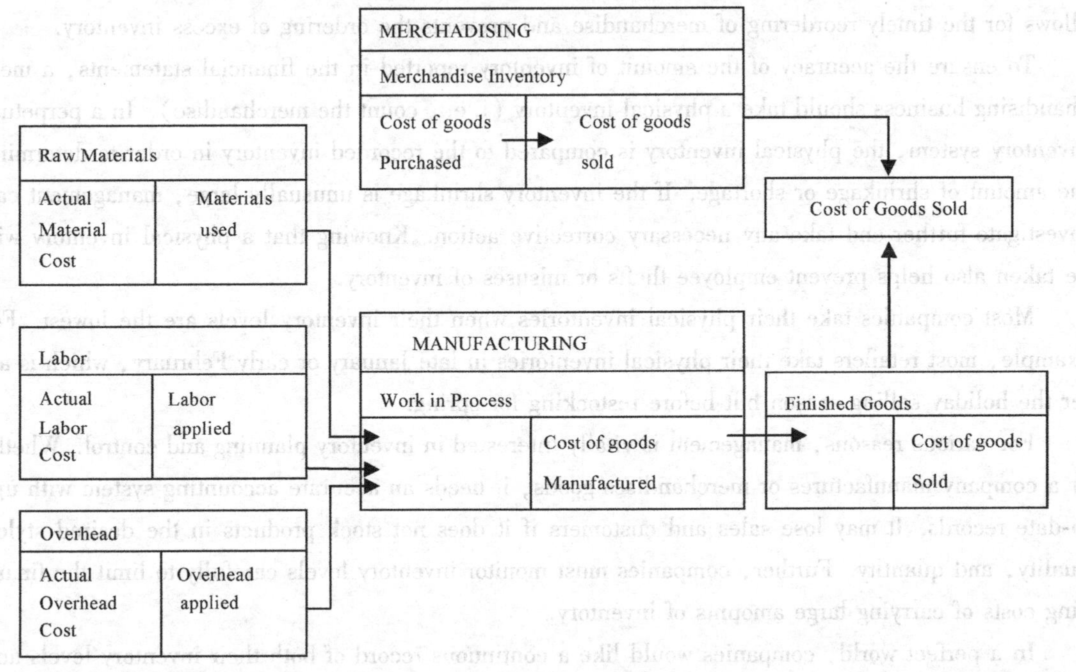


The disclosure principle holds that a company's financial statements should report enough information for outsiders to make informed decisions about the company. The company should report relevant, reliable, and comparable information about itself. That means disclosing inventory accounting methods. Without knowledge of the accounting method, a banker could make an unwise lending decision. Suppose the banker is comparing two companies—one using LIFO and the other, FIFO. The FIFO company reports higher net income but only because it uses FIFO. Without knowing this, the banker could loan money to the wrong business.

**Sale Price vs. Cost of Inventory.** The sale price of inventory and the cost of inventory are different: Sales revenue is based on the sale price of the inventory sold; Cost of goods sold is based on the cost of the inventory sold; Inventory on the balance sheet is based on the cost of the inventory still on hand.

Controls for safeguarding inventory include developing and using security measures to prevent inventory damage or customer or employee theft. For example, inventory should be stored in a warehouse or other area to which access is restricted to authorized employees. When shopping, you may have noticed how retail stores protect inventory from customer theft. Retail stores often use suchdevices as two-way mirrors, cameras, and security guards. High-priced items are often displayed in locked cabinets. Retail clothing stores often place plastic alarm tags on valuable items such as leather coats. Sensors at the exit doors set off alarms if the tags have not been removed by the clerk. These controls are designed to prevent customers from shoplifting.

Using a perpetual inventory system for merchandise also provides an effective means of control over inventory. The amount of each type of merchandise is always readily available in a subsidiary inventory ledger. In addition, the subsidiary ledger can be an aid in maintaining inventory quantities at proper levels. Frequently, comparing balances with predetermined maximum and minimum levels allows for the timely reordering of merchandise and prevents the ordering of excess inventory.

To ensure the accuracy of the amount of inventory reported in the financial statements, a merchandising business should take a physical inventory (i. e., count the merchandise). In a perpetual inventory system, the physical inventory is compared to the recorded inventory in order to determine the amount of shrinkage or shortage. If the inventory shrinkage is unusually large, management can investigate further and take any necessary corrective action. Knowing that a physical inventory will be taken also helps prevent employee thefts or misuses of inventory.

Most companies take their physical inventories when their inventory levels are the lowest. For example, most retailers take their physical inventories in late January or early February, which is after the holiday selling season but before restocking for spring.

For various reasons, management is vitally interested in inventory planning and control. Whether a company manufactures or merchandises goods, it needs an accurate accounting system with up-to-date records. It may lose sales and customers if it does not stock products in the desired style, quality, and quantity. Further, companies must monitor inventory levels carefully to limit the financing costs of carrying large amounts of inventory.

In a perfect world, companies would like a continuous record of both their inventory levels and their cost of goods sold. The popularity and affordability of computerized accounting software makes the perpetual system cost-effective for many kinds of businesses. Companies like Target, Best Buy, and Sears Holdings now incorporate the recording of sales with optical scanners at the cash register into perpetual inventory systems.

However, many companies cannot afford a complete perpetual system. But, most of these companies need current information regarding their inventory levels, to protect against stock outs or over purchasing and to aid in preparation of monthly or quarterly financial data. As a result, these companies use a modified perpetual inventory system. This system provides detailed inventory records of increases and decreases in quantities only—not dollar amounts. It is merely a memorandum device outside the double-entry system, which helps in determining the level of inventory at any point in time.

Whether a company maintains a complete perpetual inventory in quantities and dollars or a modified perpetual inventory system, it probably takes a physical inventory once a year. No matter what type of inventory records companies use, they all face the danger of loss and error. Waste, breakage, theft, improper entry, failure to prepare or record requisitions, and other similar possibilities may cause the inventory records to differ from the actual inventory on hand. Thus, all companies need periodic verification of the inventory records by actual count, weight, or measurement, with the counts compared with the detailed inventory records. As indicated earlier, a company corrects the records to agree with the quantities actually on hand.

Insofar as possible, companies should take the physical inventory near the end of their fiscal year, to properly report inventory quantities in their annual accounting reports. Because this is not always possible, however, physical inventories taken within two or three months of the year's end are satisfactory, if a company maintains detailed inventory records with a fair degree of accuracy.

## 2. Inventory Cost Flow Assumptions

Determining the cost of inventory is easy when the unit cost remains constant. But the unit cost usually changes. For example, prices often rise. The desk lamp that cost Darming \$10 in January may cost \$14 in June and \$18 in October. Suppose Darming sells 1,000 lamps in November. How many of those lamps cost \$10, how many cost \$14, and how many cost \$18?

To compute cost of goods sold and the cost of ending inventory still on hand, we must assign unit cost to the items. Accounting uses 4 generally accepted inventory methods:

(1) Specific unit cost.

(2) Average cost.

(3) First-in, first-out (FIFO) cost.

(4) Last-in, first-out (LIFO) cost.

The methods can have very different effects on reported profits, income taxes, and cash flow. Therefore, companies select their inventory method with great care.

**Specific Unit Cost.** Some businesses deal in unique inventory items, such as automobiles, antique furniture, jewels, and real estate. These businesses cost their inventories at the specific cost of the particular unit. For instance, a Toyota dealer may have 2 vehicles in the showroom—a "stripped-down" model that cost the dealer \$19,000 and a "loaded" model that cost the dealer \$24,000. If the dealer sells the loaded model, the cost of goods sold is \$24,000.

The stripped-down auto will be the only unit left in inventory, and so ending inventory is $19,000. The **specific-unit-cost method** is also called the specific identification method. This method is too expensive to use for inventory items that have common characteristics, such as bushels of wheat, gallons of paint, or auto tires.

The other inventory accounting methods—average, FIFO, and LIFO—are fundamentally different. These other methods do not use the specific cost of a particular unit. Instead, they assume different flows of inventory costs. To illustrate average, FIFO, and LIFO costing, we use a common set of data, given in Exhibit 7-3.

**Exhibit 7-3 Inventory data on various inventory costing methods**

| | | | | |
|---|---|---|---|---|
| Begin. bal. | (10 units @ 10) | 100 | | |
| Purchases: | | | Costs of goods sold | |
| No. 1 | (25 units @ 14) | 350 | (40 units @ ?) | ? |
| No. 2 | (25 units @ 18) | 450 | | |
| Ending balance | (20 units @ ?) | ? | | |

In Exhibit 7-3, Darming began the period with 10 lamps that cost $10 each; the beginning inventory was therefore $100. During the period, Darming bought 50 more lamps, sold 40 lamps, and ended the period with 20 lamps, summarized in the T-account as follows.

| Goods Available | | Number of Units | Total Cost |
|---|---|---|---|
| Goods Available | = | 10units + 25 units + 25 units = 60 units | $100 + $350 + $450 = $900 |
| Cost of goods sold | = | 40 units | ? |
| Ending inventory | = | 20 units | ? |

The big accounting questions are:

(1) What is the cost of goods sold for the income statement?

(2) What is the cost of the ending inventory for the balance sheet?

**Average Cost.** The **average-cost method**, sometimes called the weighted-average method, is based on the average cost of inventory during the period. Average cost per unit is determined as follows (data from Exhibit 7-3).

$$\text{Average cost per unit} = \frac{\text{Cost of goods available}}{\text{Number of units available}} = \frac{\$900}{60\text{units}} = \$15$$

$$\text{Goods available} = \text{Beginning inventory} + \text{Purchases}$$

$$\text{Costs of goods sold} = \text{Number of units sold} \times \text{Average cost per unit} = 40\text{units} \times \$15 = \$600$$

$$\text{Ending inventory} = \text{Number of units on hand} \times \text{Average cost per unit} = 20\text{units} \times \$15 = \$300$$

The following T-account shows the effects of average costing.

**Inventory** (at Average Cost)

| | | | |
|---|---|---|---|
| Begin. bal. | (10 units @ $10) | $100 | |
| Purchase: | | | |
| No. 1 | (25 units @ $14) | $350 | |
| No. 2 | (25 units @ $18) | $450 | Cost of goods sold (40 units @ average cost of $15 per unit) $600 |
| Ending balance | (20 units @ average cost of $15 per unit) | $300 | |

**FIFO Cost.** Under the FIFO method, the first costs into inventory are the first costs assigned to cost of goods sold—hence, the name first-in, first-out. The following T-account shows how to compute FIFO cost of goods sold and ending inventory for the Darming lamps (data from Exhibit 7-3).

**Inventory** (at FIFO cost)

| | | | | | |
|---|---|---|---|---|---|
| Begin. bal. | (10 units @ $10) | $100 | Cost of goods sold (40 units): | | |
| Purchase: | | | (10 units @ $10) | $100 | |
| No. 1 | (25 units @ $14) | $350 | (25 units @ $14) | $350 | $540 |
| No. 2 | (25 units @ $18) | $450 | (5 units @ $18) | $90 | |
| Ending balance | (20 units @ $18) | $360 | | | |

Under FIFO, the cost of ending inventory is always based on the latest costs incurred—in this case $18 per unit.

**LIFO Cost.** LIFO costing is the opposite of FIFO. Under LIFO, the last costs into inventory go immediately to cost of goods sold. Compare LIFO and FIFO, and you will see a vast difference.

The following T-account shows how to compute the LIFO inventory amounts for the Darming lamps (data from Exhibit 7-3).

**Inventory** (at LIFO cost)

| | | | | | |
|---|---|---|---|---|---|
| Begin. bal. | (10 units @ $10) | $100 | | | |
| Purchase: | | | Cost of goods sold (40 units): | | |
| No. 1 | (25 units @ $14) | $350 | (25 units @ $18) | $450 | $660 |
| No. 2 | (25 units @ $18) | $450 | (15 units @ $14) | $210 | |
| Ending balance | (10 units @ $10)<br>(10 units @ $14) | $240 | | | |

Under LIFO, the cost of ending inventory is always based on the oldest costs—from beginning inventory plus the early purchases of the period—$10 and $14 per unit.

Study Exhibit 7-4 carefully, focusing on cost of goods sold and gross profit.

Exhibit 7-5 graphs the flow of costs under FIFO and LIFO during both increasing costs and decreasing costs. Study this exhibit carefully; it will help you really understand FIFO and LIFO.

Financial analysts search the stock markets for companies with good prospects for income growth. Analysts sometimes need to compare the net income of a company that uses LIFO with the net income of a company that uses FIFO.

**Exhibit 7-4 Income effects of FIFO, LIFO, and average inventory methods**

| | FIFO | LIFO | Average |
|---|---|---|---|
| Sales revenue (assumed) | 1,000 | 1,000 | 1,000 |
| Cost of goods sold | 540 (lowest) | 660 (highest) | 600 |
| Gross profit | 460 (highest) | 340 (lowest) | 400 |

**Exhibit 7-5 Cost of goods sold and ending inventory**

| | FIFO | LIFO | Average |
|---|---|---|---|
| Sales revenue (assumed) | 1,000 | 1,000 | 1,000 |
| Cost of goods sold | 540 (lowest) | 660 (highest) | 600 |
| Ending Inventory | 360 (highest) | 240 (lowest) | 300 |

## COMPARISON OF THE INVENTORY METHODS

Let's compare the average, FIFO, and LIFO inventory methods.

(1) Measuring Cost of Goods Sold. How well does each method match Inventory expense—cost of goods sold—against revenue? LIFO results in the most realistic net income figure because LIFO assigns the most recent inventory costs to expense. In contrast, FIFO matches old inventory costs against revenue—a poor measure of expense. FIFO income is therefore less realistic than LIFO income.

(2) Measuring Ending Inventory. Which method reports the most up-to-date inventory cost on the balance sheet? FIFO. LIFO can value inventory at very old costs because LIFO leaves the oldest prices in ending inventory.

### LIFO and Managing Reported Income

LIFO allows managers to manipulate net income by timing their purchases of inventory. When inventory prices are rising rapidly and a company wants to show less income (in order to pay less taxes), managers can buy a large amount of inventory near the end of the year. Under LIFO, these high inventory costs go straight to cost of goods sold. As a result, net income is decreased.

If the business is having a bad year, management may wish to report higher income. The company can delay the purchase of high-cost inventory until next year.

This avoids decreasing current-year income. In the process, the company draws down inventory quantities, a practice known as LIFO inventory liquidation.

### LIFO Liquidation

When LIFO is used and inventory quantities fall below the level of the previous period, the situation is called a LIFO liquidation. To compute cost of goods sold, the company must dip into older layers of inventory cost. Under LIFO, and when prices are rising, that action shifts older, lower costs into cost of goods sold. The result is higher net income. Managers try to avoid a LIFO liquidation because it increases income taxes.

### International Perspective

Many U. S. companies that use LIFO must use another method in foreign countries. Why? LIFO is not allowed in Australia, the United Kingdom, and some other British common wealth countries. Virtually all countries permit FIFO and the average cost method.

## THE TAX ADVANTAGE OF LIFO

Inventory methods directly affect income taxes, which must be paid in cash. When prices are rising, LIFO results in the lowest taxable income and thus the lowest income taxes. Let's use the gross profit data of Exhibit 7-4 to illustrate. The illustration is shown in Exhibit 7-6.

**Exhibit 7-6 FIFO and LIFO's effects on income taxes**

| | FIFO | LIFO |
|---|---|---|
| Gross profit (from Exhibit 7-4) | 460 | 340 |
| Operating expenses (assumed) | 260 | 260 |
| Income before income tax | 200 | 80 |
| Income tax expense (40%) | 80 | 32 |

Income tax expense is lowest under LIFO ($32). **This is the most attractive feature of LIFO—low income tax payments**, which is why about one-third of all companies use LIFO. During periods of inflation, many companies switch to LIFO for its tax and cash-flow advantage.

## LIFO RESERVE

Many companies use LIFO for tax and external reporting purposes. However, they maintain a FIFO, average cost, or standard cost system for internal reporting purposes. There are several reasons to do so: ① Companies often base their pricing decisions on a FIFO, average, or standard cost assumption, rather than on a LIFO basis. ② Record-keeping on some other basis is easier because the LIFO assumption usually does not approximate the physical flow of the product. ③ Profit-sharing and other bonus arrangements often depend on a non-LIFO inventory assumption. ④ The use of a pure LIFO system is troublesome for interim periods, which require estimates of year-end quantities and prices.

The difference between the inventory method used for internal reporting purposes and LIFO is the Allowance to Reduce Inventory to LIFO or the LIFO reserve. The change in the allowance balance from one period to the next is the LIFO effect. The LIFO effect is the adjustment that companies must make to the accounting records in a given year.

To illustrate, assume that Acme Boot Company uses the FIFO method for internal reporting purposes and LIFO for external reporting purposes. At January 1, 2010, the Allowance to Reduce Inventory to LIFO balance is $20,000. At December 31, 2010, the balance should be $50,000. As a result, Acme Boot Company realizes a LIFO effect of $30,000 and makes the following entry at year-end.

| | | |
|---|---|---|
| Dr. Cost of Merchandise Sold | $30,000 | |
| Cr. Allowance to Reduce Inventory to LIFO | | $30,000 |

Acme Boot Company deducts the Allowance to Reduce Inventory to LIFO from inventory to ensure that it states the inventory on a LIFO basis at year-end.

## 3. Cost of Inventory on Perpetual Inventory System

### INVENTORY COSTING METHODS UNDER A PERPETUAL INVENTORY SYSTEM

In a perpetual inventory system, as we discussed in Chapter 6, all merchandise increases and decreases are recorded in a manner similar to recording increases and decreases in cash. The merchandise inventory account at the beginning of an accounting period indicates the merchandise in stock on that date. Purchases are recorded by debiting Merchandise Inventory and crediting Cash or Accounts Payable. On the date of each sale, the cost of the merchandise sold is recorded by debiting Cost of Merchandise Sold and crediting Merchandise Inventory.

There are 2 main types of inventory accounting systems: the periodic system and the perpetual system. The periodic inventory system is used for inexpensive goods. A fabric store or a lumber yard won't keep a running record of every bolt of fabric or every two-by-four. Instead, these stores count their inventory periodically—at least once a year—to determine the quantities on hand. Businesses such as restaurants and hometown nurseries also use the periodic system because the accounting cost of a periodic system is low.

A perpetual inventory system uses computer software to keep a running record of inventory on hand. This system achieves control over goods such as furniture, automobiles, jewelry, and most other types of inventory. Most businesses use the perpetual inventory system.

Even with a perpetual system, the business still counts the inventory on hand annually. The physical count establishes the correct amount of ending inventory for the financial statements and also serves as a check on the perpetual records.

### RECORDING TRANSACTIONS IN THE PERPETUAL SYSTEM

All accounting systems record each purchase of inventory. When Darming makes a sale, 2 entries are needed in the perpetual system.

(1) The company records the sale—debits Cash or Accounts Receivable and credits Sales for the sale price of the goods.

(2) Darming also debits Cost of Goods Sold and credits Inventory for the cost of the inventory sold.

Exhibit 7-7 shows the accounting for inventory in a perpetual system. Panel A gives the journal entries and the T-accounts, and Panel B shows the income statement and the balance sheet. All amounts are assumed.

**Exhibit 7-7 Recording and reporting inventory—perpetual system**

Panel A-Recording Transaction and the T-accounts (All amounts are assumed)

Journal Entry

| | | | |
|---|---|---|---|
| 1. | Merchandise Inventory | 560,000 | |
| | Accounts Payable | | 560,000 |
| | Purchased inventory on account | | |
| 2. | Accounts Receivable | 900,000 | |
| | Sales | | 900,000 |
| | Sold inventory on account | | |
| | Cost of Merchandise sold | 540,000 | |
| | Merchandise Inventory | | 540,000 |
| | Recorded cost of goods sold | | |

Merchandise Inventory

| Debit | | Credit |
|---|---|---|
| Beginning balance | 100,000 | |
| Purchases | 560,000 | Cost of merchandise sold 540,000 |
| Ending balance | 120,000 | |

Cost of Merchandise Sold

| Debit | | Credit |
|---|---|---|
| Cost of merchandise sold | 540,000 | |

Panel B-Reporting in the Financial Statements

| Income Statement (Partial) | | | |
|---|---|---|---|
| Sales | 900,000 | | |
| Cost of merchandise sold | | 540,000 | |
| Gross profit | | 360,000 | |

| Ending Balance Sheet (Partial) | |
|---|---|
| Current assets : | |
| Cash | XXX |
| Short-Term investment | XXX |
| Accounts Receivable | XXX |
| Inventory | 120,000 |
| Prepaid expense | XXX |

In Exhibit 7-7, the first entry to Inventory summarizes a lot of detail. The cost of the inventory, $560,000, is the net amount of the purchases, determined as shown in Exhibit 7-8 (using assumed amounts).

**Exhibit 7-8 The calculation of net purchase of inventory**

| | | |
|---|---|---|
| | Purchase price of the inventory | 600,000 |
| + | Freight-in (the cost to transport the goods from the seller to the buyer) | 4,000 |
| - | Purchase returns for unsuitable goods returned to the seller | 25,000 |
| - | Purchase allowances granted by the seller | 5,000 |
| - | Purchase discounts for early payment by the buyer | 14,000 |
| = | Net purchase of inventory —Cost to the buyer | 560,000 |

Freight-in is the transportation cost, paid by the buyer, to move goods from the seller to the buyer. Freight-in is accounted for as part of the cost of inventory. A purchase return is a decrease in the cost of inventory because the buyer returned the goods to the seller. A purchase allowance also decreases the cost of inventory because the buyer got an allowance (a deduction) from the amount owed. Throughout this book, we often refer to net purchases simply as Purchases.

## 4. Inventory Costing Methods under a Periodic Inventory System

Under a periodic inventory system, a company determines the quantity of inventory on hand only periodically, as the name implies. It records all acquisitions of inventory during the accounting period by debiting the Purchases account. A company then adds the total in the Purchases account at the end of the accounting period to the cost of the inventory on hand at the beginning of the period. This sum determines the total cost of the goods available for sale during the period.

To compute the cost of goods sold, the company then subtracts the ending inventory from the cost of goods available for sale. Note that under a periodic inventory system, the cost of goods sold is a residual amount that depends on a physical count of ending inventory. This process is referred to as "taking a physical inventory". Companies that use the periodic system take a physical inventory at least once a year.

**Comparing Perpetual and Periodic Systems.** To illustrate the difference between a perpetual and a periodic system, assume that Fesmire Company had the following transactions during the current year. As shown in Exhibit 7-9.

**Exhibit 7-9 Fesmire company's transaction**

| | |
|---|---|
| Beginning inventory | 100 units × 6 = 600 |
| Purchases | 900 units × 6 = 5,400 |
| Sales | 600 units × 12 = 7,200 |
| Ending inventory | 400 units × 6 = 2,400 |

Fesmire Company records these transactions during the current year as shown in Exhibit 7-10.

When a company uses a perpetual inventory system and a difference exists between the perpetual inventory balance and the physical inventory count, it needs a separate entry to adjust the perpetual inventory account. To illustrate, assume that at the end of the reporting period, the perpetual inventory account reported an inventory balance of $4,000. However, a physical count indicates inventory of $3,800 is actually on hand. The entry to record the necessary write-down is as follows.

| | | |
|---|---|---|
| Dr. Inventory Over and Short | $200 | |
| Cr. Merchandise Inventory | | $200 |

Perpetual inventory overages and shortages generally represent a misstatement of cost of goods sold. The difference results from normal and expected shrinkage, breakage, shoplifting, incorrect record keeping, and the like. Inventory Over and Short therefore adjusts Cost of Merchandise Sold. In practice, companies sometimes report Inventory Over and Short in the "Other revenues and gains" or "Other expenses and losses" section of the income statement.

**Exhibit 7-10 Comparative entries—perpetual vs. periodic**

| Perpetual inventory System | | | Periodic inventory System | | |
|---|---|---|---|---|---|
| 1. Beginning inventory, 100 units @ $6: The inventory account shows the inventory on hand at $600 | | | The inventory account shows the inventory on hand at $600 | | |
| 2. Purchase 900 units at @ $6: | | | | | |
| Merchandise Inventory | 5,400 | | Purchases | 5,400 | |
| Accounts Payable | | 5,400 | Accounts Payable | | 5,400 |
| 3. Sale of 600 units @ $12: | | | | | |
| Accounts Receivable | 7,200 | | Accounts Receivable | 7,200 | |
| Sales | | 7,200 | Sales | | 7,200 |
| Cost of Merchandise Sold (600 units × $6) | 3,600 | | (No entry) | | |
| Inventory | | 3,600 | | | |
| 4. End-of-period entries for inventory accounts, 400 units @ $6: | | | Merchandise Inventory (ending, by count) | 2,400 | |
| | | | Cost of Merchandise Sold | 3,600 | |
| No entry necessary. The accounts, inventory, shows the ending balance of $ 2,400 ($600 + $5,400 − $3,600) | | | Purchases | | 5,400 |
| | | | Merchandise Inventory (beginning) | | 600 |

Note that a company using the periodic inventory system does not report the account Inventory Over and Short. The reason: The periodic method does not have accounting records against which to compare the physical count. As a result, a company buries inventory overages and shortages in cost of goods sold. Exhibit 7-11 is a quick summary of the two main inventory accounting systems.

**Exhibit 7-11 A summary of perpetual and periodic inventory system**

| Perpetual Inventory System | Periodic Inventory System |
|---|---|
| 1. Used for all types of goods | Used for inexpensive goods |
| 2. Keeps a running record of all goods bought, sold, and on hand | Does not keep a running record of all goods bought, sold, and on hand |
| 3. Inventory counted at least once a year | Inventory counted at least once a year |

# 5. Reporting Merchandise Inventory in the Financial Statements

## CONSISTENCY PRINCIPLE

The consistency principle states that businesses should use the same accounting methods and procedures from period to period. Consistency enables investors to compare a company's financial statements from one period to the next. Suppose you are analyzing Interfax Corporation's net income pattern over a 2-year period. Interfax Corporation switched from LIFO to FIFO during that time. Its net income increased dramatically but only because of the change in inventory method.

## LOWER-OF-COST-OR-MARKET RULE

The **lower-of-cost-or-market rule** (abbreviated as LCM) is based on accounting conservatism. LCM requires that inventory be reported in the financial statements at whichever is lower—the inventory's historical cost or its market value. Applied to inventories, market value generally means current replacement cost (that is, how much the business would have to pay now to replace its inventory). If the replacement cost of inventory falls below its historical cost, the business must write down the value of its goods to market value. **The business reports ending inventory at its LCM value on the balance sheet.** All this can be done automatically by a computerized accounting system. How is the write-down accomplished?

Suppose Darming paid \$3,000 for inventory on September 26. By December 31, the inventory can be replaced for \$2,000. Darming's December 31 balance sheet must report this inventory at LCM value of \$2,000. Exhibit 7-12 presents the accounting entry to write inventory down to market value, and Exhibit 7-13 presents the effects of LCM on the balance sheet and the income statement. Before any LCM effect, cost of goods sold is \$9,000. An LCM write-down decreases Merchandise Inventory and increases Cost of Merchandise Sold, as follows.

**Exhibit 7-12 Wrote inventory down to market value**

| Date | | Description | Post. Ref. | Debit | Credit |
|---|---|---|---|---|---|
| Dec. | 31 | Cost of Merchandise Sold | | 1,000 | |
| | | Merchandise Inventory | | | 1,000 |
| | | Wrote inventory down to market value | | | |

**Exhibit 7-13 LCM effects on inventory and cost of merchandise sold**

| Balance Sheet | |
|---|---|
| Current assets: | |
| Cash | ××× |
| Short-term investments | ××× |
| Accounts receivable | ××× |
| Inventories, at market | |
| (which is lower than \$3,000 cost) | 2,000 |
| Prepaid expenses | ××× |
| Total current assets | ×,××× |
| Income Statement | |
| Sales revenue | 21,000 |
| Cost of goods sold (\$9,000 + \$1,000) | 10,000 |
| Gross profit | 11,000 |

If the market value of Darming's inventory had been above cost, Darming would have made no adjustment for LCM. In that case, simply report the inventory at cost, which is the lower of cost or market.

## VALUATION AT NET REALIZABLE VALUE

Merchandise that is out of date, spoiled, or damaged or that can be sold only at prices below cost should be written down. Such merchandise should be valued at net realizable value. Net realizable value is the estimated selling price less any direct cost of disposal, such as sales commissions. For example, assume that damaged merchandise costing \$1,000 can be sold for only \$800, and direct selling expenses are estimated to be \$150. This inventory should be valued at \$650 (\$800 − \$150), which is its net realizable value.

## MERCHANDISE INVENTORY ON THE BALANCE SHEET

Merchandise inventory is usually presented in the Current Assets section of the balance sheet, following receivables. Both the method of determining the cost of the inventory (FIFO, LIFO, or average) and the method of valuing the inventory (cost or the lower of cost or market) should be shown. It is not unusual for large businesses with varied activities to use different costing methods for different segments of their inventories.

The details may be disclosed in parentheses on the balance sheet or in a note to the financial statements. Exhibit 7-14 shows how parentheses may be used.

**Exhibit 7-14 Merchandise inventory on the balance sheet**

Metro Arts

Balance Sheet

December 31, 2008

| Assets | | |
|---|---|---|
| Current assets | | |
| Cash | | 1,940,000 |
| Accounts receivable | 8,000,000 | |
| Less allowance for doubtful accounts | 300,000 | 7,700,000 |
| Merchandise inventory —at lower of cost (first-in, first-out method) or market | | 21,630,000 |

A company may change its inventory costing methods for a valid reason. In such cases, the effect of the change and the reason for the change should be disclosed in the financial statements for the period in which the change occurred.

## EFFECT OF INVENTORY ERRORS ON THE FINANCIAL STATEMENTS

Inventory errors sometimes occur. An error in ending inventory creates errors for 2 accounting periods. In Exhibit 7-15 start with period 1, in which ending inventory is overstated by \$5,000 and cost of goods sold is therefore understated by $5,000. Then compare period 1 with period 3, which is correct. Period 1 should look exactly like period 3.

**Exhibit 7-15 Inventory errors: an example**

| | Period 1 | | Period 2 | | Period 3 | |
|---|---|---|---|---|---|---|
| | Ending Inventory Overstated by $ 5,000 | | Beginning Inventory Overstated by $ 5,000 | | Correct | |
| Sales revenue | | 100,000 | | 100,000 | | 100,000 |
| Cost of goods sold: | | | | | | |
| Beginning inventory | 10,000 | | 15,000 | | 10,000 | |
| Purchases | 50,000 | | 50,000 | | 50,000 | |
| Cost of goods available | 60,000 | | 65,000 | | 60,000 | |
| Ending inventory | (15,000) | | (10,000) | | (10,000) | |
| Cost of goods sold | | 45,000 | | 55,000 | | 50,000 |
| Gross profit | | 55,000 | | 45,000 | | 50,000 |

Inventory errors counterbalance in 2 consecutive periods. Why? Recall that period 1's ending inventory becomes period 2's beginning amount. Thus, the period 1 error carries over into period 2. Trace the ending inventory of $15,000 from period 1 to period 2. Then compare periods 2 and 3. All 3 periods should look exactly like period 3.

Beginning inventory and ending inventory have opposite effects on cost of goods sold (beginning inventory is added; ending inventory is subtracted). Therefore, after two periods, an inventory error washes out (counterbalances). Notice that total gross profit is correct for periods 1 and 2 combined ($100,000) even though each year's gross profit is off by $5,000. The correct gross profit is $50,000 for each period, as shown in Period 3.

We must have accurate information for all periods. Exhibit 7-16 summarizes the effects of inventory accounting errors.

**Exhibit 7-16 Effects of inventory errors**

| Inventory Error | Period 1 | | Period 2 | |
|---|---|---|---|---|
| | Cost of Goods Sold | Gross Profit and Net Income | Cost of Goods Sold | Gross Profit and Net Income |
| Period 1 | | | | |
| Ending inventory overstated | Understated | Overstated | Overstated | Understated |
| Period 1 | | | | |
| Ending inventory understated | Overstated | Understated | Understated | Overstated |

**TERMINOLOGY:**

Inventory: 存货

Control of Inventory: 存货控制

Average Cost Method: 平均成本法

First-in, First-out (FIFO) Method: 先进先出法

Last-in, First-out (LIFO) Method:后进先出法

Lower-of-cost-or-market (LCM) Method:成本市价孰低法

Net Realizable Value:可实现净值

Physical Inventory:实物存货

Perpetual Inventory System:永续盘存制

Periodic Inventory System:定期盘存制

Inventory Errors:库存错误

## QUESTIONS:

**1. Describe the effect of inventory errors on the financial statements.**

Any errors in reporting inventory based upon the physical inventory will misstate the ending inventory, current assets, total assets, and total owner's equity (retained earnings) on the balance sheet. In addition, the cost of goods sold, gross profit, and net income will be misstated on the income statement.

**2. Describe three inventory cost flow assumptions and how they impact the income statement and balance sheet.**

The three common cost flow assumptions used in business are the first-in, first-out method, last-in, first-out method, and average cost method. Each method normally yields different amounts for the cost of merchandise sold and the ending merchandise inventory. Thus, the choice of a cost flow assumption directly affects the income statement and balance sheet.

**3. Compare the use of the three inventory costing methods.**

The three inventory costing methods will normally yield different amounts for the ending inventory, the cost of the merchandise sold for the period, and the gross profit (and net income) for the period. During periods of inflation, the FIFO method yields the lowest amount for the cost of merchandise sold, the highest amount for gross profit (and net income), and the highest amount for the ending inventory. The LIFO method yields the opposite results. During periods of deflation, the preceding effects are reversed. The average cost method yields results that are between those of FIFO and LIFO.

## PROBLEM:

Fossil specializes in designer watcher and leather goods. Assume Fossil began June holding 10 wristwatches that cost $50 each. Fossil sells these watches for $100 each. During June, Fossil bought and sold inventory as shown in Exhibit 7-17.

**Exhibit 7-17 Fossil's inventory bought and sold**

| | |
|---|---|
| June 3 | Sold 8 units for $100 each |
| 16 | Purchased 10 units for $55 each |
| 23 | Sold 8 units for $100 each |

**Requirements**

1. Prepare a perpetual inventory record for Fossil under:

(1) FIFO (2) LIFO (3) Average Cost

Round unit cost to the nearest cent and all other amounts to the nearest dollar.

2. Journalize all of Fossil's inventory transactions for June under all three costing methods.

3. Show the computation of gross profit for each method.

4. Which method maximizes net income? Which method minimizes income taxes?

**Solutions**

Requirement 1.

(1) The perpetual inventory record for Fossil under FIFO is shown in Exhibit 7-18.

**Exhibit 7-18 The perpetual inventory record under FIFO**

| Wristwatches | | | | | | | | | |
|---|---|---|---|---|---|---|---|---|---|
| Date | Purchases | | | Cost of Goods sold | | | Inventory on Hand | | |
| | Quantity | Unit Cost | Total Cost | Quantity | Unit Cost | Total Cost | Quantity | Unit Cost | Total Cost |
| June 1 | | | | | | | 10 units | 50 | 500 |
| 3 | | | | 8units | 50 | 400 | 2 units | 50 | 100 |
| 16 | 10 units | 55 | 550 | | | | 2 units<br>10 units | 50<br>55 | 100<br>550 |
| 23 | | | | 2 units<br>6 units | 50<br>55 | 100<br>330 | 4 units | 55 | 220 |
| 30 | 10 units | | 550 | 16 units | | 830 | 4 units | | 220 |

(2) The perpetual inventory record for Fossil under LIFO as shown in Exhibit 7-19.

**Exhibit 7-19 The perpetual inventory record under LIFO**

| Wristwatches | | | | | | | | | |
|---|---|---|---|---|---|---|---|---|---|
| Date | Purchases | | | Cost of Goods sold | | | Inventory on Hand | | |
| | Quantity | Unit Cost | Total Cost | Quantity | Unit Cost | Total Cost | Quantity | Unit Cost | Total Cost |
| June 1 | | | | | | | 10 units | 50 | 500 |
| 3 | | | | 8 units | 50 | 400 | 2 units | 50 | 100 |
| 16 | 10 units | 55 | 550 | | | | 2 units<br>10 units | 50<br>55 | 100<br>550 |
| 23 | | | | 8 units | 55 | 440 | 2 units<br>2 units | 50<br>55 | 100<br>110 |
| 30 | 10 units | | 550 | 16 units | | 840 | 4 units | | 210 |

(3) The perpetual inventory record for Fossil under Average Cost as shown in Exhibit 7-20.

Requirement 2. All of Fossil's inventory transactions for June under all three costing methods as shown in Exhibit 7-21.

**Exhibit 7-20 The perpetual inventory record under average cost**

| Date | Wristwatches | | | | | | | | |
|---|---|---|---|---|---|---|---|---|---|
| | Purchases | | | Cost of Goods sold | | | Inventory on Hand | | |
| | Quantity | Unit Cost | Total Cost | Quantity | Unit Cost | Total Cost | Quantity | Unit Cost | Total Cost |
| June 1 | | | | | | | 10 units | 50.00 | 500 |
| 3 | | | | 8 units | 50.00 | 400 | 2 units | 50.00 | 100 |
| 16 | 10 units | 55 | 550 | | | | 12 units | 54.17 | 650 |
| 23 | | | | 8 units | 54.17 | 433 | 4 units | 54.17 | 217 |
| 30 | 10 units | | 550 | 16 units | | 833 | 4 units | | 217 |

**Exhibit 7-21 All inventory transactions under all three costing methods**

| | | FIFO | | LIFO | | Average Cost | |
|---|---|---|---|---|---|---|---|
| June 3 | Accounts Receivable | 800 | | 800 | | 800 | |
| | Sales | | 800 | | 800 | | 800 |
| 3 | Cost of Merchandise Sold | 400 | | 400 | | 400 | |
| | Merchandise Inventory | | 400 | | 400 | | 400 |
| 16 | Merchandies Inventory | 550 | | 550 | | 550 | |
| | Accounts Payable | | 550 | | 550 | | 550 |
| 23 | Accounts Receivable | 800 | | 800 | | 800 | |
| | Sales | | 800 | | 800 | | 800 |
| 23 | Cost of Merchandise Sold | 430 | | 440 | | 433 | |
| | Merchandise Inventory | | 430 | | 440 | | 433 |

Requirement 3. The computation of gross profit for each method as shown in Exhibit 7-22.

**Exhibit 7-22 Computation of gross profit for each method**

| | FIFO | LIFO | Average Cost |
|---|---|---|---|
| Sales revenue( \$800 + \$800) | 1,600 | 1,600 | 1,600 |
| Cost of goods sold( \$400 + \$430) | 830 | | |
| ( \$400 + \$440) | | 840 | |
| ( \$400 + \$433) | | | 833 |
| Gross profit | 770 | 760 | 767 |

Requirement 4. FIFO maximizes net income; LIFO minimizes income taxes.

# Chapter 8

## Internal Control and Cash

**Objectives**

1. Describe internal controls of cash and financial reporting.
2. Illustrate the objectives and elements of internal control.
3. Illustrate the application of internal controls to cash.
4. Describe the nature of a bank account and its use in controlling cash.
5. Illustrate the use of bank reconciliation in controlling cash.
6. Describe the accounting for special-purpose cash funds.
7. Reporting cash and cash equivalents in the financial statements.

# 1. Internal Control

As indicated in the prior section, effective internal controls are required by Sarbanes-Oxley. In addition, effective internal controls help businesses guide their operations and prevent theft and other abuses. For example, assume that you own and manage a lawn care service. Your business uses several employee teams, and you provide each team with vehicle and lawn equipment. What issues might you face as a manager in controlling the operations of this business? Below are some examples.

(1) Lawn care must be provided on time.

(2) The quality of lawn care services must meet customer expectations.

(3) Employees must provide work for the hours they are paid.

(4) Lawn care equipment should be used for business purposes only.

(5) Vehicles should be used for business purposes only.

(6) Customers must be billed and payments collected for services rendered.

How would you address these issues? You could, for example, develop a schedule at the beginning of each day and then inspect the work at the end of the day to verify that it was completed according to quality standards. You could have "surprise" inspections by arriving on site at random times to verify that the teams are working according to schedule. You could require employees to "clock in" at the beginning of the day and "clock out" at the end of the day to make sure that they are paid for hours worked. You could require the work teams to return the vehicles and equipment to a central location to prevent unauthorized use. You could keep a log of odometer readings at the end of each day to verify that the vehicles have not been used for "joy riding". You could bill customers after you have inspected the work and then monitor the collection of all receivables. All of these are examples of internal control.

In this section, we describe and illustrate internal control using the framework developed by the Committee of Sponsoring Organizations (COSO), which was formed by five major business associations. The committee's deliberations were published in Internal Control—Integrated Framework. This framework, cited by GE in Exhibit 8-1, has become the standard by which companies design, analyze, and evaluate internal control. We describe and illustrate the framework by first describing the objectives of internal control and then showing how these objectives can be achieved through the five elements of internal control.

**Exhibit 8-1 Objectives of internal control**

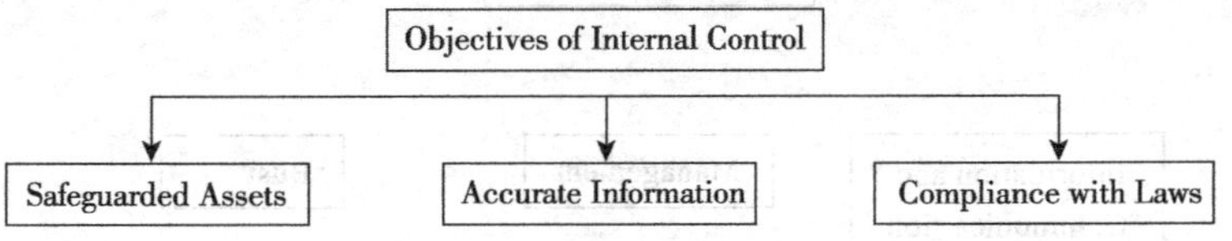

## 2. The Limitations of Internal Control—Costs and Benefits

Unfortunately, most internal controls can be overcome. Collusion—2 or more people working together—can beat internal controls. Consider Galaxy Theater. Ralph and Lana can design a scheme in which Ralph sells tickets and pockets the cash from 10 customers. Lana, the ticket taker, admits 10 customers without tickets. Ralph and Lana split the cash. To prevent this situation, the manager must take additional steps, such as matching the number of people in the theater against the number of ticket stubs retained. But that takes time away from other duties.

The stricter the internal control system, the more it costs. A complex system of internal control can strangle the business with red tape. How tight should the controls be? Internal controls must be judged in light of their costs and benefits. An example of a good cost/benefit relationship: A security guard at a Wal-Mart store costs about \$28,000 a year. On average, each guard prevents about \$50,000 of theft. The net savings to Wal-Mart is \$22,000.

## 3. Elements of Internal Control

Internal control can be broken down into 5 components.

(1) Control environment.

(2) Monitoring of controls.

(3) Risk assessment.

(4) Information system.

(5) Control procedures.

The Exhibit 8-2 shows the elements of internal control, these elements protect the company from control threats like an umbrella.

**Exhibit 8-2 Elements of internal control**

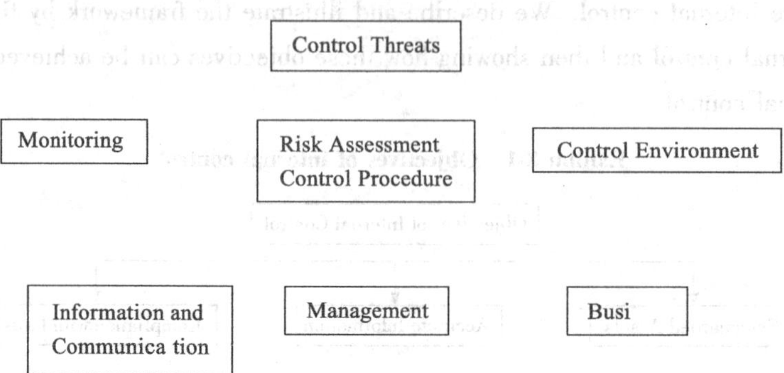

## CONTROL ENVIRONMENT

The control environment is the "tone at the top" of the business. It starts with the owner and the top managers. They must behave honorably to set a good example for company employees. The owner must demonstrate the importance of internal controls if he or she expects employees to take the controls seriously. Former executives of Enron, WorldCom, and Tyco failed to establish a good control environment, and they are in prison as a result.

The Exhibit 8-3 shows the elements influencing the construction of the control environment, these elements exist in different level of a company.

**Exhibit 8-3 Elements of control environment**

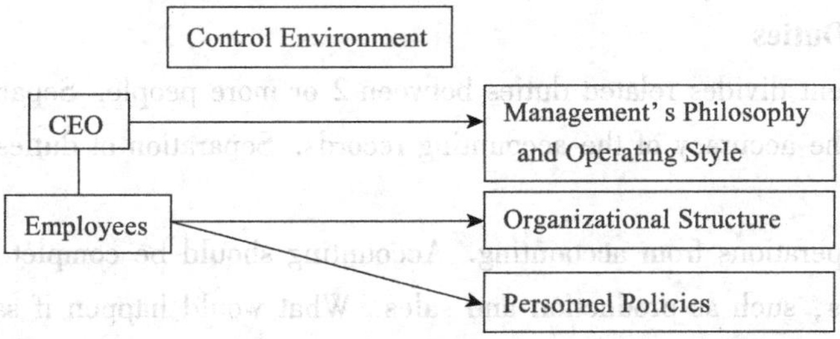

Control Environment

CEO

Employees

Management' s Philosophy and Operating Style

Organizational Structure

Personnel Policies

## RISK ASSESSMENT

A company must identify its risks. For example, Kraft Foods faces the risk that its food products may harm people. American Airlines planes may crash. And all companies face the risk of bankruptcy. Companies facing difficulties are tempted to falsify the financial statements to make themselves look better than they really are.

## CONTROL PROCEDURES

These are the procedures designed to ensure that the business's goals are achieved. Examples include assigning responsibilities, separating duties, and using security devices to protect assets from theft. The Exhibit 8-4 discusses internal control procedures.

**Exhibit 8-4 Internal control procedures**

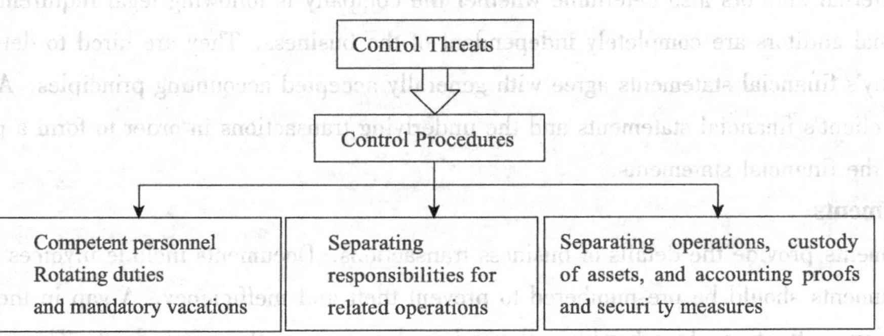

Whether the business is AMEX Products, Microsoft, or an Exxon gas station, you need the following internal control procedures.

**Competent, Reliable, and Ethical Personnel**

Employees should be competent, reliable, and ethical. Paying good salaries will attract high-quality employees. You also must train them to do the job, supervise their work, and reward them fairly. This will build a competent staff.

**Assignment of Responsibilities**

In a business with good internal controls, no important duty is overlooked. Each employee has certain responsibilities. In a company such as AMEX Products, the person in charge of writing checks is called the treasurer. The chief accounting officer is called the controller. With clearly assigned responsibilities, all important jobs get done.

**Separation of Duties**

Smart management divides related duties between 2 or more people. Separation of duties limits fraud and promotes the accuracy of the accounting records. Separation of duties can be divided into 2 parts.

(1) Separate operations from accounting. Accounting should be completely separate from the operating departments, such as production and sales. What would happen if sales personnel recorded the company's revenue? Sales figures could be inflated, and top managers wouldn't know how much the company actually sold. This is why you should separate accounting and sales duties.

(2) Separate the custody of assets from accounting. Accountants must not handle cash, and cashiers must not have access to the accounting records. If one employee has both cash-handling and accounting duties, that person can steal cash and conceal the theft. This is what happened at AMEX Products. The treasurer of a company should handle cash, and the controller should account for the cash. Neither person should have both jobs.

**Audits**

To validate their accounting records, most companies have an audit. An audit is an examination of the company's financial statements and accounting system. To evaluate the system, auditors examine the internal controls. Audits can be internal or external. Internal auditors are employees of the business. They ensure that employees are following company policies and operations are running efficiently. Internal auditors also determine whether the company is following legal requirements.

External auditors are completely independent of the business. They are hired to determine that the company's financial statements agree with generally accepted accounting principles. Auditors examine the client's financial statements and the underlying transactions in order to form a professional opinion of the financial statements.

**Documents**

Documents provide the details of business transactions. Documents include invoices and fax orders. Documents should be pre-numbered to prevent theft and inefficiency. A gap in the numbered sequence draws attention. In a bowling alley a key document is the score sheet. The manager can compare the number of games scored with the amount of cash received. Multiply the number of games by the charge per game and compare the revenue with cash receipts. You can see whether the business is collecting all the revenue.

**Electronic Devices**

Accounting systems are relying less on documents and more on digital storage devices. For example, retailers such as Target Stores and Macy's control inventory by attaching an electronic sensor to merchandise. The cashier removes the sensor. If a customer tries to leave the store with the sensor attached, an alarm sounds. According to Checkpoint Systems, these devices reduce theft by as much as 50%.

**Other Controls**

Businesses keep important documents in fire proof vaults. Burglar alarms protect buildings, and security cameras protect other property. Loss-prevention specialists train employees to spot suspicious activity. Employees who handle cash are in a tempting position. Many businesses purchase fidelity bonds on cashiers. The bond is an insurance policy that reimburses the company for any losses due to employee theft. Before issuing a fidelity bond, the insurance company investigates the employee's background.

Mandatory vacation sand job rotation improve internal control. Companies move employees from job to job. This improves morale by giving employees a broad view of the business. Also, knowing someone else will do your job next month keeps you honest. AMEX Products didn't rotate employees to different jobs, and it cost the company $622,000.

Separating Responsibilities for Related Operations. To decrease the possibility of inefficiency, errors, and fraud, the responsibility for related operations should be divided among two or more persons. For example, the responsibilities for purchasing, receiving, and paying for computer supplies should be divided among three persons or departments. If the same person orders supplies, verifies the receipt of the supplies, and pays the supplier, the following abuses are possible:

(1) Orders may be placed on the basis of friendship with a supplier, rather than on price, quality, and other objective factors.

(2) The quantity and quality of supplies received may not be verified, thus causing payment for supplies not received or poor-quality supplies.

(3) Supplies may be stolen by the employee.

(4) The validity and accuracy of invoices may be verified carelessly, thus causing the payment of false or inaccurate invoices.

The "checks and balances" provided by dividing responsibilities among various department requires no duplication of effort. The business documents prepared by one department are designed to coordinate with and support those prepared by other departments.

To illustrate, consider the case where an accounts payable clerk created false in voices and submitted them for payment. The clerk obtained the resulting checks, opened a bank account, and cashed the checks under an assumed name. The clerk was able to steal thousands of dollars because no one was required to approve the payments other than the accounts payable clerk.

Separating Operations, Custody of Assets, and Accounting Control policies should establish the responsibilities for various business activities. To reduce the possibility of errors and fraud, the responsibilities for operations, custody of assets, and accounting should be separated. The accounting records then serve as an independent check on the individuals who have custody of the assets and who engage in the business operations. For example, the employees entrusted with handling cash receipts from credit customers should not record cash receipts in the accounting records. To do so would allow employees to borrow or steal cash and hide the theft in the records. Likewise, if those engaged in operating activities also record the results of operations, they could distort the accounting reports to show favorable results. For example, a store manager whose year-end bonus is based upon operating profits might be tempted to record fictitious sales in order to receive a larger bonus.

To illustrate, consider the case where a payroll clerk was responsible for preparing the payroll and distributing the payroll checks. The clerk stole almost $40,000 over two months by preparing duplicate payroll checks and checks for fictitious part-time employees. After the theft was detected, the duties of preparing payroll checks and distributing payroll checks were assigned to separate employees.

**Proofs and Security Measures**

Proofs and security measures should be used to safe guard assets and ensure reliable accounting data. This control procedure applies to many different techniques, such as authorization, approval, and reconciliation procedures. For example, employees who travel on company business may be required to obtain a department manager's approval on a travel request form.

Other examples of control procedures include the use of bank accounts and other measures to ensure the safety of cash and valuable documents. A cash register that dis-plays the amount recorded for each sale and provides the customer a printed receipt can be an effective part of the internal control structure. An all-night convenience store could use the following security measures to deter robberies.

(1) Locate the cash register near the door, so that it is fully visible from outside the store; have two employees work late hours; employ a security guard.

(2) Deposit cash in the bank daily, before 5 p. m.

(3) Keep only small amounts of cash on hand after 5 p. m. by depositing excess cash in a store safe that can't be opened by employees on duty.

(4) Install cameras and alarm systems.

To illustrate, consider the case where someone stole thousands of dollars in parking fines from a small town. Citizens would pay their parking fines by placing money in ticket envelopes and putting them in a locked box outside the town hall. The key to the locked box was not safeguarded and was readily available to a variety of people. As a result, the person who stole the money was never discovered. The town later gave one person the responsibility of safeguarding the key and emptying the locked box.

## MONITORING

Companies hire auditors to monitor their controls. Internal auditors monitor company controls to safeguard the company's assets, and external auditors monitor the controls to ensure that the accounting records are accurate.

### INFORMATION AND COMMUNICATION

As we have seen, the information system is critical. The owner of a business needs accurate information to keep track of assets and measure profits and losses. Exhibit 8-5 shows the warning signs of internal control problems.

**Exhibit 8-5 Warning signs of internal control problems**

**Warning signs with regard to people**

(1) Abrupt change in lifestyle (without winning the lottery).

(2) Close social relationships with suppliers.

(3) Refusing to take a vacation.

(4) Frequent borrowing from other employees.

---

**Warning signs from the accounting system**

(1) Missing documents or gaps in transaction numbers(could mean documents are being used for fraudulent transactions).

(2) An unusual increase in customer refunds (refunds maybe phony).

(3) Differences between daily cash receipts and bank deposits(could mean receipts are being pocketed before being deposited).

(4) Sudden increase in slow payments(employee may be pocketing the payment).

(5) Backlog in recording transactions(possibly an attempt to delay detection of fraud).

## 4. Cash Controls over Receipts and Payments

Cash includes coins, currency (paper money), checks, money orders, and money on deposit that is available for unrestricted withdrawal from banks and other financial institutions. Normally, you can think of cash as anything that a bank would accept for deposit in your account. For example, a check made payable to you could normally be deposited in a bank and thus is considered cash.

We will assume in this chapter that a business maintains only one bank account, represented in the ledger as Cash. In practice, however, a business may have several bank accounts, such as one for general cash payments and another for payroll. For each of its bank accounts, the business will maintain a ledger account, one of which may be called Cash in Bank—First Bank, for example. It will also maintain separate ledger ac counts for special-purpose cash funds, such as travel reimbursements. We will introduce some of these other cash accounts later in this chapter.

Because of the ease with which money can be transferred, cash is the asset most likely to be diverted and used improperly by employees. In addition, many transactions either directly or indirectly affect the receipt or the payment of cash. Businesses must therefore design and use controls that safeguard cash and control the authorization of cash transactions. In the following paragraphs, we will discuss these controls.

## CONTROL OF CASH RECEIPTS

To protect cash from theft and misuse, a business must control cash from the time it is received until it is deposited in a bank. Businesses normally receive cash from two main sources: customers purchasing products or services and customers making payments on account. For example, fast-food restaurants, such as McDonald's, Wendy's International, Inc., and Burger King Corporation, receive cash primarily from over- the-counter sales to customers. Mail-order and Internet retailers, such as Lands' End, Inc., The Orvis Company, Inc., L. L. Bean, Inc., and Amazon. com, receive cash primarily through electronic funds transfers from credit card companies.

### Cash Received from Cash Sales

Regardless of the source of cash receipts, every business must properly safeguard and record its cash receipts. One of the most important controls to protect cash received in over-the-counter sales is a cash register. When a clerk (cashier) enters the amount of a sale, the cash register normally displays the amount. This is a control to ensure that the clerk has charged you the correct amount. You also receive a receipt to verify the accuracy of the amount.

At the beginning of a work shift, each cash register clerk is given a cash drawer that contains a predetermined amount of cash for making change for customers. The amount in each drawer is sometimes called a change fund. At the end of the shift, the clerk and the supervisor count the cash in that clerk's cash drawer. The amount of cash in each drawer should equal the beginning amount of cash plus the cash sales for the day. However, errors in recording cash sales or errors in making change cause the amount of cash on hand to differ from this amount. Such differences are recorded in a cash short and over account.

At the end of the accounting period, a debit balance in the cash short and over account is included in Miscellaneous Expense in the income statement. A credit balance is included in the Other Income section. If a clerk consistently has significant cash short and over amounts, the supervisor may require the clerk to take additional training.

After a cash register clerk's cash has been counted and recorded on a memorandum form, the cash is then placed in a store safe in the Cashier's Department until it can be deposited in the bank. The supervisor forwards the clerk's cash register receipts to the Accounting Department, where they serve as the basis for recording the transactions for the day.

The Exhibit 8-6 below shows the control of cash receipts, which run through the course from a trade's beginning to the ending.

**Exhibit 8-6 Control of Cash Receipts**

Some retail companies use debit card systems to transfer and record the receipt of cash. In a debit card system, a customer pays for goods at the time of purchase by presenting a plastic card. The card authorizes the electronic transfer of cash from the customer's checking account to the retailer's bank account.

At the end of the day—or several times a day if business is brisk—the cashier deposits the cash in the bank. The machine tape then goes to the accounting department for the journal entry to record sales revenue. These measures, coupled with oversight by a manager, discourage theft.

**Cash Received in the Mail**

Many companies receive cash by mail. Exhibit 8-7 shows how companies control cash received by mail. All incoming mail is opened by a mailroom employee. The mailroom then sends all customer checks to the treasurer, who has the cashier deposit the money in the bank. The remittance advices go to the accounting department for journal entries to Cash and customer accounts receivable. As a final step, the controller compares the following records for the day.

(1) Bank deposit amount from the treasurer.

(2) Debit to Cash from the accounting department.

**Exhibit 8-7 Cash receipts by mail**

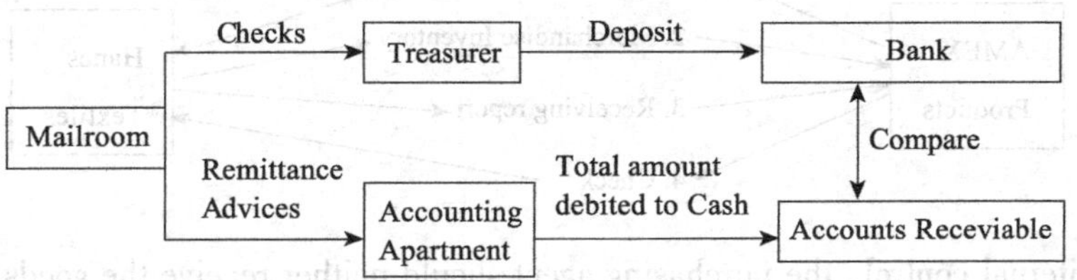


The debit to Cash should equal the amount deposited in the bank. All cash receipts are safe in the bank, and the company books are up-to-date.

Many companies use a lock-box system. Customers send their checks directly to the company's bank account. Internal control is tight because company personnel never touch incoming cash. The lock-box system puts your cash to work immediately.

**Electronic funds transfer (EFT)**

Electronic funds transfer (EFT) moves cash by electronic communication. It is cheaper to pay without having to mail a check, so many people pay their mortgage, rent, utilities, and insurance by EFT. The bank may receive or pay cash on your behalf. An EFT may be a cash receipt or a cash payment. Add EFT receipts and subtract EFT payments.

## CONTROL OF CASH PAYMENTS

Companies make most payments by check. Let's see how to control cash payments by check.

**Controls over Payment by Check**

As we have seen, you need a good separation of duties between operations and writing checks for cash payments. Payment by check is an important internal control, as follows.

(1) The check provides a record of the payment.

（2）The check must be signed by an authorized official.

（3）Before signing the check, the official should study the evidence supporting the payment.

**Controls over Purchase and Payment**

To illustrate the internal control over cash payments by check, suppose AMEX Products buys some of its inventory from Hanes Textiles. The purchasing and payment process follows these steps, as shown in Exhibit 8-8. Start with the box for AMEX Products on the left side.

（1）AMEX Products faxes a purchase order to Hanes Textiles. AMEX Products says, "Please send us 100 T-shirts."

（2）Hanes Textiles ships the goods and faxes an invoice back to AMEX Products. Hanes Textiles sent the goods.

（3）AMEX Products receives the inventory and prepares a receiving report to list the goods received. AMEX Products got its T-shirts.

（4）After approving all documents, AMEX Products sends a check to Hanes Textiles. AMEX Products says, "Okay, we'll pay you."

**Exhibit 8-8　Cash payments by check**

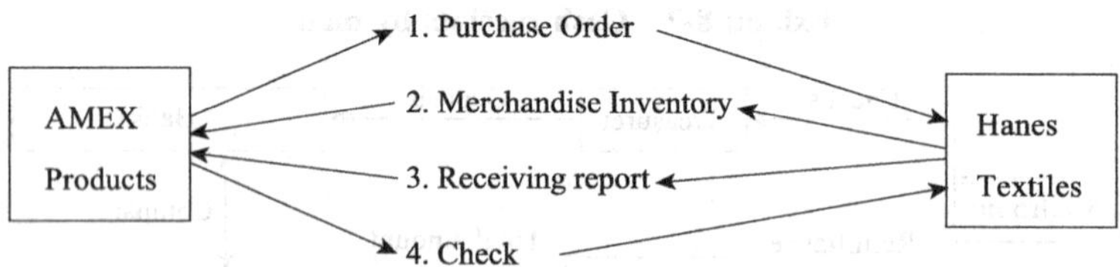


For good internal control, the purchasing agent should neither receive the goods nor approve the payment. If these duties aren't separated, a purchasing agent can buy goods and have them shipped to his or her home. Or a purchasing agent can spend too much on purchases, approve the payment, and split the excess with the supplier. To avoid these problems, companies split the following duties among different employees.

（1）purchasing goods.

（2）receiving goods.

（3）approving and paying for goods.

Exhibit 8-9 shows AMEX Products' payment packet of documents. Before signing the check, the controller or the treasurer should examine the packet to prove that all the documents agree. Only then does the company know that:

（1）It received the goods ordered.

（2）It is paying only for the goods received.

**Exhibit 8-9　Payment packet**

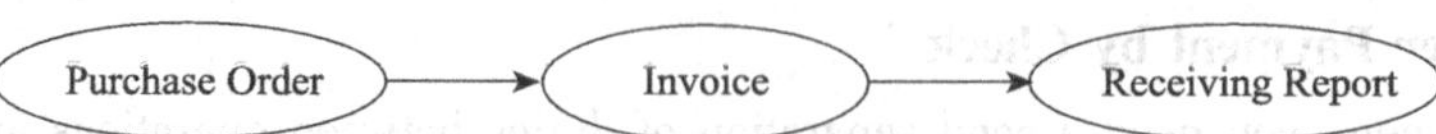


After payment, the check signer punches a hole through the payment packet. Dishonest people have tried to run a bill through twice for payment. This hole shows that the bill has been paid.

# 5. Bank Accounts

Most of you are familiar with bank accounts. You probably have a checking account at a local bank, credit union, savings and loan association, or other financial institution. In this section, we discuss the use of bank accounts by businesses. We then discuss the use of bank accounts as an additional control over cash.

## USE OF BANK ACCOUNTS

A business often maintains several bank accounts. For example, a business with several branches or retail outlets such as Sears Holdings, Inc. or Gap, Inc. will often maintain a bank account for each location. In addition, businesses usually maintain a separate bank account for payroll and other special purposes.

A major reason that businesses use bank accounts is for control purposes. Use of bank accounts reduces the amount of cash on hand at any one time. For example, many merchandise businesses deposit cash receipts twice daily to reduce the amount of cash on hand that is susceptible to theft. Likewise, using a payroll account allows for paying employees by check or electronic funds transfer rather than by distributing a large amount of cash each payroll period.

In addition to reducing the amount of cash on hand, bank accounts provide an in dependent recording of cash transactions that can be used as a verification of the busi ness's recording of transactions. That is, the use of bank accounts provides a double recording of cash transactions. The company's cash account corresponds to the bank's liability (deposit) account for the company. As we will discuss and illustrate in the next section, this double recording of cash transactions allows for a reconciliation of the cash account on the company's records with the cash balance recorded by the bank.

Finally, the use of bank accounts facilitates the transfer of funds. For example, electronic funds transfer systems require bank accounts for the transfer of funds between companies. Within a company, cash can be transferred between bank accounts through the use of wire transfers. In addition, online banking allows companies to transfer funds and pay bills electronically as well as monitor their cash balances on a real-time basis.

## BANK STATEMENT

Banks send monthly statements to customers. A bank statement reports what the bank did with the customer's cash. The statement shows the account's beginning and ending balances, cash receipts, and payments. Included with the statement are copies of the maker's canceled checks (or the actual paid checks). Exhibit 8-10 is the January bank statement of the Palo Alto office of AMEX

Products.

**Exhibit 8-10 Bank statement**

Bank Statement
CHECKING ACCOUNT
136 – 213733

AMEX products
3814 Glenwood Parkway
Palo Alto, CA 94306

DECEMBER 31, 2007

| BEGINNING BALANCE | TOTAL DEPOSITS | TOTAL WITHDRAWALS | SERVICE CHARGES | ENDING BALANCE |
|---|---|---|---|---|
| 6,550 | 4,370 | 5,000 | 20 | 5,900 |

TRANSACTIONS

| DEPOSITS | DATE | AMOUNT |
|---|---|---|
| Deposit | 12/04 | 1,150 |
| Deposit | 12/08 | 190 |
| EFT-Receipt of cash dividend | 12/17 | 900 |
| Bank Collection | 12/26 | 2,100 |
| Interest | 12/31 | 30 |

| CHARGES | DATE | AMOUNT |
|---|---|---|
| Service Charge | 12/31 | 20 |

CHECKS

| Number | Amount | Number | Amount | Number | Amount |
|---|---|---|---|---|---|
| 307 | 100 | 333 | 150 | 335 | 100 |
| 332 | 3,000 | 334 | 100 | 336 | 1,100 |

| OTHER DEDUCTIONS | DATE | AMOUNT |
|---|---|---|
| NSF | 12/04 | 50 |
| EFT-insurance | 12/20 | 400 |

## BANK ACCOUNTS AS A CONTROL OVER CASH

Cash is the most liquid asset because it's the medium of exchange. Cash is easy to conceal and relatively easy to steal. As a result, most businesses create specific controls for cash. Keeping cash in a bank account helps control cash because banks have established practices for safeguarding customers' money. The documents used to control a bank account include the:

(1) Signature card.

(2) Bank statement.

(3) Deposit ticket.

(4) Bank reconciliation.

(5) Check.

### Signature Card

Banks require each person authorized to sign on an account to provide a signature card. This protects against forgery.

**Deposit Ticket**

Banks supply standard forms such as deposit tickets. The customer fills in the amount of each deposit. As proof of the transaction, the customer keeps a deposit receipt.

**Check**

To pay cash, the depositor can write a check, which tells the bank to pay the designated party a specified amount. There are 3 parties to a check:

(1) The maker, who signs the check.

(2) The payee, to whom the check is paid.

(3) The bank on which the check is drawn.

Exhibit 8-11 shows a check drawn by AMEX Products, the maker. The check has 2 parts, the check itself and the remittance advice below. This optional attachment tells the payee the reason for the payment.

**Exhibit 8-11 Check with remittance advice**

Bank
Payee
Check Serial Number

BAY AREA NATIONAL BANK
South Palo Alto #136
P.O. Box 22985
Palo Alto, CA 94306

338

Dec. 28, 2007 11-8/1210

PAY TO THE ORDER OF California Office Products $ 320.00

Amount — Three hundred twenty and no/100 ---------------- DOLLARS

AMEX PRODUCTS
3814 Glenwood Parkway
Palo Alto, CA 94306

Edward G. Lee Treasurer
Horace R. Nash Vice-President
Makers

⑆121000086⑆0 338 136213733⑈ 33

| Date | Description | Amount |
|---|---|---|
| 12/28/2007 | Office Supplies | $320.00 |

Remittance Advice

## 6. Bank Reconciliation

For effective control, the reasons for the difference between the cash balance on the bank statement and the cash balance in the accounting records should be analyzed by preparing a bank reconciliation. A **bank reconciliation** is an analysis of the items and amounts that cause the cash balance reported in the bank statement to differ from the balance of the cash account in the ledger in order to determine the adjusted cash balance.

A bank reconciliation is usually divided into two sections. The first section, referred to as the bank section, begins with the cash balance according to the bank statement and ends with the adjusted balance. The second section, referred to as the company section, begins with the cash balance according to the company's records and ends with the adjusted balance. The two amounts designated as the adjusted balance must be equal.

The content of the bank reconciliation is shown in Exhibit 8-12.

**Exhibit 8-12 The content of the bank reconciliation**

| | | | |
|---|---|---|---|
| Cash balance according to bank | | ××× | |
| Add: Debits to cash not on bank statement (deposits in transit, etc.) | ×× | | |
| Deduct: Credits to cash not on bank statement (outstanding checks, etc.) | ×× | ××× | |
| Adjusted balance | | ××× | ← |
| Cash balance according to company | | ××× | |
| Add: Unrecorded bank credits (notes collected by bank) | ×× | | Must be equal |
| Deduct: Unrecorded bank debits (NSF checks, service charges, etc.) | ×× | ××× | |
| Adjusted balance | | ××× | ← |

The following steps are useful in finding the reconciling items and determining the adjusted balance of Cash.

(1) Compare each deposit listed on the bank statement with unrecorded deposits appearing in the preceding period's reconciliation and with the current period's deposits. Add deposits not recorded by the bank to the balance according to the bank statement.

(2) Compare paid checks with outstanding checks appearing on the preceding period's reconciliation and with recorded checks. Deduct checks outstanding that have not been paid by the bank from the balance according to the bank statement.

(3) Compare bank credit memorandums to entries in the journal. For example, a bank would issue a credit memorandum for a note receivable and interest that it collected for a company. Add credit memorandums that have not been recorded to the balance according to the company's records.

(4) Compare bank debit memorandums to entries recording cash payments. For example, a bank normally issues debit memorandums for service charges and check printing charges. A bank also issues debit memorandums for not sufficient funds checks. NSF checks are normally charged back

to the customer as an account receivable. Deduct debit memorandums that have not been recorded from the balance according to the company's records.

(5) List any errors discovered during the preceding steps. For example, if an amount has been recorded incorrectly by the company, the amount of the error should be added to or deducted from the cash balance according to the company's records. Similarly, errors by the bank shouldbe added to or deducted from the cash balance according to the bank statement.

To illustrate a bank reconciliation, we will use the bank statement for Power Networking. This bank statement shows a balance of $3,360 as of July 31. The cash balance in Power Networking's ledger as of the same date is $2,550. The following reconciling items are revealed by using the steps outlined above.

Deposit of July 31, not recorded on bank statement ······························ $816

Checks outstanding: No. 812, $1,061; No. 878, $435;
No. 883, $49 ······························································ $1,545

Note plus interest of $8 collected by bank (credit memorandum), not
recorded in the journal ······················································ $408

Check from customer (Thomas Ivey) returned by bank because of
insufficient funds (NSF) ·················································· $300

Bank service charges (debit memorandum), not recorded in the journal ·············· $18

Check No. 879 for $732.26 to Taylor Co. on account, recorded
in the journal as $723.26 ··················································· $9

No entries are necessary on the company's records as a result of the information included in the bank section of the reconciliation. This section begins with the cash balance according to the bank statement. However, the bank should be notified of any errors that need to be corrected on its records.

The bank reconciliation, based on the bank statement and the reconciling items, is shown in Exhibit 8-13.

**Exhibit 8-13 Bank reconciliation for Power Networking**

Power Networking

Bank Reconciliation

July 31, 2007

| | | |
|---|---|---|
| Cash balance according to bank statement | | 3,360 |
| Add deposit of July 31, not recorded by bank | | 816 |
| | | 4,176 |

(Continued)

| | | |
|---|---|---|
| Deduct outstanding checks: | | |
| No. 812 | 1,061 | |
| No. 878 | 435 | |
| No. 883 | 49 | 1,545 |
| Adjusted balance | | 2,631 |
| | | |
| Cash balance according to Power Networking records | | 2,550 |
| Add note and interest collected by bank | | 408 |
| | | 2,958 |
| Deduct: Check returned because of insufficient funds | 300 | |
| Bank service charge | 18 | |
| Error in recording Check No. 879 | 9 | 327 |
| Adjusted balance | | 2,631 |

Any items in the company's section of the bank reconciliation must be recorded in the company's accounts. For example, journal entries should be made for any un-recorded bank memorandums and any company errors. The journal entries for Power Networking, based on the preceding bank reconciliation, are as shown in Exhibit 8-14.

**Exhibit 8-14 Journal entry based on the banking reconciliation**

| Date | | Description | Post. Ref. | Debit | Credit |
|---|---|---|---|---|---|
| July | 31 | Cash | | 408 | |
| | | Note Receivable | | | 400 |
| | | Interest Revenue | | | 8 |
| | | | | | |
| | 31 | Accounts Receivable—Thomas Ivey | | 300 | |
| | | Miscellaneous Expense | | 18 | |
| | | Accounts Payable—Taylor Co. | | 9 | |
| | | Cash | | | 327 |

After the entries above have been posted, the cash account will have a debit balance of $2,631. This balance agrees with the adjusted cash balance shown on the bank reconciliation. This is the amount of cash available as of July 31 and the amount that would be reported on Power Networking's July 31 balance sheet.

Although businesses may reconcile their bank accounts in a slightly different format from what we described above, the objective is the same: to control cash by reconciling the company's records to the records of an independent outside source, the bank. In doing so, any errors or misuse of cash may be detected.

For effective control, the bank reconciliation should be prepared by an employee who does not take part in or record cash transactions. When these duties are not properly separated, mistakes are likely to occur, and it is more likely that cash will be stolen or otherwise misapplied. For example, an employee who takes part in all of these duties could prepare and cash an unauthorized check, omit it from the accounts, and omit it from the reconciliation.

A bank reconciliation is also appropriate in a computerized environment where the deposits and checks are stored in electronic files and records. In some systems, the computer determines the difference between the ending bank balance and the balance per the company's records and then adjusts for deposits in transit and outstanding checks. Any remaining differences are reported for further analysis.

## 7. Special-Purpose Cash Funds

Petty Cash. It would be wasteful to write separate checks for an executive's taxi fare, name tags needed right away, or delivery of a package across town. Therefore, companies keep a petty cash fund on hand to pay such minor amounts.

The petty cash fund is opened with a particular amount of cash. A check for that amount is then issued to Petty Cash. Assume that on February 28, Cisco Systems, the worldwide leader in networks for the Internet, establishes a petty cash fund of $500 in a sales department. The custodian of the petty cash fund cashes the check and places $500 in the fund, which may be a cash box or other device.

For each petty cash payment, the custodian prepares a petty cash ticket to list the item purchased. The sum of the cash in the petty cash fund plus the total of the ticket amounts should equal the opening balance at all times—in this case, $500. The Petty Cash account keeps its $500 balance at all times. Maintaining the Petty Cash account at this balance, supported by the fund (cash plus tickets), is how an imprest system works. The control feature is that it clearly identifies the amount for which the custodian is responsible.

To illustrate normal petty cash fund entries, assume that a petty cash fund of $400 is established on June 1. The entry to record this transaction is as shown in Exhibit 8-15.

**Exhibit 8-15 Established a petty cash fund**

| Date | | Description | Post. Ref. | Debit | Credit |
|---|---|---|---|---|---|
| June | 1 | Petty Cash | | 400 | |
| | | Cash | | | 400 |

At the end of June, the petty cash receipts indicate expenditures for the following items: office supplies, $380; miscellaneous administrative expense, $10; and store supplies, $25. The entry to replenish the petty cash fund on June 31 is as shown in Exhibit 8-16.

**Exhibit 8-16 Replenish the petty cash fund**

| Date | | Description | Post. Ref. | Debit | Credit |
|---|---|---|---|---|---|
| Aug. | 31 | Office Supplies | | 380 | |
| | | Miscellaneous Administrative Expense | | 10 | |
| | | Store Supplies | | 25 | |
| | | Cash | | | 415 |

## 8. Financial Statements Reporting of Cash

Most companies have numerous bank accounts, but they usually combine all cash amounts into a single total called "Cash and Cash Equivalents". Cash equivalents include liquid assets such as time deposits and certificates of deposit, which are interest-bearing accounts that can be withdrawn with no penalty. Slightly less liquid than cash, cash equivalents are sufficiently similar to be reported along with cash. The balance sheet of AMEX Products reported in Exhibit 8-17.

**Exhibit 8-17 The balance sheet of AMEX Products**

AMEX Products Inc.
Balance Sheet (Excerpts, adapted)
For the Year Ended December 31, 2007

(amounts in millions)

| Assets | |
|---|---|
| Cash and cash equivalent | 6,260 |
| Cash pledged as collateral | 2,000 |

### COMPENSATING BALANCE AGREEMENTS

The Cash account on the balance sheet reports the liquid assets available for day-to-day use. None of the Cash balance is restricted in any way.

Any restricted amount of cash should not be reported as Cash on the balance sheet. For example, on the AMEX Products balance sheet, cash pledged as collateral is reported separately because that cash is not available for day-to-day use. Instead, AMEX Products has pledged the cash as security (collateral) for a loan. If AMEX Products fails to pay the loan, the lender can take the pledged cash. For this reason, the pledged cash is less liquid.

Also, banks often lend money under a compensating balance agreement. The borrower agrees to maintain a minimum balance in a checking account at all times. This minimum balance becomes a long-term asset and is therefore not cash in the normal sense.

Suppose AMEX Products borrowed $10,000 at 8% from First Interstate Bank and agreed to keep 20% ( $2,000) on deposit at all times. The net result of the compensating balance agreement is that AMEX Products actually borrowed only $8,000. And by paying 8% interest on the full $10,000, AMEX Products actual interest rate is really 10%, as shown here:

$$\$10,000 \times 0.08 = \$800 \text{ interest}$$

$$\$800/\$8,000 = 10\% \text{ interest rate}$$

## SUMMARY OF CASH-RELATED ITEMS

Cash and cash equivalents include the medium of exchange and most negotiable instruments. If the item cannot be quickly converted to coin or currency, a company separately classifies it as an investment, receivable, or prepaid expense. Companies segregate and classify cash that is unavailable for payment of currently maturing liabilities in the long-term assets section. Exhibit 8-18 summarizes the classification of cash-related items.

**Exhibit 8-18 Classification of cash-related items**

Classification of Cash, Cash Equivalents, and Noncash Items

| Item | Classification | Comment |
|---|---|---|
| Cash | Cash | If unrestricted, report as cash.<br>If restricte, identify and classify as current and non-current assets |
| Petty cash and change funds | Cash | Report as cash |
| Short-term paper | Cash equivalents | Investments with maturity of less than 3 months, often combined with cash |
| Short-term paper | Temporary investments | Investments with maturity of 3 to 12 months |
| Postdated checks and IOUs | Receivables | Assumed to be collectible |
| Travel advances | Receivables | Assumed to be collected from employees or deducted from their salaries |
| Postage on hand (as stamps or in postage Meters) | Prepaid expenses | Inventory. May also be classified as office supplies |
| Bank overdrafts | Current liability | If right of offset exists, reduce cash |
| Compensating balances | Cash separately classified as a deposit maintained as compensating balance | Classify as current or noncurrent in the balance sheet. Disclose separately in notes details of the arrangement. |

**TERMINOLOGY:**

Internal Control: 内部控制

Cash: 现金

Internal Control of Cash: 现金内部控制

Internal Control of Financial Statements: 财务报表内部控制

Control Environment: 控制环境

Risk Assessment：风险评估
Control Procedures：控制程序
Cash Receipts：现金收入
Petty Cash：备用金
Check：支票
Bank Accounts：银行存款
Remittance Advice：汇款通知单
Bank Reconciliation：银行对账单
Special-purpose Cash Funds：专用资金
Cash and Cash Equivalents：现金和现金等价物
Compensating Balance Agreements：补偿性余额协议
Postdated Checks：期票

**QUESTIONS：**

**1. List the three objectives of internal control, and define and give examples of the five elements of internal control.**

Internal control provides reasonable assurance that assets are safeguarded and used for business purposes, business information is accurate, and laws and regulations are complied with. The five elements of internal control are the control environment, risk assessment, control procedures, monitoring, and information and communication.

**2. Summarize basic procedures for achieving internal control over cash receipts.**

One of the most important controls to protect cash received in over-the-counter sales is a cash register. A remittance advice is a preventive control for cash received through the mail. Separating the duties of handling cash and recording cash is also a preventive control.

**3. Prepare a bank reconciliation and journalize any necessary entries.**

The first section of the bank reconciliation begins with the cash balance according to the bank statement. This balance is adjusted for the depositor's changes in cash that do not appear on the bank statement and for any bank errors. The second section begins with the cash balance according to the depositor's records. This balance is adjusted for the bank's changes in cash that do not appear on the depositor's records and for any depositor errors. The adjusted balances for the two sections must be equal.

No entries are necessary on the depositor's records as a result of the information included in the first section of the bank reconciliation. However, the items in the second section must be journalized on the depositor's records.

**PROBLEM：**

The cash account of Baylor Associates at February 28, 2007, shown in Exhibit 8-19.

**Exhibit 8-19 The cash account**

Cash

| | | | |
|---|---|---|---|
| Feb. 1 | Bal. 3,995 | Feb. 3 | 400 |
| 6 | 800 | 12 | 3,100 |
| 15 | 1,800 | 19 | 1,100 |
| 23 | 1,100 | 25 | 500 |
| 28 | 2,400 | 27 | 900 |
| Feb. 28 | Bal. 4,095 | | |

Baylor Associates received the bank statement on February 28, 2007 (negative amounts are in parentheses), as shown in Exhibit 8-20.

**Exhibit 8-20 The bank statement**

| | | |
|---|---|---|
| Beginning balance | | 3,995 |
| Deposits: | | |
| Feb. 7 | 800 | |
| 15 | 1,800 | |
| 24 | 1,100 | 3,700 |
| Checks (total per day): | | |
| Feb. 8 | 400 | |
| 16 | 3,100 | |
| 23 | 1,100 | (4,600) |
| Other items: | | |
| Service charge | | (10) |
| NSF check from M. E. Crown | | (700) |
| Bank collection of note receivable for the company | | 1,000 |
| EFT-monthly rent expense | | (330) |
| Interest revenue earned on account balance | | 15 |
| Ending balance | | 3,070 |

Additional data: Baylor Associates deposits all cash receipts in the bank and makes all payments by check.

**Requirements**

Prepare the bank reconciliation of Baylor Associates at February 28, 2007. Journalize the entries based on the bank reconciliation.

Solution the Exhibit 8-21 presents the bank reconciliation, and Exhibit 8-22 is the entries based on the bank reconciliation.

**Exhibit 8-21　The bank reconciliation**

Baylor Associates

Bank Reconciliation

February 28, 2007

| | | |
|---|---|---|
| Bank: | | |
| Balance, February 28, 2007 | | 3,070 |
| Add: Deposit of February 28 in transit | | 2,400 |
| | | 5,470 |
| Less: Outstanding checks issued on Feb. 25 ( $500) | 500 | |
| and Feb. 27 ( $900) | 900 | 1,400 |
| Adjusted bank balance , February 28, 2007 | | 4,070 |
| | | |
| Books: | | |
| Balance, February 28, 2007 | | 4,095 |
| Add: Bank collection of note receivable | | 1,000 |
| Interest revenue earned on bank balance | | 15 |
| | | 5,110 |
| Less: Service charge | 10 | |
| NSF check | 700 | |
| EFT-Rent expense | 330 | 1,040 |
| Adjusted book balance, February 28, 2007 | | 4,070 |

**Exhibit 8-22　The entries based on the bank reconciliation**

| Date | Description | Post. Ref. | Debit | Credit |
|---|---|---|---|---|
| Feb. 28 | Cash | | 1,000 | |
| | Note receivable | | | 1,000 |
| | Note receivable collected by bank | | | |
| 28 | Cash | | 15 | |
| | Interest Revenue | | | 15 |
| | Interest earned on bank balance | | | |
| 28 | Miscellaneous Expense | | 10 | |
| | Cash | | | 10 |
| | Bank service charge | | | |
| 28 | Accounts Receivable-M. E. Crown | | 700 | |
| | Cash | | | 700 |
| | NSF check returned by bank | | | |
| 28 | Rent Expense | | 330 | |
| | Cash | | | 330 |
| | Monthly rent expense | | | |

# Chapter 9

## Receivables

**Objectives**

1. Describe the common classifications of receivables.
2. Describe the accounting for uncollectible receivables.
3. Describe the direct write-off method of accounting for uncollectible receivables.
4. Describe the allowance method of accounting for uncollectible receivables.
5. Compare direct write-off and allowance methods of accounting for uncollectible accounts.
6. Describe the accounting for notes receivable.
7. Describe the reporting of receivables on the balance sheet.

# 1. Classification of Receivables

Receivables are the third most liquid asset—after cash and short-term investments.

Most of the remainder of this chapter shows how to account for receivables.

Receivables are monetary claims against others. Receivables are acquired mainly by selling goods and services (accounts receivable) and by lending money (notes receivable). The journal entries to record the receivables can be shown in Exhibit 9-1.

**Exhibit 9-1 The journal entries to record the receivables**

| Performing a Service on Account | | Lending Money on a Note Receivable | |
|---|---|---|---|
| Accounts Receivable ………… | XXX | Note Receivable ………… | XXX |
| Service Income ………… | XXX | Cash ………… | XXX |
| Performed a service on account | | Loaned money to another company | |

The 2 major types of receivables are accounts receivable and notes receivable. A business's accounts receivable are the amounts collectible from customers from the sale of goods and services. Accounts receivable, which are current assets, are sometimes called trade receivables or merely receivables.

## ACCOUNTS RECEIVABLE

The Accounts Receivable account in the general ledger serves as a control account that summarizes the total amount receivable from all customers. Companies also keep a subsidiary record of accounts receivable with a separate account for each customer, illustrated in Exhibit 9-2.

**Exhibit 9-2 The general ledger and the subsidiary record**

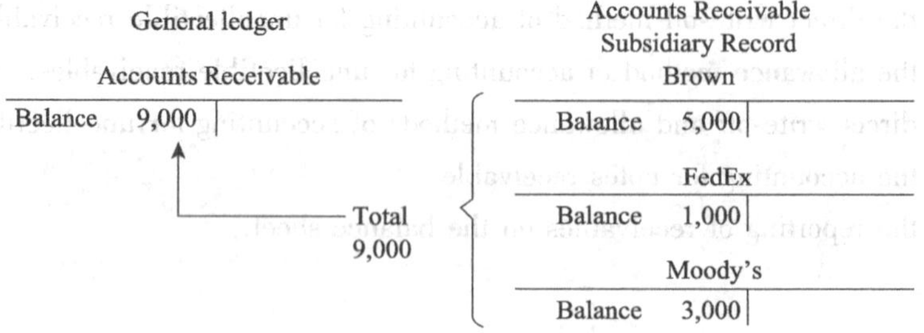


## NOTES RECEIVABLE

Notes receivable are more formal contracts than accounts receivable. For a note, the borrower signs a written promise to pay the lender a definite sum at the maturity date. This is why notes are also called promissory notes. The note may require the borrower to pledge security for the loan. This means that the borrower gives the lender permission to claim certain assets, called collateral, if the borrower fails to pay the amount due. We cover the details of notes receivable later in this chapter.

### OTHER RECEIVABLES

Other receivables is a miscellaneous category for all receivables other than accounts receivable and notes receivable. Examples include loans to employees and to related companies . Other receivables are normally listed separately on the balance sheet. They are classified as current assets if they are expected to be collected within one year. If collection is expected beyond one year, they are classified as noncurrent assets and reported under the caption Investments. Other receivables include interest receivable, taxes receivable, and receivables from officers or employees.

## 2. Uncollectible Receivables

A company gets an account receivable only when it sells its product or service on credit(on account). You'll recall that the entry to record the earning of revenue on account is(amount assumed) as Exhibit 9-3.

**Exhibit 9-3 The entry to record the earning of revenue**

| Date | Description | Post. Ref. | Debit | Credit |
|---|---|---|---|---|
| | Accounts Receivable | | 1,000 | |
| | Sales(or Service Income) | | | 1,000 |
| | Earned revenue on account | | | |

Ideally, the company would collect cash for all of its receivables. But unfortunately the entry to record cash collections on account is for only $950, as shown in Exhibit 9-4.

**Exhibit 9-4 The entry to record cash collections**

| Date | Description | Post. Ref. | Debit | Credit |
|---|---|---|---|---|
| | Cash | | 950 | |
| | Accounts Receivable | | | 950 |
| | Collections on account | | | |

You can see that companies rarely collect all of their accounts receivables. So companies must account for their uncollectible accounts— $50 in this example. Selling on credit creates both a benefit and a cost:

(1) Benefit: Customers who cannot pay cash immediately can buy on credit, so sales and profits increase.

(2) Cost: The company cannot collect from some customers. Accountants label this cost uncollectible-account expense, doubtful-account expense, or bad debt expense.

PepsiCo reports receivables as follows on its 2006 balance sheet (amounts in millions):

| | |
|---|---|
| Accounts and notes receivable, net of allowance for doubtful accounts of \$64 ········ | \$3,725 |

The allowance (\$64) represents the amount that PepsiCo does not expect to collect. The net amount of the receivables (\$3,725 million) is the amount that PepsiCo does expect to collect. This is called the net realizable value because it's the amount of cash PepsiCo expects to realize in cash receipts.

Bad debt expense is an operating expense along with salaries, depreciation, rent, and utilities. To measure bad debt expense, accountants use the allowance method or, in certain limited cases, the direct write-off method.

## 3. Direct Write-Off Method for Uncollectible Accounts

There is another, less preferable, way to account for uncollectible receivables. Under the direct write-off method, the company waits until a specific customer's receivable proves uncollectible. Then the accountant writes off customer's account and records Bad Debt Expense, as shown in Exhibit 9-5 (using assumed data).

**Exhibit 9-5 The bad debt expense**

| Date | Description | Post. Ref. | Debit | Credit |
|---|---|---|---|---|
| 2007 Jan. 2 | Bad Debt Expense | | 12 | |
| | Accounts Receivable—Fiesta | | | 9 |
| | Accounts Receivable—Stop-N-Shop | | | 3 |
| | Wrote off bad accounts by direct write-off method | | | |

The direct write-off method is defective for 2 reasons.

(1) The direct write-off method uses no allowance for uncollectibles. As a result, receivables are always reported at their full amount, which is more than the business expects to collect. Assets on the balance sheet are overstated.

(2) The direct write-off method causes a poor matching of bad debt expense against revenue. In

this example, PepsiCo made the sales to Fiesta and Stop - N - Shop in 2006 and should have recorded the bad debt expense during 2006, not in 2007 when it wrote off the accounts.

Because of these deficiencies, PepsiCo and virtually all other large companies use the allowance method. The direct write-off method is acceptable only when uncollectibles are so low that there would be no allowance for uncollectible accounts.

## 4. Allowance Method for Uncollectible Accounts

As we mentioned earlier, the allowance method is required by generally accepted accounting principles for companies with large accounts receivable. As a result, most well-known companies such as Coca-cola Company, PepsiCo Inc., Intel Corporation, and FedEx use the allowance method.

As discussed in the preceding section, the direct write-off method records bad debt expense only when an account is determined to be worthless. In contrast, the allowance method estimates the accounts receivable that will not be collected and records bad debt expense for this estimate at the end of each accounting period. Based upon this estimate, Bad Debt Expense is then recorded by adjusting entry.

To illustrate, assume that Anta Company began operations in August and chose to use the calendar year as its fiscal year. As of December 31, 2007, Anta Company has an accounts receivable balance of $1,000,000 that includes some accounts that are past due. However, Anta Company doesn't know which customer accounts will be uncollectible. Based upon industry data, Anta Company estimates that $40,000 of its accounts receivable will be uncollectible. Using this estimate, the adjusting entry is made on December 31 as shown in Exhibit 9-6.

**Exhibit 9-6 Bad debt expense on Dec. 31**

| Date | | Description | Post. Ref. | Debit | Credit |
|---|---|---|---|---|---|
| Dec. | 31 | Bad Debt Expense | | 40,000 | |
| | | Allowance for Doubtful Accounts | | | 40,000 |
| | | Uncollectible accounts estimate | | | |

Since the $40,000 reduction in accounts receivable is an estimate, specific customer accounts cannot be reduced or credited. Instead, a contra asset account entitled Allowance for Doubtful Accounts is credited.

The preceding adjusting entry affects the balance sheet and income statement. First, the adjusting entry records $40,000 of Bad Debt Expense, which will be matched against the related revenues of the period on the income statement. Second, the adjusting entry reduces the value of the receivables to the amount of cash expected to be realized in the future. This amount, $960,000

( $1,000,000 − $40,000), is called the **net realizable value** of the receivables. The net realizable value of the receivables is reported on the balance sheet.

After the preceding adjusting entry has been recorded, Ac counts Receivable still has a debit balance of $1,000,000. This balance represents the total amount owed by customers on account and is supported by the individual customer accounts in the accounts receivable subsidiary ledger. The accounts receivable contra account, Allowance for Doubtful Accounts, has a credit balance of $40,000.

## WRITE-OFFS TO THE ALLOWANCE ACCOUNT

Assume that at the beginning of 2007 a division of PepsiCo had accounts receivable shown in Exhibit 9-7 (amounts in thousands).

**Exhibit 9-7 The accounts receivable and allowance**

| Accounts Receivable—Fiesta | | Accounts Receivable—Stop-N-Shop | | Allowance for Doubtful Accounts | |
|---|---|---|---|---|---|
| 9 | | 3 | | | 20 |

| Accounts Receivable—Other | |
|---|---|
| 88 | |

Total Accounts Receivable = 100　　Allowance = 20

Accounts Receivable, Net = 80

Suppose that early in 2007, PepsiCo's credit department determines that PepsiCo cannot collect from customers Fiesta and Stop − N − Shop. PepsiCo then writes off the receivables from these 2 customers with the entry shown in Exhibit 9-8.

**Exhibit 9-8 The allowance for doubtful accounts on Jan. 31**

| Date | Description | Post. Ref. | Debit | Credit |
|---|---|---|---|---|
| 2007 Jan. 31 | Allowance for Doubtful Accounts | | 12 | |
| | Accounts Receivable—Fiesta | | | 9 |
| | Accounts Receivable—Stop-N-Shop | | | 3 |
| | Wrote off uncollectible receivables | | | |

After the write-off, PepsiCo's accounts show these amounts in Exhibit 9-9.

**Exhibit 9-9 The PepsiCo's accounts after the write-off**

| Accounts Receivable—Fiesta | |
|---|---|
| 9 | 9 |

| Accounts Receivable—Stop-N-Shop | |
|---|---|
| 3 | 3 |

| Allowance for Doubtful Accounts | |
|---|---|
| 12 | 20 |
| | 8 |

| Accounts Receivable—Other | |
|---|---|
| 88 | |

Total Accounts Receivable =88 Allowance =8

Accounts Receivable, Net =80

The accounting equation shows that the write-off ofuncollectibles has no effect on PepsiCo's total assets. Accounts Receivable, Net is still $80. There is no effect on net income either. Why is there no effect on net income? Net income is unaffected because the write-off of uncollectibles affects no expense account. The exhibit 9-10 shows how the write-off of uncollectibles affects the Balance Sheet.

**Exhibit 9-10 The influence on balance sheet**

| Assets | = | Liabilities | + | Stockholders' Equity |
|---|---|---|---|---|
| +12 | | | | |
| −12 | = | 0 | + | 0 |

## ESTIMATING UNCOLLECTIBLES

As we indicated earlier in this section, the allowance method estimates bad debt expense at the end of the period. How is the amount of uncollectible accounts estimated? The estimate ofuncollectibles at the end of a fiscal period is based on past experience and forecasts of the future. When the general economy is doing well, the estimate of bad debt expense is normally less than it would be when the economy is doing poorly.

Two methods are commonly used to estimate uncollectible accounts receivable at the end of the period. The estimate may be based upon a percent of sales or an analysis of the receivables. We describe and illustrate each method next.

### Estimate Based on Percent of Sales

Since accounts receivable are created by credit sales, bad debt expense can be estimated as a percent of credit sales. To illustrate, assume that onDecember 31, 2008, the Allowance for Doubtful Accounts for Coca-cola Company has a credit balance of $3,250. In addition, Coca-cola Company estimates that 1.5% of 2008 credit sales will be uncollectible. If credit sales for the year are $3,000,000, the adjusting entry for uncollectible accounts on December 31 is as shown in Exhibit 9-11.

**Exhibit 9-11 The adjusting entry**

| Date | | Description | Post. Ref. | Debit | Credit |
|---|---|---|---|---|---|
| Dec. | 31 | Bad Debt Expense | | 45,000 | |
| | | Allowance for Doubtful Accounts | | | 45,000 |
| | | Uncollectible accounts estimate (3,000,000 ×0.015 = $45,000) | | | |

After the preceding adjusting entry is posted to the ledger, Bad Debt Expense will have a balance of $45,000, and the Allowance for Doubtful Accounts will have a balance of $48,250, as shown in Exhibit 9-12.

**Exhibit 9-12 Bad debt expense**

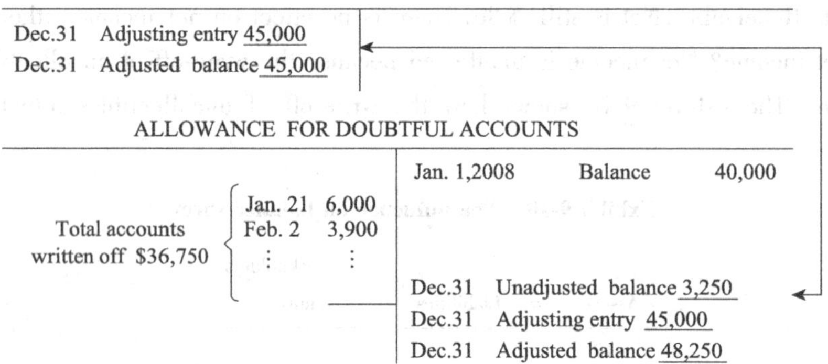


After the adjusting entry is recorded, the Allowance for Doubtful Accounts has a credit balance of $48,250. If there had been a debit balance of $4,100 in the allowance account before the year-end adjustment, the amount of the adjustment would still have been $45,000. However, the December 31 ending balance of the allowance account would have been $40,900($45,000 - $4,100). In other words, under the percent of sales method, the amount of the adjusting entry for Bad Debt Expense is credited to whatever balance exists in the Allowance for Doubtful Accounts.

**Estimate Based on Analysis of Receivables**

The longer an account receivable is out- standing, the less likely that it will be collected. Thus, we can base the estimate of un- collectible accounts on how long specific accounts have been outstanding. For this purpose, we can use a process called **aging the receivables.**

Receivables are aged by classifying each customer's receivable by its due date. The number of days an account is past due is the number of days between the due date of the account and the date the aging schedule is prepared. To illustrate, assume that Coca-cola Company is preparing an aging schedule for its accounts receivable of $86,300 as of August 31, 2008. The $160 account receivable for Saxon Woods Company was due on May 29. As of August 31, Saxon Woods Company's account is 94 days past due, as shown below.

Number of days past due in May 2 days
Number of days past due in June 30 days
Number of days past due in July 31 days
Number of days past due in August 31 days
Total number of days past due 94 days

A portion of the aging schedule for Coca-cola Company is shown in Exhibit 9-13. The schedule shows the total amount of receivables in each aging class.

**Exhibit 9-13 Aging of accounts receivable**

| | | | Not | Days Past Due | | | | | | |
|---|---|---|---|---|---|---|---|---|---|---|
| | Customer | Balance | Past Due | 1 ~ 30 days | 31 ~ 60 days | 61 ~ 90 days | 91 ~ 180 days | 181 ~ 365 days | Over 365 days | |
| 1 | Ashby | 150 | | | 150 | | | | | 1 |
| 2 | B. T Barr | 610 | | | | | 350 | 260 | | 2 |
| 3 | Brock Co. | 470 | 47 | | | | | | | 3 |
| ⋮ | ⋮ | ⋮ | | | | | | | | ⋮ |
| 22 | Saxon Woods Company | 160 | | | | | 160 | | | 22 |
| 23 | Total | 86,300 | 75,000 | 4,000 | 3,100 | 1,900 | 1,200 | 800 | 300 | 23 |

Coca-cola Company uses a sliding scale of percentages, based on industry or company experience, to estimate the amount of uncollectibles in each aging class. As shown in Exhibit 9-14, the percent estimated as uncollectible increases the longer the account is past due. For accounts not past due, the percent is 2%, while for accounts over 365 days past due the percent is 80%. The total of these amounts is the desired end-of-period balance for the Allowance for Doubtful Accounts. For Coca-cola Company, the desired August 31 balance of the Allowance for Doubtful Accounts is $3,390.

**Exhibit 9-14 Estimate of uncollectible accounts**

| | | | Estimated Uncollectible Accounts | | |
|---|---|---|---|---|---|
| | Age Interval | Balance | Percent | Amount | |
| 1 | Not past due | 75,000 | 2 % | 1,500 | 1 |
| 2 | 1 ~ 30 days past due | 4,000 | 5% | 200 | 2 |
| 3 | 31 ~ 60 days past due | 3,100 | 10% | 310 | 3 |
| 4 | 61 ~ 90 days past due | 1,900 | 20% | 380 | 4 |
| 5 | 91 ~ 180 days past due | 1,200 | 30% | 360 | 5 |
| 6 | 181 ~ 365 days past due | 800 | 50% | 400 | 6 |
| 7 | Over 365 days past due | 300 | 80% | 240 | 7 |
| 8 | Total | 86,300 | | 3,390 | 8 |

Comparing the estimate of $3,390 with the unadjusted balance of the allowance account determines the amount of the adjustment for Bad Debt Expense. For example, assume that the unadjusted balance of the allowance account is a credit balance of $510. The amount to be added to this balance is therefore $2,880($3,390- $510), and the adjusting entry is shown in Exhibit 9-15.

**Exhibit 9-15 The adjusting entry**

| | | | | | | |
|---|---|---|---|---|---|---|
| | Aug. | 31 | Bad Debt Expense | | 2,880 | |
| | | | Allowance for Doubtful Accounts | | | 2,880 |
| | | | Uncollectible accounts estimate($3,390 - $510) | | | |

After the preceding adjusting entry is posted to the ledger, Bad Debt Expense will have a balance of $2,880, and the Allowance for Doubtful Accounts will have a balance of $3,390, as shown in Exhibit 9-16.

**Exhibit 9-16 The allowance for doubtful accounts**

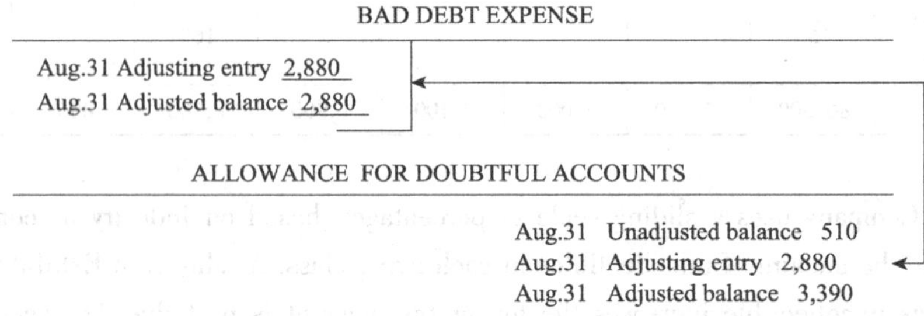


After the adjustment is recorded, the balance of the bad debt expense account is $2,880, and the balance of the allowance account is $3,390. The net realizable value of the receivables is $82,910($86,300 - $3,390). If the unadjusted balance of the allowance account had been a debit balance of $300, the amount of the adjustment would have been $3,690($3,390 + $300). In this case, the bad debt expense account would have a $3,690 balance, but the balance of the allowance account would still have been $3,390, as shown in Exhibit 9-17.

**Exhibit 9-17 The bad debt expense and allowance**

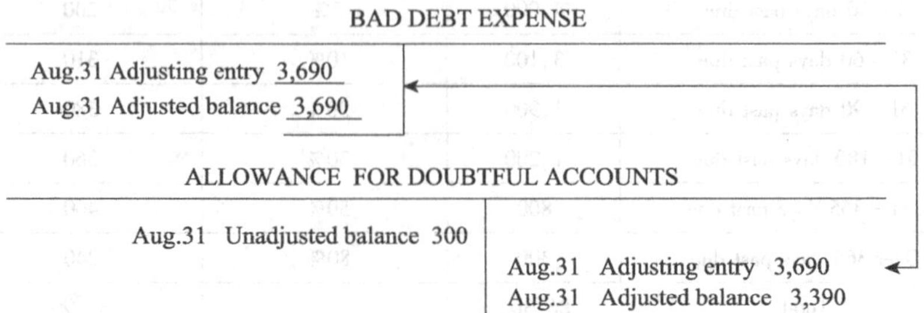

### Comparing Estimation Methods

The percent of sales and analysis of receivables methods can be compared in two different ways. First, the methods can be compared based on their financial statement emphasis. Second, the methods can be compared based on whether Bad Debt Expense or the Allowance for Doubtful Accounts is the focus of the estimate.

The percent of sales method emphasizes the matching of bad debt expense with the related credit sales of the period. In doing so, the percent of sales method places more emphasis on the income statement. The analysis of receivables method emphasizes the end-of-period net realizable value of the receivables and the related balance of the allowance account. Thus, the analysis of receivables method places more emphasis on the balance sheet.

Under the percent of sales method, Bad Debt Expense is the focus of the estimation process. In other words, the percent of sales method emphasizes obtaining the best estimate for Bad Debt Expense for the period. The ending balance for Allowance for Doubtful Accounts is the result of estimating bad debt expense. For example, in the Coca-cola Company illustration, bad debt expense was estimated as \$45,000(\$3,000,000 × 1.5%) and thus, \$45,000 was credited to the Allowance for Doubtful Accounts. Since the Allowance for Doubtful Accounts had an unadjusted credit balance of \$3,250, its ending balance became a credit balance of \$48,250.

Under the analysis of receivables method, Allowance for Doubtful Accounts is the focus of the estimation process. Bad Debt Expense becomes the end result of estimating Allowance for Doubtful Accounts. For example, in the Coca-cola Company illustration, the adjusted balance for the Allowance for Doubtful Accounts was estimated using the aging method as \$3,390. Since the Allowance for Doubtful Accounts had an unadjusted credit balance of \$510, it was credited for \$2,880(\$3,390 − \$510). The related debit of \$2,880 was to Bad Debt Expense. Thus, the ending balance of Bad Debt Expense became \$2,880. Exhibit 9-18 summarizes the differences between the percent of sales and the analysis of receivables methods.

**Exhibit 9-18 The difference between the percent of sales and the analysis of receivables method**

| | Percent of Sales Method | Analysis of Receivables Method |
|---|---|---|
| Financial statement | Income statement | Balance sheet |
| Focus of estimate | Bad Debt Expense | Allowance for Doubtful Accounts |
| End result of estimate | Allowance for Doubtful Accounts | Bad Debt Expense |

## 5. Comparing Direct Write-Off and Allowance Methods

The primary differences between these two methods are summarized in Exhibit 9-19.

**Exhibit 9-19　Compare the direct write-off and allowance method**

| | Amount of bad debt and Expense recorded | Allowance account | Primary users |
|---|---|---|---|
| Direct Write-Off Method | When the actual accounts receivable are determined to be uncollectible | No allowance account is used | Small companies and companies with relatively few receivables |
| Allowance Method | Using estimate based on either a percent of sales or an analysis of receivables | The allowance account is used | Large companies and those with a large amount of receivables |

# 6. Notes Receivable

Notes receivable are more formal than accounts receivable. Notes receivable due within 1 year or less are current assets. Notes due beyond 1 year are long-term receivables and are reported as long-term assets. Some notes receivable are collected in installments. The portion due within 1 year is a current asset and the remainder is long-term assets. PepsiCo may hold a \$20,000 note receivable from a customer, but only the \$6,000 the customer must pay within 1 year is a current asset of PepsiCo.

## CHARACTERISTICS OF NOTES RECEIVABLE

A note receivable, or promissory note, is a written promise to pay a sum of money (face amount) on demand or at a definite time. It can be payable either to an individual or a business, or to the bearer or holder of the note. It is signed by the person or firm that makes the promise. The one to whose order the note is payable is called the payee, and the one making the promise is called the maker.

The date a note is to be paid is called the due date or maturity date. The period of time between the issuance date and the due date of a short-term note may be stated in either days or months. When the term of a note is stated in days, the due date is the specified number of days after its issuance. To illustrate, the due date of a 90-day note dated March 16 is June 14, as shown in Exhibit 9-20.

**Exhibit 9-20　The term of the note**

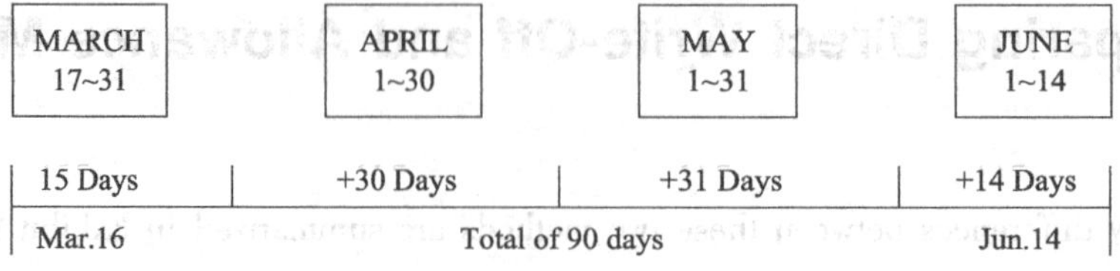


The term of a note may be stated as a certain number of months after the issuance date. In such cases, the due date is determined by counting the number of months from the issuance date. For example, a three-month note dated June 5 would be due on September 5. A two-month note dated July 31 would be due on September 30.

A note normally specifies that interest be paid for the period between the issuance date and the due date. Notes covering a period of time longer than one year normally provide for interest to be paid annually, semiannually, quarterly, or monthly. When the term of the note is less than one year, the interest is usually payable at the time the note is paid.

The interest rate on notes is normally stated in terms of a year, regardless of the actual period of time involved. Thus, the interest on \$2,000 for one year at 12% is \$240 (12% × \$2,000). The interest on \$2,000 for 90 days at 12% is \$60 (\$2,000 × 12% × 90days/360days). To simplify computations, we will use 360 days per year. In practice, companies such as banks and mortgage companies use the exact number of days in a year, 365.

The amount that is due at the maturity or due date of a note receivable is its maturity value. The maturity value of a note is the sum of the face amount and the interest. For example, the maturity value of a \$25,000, 9%, 120-day note receivable is \$25,750 (\$25,000 + (\$25,000 × 9% × 120days/360days)).

Before launching into the accounting for notes receivable, let's define some key terms.

**Creditor.** The party to whom money is owed. The creditor is also called the lender.

**Debtor.** The party that borrowed and owes money on the note. The debtor is also called the maker of the note or the borrower.

**Interest.** Interest is the cost of borrowing money. The interest is stated in an annual percentage rate.

**Maturity date.** The date on which the debtor must pay the note.

**Maturity value.** The sum of principal and interest on the note.

**Principal.** The amount of money borrowed by the debtor.

**Term.** The length of time from when the note was signed by the debtor to when the debtor must pay the note.

A promissory note is shown in Exhibit 9-21, we can know that the principal amount of the note (\$1,000) is the amount borrowed by the debtor, lent by the creditor. This 6-month note receivable runs from August 31, 20×8, to February 28, 20×9, when Lauren Holland (the maker) promises to pay Continental Bank (the creditor) the principal of \$1,000 plus 9% interest. Interest is revenue to the creditor (Continental Bank, in this case).

## ACCOUNTING FOR NOTES RECEIVABLE

Consider the promissory note in Exhibit 9-21. After Lauren Holland signs the note, Continental Bank gives her \$1,000 cash. The bank's entries is shown in Exhibit 9-22, assuming a December 31 year end for Continental Bank.

**Exhibit 9-21 A promissory note**

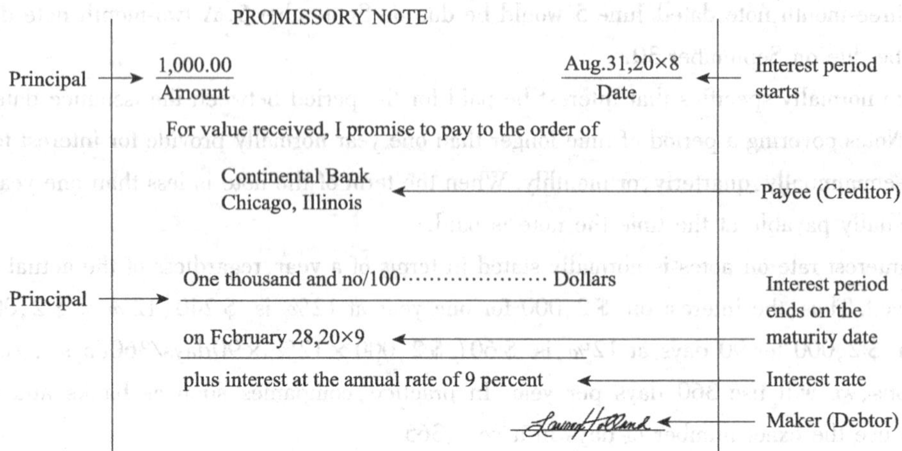


**Exhibit 9-22 The bank's entry on making a loan**

| Date | Description | Post. Ref. | Debit | Credit |
|---|---|---|---|---|
| 20×8 Aug. 31 | Note Receivable—L. Holland | | 1,000 | |
| | Cash | | | 1,000 |
| | Made a loan | | | |

| Note Receivable—L. Holland | |
|---|---|
| 1,000 | |

The bank gave one asset, cash, in return for another asset, a note receivable, so total assets did not change.

Continental Bank earns interest revenue during September, October, November, and December. At December 31, the bank accrues 9% interest revenue for 4 months as shown in Exhibit 9-23.

**Exhibit 9-23 Record the bank's interest revenue**

| Date | Description | Post. Ref. | Debit | Credit |
|---|---|---|---|---|
| 20×8 Dec. 31 | Interest Receivable ($1,000×9%×4months/12months) | | 30 | |
| | Interest Revenue | | | 30 |
| | Accrued interest revenue | | | |

The bank's assets and revenues increase.

Continental Bank reports these amounts in its financial statements at December 31, 20×8, as shown in Exhibit 9-24.

**Exhibit 9-24 The financial statements**

| | |
|---|---|
| Balance sheet | |
| Current assets: | |
| Note receivable | 1,000 |
| Interest receivable | 30 |
| Income statement | |
| Interest revenue | 30 |

The bank collects the note on February 28, 20 ×9, and records as in Exhibit 9-25.

**Exhibit 9-25 The bank collect the note at maturity**

| Date | Description | Post. Ref. | Debit | Credit |
|---|---|---|---|---|
| 20 ×9 Feb. 28 | Cash | | 1,045 | |
| | Note Receivable—L. Holland | | | 1,000 |
| | Interest Receivable | | | 30 |
| | Interest Revenue ( $1,000 ×9% ×2months/12months) | | | 15 |
| | Collected note at maturity | | | |

This entry zeroes out Note Receivable and Interest Receivable and also records the interest revenue earned in 20 ×9.

| Note Receivable—L. Holland | |
|---|---|
| $1,000 | $1,000 |

In its 20 ×9 financial statements the only item that Continental Bank will report is the interest revenue of $15 that was earned in 20 ×9. There's no note receivable or interest receivable on the balance sheet because those items were zeroed out when the bank collected the note at maturity.

## 7. Reporting Receivables on the Balance Sheet

The balances of Crabtree Co's notes receivable, accounts receivable, and interest receivable accounts are disclosed in Exhibit 9-26. The allowance for doubtful accounts is subtracted from the accounts receivable. Alternatively, the accounts receivable may be listed on the balance sheet at its net realizable value of $430,000, with a note showing the amount of the allowance. If the allowance account includes provisions for doubtful notes as well as accounts, it should be deducted from the total of Note Receivable and Accounts Receivable.

**Exhibit 9-26 Receivables on balance sheet**

Crabtree Co.

Balance Sheet

December 31,2008

| | | | |
|---|---|---|---|
| | Assets | | |
| | Current assets: | | |
| | Cash | | 119,500 |
| | Notes receivable | | 250,000 |
| | Accounts receivable | 445,000 | |
| | Less allowance for doubtful accounts | 15,000 | 430,000 |
| | Interest receivable | | 14,500 |

Other disclosures related to receivables are presented either on the face of the financial statements or in the accompanying notes. Such disclosures include the market(fair) value of thereceivables. In addition, if unusual credit risks exist within the receivables, the nature of the risks should be disclosed. For example, if the majority of the receivables are due from one customer or are due from customers located in one area of the country or one industry, these facts should be disclosed.

## FINANCIAL ANALYSIS AND INTERPRETATION

Investors and creditors use ratios to evaluate the financial health of a company. The quick (or acid-test) rstio and the number of days' sales in receivables help investors measure liquidity.

### Acid-Test (or Quick) Ratio

The balance sheet lists assets in the order of relative liquidity.

(1) Cash and cash equivalents.

(2) Short-term investments.

(3) Accounts(or notes) receivable.

PepsiCo's balance sheet in the chapter-opening story lists these accounts in order.

Managers, stockholders, and creditors care about the liquidity of a company's assets. The current ratio measures ability to pay current liabilities with current assets. A more stringent measure of ability to pay current liabilities is the acid-test(or quick) ratio, the calculation is shown in Exhibit 9-27.

**Exhibit 9-27 The acid-test ratio**

Pepsi Co 2006

(amounts in millions, taken from Pepsi Co balance sheet)

$$\text{Acid-test ratio} = \frac{\text{Cash + Short-term investments + Net current receivables}}{\text{Total current liabilities}}$$

$$= \frac{1,651 + 1,171 + 3,725}{6,860} = 0.95$$

The higher the acid-test ratio, the easier it is to pay current liabilities. PepsiCo's acid-test ratio of 0.95 means that PepsiCo has 95 cents of quick assets to pay each \$1 of current liabilities. This ratio value is close to perfect. Traditionally, companies have wanted an acid-test ratio of 1.0 to be safe. The ratio needs to be high enough for safety, but not too high. After all, cash and the other liquid assets don't earn very high rates of return, as inventory and plant assets do.

What is an acceptable acid-test ratio? The answer depends on the industry. Auto dealers can operate smoothly with an acid-test ratio of 0.20, roughly one-fourth of PepsiCo's ratio value. How can auto dealers survive with so low an acid-test ratio? The auto manufacturers help finance their dealers' inventory. Most dealers, therefore, have a financial safety net. Companies without a big brother like Ford Motor Company need a higher acid-test ratio.

### Days' Sales in Receivables

After a business makes a credit sale, the next step is collecting the receivable. Days' sales in receivables, also called the collection period, tells a company how long it takes to collect its average level of receivables. Shorter is better because cash is coming in quickly. The longer the collection period, the less cash is available to pay bills and expand.

Days' sales in receivables can be computed in 2 logical steps. First, compute one day's sales (or total revenues). Then divide one day's sales into average receivables for the period. We show days' sales in receivables for PepsiCo in Exhibit 9-28.

**Exhibit 9-28 The calculation of day's sales in receivable**

(amounts in millions, taken from PepsiCo's financial statement)

| Days' Sales in Receivables | PepsiCo |
|---|---|
| 1. One day's sales = | $\frac{\text{Net sale}}{365\text{ days}} = \frac{35,137}{365\text{ days}} = 96$ per day |
| 2. Days'sales in average receivables = | $\frac{\text{Average receivables}}{\text{One day's sales}} = \frac{3,493}{96\text{ per day}} = 36$days |
| Average net receivables = | $\frac{\text{Beginning net receivable + Ending net receivables}}{2}$ |
| | $= \frac{3,261 + 3,725}{2} = 3,493$ |

Net sales come from the income statement, and the receivables amounts are taken from the balance sheet. Average receivables is the simple average of the beginning and ending balance.

It takes PepsiCo 36 days to collect its average level of receivables. To evaluate PepsiCo's collection period of 36 days, we need to compare 36 days to the credit terms that PepsiCo offers customers when the company makes a sale. Suppose PepsiCo makes sales on net 30 terms, which means that customers should pay PepsiCo within 30 days of the sale. PepsiCo's collection period of 36 days is pretty good in comparison to the ideal measure of 30 days. After all, some customers drag out their payments. And, as we've seen, some customers don't pay at all.

Companies watch their collection periods closely. Whenever collections slow down, the business must find other sources of financing, such as borrowing or selling receivables. During recessions, customers pay more slowly, and a longer collection period may be unavoidable.

## DISCOUNTING NOTES RECEIVABLE

Although it is not a common transaction, a company may endorse its notes receivable by transferring them to a bank in return for cash. The bank transfers cash (the proceeds) to the company after deducting a discount (interest) that is computed on the maturity value of the note for the discount period. The discount period is the time that the bank must hold the note before it becomes due.

To illustrate, assume that a 90-day, 12%, $ 1,800 note receivable from Pryor & Co., dated April 8, is discounted at the payee's bank on May 3 at the rate of 14%. The data used in determining the effect of the transaction are as follows:

| | |
|---|---|
| Face value of note dated April 8 | $ 1,800 |
| Interest on note (90 days at 12%) | $ 54 |
| Maturity value of note due July 7 | $ 1,854 |
| Discount on maturity value (65 days from May 3 to July 7, at 14%) | $ 47 |
| Proceeds | $ 1,807 |

The endorser records as interest revenue the excess of the proceeds from dis counting the note, $ 1,807, over its face value, $ 1,800, as shown in Exhibit 9-29.

**Exhibit 9-29 The record of the excess of proceeds from discounting the note**

| Date | | Description | Post. Ref. | Debit | Credit |
|---|---|---|---|---|---|
| | May 3 | Cash | | 1,807 | |
| | | Note Receivable | | | 1,800 |
| | | Interest Revenue | | | 7 |
| | | Discounted $ 1,800, 90-day, 12% note at 14% | | | |

What if the proceeds from discounting a note receivable are less than the face value? When this situation occurs, the endorser records the excess of the face value over the proceeds as interest expense. The length of the discount period and the difference between the interest rate and the discount rate determine whether interest expense or interest revenue will result from discounting.

Without a statement limiting responsibility, the endorser of a note is committed to paying the note if the maker defaults. This potential liability is called a contingent liability. Thus, the endorser of a note that has been discounted has a contingent liability until the due date. If the maker pays the promised amount at maturity, the contingent liability is removed without any action on the part of the endorser. If, on the other hand, the maker dishonors the note and the endorser is notified according to legal requirements, the endorser's liability becomes an actual one.

When a discounted note receivable is dishonored, the bank notifies the endorser and asks for payment. In some cases, the bank may charge a protest fee for notifying the endorser that a note has been dishonored. The entire amount paid to the bank by the endorser, including the interest and protest fee, should be debited to the account receivable of the maker.

**TERMINOLOGY:**

AccountsReceivable:应收账款
Notes Receivable:应收票据
Other Receivables:其他应收款
Uncollectible Receivables:坏账
Direct Write-off Method:直接冲销法
Percent of Sales Method:销货百分比法
Analysis of Receivables Method:应收账款分析法
Aging of Accounts Receivable:应收账款账龄
Bad Debt Expense:坏账费用
Allowance Method:备抵法
Maturity Date:到期日
Maturity Value:到期价值
Principal:面值
Days' Sales in Receivables:应收账款周转天数
Acid-test Ratio(Quick Ratio):酸性测试比率(速动比率)
Discounting Notes Receivable:应收票据贴现

**QUESTIONS:**

**1. Journalize the entries for the allowance method of accounting for uncollectibles, and estimate uncollectible receivables based on sales and on an analysis of receivables.**

A year-end adjusting entry provides for the reduction of the value of the receivables to the amount of cash expected to be realized from them in the future and the allocation to the current period of the expected expense resulting from such reduction. The adjusting entry debits Bad Debt Expense and credits Allowance for Doubtful Accounts. When an account is believed to be uncollectible, it is written off against the allowance account.

When the estimate of uncollectibles is based on the amount of sales for the fiscal period, the adjusting entry is made without regard to the balance of the allowance account. When the estimate of uncollectibles is based on the amount and the age of the receivable accounts at the end of the period, the adjusting entry is recorded so that the balance of the allowance account will equal the estimated uncollectibles at the end of the period.

The allowance account, which will have a credit balance after the adjusting entry has been posted, is a contra asset account. The bad debt expense is generally reported on the income statement as an administrative expense.

**2. Describe the nature and characteristics of promissory notes.**

A note is a written promise to pay a sum of money on demand or at a definite time. Characteristics of notes that affect how they are recorded and reported include the due date, interest rate, and maturity value. The basic formula for computing interest on a note is: Principal × Rate × Time = Interest. The due date is the date a note is to be paid, and the period of time between the issuance date and the due date is normally stated in either days or months. The maturity value of a note is the sum of the face amount and the interest.

**3. Journalize the entries for notes receivable transactions.**

A note received in settlement of an account receivable is recorded as a debit to Note Receivable and a credit to Accounts Receivable. When a note matures, Cash is debited, Note Receivable is credited, and Interest Revenue is credited. If the maker of a note fails to pay the debt on the due date, the note is said to be dishonored. When a note is dishonored, the maturity value of the note is debited to an accounts receivable account, while the face value is credited to Note Receivable and Interest Revenue is credited for the difference.

**4. Compute and interpret the accounts receivable turnover and the number of days' sales in receivables.**

The accounts receivable turnover is net sales divided by average accounts receivable. It measures how frequently accounts receivable are being converted into cash. The number of days' sales in receivables is the end-of-year accounts receivable divided by the average daily sales. It measures the length of time the accounts receivable have been outstanding.

## PROBLEM:

**1. Monarch Map Company's balance sheet at December 31, 2007, reported in Exhibit 9-30.**

**Exhibit 9-30 Monarch Map Company's balance sheet**

| | |
|---|---|
| Accounts receivable | 60,000 |
| Allowance for doubtful accounts | 2,000 |

### Requirements

(1) How much of the receivable did Monarch expect to collect? Stated differently what was the net realizable value of these receivables?

(2) Journalize, without explanations, 2008 entries for Monarch:

a. Total estimated Bad Debt Expense was $2,400 for the firm.

Three quarters of the year, based on the percent-of-sales method.

b. Write-offs of accounts receivable totaled $2,700.

c. December 31, 2008, aging of receivable indicates that $2,200 of the receivables is uncollectible.

Prepare a T-account for Allowance for Doubtful Accounts, as shown in Exhibit 9-31.

**Exhibit 9-31 Allowance for doubtful accounts**

| | |
|---|---|
| 2008 Write-offs ? | Dec. 31, 2007 Bal. 2,000<br>2008 Expense ? |
| | Bal. before Adj.<br>Dec. 31, 2008 Adj. ? |
| | Dec. 31, 2008 Bal. 2,200 |

Post all three transactions to the allowance account.

(3) Report Monarch's receivable and related allowance on the December 31, 2008, balance sheet. Accounts receivable total $63,000.

What is the net realizable value of receivables at December 31, 2008?

How much is bad debt expense for 2008?

**Solution**

Requirement (1).

| | |
|---|---|
| Net realizable value of receivables ($60,000 − $2,000) | $58,000 |

Requirement (2).

| | | |
|---|---|---|
| a. Bad Debt Expense | $2,400 | |
| Allowance for Doubtful Accounts | | $2,400 |
| b. Allowance for Doubtful Accounts | $2,700 | |
| Accounts Receivable | | $2,700 |
| c. Bad Debt Expense ($2,200 − $1,700) | $500 | |
| Allowance for Doubtful Accounts | | $500 |

**Allowance for Doubtful Accounts**

| | | | |
|---|---|---|---|
| 2008 Write-offs | $2,700 | Dec. 31, 2007 Bal.<br>2008 Expense | $2,000<br>$2,400 |
| | | Bal. before Adj.<br>Dec. 31, 2008 Adj. | $1,700<br>$500 |
| | | Dec. 31, 2008 Bal. | $2,200 |

Requirement (3).

| | |
|---|---|
| Accounts receivable | $63,000 |
| Less: Allowance for doubtful accounts | $2,200 |
| Accounts receivable, net | $60,800 |
| Bad debt expense for 2008 ($2,400 + $500) | $2,900 |

**2. Suppose First Fidelity Bank engaged in the following transactions.**

2007

Apr. 1 Loaned out $8,000 to Bland Co. Received a six-month, 10% note.

Oct. 1 Collected the Bland note at maturity.

Dec. 1 Loaned $6,000 to Flores, Inc., on a 180-day, 12% note.

Dec. 31 Accrued interest revenue on theFlores note.

2008

May 30 Collected the Flores note at maturity.

First Fidelity Bank's accounting period ends on December 31.

Requirements (Explanations are not needed. Use a 360-day year to compute interest.)

(1) Record the 2007 transactions on April 1 through December 1 on Fidelity's books.

(2) Make the adjusting entry needed on December 31, 2007.

(3) Record the May 30, 2008, collection of theFlores note.

Solution

Requirement(1). The 2007 transactions on April 1 through December 1 on Fidelity's books are shown in the Exhibit 9-32.

**Exhibit 9-32 The 2007 transactions on April 1 through December 1 on Fidelity's books**

| 2007 | | | |
|---|---|---|---|
| Apr. 1 | Note receivable—Bland Co. | 8,000 | |
| | Cash | | 8,000 |
| Oct. 1 | Cash($8,000 + $400) | 8,400 | |
| | Note Receivable—Bland Co. | | 8,000 |
| | Interest Revenue($8,000 × 10% × 6months/12months) | | 400 |
| Dec. 1 | Note Receivable—Flores, Inc. | 6,000 | |
| | Cash | | 6,000 |

Requirement(2). The adjusting entry needed on December 31, 2007 is shown in the Exhibit 9-33.

**Exhibit 9-33 The adjusting entry needed on December 31, 2007**

| 2007 | | | |
|---|---|---|---|
| Dec. 31 | Interest Receivable | 60 | |
| | Interest Revenue($6,000 × 12% × 30days/360days) | | 60 |

Requirement (3). The collection of the Flores note on May 30, 2008 is shown in the Exhibit 9-34.

**Exhibit 9-34 The collection of the Flores note on May 30,2008**

| 2008 | | | |
|---|---|---|---|
| May. 30 | Cash( $6,000 + ( $6,000 × 12% × 180days/360 days)) | 6,360 | |
| | Note Receivable—Flores, Inc. | | 6,000 |
| | Interest Receivable | | 60 |
| | Interest Revenue( $6,000 × 12% × 150days/360days) | | 300 |

# Chapter 10

## Fixed Assets and Intangible Assets

**Objectives**

1. Define, classify, and account for the cost of fixed assets.
2. Compute depreciation using straight-line method, units-of-production method, and double-declining-balance method.
3. Journalize entries for the disposal of fixed assets.
4. Compute depletion and journalize the entry for depletion.
5. Describe the accounting for intangible assets.
6. Describe the presentation of fixed assets and intangible assets in financial statement.

# 1. Nature of Fixed Assets

Fixed assets such as equipment, furniture, tools, machinery, buildings, and land are long-term or relatively permanent assets. They are tangible assets because they exist physically. They are owned and used by the business and are not offered for sale as part of normal operations. Other descriptive titles for these assets are plant assets or property, plant, and equipment.

The fixed assets can be a significant part of the total assets. Exhibit 10-1 shows the percent of fixed assets to total assets for some select companies, divided between service, manufacturing, and merchandising firms. As you can see, the fixed assets for most firms comprise a significant proportion of their total assets. In contrast, Computer Associates International, Inc., is a consulting firm that relies less on fixed assets to deliver value to customers.

**Exhibit 10-1 Fixed assets as a percent of total assets—selected companies**

| | |
|---|---|
| Service Firms: | |
| Computer AssociatesInternational Inc. | 6% |
| Marriott International Inc. | 31% |
| Verizon Communications | 45% |
| Manufacturing Firms: | |
| Alcoa Inc. | 40% |
| FordMotor Company | 35% |
| ExxonMobil Corporation | 60% |
| Merchandising Firms: | |
| Kroger | 55% |
| Walgreen Co. | 46% |
| Wal-Mart | 53% |

## CLASSIFYING COSTS

Exhibit 10-2 displays questions on classifying costs. If the purchased item is long-lived, then it should be capitalized, which means it should appear on the balance sheet as an asset. Otherwise, the cost should be reported as an expense on the income statement. Capitalized costs are normally expected to last more than a year. If the asset is also used for a productive purpose, which involves a repeated use or benefit, then it should be classified as a fixed asset, such as land, buildings, or equipment. An asset does not need to be used regularly to be a fixed asset. For example, standby equipment for use in the event of a breakdown of regular equipment or for use only during peak periods is included in fixed assets. Fixed assets that have been abandoned or are no longer used should not be classified as fixed assets.

**Exhibit 10-2 Classifying costs**

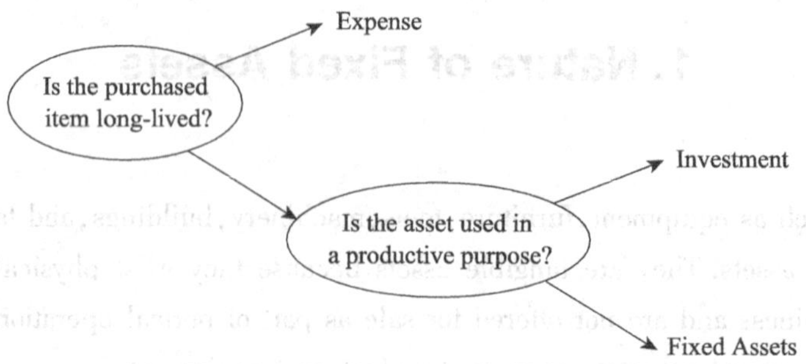


Fixed assets are owned and used by the business and are not offered for resale. Long-lived assets held for resale are not classified as fixed assets, but should be listed on the balance sheet in a section entitled Investments. For example, undeveloped land acquired as an investment for resale would be classified as an investment, not land.

## THE COST OF FIXED ASSETS

The costs of acquiring fixed assets include all amounts to get the asset in place and ready for use. The direct costs associated with new construction, such as labor and materials, should be debited to a "construction in progress" asset account. When the construction is complete, the costs should be reclassified by crediting the construction in progress account and debiting the appropriate fixed asset account. For growing companies, construction in progress can be significant.

Exhibit 10-3 summarizes some of the common costs of acquiring fixed assets. These costs should be recorded by debiting the related fixed asset account, such as Machinery&Equipment, Land, or Building.

**Exhibit 10-3 Costs of acquiring fixed assets**

| Building | Machinery&Equipment | Land |
|---|---|---|
| Permits from government agencies | Modifying for use | Title fees |
| Modifying for use | Freight | Paving a public street bordering |
| Reconditioning (purchase of existing building) | Assembly | Permits from government agencies |
| Repairs (purchase of existing building) | Permits from government agencies | Removing unwanted buildings, less any salvage |
| Walkways to and around the building | Reconditioning (purchase of used equipment) | Purchase price |
| Engineers' fees | Insurance while in transit | Surveying fees |
| Interest on money borrowed to finance construction | Installation | Delinquent real estate taxes |
| Insurance costs incurred during construction | Sales taxes | Broker's commissions |
| Sales taxes | Testing for use | Grading and leveling |
| Architects' fees | Repairs (purchase of used equipment) | Sales taxes |

## CAPITAL AND REVENUE EXPENDITURES

Expenditures on fixed asset may be incurred for ordinary maintenance and repairs. In addition, expenditures may be incurred for improving an asset or for extraordinary repairs that extend the asset's useful life. Expenditures that benefit only the current period are called revenue expenditures. Expenditures that improve the asset or extend its useful life are capital expenditures.

### Ordinary Maintenance and Repairs

Expenditures related to the ordinary maintenance and repairs of a fixed asset are recorded as an expense of the current period. Such expenditures are revenue expenditures and are recorded as increases to Repairs and Maintenance Expense. For example, $500 paid for a tune-up of a delivery truck would be recorded in Exhibit 10-4.

**Exhibit 10-4 Journal entry for ordinary maintenance and repairs**

| Description | Debit | Credit |
|---|---|---|
| Repairs and Maintenance Expense | 500 | |
| Cash | | 500 |

### Asset Improvements

After a fixed asset has been placed in service, expenditures may be incurred to improve an asset. For example, the service value of a delivery truck might be improved by adding a $6,500 hydraulic lift to allow for easier and quicker loading of heavy cargo. Such expenditures are capital expenditures and are recorded as increases to the fixed asset account. In the case of the hydraulic lift, the expenditure is recorded in Exhibit 10-5.

**Exhibit 10-5 Journal entry for asset improvement**

| Description | Debit | Credit |
|---|---|---|
| Delivery Truck | 6 500 | |
| Cash | | 6 500 |

Because the cost of the delivery truck has increased, depreciation for the truck would also change over its remaining useful life.

### Extraordinary Repairs

Expenditures may be incurred to extend the asset's useful life. For example, the engine of a forklift that is near the end of its useful life may be overhauled at a cost of $5,500, which would extend its useful life by eight years. Such expenditures are capital expenditures and are recorded as a decrease in an accumulated depreciation account. In the case of the forklift, the expenditure is recorded in Exhibit 10-6.

**Exhibit 10-6 Journal entry of extraordinary repairs**

| Description | Debit | Credit |
|---|---|---|
| Accumulated Depreciation—Forklift | 5 500 | |
| Cash | | 5 500 |

Because the forklift's remaining useful life has changed, depreciation for the forklift would also change based upon the new book value of the forklift.

The accounting for revenue and capital expenditures is summarized in Exhibit 10-7.

**Exhibit 10-7 The accounting for revenue and capital expenditures**

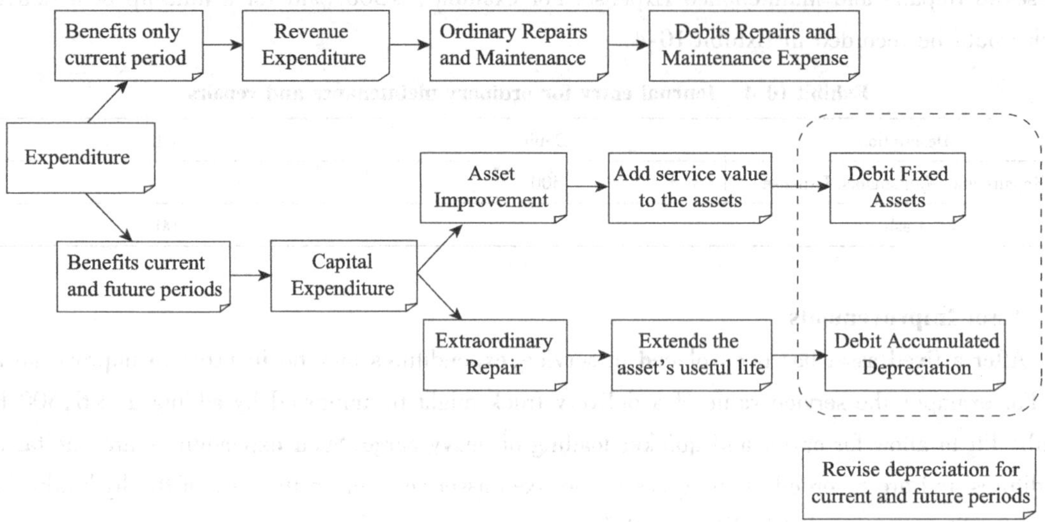


## LEASING FIXED ASSETS

A lease is a contract for the use of an asset for a stated period of time. Leases are frequently used in business. For example, automobiles, computers, medical equipment, buildings, and airplanes are often leased.

The two parties to a lease contract are the lessor and the lessee. The lessor is the party who owns the asset. The lessee is the party to whom the rights to use the asset are granted by the lessor. The lessee is obligated to make periodic rent payments for the lease term. All leases are classified by the lessee as either capital leases or operating leases.

A capital lease is accounted for as if the lessee has, in fact, purchased the asset. The lessee debits an asset account for the fair market value of the asset and credits a long-term lease liability account. The asset is then written off as expense (amortized) over the life of the capital lease. The accounting for capital leases and the criteria that a capital lease must satisfy are discussed in more advanced accounting texts.

A lease that is not classified as a capital lease is classified as anoperating lease. The lessee records the payments under an operating lease by debiting Rent Expense and crediting Cash. Neither future lease obligations nor the future rights to use the leased asset are recognized in the accounts. However, the lessee must disclose future lease commitments in notes to the financial statements.

The asset rentals described in earlier chapters of this text were accounted for as operating leases. To simplify, we will continue to treat asset leases as operating leases.

# 2. Accounting for Depreciation

Land has an unlimited life and therefore can provide unlimited services. On the other hand, other fixed assets such as equipment, buildings, and land improvements lose their ability, over time, to provide services. As a result, the costs of equipment, buildings, and land improvements should be transferred to expense accounts in a systematic manner during their expected useful lives. This periodic transfer of cost to expense is called depreciation.

The adjusting entry to record depreciation is usually made at the end of each month or at the end of the year. This entry debits Depreciation Expense and credits a contra asset account entitled Accumulated Depreciation or Allowance for Depreciation. The use of a contra asset account allows the original cost to remain unchanged in the fixed asset account.

Factors that cause a decline in the ability of a fixed asset to provide services may be identified as physical depreciation or functional depreciation. Physical depreciation occurs from wear and tear while in use and from the action of the weather. Functional depreciation occurs when a fixed asset is no longer able to provide services at the level for which it was intended. For example, a personal computer made in the 1980s would not be able to provide an Internet connection. Such advances in technology during this century have made functional depreciation anincreasingly important cause of depreciation.

The amount of a fixed asset's unexpired cost reported in the balance sheet usually does not agree with the amount that could be realized from its sale. Fixed assets are held for use in a business rather than for sale. It is assumed that the business will continue as a going concern. Thus, a decision to dispose of a fixed asset is based mainly on the usefulness of the asset to the business and not on its market value.

Another common misunderstanding is that accounting for depreciation provides cash needed to replace fixed assets as they wear out. This misunderstanding probably occurs because depreciation, unlike most expenses, does not require an outlay of cash in the period in which it is recorded. The cash account is neither increased nor decreased by the periodic entries that transfer the cost of fixed assets to depreciation expense accounts.

## FACTORS IN COMPUTING DEPRECIATION EXPENSE

Three factors are considered in determining the amount of depreciation expense to be recognized each period. These three factors are the fixed asset's initial cost, its expected useful life, and its estimated value at the end of its useful life. This third factor is called the residual value, scrap value, salvage value, or trade-in value.

Estimated residual value—scrap value or salvage value—is the expected cash value of an asset at the end of its useful life. For example, FedEx may believe that a package-handling machine will be useful for 7 years. After that time, FedEx may expect to sell the machine as scrap metal. The amount FedEx believes it can get for the machine is the estimated residual value. In computing depreciation, the estimated residual value is not depreciated because FedEx expects to receive this amount from selling the asset. If there's no expected residual value, the full cost of the asset is depreciated. Exhibit 10-8 shows the relationship among the three factors and the periodic depreciation expense.

**Exhibit 10-8 Depreciation expense factors**

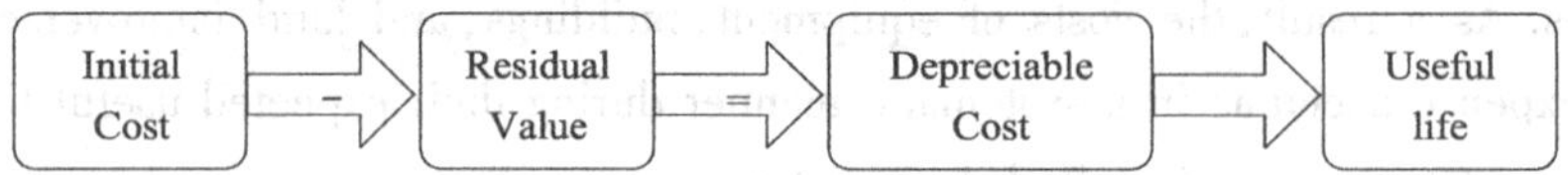


Estimates of expected useful lives are available from various trade associations and other publications. For federal income tax purposes, the Internal Revenue Service has established guidelines for useful lives. These guidelines may also be helpful in determining depreciation for financial reporting purposes. However, it is common for different companies to use a different useful life for similar assets.

In practice, many businesses use the guideline that all assets placed in or taken out of service during the first half of a month are treated as if the event occurred on the first day of that month. That is, these businesses compute depreciation on these assets for the entire month. Likewise, all fixed asset additions and deductions during the second half of a month are treated as if the event occurred on the first day of the next month. We will follow this practice in this chapter.

A business can use the different methods of computing depreciation for all its depreciable assets. The methods used in the accounts and financial statements may also differ from the methods used in determining income taxes and property taxes. The three methods used most often are straight-line, units-of-production, and double-declining-balance. Exhibit 10-9 shows the extent of the use of these methods in financial statements.

**Exhibit 10-9 Use of depreciation methods**

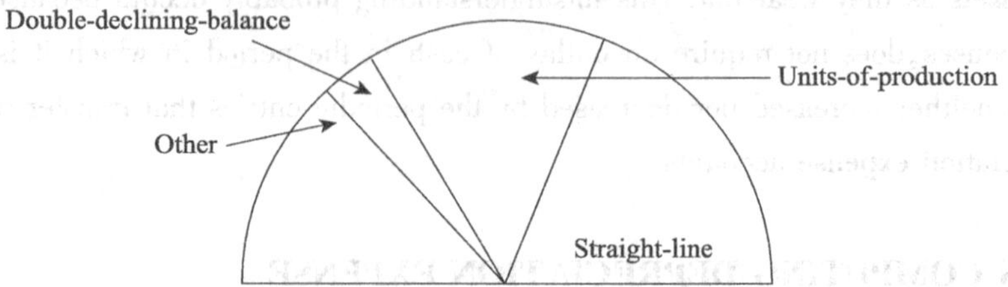

## STRAIGHT-LINE METHOD

In the straight-line (SL) method, an equal amount of depreciation is assigned to each year (or period) of asset use. Depreciable cost is divided by useful life in years to determine the annual depreciation expense. Applied to the FedEx truck data, straight-line depreciation is computed as follows.

$$\text{Straight-line depreciation per year} = \frac{\text{Cost} - \text{Residual value}}{\text{Useful life, in years}}$$

$$= \frac{\$41,000 - \$1,000}{5}$$

$$= \$8,000$$

The entry to record depreciation is Dr. Depreciation Expense $8,000, Cr. Accumulated Depreciation $8,000. Observe that depreciation decreases the asset (through Accumulated Depreciation) and also decreases equity (through Depreciation Expense). Let's assume that FedEx purchased this truck on Jan. 1, 20×3. Assume that FedEx's accounting year ends on Dec. 31. The final column of the Exhibit 10-10 shows the asset's book value, which is cost less accumulated depreciation. The asset's book value at end of year, which is the asset's book value at beginning of year minus current depreciation for year.

**Exhibit 10-10 The straight-line depreciation**

| Year | Cost | Accum. Depr. at Beginning of Year | Book Value at Beginning of Year | Depreciation for Year | Book Value at End of Year |
|---|---|---|---|---|---|
| 1 | 41,000 | | 41,000.00 | 8,000.00 | 33,000.00 |
| 2 | 41,000 | 8,000.00 | 33,000.00 | 8,000.00 | 25,000.00 |
| 3 | 41,000 | 16,000.00 | 25,000.00 | 8,000.00 | 17,000.00 |
| 4 | 41,000 | 24,000.00 | 17,000.00 | 8,000.00 | 9,000.00 |
| 5 | 41,000 | 32,000.00 | 9,000.00 | 8,000.00 | 1,000.00 |

## UNITS-OF-PRODUCTION METHOD

When the amount of use of a fixed asset varies from year to year, the units-of-production method is more appropriate than the straight-line method. In such cases, the units-of-production method better matches the depreciation expense with the related revenue.

The units-of-production method provides for the same amount of depreciation expense for each unit produced or each unit of capacity used by the asset. To apply this method, the useful life of the asset is expressed in terms of units of productive capacity such as hours or miles. The total depreciation expense for each accounting period is then determined by multiplying the unit depreciation by the number of units produced or used during the period. For example, assume that a machine with a cost of $25,000 and an estimated residual value of $2,000 is expected to have an estimated life of 10,000 operating hours. The depreciation for a unit of one hour is computed as follows.

$$\frac{\$25,000 \text{ cost} - \$2,000 \text{ estimated residual value}}{10,000 \text{ estimated hours}} = \$2.30 \text{ hourly depreciation}$$

Assuming that the machine was in operation for 2,100 hours during a year, the depreciation for that year would be \$4,830(\$2.30 ×2,100 hours).

## DOUBLE-DECLINING-BALANCE METHOD

The double-declining-balance method provides for a declining periodic expense over the estimated useful life of the asset. In using this method, a double-declining-balance rate is determined by doubling the straight-line rate. To illustrate, assume that an asset has a useful life of four years. The double-declining-balance rate of 50% is determined as shown below.

Double-Declining-Balance Rate = Straight-Line Rate ×2
= (1/4) ×2 =25% ×2 =50%

For the first year of use, the cost of the asset is multiplied by the double-declining- balance rate. After the first year, the declining book value(cost minus accumulated depreciation) of the asset is multiplied by this rate. To illustrate, the annual double- declining-balance depreciation for an asset with an estimated four-year life and a cost of \$36,000 is shown in Exhibit 10-11.

**Exhibit 10-11 The annual double- declining-balance depreciation**

| Year | Cost | Accum. Depr. at Beginning of Year | Book Value at Beginning of Year | Double Declining Balance Rate | Depreciation for Year | Book Value at End of Year |
|---|---|---|---|---|---|---|
| 1 | 36,000 | | 36,000.00 | 50% | 18,000.00 | 18,000.00 |
| 2 | 36,000 | 18,000.00 | 18,000.00 | 50% | 9,000.00 | 9,000.00 |
| 3 | 36,000 | 27,000.00 | 9,000.00 | 50% | 4,500.00 | 4,500.00 |
| 4 | 36,000 | 31,500.00 | 4,500.00 | 50% | 2,250.00 | 2,250.00 |

We assumed that the first use of the asset occurred at the beginning of the fiscal year. This is normally not the case in practice, however, and depreciation for the first partial year of use must be computed. For example, assume that the asset above was in service at the end of the third month of the fiscal year. In this case, only a portion(9/12) of the first full year's depreciation of \$18,000 is allocated to the first fiscal year. Thus, depreciation of \$13,500(9/12 × \$18,000) is allocated to the first partial year of use. The depreciation for the second fiscal year would then be \$11,250 (50% × (\$36,000 - \$13,500)).

## COMPARING DEPRECIATION METHODS

The differences among the three depreciation methods are summarized in Exhibit 10-12. All three methods assign a portion of the total cost of an asset to an accounting period, while never depreciating an asset below its residual value.

**Exhibit 10-12 Summary of depreciation methods**

| Method | Useful Life | Depreciable Cost | Depreciation Rate | Depreciation Expense |
|---|---|---|---|---|
| Straight-line | Years | Costless residualvalue | Straight-linerate | Constant |
| Units-of-production | Totalestimated units of production | Costless residualvalue | (Cost − Residual value)/Total estimated units of production | Variable |
| Double-declining-balance | Years | Decliningbook value, but not below residual value | Straight-linerate × 2 | Declining |

Generally Accepted Accounting Principles(GAAP) say to match an asset's depreciation against the revenue the asset produces. For a plant asset that generates revenue evenly over time, the straight-line method best meets the matching principle.

The units-of-production method best fits those assets that wear out because of physical use rather than obsolescence. The double-declining balance method applies best to assets that generate more revenue earlier in their useful lives and less in later years.

## DEPRECIATION FOR FEDERAL INCOME TAX

Most other companies use straight-line depreciation for reporting to stockholders and creditors on their financial statements. But for their income taxes they also keep a separate set of depreciation records. For tax purposes, FedEx and most other companies use an accelerated depreciation method (Double-declining-balance method). This is legal, ethical, and honest. U. S. law permits it.

Suppose you are a business manager, and the Internal Revenue Service(IRS) allows an accelerated depreciation method. Why do FedEx managers prefer accelerated over straight-line depreciation for income-tax purposes? Accelerated depreciation provides the fastest tax deductions, thus decreasing immediate tax payments. FedEx can reinvest the tax savings back in the business. FedEx has a choice—pay taxes or buy equipment. This choice is easy.

For income-tax purposes, accelerated depreciation helps conserve cash for the business. That's why virtually all companies use accelerated depreciation to compute their income tax.

There is a special depreciation method, used only for income tax purposes, called the Modified Accelerated Cost Recovery System(MACRS). Under MACRS assets are grouped into 1 of 8 classesidentified by asset life. Depreciation for the first 4 classes is computed by the double-declining-balance method. Depreciation for 15-year assets and 20-year assets is computed by the 150%-declining-balance method. Under 150%-declining-balance, annual depreciation is computed by multiplying the straight-line rate by 1.50(instead of 2.00, as for double-declining-balance).

## REVISING DEPRECIATION ESTIMATES

Revising the estimates of the residual value and the useful life is normal. When these estimates are revised, they are used to determine the depreciation expense in future periods. They do not affect the amounts of depreciation expense recorded in earlier years.

To illustrate, assume that a fixed asset purchased for \$160,000 was originally estimated to have a useful life of five years and a residual value of \$10,000. The asset has been depreciated for two years by the straight-line method at a rate of \$30,000 per year ((\$160,000 - \$10,000)/5 years). At the end of two years, the asset's book value (undepreciated cost) is \$100,000, determined as follows.

| | |
|---|---|
| Asset cost | \$160,000 |
| Lessaccumulated depreciation (\$30,000 per year × 2 years) | \$60,000 |
| Book value (undepreciated cost), end of second year | \$100,000 |

During the third year, the company estimates that the remaining useful life is eight years (instead of three) and that the residual value is \$4,000 (instead of \$10,000). The depreciation expense for each of the remaining eight years is \$12,000, computed as follows.

| | |
|---|---|
| Book value (undepreciated cost), end of second year | \$100,000 |
| Less revised estimated residual value | \$4,000 |
| Revised remaining depreciable cost | \$96,000 |
| Revised annual depreciation expense (\$96,000 ÷ 8 years) | \$12,000 |

Notice that the book value declines at a slower rate beginning at the end of year 2 and continuing until it reaches the residual value of \$4,000 at the end of year 10, which is the revised end of the asset's useful life.

## 3. Disposal of Fixed Assets

The details of the entry to record fixed assets discarded, sold, or traded for other fixed assets will vary. In all cases, however, the book value of the asset must be removed from the accounts. The entry for this purpose debits the asset's accumulated depreciation account for its balance on the date of disposal and credits the asset account for the cost of the asset.

A fixed asset should not be removed from the accounts only because it has been fully depreciated. If the asset is still used by the business, the cost and accumulated depreciation should remain in the ledger. This maintains accountability for the asset in the ledger. If the book value of the asset was removed from the ledger, the accounts would contain no evidence of the continued existence of the asset. In addition, the cost and the accumulated depreciation data on such assets are often needed for property tax and income tax reports.

### DISCARDING FIXED ASSETS

When fixed assets are no longer useful to the business and have no residual or market value, they are discarded. To illustrate, assume that an item of equipment acquired at a cost of $26,000 is fully depreciated at December 31, the end of the preceding fiscal year. On February 15, the equipment is discarded. The entry to record this is as shown in Exhibit 10-13.

**Exhibit 10-13 Entry to write off the discarding fixed asset**

| Date | | Description | Debit | Credit |
|---|---|---|---|---|
| Feb. | 15 | Accumulated Depreciation—Equipment | 26 000 | |
| | | Equipment | | 26 000 |
| | | To write off equipment discarded | | |

Depreciation should be recorded prior to removing it from service and from the accounting records if an asset has not been fully depreciated. To illustrate, assume that equipment costing $6,000 with no estimated residual value is depreciated at an annual straight-line rate of 10%. In addition, assume that on December 31 of the preceding fiscal year, the accumulated depreciation balance, after adjusting entries, is $4,750. Finally, assume that the asset is removed from service on the following March 25. The entry to record the depreciation for the three months of the current period prior to the asset's removal from service is as shown in Exhibit 10-14.

**Exhibit 10-14 Entry to record the depreciation before removing it from service**

| Date | | Description | Debit | Credit |
|---|---|---|---|---|
| Mar. | 25 | Depreciation Expense—Equipment | 150 | |
| | | Accumulated Depreciation—Equipment | | 150 |
| | | To record current depreciation on equipment discarded( $ 600/12 ×3) | | |

The discarding of the equipment is then recorded in Exhibit 10-15.

**Exhibit 10-15 Record the discarding equipment**

| Date | | Description | Debit | Credit |
|---|---|---|---|---|
| Mar. | 25 | Accumulated Depreciation—Equipment | 4 900 | |
| | | Loss on Disposal of Fixed Assets | 1 100 | |
| | | Equipment | | 6 000 |
| | | To write off equipment discarded | | |

The loss of $1,100 is recorded because the balance of the accumulated depreciation account ($4,900) is less than the balance in the equipment account($6,000). Losses on the discarding offixed assets are non-operating items and are normally reported in the Other Expense section of the income statement.

## SELLING FIXED ASSETS

The entry to record the sale of a fixed asset is similar to the entries illustrated above, except that the cash or other asset received must also be recorded. If the selling price is more than the book value of the asset, the transaction results in a gain. If the selling price is less than the book value, there is a loss.

Assume that equipment is acquired at a cost of $12,000 with no estimated residual value and is depreciated at an annual straight-line rate of 10%. The equipment is sold for cash on October 12 of the eighth year of its use. The balance of the accumulated depreciation account as of the preceding December 31 is $8,400. The entry to update the depreciation for the nine months of the current year is as shown in Exhibit 10-16.

**Exhibit 10-16 Record the depreciation for the nine months of current year**

| Date | | Description | Debit | Credit |
|---|---|---|---|---|
| Oct. | 12 | Depreciation Expense—Equipment | 900 | |
| | | Accumulated Depreciation—Equipment | | 900 |
| | | To record current depreciation on equipment sold ( $12,000 ×9/12 ×10% ) | | |

After the current depreciation is recorded, the book value of the asset is $2,700( $12,000 - $9,300). The entries to record the sale, assuming three different selling prices, are as shown in Exhibit 10-17.

**Exhibit 10-17 Entry to sell the equipment at three different prices**

| Date | | Description | Debit | Credit |
|---|---|---|---|---|
| Oct. | 12 | Cash | 2 700 | |
| | | Accumulated Depreciation—Equipment | 9 300 | |
| | | Equipment | | 12 000 |
| Date | | Description | Debit | Credit |
| Oct. | 12 | Cash | 1 300 | |
| | | Accumulated Depreciation—Equipment | 9 300 | |
| | | Loss on Disposal of Fixed Assets | 1 400 | |
| | | Equipment | | 12 000 |
| Date | | Description | Debit | Credit |
| Oct. | 12 | Cash | 3 000 | |
| | | Accumulated Depreciation—Equipment | 9 300 | |
| | | Equipment | | 12 000 |
| | | Gain on Disposal of Fixed Assets | | 300 |

## EXCHANGING SIMILAR FIXED ASSETS

Old equipment is often traded in for new equipment having a similar use. The seller allows the buyer an amount for the old equipment traded in. This amount, called the trade-in allowance, may be either greater or less than the book value of the old equipment. The remaining balance—the amount owed—is either paid in cash or recorded as a liability. It is normally called boot, which is its tax name.

**Gains on Exchanges**

Gains on exchanges of similar fixed assets are not recognized for financial reporting purposes. This is based on the theory that revenue occurs from the production and sale of goods produced by fixed assets and not from the exchange of similar fixed assets.

When the trade-in allowance exceeds the book value of an asset traded in and no gain is recognized, the cost recorded for the new asset can be determined in either of two ways.

(1) Cost of new asset = List price of new asset − Unrecognized gain

(2) Cost of new asset = Cash given (or liability assumed) + Book value of old asset

To illustrate, assume the following exchange.

Similar equipment acquired (new):

List price of new equipment ........ $5,000

Trade-in allowance on old equipment ........ $1,100

Cash paid at June 19, date of exchange ........ $3,900

Equipment traded in (old):

Cost of old equipment ........ $4,000

Accumulated depreciation at date of exchange ........ $3,200

Book value at June 19, date of exchange ........ $800

Recorded cost of new equipment:

Method One:

List price of new equipment ........ $5,000

Trade-in allowance ........ $1,100

Book value of old equipment ........ $800

Unrecognized gain on exchange ........ $300

Cost of new equipment ........ $4,700

Method Two:

Book value of old equipment ........ $800

Cash paid at date of exchange ........ $3,900

Cost of new equipment ........ $4,700

The entry to record this exchange and the payment of cash is as shown in Exhibit 10-18.

**Exhibit 10-18 Entry to record the exchange of equipment**

| Date | | Description | Debit | Credit |
|---|---|---|---|---|
| June | 19 | Accumulated Depreciation—Equipment | 3 200 | |
| | | Equipment (new equipment) | 4 700 | |
| | | Equipment (old equipment) | | 4 000 |
| | | Cash | | 3 900 |
| | | To record exchange of equipment | | |

Not recognizing the $300 gain ($1,100 trade-in allowance minus $800 book value) at the time of the exchange reduces future depreciation expense. That is, the depreciation expense for the new asset is based on a cost of $4,700 rather than on the list price of $5,000. In effect, the unrecognized gain of $300 reduces the total amount of depreciation taken during the life of the equipment by $300.

**Losses on Exchanges**

For financial reporting purposes, losses are recognized on ex changes of similar fixed assets if the trade-in allowance is less than the book value of the old equipment. When there is a loss, the cost recorded for the new asset should be the market (list) price. To illustrate, assume the following exchange.

Similar equipment acquired (new):
List price of new equipment ........ $10,000
Trade-in allowance on old equipment ........ $2,000
Cash paid at September 7, date of exchange ........ $8,000

Equipment traded in (old):
Cost of old equipment ........ $7,000
Accumulated depreciation at date of exchange ........ $4,600
Book value at September 7, date of exchange ........ $2,400
Trade-in allowance on old equipment ........ $2,000
Loss on exchange ........ $400

The entry to record the exchange is as shown in Exhibit 10-19.

**Exhibit 10-19 Entry to record exchange of equipment with loss**

| Date | | Description | Debit | Credit |
|---|---|---|---|---|
| Sept. | 7 | Accumulated Depreciation—Equipment | 4 600 | |
| | | Equipment | 10 000 | |
| | | Loss on Disposal of Fixed Assets | 400 | |

(Continued)

| Date | | Description | Debit | Credit |
|---|---|---|---|---|
| | | Equipment | | 7 000 |
| | | Cash | | 8 000 |
| | | To record exchange of equipment with loss | | |

**Review of Accounting for Exchanges of Similar Fixed Assets**

Exhibit 10-20 reviews the accounting for exchanges of similar fixed assets, using the following data.

List price of new equipment acquired ································ $ 15,000
Cost of old equipment traded in ································ $ 12,500
Accumulated depreciation at date of exchange ······················ $ 10,100
Book value at date of exchange ································ $ 2,400

**Exhibit 10-20 Accounting for exchanges of similar fixed assets**

| CASE ONE(GAIN): Trade-in allowance is more than book value of asset traded in | | |
|---|---|---|
| Trade-in allowance, $ 3,000; cash paid, $ 12,000( $ 15,000- $ 3,000) | | |
| Cost of new asset | List price of new asset acquired, less unrecognized gain:<br>$ 14,400( $ 15,000-( $ 3,000- $ 2,400))<br>or<br>Cash paid plus book value of asset traded in:<br>$ 14,400( $ 12,000 + $ 2,400) | |
| Gain recognized | None | |
| Entry | Equipment<br>Accumulated Depreciation<br>Equipment<br>Cash | 14,400<br>10,100<br>12,500<br>12,000 |
| CASE TWO(LOSS): Trade-in allowance is less than book value of asset traded in | | |
| Trade-in allowance, $ 2,000; cash paid, $ 13,000( $ 15,000- $ 2,000) | | |
| Cost of new asset | List price of new asset acquired:<br>$ 15,000 | |
| Loss recognized | $ 400 | |
| Entry | Equipment<br>Accumulated Depreciation<br>Loss on Disposal of Fixed Assets<br>Equipment<br>Cash | 15,000<br>10,100<br>400<br>12,500<br>13,000 |

## 4. Natural Resources

A portion of the cost of acquiring timber, metal ores, minerals, or other natural resources must be debited to an expense account. This process of transferring the cost of natural resources to an expense account is called depletion. The amount of depletion is determined by multiplying the quantity extracted during the period by the depletion rate. This rate is computed by dividing the cost of the mineral deposit by its estimated size.

Computing depletion is similar to computing units-of-production depreciation. To illustrate, assume that a business paid $400,000 for the mining rights to a mineral deposit estimated at 1,000,000 tons of ore. The depletion rate is $0.40 per ton($400,000/1,000,000 tons). If 80,000 tons are mined during the year, the periodic depletion is $32,000(80,000 tons × $0.40). The adjusting entry to record the depletion is shown in Exhibit 10-21.

**Exhibit 10-21 The adjusting entry to record the depletion**

| Date | | Description | Debit | Credit |
|---|---|---|---|---|
| Dec. | 31 | Depletion Expense | 32 000 | |
| | | Accumulated Depletion | | 32 000 |
| | | Depletion of mineral deposit | | |

Like the accumulated depreciation account, Accumulated Depletion is a contra asset account. It is reported on the balance sheet as a deduction from the cost of the mineral deposit.

## 5. Intangible Assets

Patents, copyrights, trademarks, and goodwill are long-lived assets that are useful in the operations of a business and are not held for sale. These assets are calledintangible assets because they do not exist physically.

The basic principles of accounting for intangible assets are like those described earlier for fixed assets. The major concerns are determining the initial cost and the amortization—the amount of cost to transfer to expense. Amortization results from the passage of time or a decline in the usefulness of the intangible asset.

### PATENTS

Manufacturers may acquire exclusive rights to produce and sell goods with one or more unique features. Such rights are granted by patents, which the federal government issues to inventors. These rights continue in effect for 20 years. A business may purchase patent rights from others, or it may obtain patents developed by its own research and development efforts.

The initial cost of a purchased patent, including any related legal fees, is debited to an asset account. This cost is written off, or amortized, over the years of the patent's expected usefulness. This period of time may be less than the remaining legal life of the patent. The estimated useful life of the patent may also change as technology or consumer tastes change.

The straight-line method is normally used to determine the periodic amortization. When the amortization is recorded, it is debited to an expense account and credited directly to the patents account. A separate contra asset account is usually not used for intangible assets.

Assume that at the beginning of its fiscal year, a business acquires patent rights for $200,000. The patent had been granted six years earlier by the Federal Patent Office. Although the patent will not expire for 14 years, its remaining useful life is estimated as five years. The adjusting entry to amortize the patent at the end of the year is as shown in Exhibit 10-22.

**Exhibit 10-22 The adjusting entry to amortize the patent**

| Date | | Description | Debit | Credit |
|---|---|---|---|---|
| Dec. | 31 | Amortization Expense—Patents | 40 000 | |
| | | Patents | | 40 000 |
| | | Patent amortization( $200,000/5years) | | |

A business may incur significant costs in developing patents through its own research and development efforts rather than purchase patent rights. Such research and development costs are usually accounted for as current operating expenses in the period in which they are incurred. Expensing research and development costs is justified because the future benefits from research and development efforts are highly uncertain.

## COPYRIGHTS AND TRADEMARKS

### Copyrights

Copyrights are exclusive rights to reproduce and sell a book, musical composition, film, or other work of art. Copyrights also protect computer software programs, such as Microsoft's Windows ® and Excel. Issued by the federal government, copyrights extend 70 years beyond the author's (composer's, artist's, or programmer's) life. The cost of obtaining a copyright from the government is low, but a company may pay a large sum to purchase an existing copyright from the owner. For example, a publisher may pay the author of a popular novel $1 million or more for the book copyright. Because the useful life of a copyright is usually no longer than 2 or 3 years, each period's amortization amount is a high proportion of the copyright cost.

### Trademarks and Trade Names

Trademarks and trade names (or brand names) are distinctive identification of a product or service. The "eye" symbol that flashes across our television screens is the trademark that identifies the CBS television network. You are probably also familiar with NBC's peacock. Advertising slogans that are legally protected include United Airlines' "Fly the friendly skies ®" and Avis Car Rental's "We try harder ®." These are distinctive identifications of products or services, marked with the symbol™ or ®.

Some trademarks may have a definite useful life set by contract. We should amortize this trademark's cost over its useful life. But a trademark or a trade name may have an indefinite life and not be amortized.

## GOODWILL

In accounting, goodwill has a very specific meaning. Goodwill is defined as the excess of the cost of purchasing another company over the sum of the market values of the acquired

company's net assets (assets minus liabilities). A purchaser is willing to pay for goodwill when the purchaser buys another company that has abnormal earning power.

Coca-cola operates in several foreign countries. Suppose Coca-cola acquires Europa Company at a cost of $10 million. Europa Company's assets have a market value of $9 million, and its liabilities total $2 million so Europa Company's net assets total $7 million at current market value. In this case, Coca-cola paid $3 million for goodwill, computed as follows.

| | |
|---|---|
| Purchase price paid for Europa Company ································ | $10 million |
| Sum of the market values of Europa Company's assets ··················· | $9 million |
| Less: Europa Company's liabilities ········································ | $2 million |
| Market value of Europa Company's net assets ···························· | $7 million |
| Excess is called goodwill ···················································· | $ 3 million |

Coca-cola's entry to record the acquisition of Europa Company is shown in Exhibit 10-23.

**Exhibit 10-23 Entry to record the acquisition of another company**

| Description | Debit | Credit |
|---|---|---|
| Assets (Cash, Receivables, Inventories, Plant Assets, | | |
| all at market value) | 9,000,000 | |
| Goodwill | 3,000,000 | |
| Liabilities | | 2,000,000 |
| Cash | | 10,000,000 |

Goodwill in accounting has special features, as follows.

(1) Goodwill is recorded only when it is purchased in the acquisition of another company. A purchase transaction provides objective evidence of the value of goodwill. Companies never record goodwill that they create for their own business.

(2) According to Generally Accepted Accounting Principles (GAAP), goodwill is not amortized

because the goodwill of many entities increases in value.

Exhibit 10-24 compares the different intangible assets.

**Exhibit 10-24 Comparison of intangible assets**

| Intangible Asset | Description | Amortization Period | Periodic Expense |
|---|---|---|---|
| Patent | Exclusive right tobenefit from an innovation | Estimated useful life not to exceed legal life | Amortization |
| Copyright | Exclusive right tobenefit from a literary, artistic, or musical composition | Estimated useful life not to exceed legal life | Amortization expense |
| Trademark | Exclusive use of a name term, or symbol | None | Impairmentloss if fair value less than carrying value(impaired) |
| Goodwill | Excess of purchase price of a business over fair value of its net assets | None | Impairment loss ifless than carrying value(impaired) |

## 6. Financial Reporting for Fixed Assets and Intangible Assets

The amount of depreciation and amortization expense of a period should be reported separately in the income statement or disclosed in a note. A general description of the method or methods used in computing depreciation should also be reported.

The amount of each major class of fixed assets should be disclosed in the balance sheet or in notes. The related accumulated depreciation should also be disclosed, either by major class or in total. The fixed assets may be shown at their book value (cost less accumulated depreciation), which can also be described as their net amount. To illustrate, the net book value of office equipment originally costing \$125,750 with accumulated depreciation of \$86,300 is shown below.

| | |
|---|---|
| Office equipment | \$125,750 |
| Less accumulated depreciation | \$86,300 |
| Net bookvalue | \$39,450 |

If there are too many classes of fixed assets, a single amount may be presented in the balance sheet, supported by a separate detailed listing. Fixed assets are normally presented under the more descriptive caption of property, plant, and equipment.

The cost of mineral rights or ore deposits is normally shown as part of the Fixed Assets section of the balance sheet. The related accumulated depletion should also be disclosed. In some cases, the mineral rights are shown net of depletion on the face of the balance sheet, accompanied by a note that discloses the amount of the accumulated depletion.

Intangible assets are usually reported in the balance sheet in a separate section immediately following fixed assets. The balance of each major class of intangible assets should be disclosed at an amount net of amortization taken to date. Exhibit 10-25 is a partial balance sheet that shows the reporting of fixed assets and intangible assets.

**Exhibit 10-25 Fixed assets and intangible assets in the balance sheet**

| Assets | | | | |
|---|---|---|---|---|
| Total current assets | | | | 462,500 |
| | Cost | Accum. Depr. | Book Value | |
| Property, plant, and equipment: | | | | |
| Land | 30,000 | | 30,000 | |
| Buildings | 110,000 | 26,000 | 84,000 | |
| Factory equipment | 650,000 | 192,000 | 458,000 | |
| Office equipment | 120,000 | 13,000 | 107,000 | |
| | 910,000 | 231,000 | | 679,000 |
| | Cost | Accum Depr. | Book Value | |
| Mineral deposits: | | | | |
| Alaska deposit | 1,200,000 | 800,000 | 400,000 | |
| Wyoming deposit | 750,000 | 200,000 | 550,000 | |
| | 1,950,000 | 1,000,000 | | 950,000 |
| Total property, plant, and equipment | | | | 1,629,000 |
| Intangible assets: | | | | |
| Patents | | | | 75,000 |
| Goodwill | | | | 50,000 |
| Total intangible assets | | | | 125,000 |

**TERMINOLOGY:**

Accelerated Depreciation Method:加速折旧法
Amortization:摊销
Book Value:账面价值
Capital Expenditure:资本支出
Double-declining-balance Method:双倍余额递减法
Straight-line Method:直线法
Fixed Assets:固定资产
Intangible Assets:无形资产
Residual Value:残值
Units-of-production Method:生产单位法
Goodwill:商誉
Depreciation:折旧
Patent:专利
Trademark:商标

Copyright:版权

## QUESTIONS:

**1. How to define fixed assets, and list types of costs that should and should not be in cluded in the cost of a fixed asset.**

Fixed assets are long-term tangible assets that are owned by the business and are used in the normal operations of the business such as equipment, buildings, and land.

The initial cost of a fixed asset includes all amounts spent to get the asset in place and ready for use. Once an asset is placed into service, revenue and capital expenditures may be incurred. Revenue expenditures include ordinary repairs and maintenance. Capital expenditures include asset improvements and extraordinary repairs. Fixed assets may also be leased and accounted for as capital or operating leases.

**2. Define and describe depreciation.**

All fixed assets except land lose their ability to provide services and should be depreciated over time. Three factors are considered in determining depreciation: ① The fixed asset's initial cost, ② The useful life of the asset. ③ The residual value of the asset.

**3. Describe straight-line depreciation, units-of-production depreciation and double-declining balance depreciation.**

The straight-line method spreads the initial cost less the residual value equally over the useful life. The units-of-production method spreads the initial cost less the residual value equally over the units expected to be produced by the asset during its useful life. The double-declining-balance method is applied by multiplying the declining book value of the asset by twice the straight-line rate.

**4. Define, describe, and provide examples of intangible assets.**

Long-term assets such as patents, copyrights, trademarks, and goodwill that are without physical attributes but are used in the business are intangible assets. The initial cost of anintangible asset should be debited to an asset account. The cost of patents and copyrights should be amortized over the years of the asset's expected usefulness by debiting an expense account and crediting the intangible asset account. Trademarks and goodwill are not amortized, but are written down only upon impairment.

## PROBLEM:

Latte On Demand purchased a coffee drink machine on January 1, 2007, for $44,000. Expected useful life is 10 years or 100,000 drinks (assuming 3,000 units of production in 2007, 14,000 units of prodution in 2008), and residual value is $4,000. Under three depreciation methods, annual depreciation and total accumulated depreciation at the end of 2007 and 2008 are as shown in Exhibit 10-26.

**Exhibit 10-26　The depreciation under the three methods**

| Year | Method A | | Method B | | Method C | |
|---|---|---|---|---|---|---|
| | Annual Depreciation Expense | Accumulated Depreciation | Annual Depreciation Expense | Accumulated Depreciation | Annual Depreciation Expense | Accumulated Depreciation |
| 2007 | 1,200 | 1,200 | 8,800 | 8,800 | 4,000 | 4,000 |
| 2008 | 5,600 | 6,800 | 7,040 | 15,840 | 4,000 | 8,000 |

**Requirements**

1. Identify the depreciation method used in each instance, and show the equation and computation for each method (Round to the nearest dollar).

2. Assume use of the same method through 2009. Computer depreciation expense, accumulated depreciation, and asset value for 2007 through 2009 under each method, assuming 12,000 units of production in 2009.

**Solution**

Requirement 1.

Method A: Units-of-Production

$$\text{Depreciation per unit} = \frac{\$44,000 - \$4,000}{100,000\text{units}} = \$0.40$$

$$2007: \$0.40 \times 3,000 \text{ units} = \$1,200$$

$$2008: \$0.40 \times 14,000 \text{ units} = \$5,600$$

Method B: Double-Declining-Balance

$$\text{Rate} = \frac{1}{10\text{years}} \times 2 = 20\%$$

$$2007: 20\% \times \$44,000 = \$8,800$$

$$2008: 20\% \times (\$44,000 - \$8,800) = \$7,040$$

Method C: Straight-Line

$$\text{Depreciable cost} = \$44,000 - \$4,000 = \$40,000$$

$$\text{Each year: } \$40,000/10 \text{ years} = \$4,000$$

Requirement 2.

Method A: Units-of-Production

The depreciation expense, accumulated depreciation, and asset value for 2007 through 2009 under Units-of-Production is shown in Exhibit 10-27.

**Exhibit 10-27　The depreciation under units-of-production**

| Year | Annual Depreciation Expense | Accumulated Depreciation | Book Value |
|---|---|---|---|
| Start | | | 44,000 |
| 2007 | 1,200 | 1,200 | 42,800 |
| 2008 | 5,600 | 6,800 | 37,200 |
| 2009 | 4,800 | 11,600 | 32,400 |

Method B: Double-Declining-Balance

The depreciation expense, accumulated depreciation, and asset value for 2007 through 2009 under Double-Declining-Balance is shown in Exhibit 10-28.

**Exhibit 10-28 The depreciation under double-declining-balance**

| Year | Annual Depreciation Expense | Accumulated Depreciation | Book Value |
|---|---|---|---|
| Start | | | 44,000 |
| 2007 | 8,800 | 8,800 | 35,200 |
| 2008 | 7,040 | 15,840 | 28,160 |
| 2009 | 5,632 | 21,472 | 22,528 |

Method C: Straight-Line

The depreciation expense, accumulated depreciation, and asset value for 2007 through 2009 under Straight-Line is shown in Exhibit 10-29.

**Exhibit 10-29 The depreciation under straight-line**

| Year | Annual Depreciation Expense | Accumulated Depreciation | Book Value |
|---|---|---|---|
| Start | | | 44,000 |
| 2007 | 4,000 | 4,000 | 40,000 |
| 2008 | 4,000 | 8,000 | 36,000 |
| 2009 | 4,000 | 12,000 | 32,000 |

Computations for 2009:

| | |
|---|---|
| Units-of-production | $0.40 × 12,000 units = $4,800 |
| Double-declining-balance | 20% × $28,160 = $5,632 |
| Straight-line | $40,000/10 years = $4,000 |

# Chapter 11

## Current Liabilities and Payroll

**Objectives**

1. Describe current liabilities related to accounts payable, current portion of long-term debt, and notes payable.

2. Determine employer liabilities for payroll, including liabilities arising from employee earnings and deductions from earnings.

3. Describe payroll accounting systems that use a payroll register, employee earnings records, and a general journal.

4. Journalize entries for employee fringe benefits, including vacation pay and pensions.

5. Describe the accounting treatment for contingent liabilities and journalize entries for product warranties.

# 1. Current Liabilities

Debt is an obligation that is recorded as a liability. Long-term liabilities are obligations due for a period of time greater than one year. Thus, a 30-year mortgage taken out to purchase property would be an example of a long-term liability. In contrast, current liabilities are obligations that will be paid out of current assets and are due within a short time, usually within one year.

Three types of current liabilities will be discussed in this section—accounts payable, current portion of long-term debt, and notes payable.

## ACCOUNTS PAYABLE

Accounts payable arise from purchasing goods or services for use in a company's operations or for purchasing merchandise for resale. We have described and illustrated accounts payable transactions in earlier chapters. For most businesses, this is often the largest current liability. Exhibit 11-1 illustrates the size of the accounts payable balance as a percent of total current liabilities for a number of different companies. The average percent of accounts payable to total current liabilities for large companies is 35.7%.

**Exhibit 11-1 Accounts payable as a percent of total current liabilities**

| Company | Current Liabilities |
|---|---|
| Alcoa Inc. | 39% |
| ChevronTexaco | 54% |
| Nissan Motor Co. Ltd. | 25% |
| IBM | 22% |
| Gap Inc. | 47% |
| Rite Aid Corp. | 51% |
| BellSouth Corp. | 16% |

## CURRENT PORTION OF LONG-TERM DEBT

Long-term liabilities are often paid back in periodic payments, called installments, much like a car loan. Long-term liability installments that are due within the coming year must beclassified as a current liability. The total amount of the installments due after the coming year is classified as a long-term liability.

## SHORT-TERM NOTES PAYABLE

Short-term notes payable, a common form of financing, are notes payable due within 1 year. Starbucks lists its short-term notes payable as short-term borrowings. Starbucks may issue short-term notes payable to borrow cash or to purchase assets. On its notes payable, Starbucks must accrue interest expense and interest payable at the end of the period. The following sequence ofentries covers the purchase of inventory, accrual of interest expense, and payment of a 10% short-term note payable that is due in 1 year. Exhibit 11-2 shows the entry to purchase assets by issuing short-term notes.

**Exhibit 11-2 Issue short-term notes to purchase assets**

| Date | Description | Debit | Credit |
|---|---|---|---|
| Jan. 1 | Inventory | 8,000 | |
| | Note Payable, Short-Term | | 8,000 |

This transaction increases both an asset and a liability.

| Assets | = | Liabilities | + | Stockholders' Equity |
|---|---|---|---|---|
| + $8,000 | = | + $8,000 | + | 0 |

The Starbucks fiscal year ends each September 30. At year end, Starbucks must accrue interest expense at 10% for January through September, the entry is shown in Exhibit 11-3.

**Exhibit 11-3 Accrue interest expense at 10%**

| Date | Description | Debit | Credit |
|---|---|---|---|
| Sept. 30 | Interest Expense ($8,000 × 10% × 9/12) | 600 | |
| | Interest Payable | | 600 |

Liabilities increase and equity decreases because of the expense.

| Assets | = | Liabilities | + | Stockholders' Equity | − | Expenses |
|---|---|---|---|---|---|---|
| 0 | = | + $600 | | | | − $600 |

The balance sheet at year end will report the Note Payable of $8,000 and the related Interest Payable of $600 as current liabilities. The income statement will report interest expense of $600.

Exhibit 11-4 records the note's payment at maturity on January 1next year.

**Exhibit 11-4 Records the note's payment at maturity**

| Date | Description | Debit | Credit |
|---|---|---|---|
| Jan. 1 | Note Payable, Short-Term | 8,000 | |
| | Interest Payable | 600 | |
| | Interest Expense ($8,000 × 10% × 3/12) | 200 | |
| | Cash ($8,000 + ($8,000 × 10%)) | | 8,800 |

The debits zero out the payables and also record Starbuck's interest expense for October, November, and December.

# 2. Payroll and Payroll Taxes

In accounting, the term payroll refers to the amount paid to employees for the services they provide during a period. A business's payroll is usually significant for several reasons. First, employees are sensitive to payroll errors and irregularities. Maintaining good employee morale requires that the payroll be paid on a timely, accurate basis. Second, the payroll is subject to various federal and state regulations. Finally, the payroll and related payroll taxes have a significant effect on the net income of most businesses. Although the amount of such expenses varies widely, it is not unusual for a business's payroll and payroll-related expenses to equal nearly one-third of its revenue.

## LIABILITY FOR EMPLOYEE EARNINGS

The term salary usually refers to payment for managerial, administrative, or similar services. The rate of salary is normally expressed in terms of a month or a year. The term wage usually refers to payment for manual labor, both skilled and unskilled. The rate of wage is normally stated on an hourly or a weekly basis. In practice, the terms salary and wage are often used interchangeably.

The basic salary or wage of an employee may be increased by commissions, profit sharing, or cost-of-living adjustments. Many businesses pay managers an annual bonus in addition to a basic salary. The amount of the bonus is often based on some measure of productivity, such as income or profit of the business. Although payment is usually made by check or in cash, it may be in the form of securities, notes, lodging.

Salary and wage rates are determined by agreement between the employer and the employees. Businesses engaged in interstate commerce must follow the requirements of the Fair Labor Standards Act. Employers covered by this legislation, which is commonly called the Federal Wage and Hour Law, are required to pay a minimum rate of 1.5 times the regular rate for all hours worked in excess of 40 hours per week. Exemptions are provided for executive, administrative, and certain supervisory positions. Premium rates for overtime or for working at night, holidays, or other less desirable times are fairly common, even when not required by law. In some cases, the premium rates may be as much as twice the base rate.

## DEDUCTIONS FROM EMPLOYEE EARNINGS

Gross pay is the total earnings of an employee for a payroll period, including bonuses and overtime pay. From this amount is subtracted one or more deductions to arrive at the net pay. The deductions for federal taxes are usually the largest deduction. Deductions may also be required for state or local income taxes. Other deductions may be made for medical insurance, contributions to pensions, and for items authorized by individual employees.

### Income Taxes

Except for certain types of employment, all employers must withhold a portion of employee earnings for payment of the employees' federal income tax. As a basis for determining the amount to be withheld, each employee completes and submits to the employer an "Employee's Withholding Allowance Certificate," often called a W-4. Exhibit 11-5 is an example of a completed W-4 form.

**Exhibit 11-5 Employee's withholding allowance certificate** (W-4 form)

<table>
<tr><td>W-4<br>Department of the Treasury Internal Revenue Service</td><td colspan="2">Employee's Withholding Allowance Certificate<br>Whether you are entitled to claim a certain number of allowances or exemption from withholding is subject to review by the IRS. Your employer may be required to send a copy of this form to the IRS.</td><td colspan="2">OMB No. 1545 – 0074<br>2006</td></tr>
<tr><td>1. Type or print your first name and middle initial.<br>John T.</td><td colspan="2">Last name<br>McGrath</td><td colspan="2">Your social security number<br>381 48 9120</td></tr>
<tr><td colspan="2">2. Home address (number and street or rural route)<br>1830 4th Street</td><td colspan="3">3. (×) Single ( ) Married ( ) Married, but withhold at higher<br>Single rate.<br>Note. If married, but legally separated, or spouse is a nonresident alien, check the "Single" box.</td></tr>
<tr><td colspan="2">City or town, state, and ZIP code<br>Clinton, Iowa 52732 – 6142</td><td colspan="3">4. If your last name differs from that shown on your social security card, check here. You must call 1 – 800 – 772 – 1213 for a new card.</td></tr>
<tr><td colspan="3">5. Total number of allowances you are claiming (from line H above or from the applicable worksheet on page 2)</td><td>5</td><td>1</td></tr>
<tr><td colspan="3">6. Additional amount, if any, you want withheld from each paycheck</td><td>6</td><td>$</td></tr>
<tr><td colspan="5">7. I claim exemption from withholding for 2006, and I certify that I meet both of the following conditions for exemption.<br>• Last year I had a right to a refund of all federal income tax withheld because I had no tax liability and<br>• This year I expect a refund of all federal income tax withheld because I expect to have no tax liability.</td></tr>
<tr><td colspan="3">If you meet both conditions, write "Exempt" here</td><td>7</td><td></td></tr>
</table>

On the W-4, an employee indicates marital status, the number of withholding allowances, and whether any additional withholdings are authorized. A single employee may claim one withholding allowance. A married employee may claim an additional allowance for a spouse. An employee may also claim an allowance for each dependent other than a spouse. Each allowance claimed reduces the amount of federal income tax withheld from the employee's check.

The amount that must be withheld for income tax differs, depending upon each employee's gross pay and completed W-4. Most employers use wage bracket withholding tables furnished by the Internal Revenue Service (IRS) to determine the amount to be withheld.

Exhibit 11-6 is an example of an IRS wage bracket withholding table for a single person who is paid weekly. Each row represents a person's wages after subtracting a standard IRS withholding allowance. The standard IRS withholding allowance is determined annually by the IRS. For a single person paid weekly, we assume the standard withholding allowance is $63.

John T. McGrath made $1,462 for the week ended December 27. Thus, the wages used in determining McGrath's withholding for the week are \$1,399(\$1,462 - \$63). If McGrath had declared two withholding allowances, the total amount deducted would have been \$126, and the wages used in determining McGrath's withholding for the week would have been \$1,336(\$1,462 - \$126).

**Exhibit 11-6 Wage bracket withholding table**

| Over— | But not over— | | of excess over— |
|---|---|---|---|
| 51 | ~192 | 10% | -51 |
| 192 | ~620 | 14.10 plus 15% | -192 |
| 620 | ~1,409 | 78.30 plus 25% | -620 |
| 1,409 | ~3,013 | 275.55 plus 28% | -1,409 |
| 3,013 | ~6,508 | 724.67 plus 33% | -3,013 |
| 6,508 | | 1,878.02 plus 35% | -6,508 |

After the person's withholding wage bracket has been identified, the amount of federal income tax withheld is determined using Exhibit 11-6 as follows.

(1). Locate the proper withholding wage bracket. Since McGrath's wages after deducting one standard IRS withholding allowance is \$1,399, the proper wage bracket for McGrath is \$620 \$1,409.

(2). Compute the withholding for the proper wage bracket using the directions in the two right-hand columns of Exhibit 11-6. For McGrath's wage bracket, Exhibit 11-6 indicates that the withholding should be "\$78.30 plus 25% of the excess over \$620". Thus, the withholding for McGrath is \$273.05, as shown below.

| | |
|---|---|
| Initial withholding from wage bracket in Exhibit 11-6 | \$ 78.30 |
| Plus additional withholding: 25% of excess over \$620 | \$194.75((\$1,399 - \$620) ×25%) |
| Total withholding | \$273.05 |

In addition to the federal income tax, employees may also be required to pay a state income tax and a city income tax. State and city taxes are withheld from employees' earnings and paid to state and city governments.

**FICA Tax**

Most of us have FICA tax withheld from our payroll checks by our employers. Employers are required by the Federal Insurance Contributions Act (FICA) to withhold a portion of the earnings of each of the employees. The amount of FICA tax withheld is the employees' contribution to two federal programs. Tax is withheld separately under each program. The first program, called social security, is for old age, survivors, and disability insurance (OASDI). The second program, called Medicare, is health insurance for senior citizens.

The amount of tax that employers are required to withhold from each employee is normally based on the amount of earnings paid in the calendar year. Although both the schedule of future tax rates and the maximum amount subject to tax are revised often by Congress, such changes have little effect on the basic payroll system. In this text, we will use a social security rate of 7% on the first \$100,000 of annual earnings and a Medicare rate of 1.5% on all annual earnings.

Assume that John T. McGrath's annual earnings prior to the current payroll period total $99,048. Assume also that the current period earnings are $1,562. The total FICA tax of $90.07 is determined as shown in Exhibit 11-7.

**Exhibit 11-7 Earnings subject to 7% social security tax**

| | |
|---|---|
| (100,000 - 99,048) | 952 |
| Social security tax rate | ×7% |
| Social security tax | 66.64 |
| Earnings subject to 1.5% Medicare tax | 1,562 |
| Medicare tax rate | ×1.5% |
| Medicare tax | 23.43 |
| Total FICA tax | 90.07 |

### Other Deductions

Neither the employer nor the employee has any choice in deducting taxes from gross earnings. However, employees may choose to have additional amounts deducted for other purposes. For example, you as an employee may authorize deductions for retirement savings, for contributions to charitable organizations, or for premiums on employee insurance. A union contract may also require the deduction of union dues.

## LIABILITY FOR EMPLOYER'S PAYROLL TAXES

Most employers are also subject to federal and state payroll taxes based on the amount paid their employees. Such taxes are an operating expense of the business. Exhibit 11-8 summarizes the responsibility for employee and employer payroll taxes.

**Exhibit 11-8 Responsibility for tax payments**

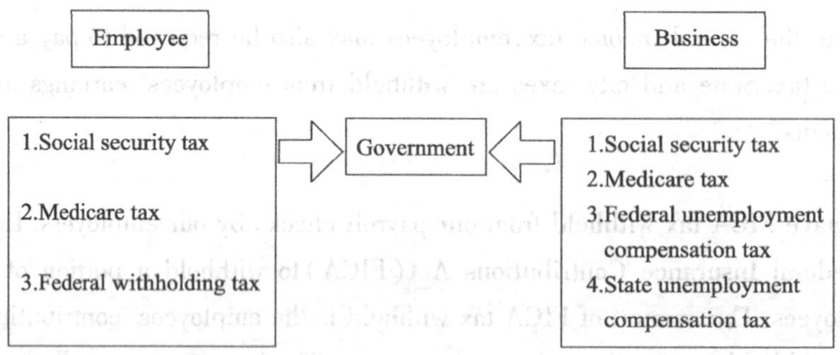


### FICA Tax

Employers are required to contribute to the social security and Medicare programs for each employee. The employer must match the employee's contribution to each program.

### Federal Unemployment Compensation Tax

The Federal Unemployment Tax Act (FUTA) provides for temporary payments to those who become unemployed as a result of layoffs due to economic causesbeyond their control. Types of employment subject to this program are similar to those covered by FICA taxes. A tax of 6.2% is levied on employers only, rather than on both employers and employees. It is applied to only the first $7,000 of the earnings of each covered employee during a calendar year. Congress often revises the rate and maximum earnings subject to federal unemployment compensation tax. The funds collected by the federal government are not paid directly to the unemployed but are allocated among the states for use in state programs.

**State Unemployment Compensation Tax**

State Unemployment Tax Acts (SUTA) also provide for payments to unemployed workers. The amounts paid as benefits are obtained, for the most part, from a tax levied upon employers only. A few states require employee contributions also. The rates of tax and the tax bases vary. In most states, employers who provide stable employment for their employees are granted reduced rates. The employment experience and the status of each employer's tax account are reviewed annually, and the tax rates are adjusted accordingly.

# 3. Accounting for Payroll and Payroll Taxes

In designing payroll systems, various federal, state, and local agencies for payroll data must also be maintained accurately for each payroll period and for each employee. Periodic reports using payroll data must be submitted to government agencies. The payroll data itself must be retained for possible inspection by the various agencies.

Payroll systems must be designed to pay employees on a timely basis. Payroll systems should also be designed to provide useful data for management decision-making needs. Such needs might include settling employee grievances and negotiating retirement or other benefits with employees.

Although payroll systems differ among businesses, the major elements common to most payroll systems are the payroll register, employee's earnings record, and payroll checks. We discuss and illustrate each of these elements next. We have kept the illustrations relatively simple, and they may be modified in practice to meet the needs of each individual business.

## PAYROLL REGISTER

The payroll register is a multicolumn report used for summarizing the data for each payroll period. Its design varies according to the number and classes of employees and the extent to which computers are used. Exhibit 11-9 illustrates a payroll register suitable for a small number of employees.

The nature of the data appearing in the payroll register is evident from the column headings. The number of hours worked and the earnings and deduction data are inserted in their proper columns. The sum of the deductions for each employee is then subtracted from the total earnings to yield the amount to be paid. The check numbers are recorded in the payroll register as evidence of payment.

The last two columns of the payroll register are used to accumulate the total wages or salaries to be debited to the various expense accounts. This process is usually called payroll distribution.

Exhibit 11-9 Payroll register

| Employee Name | Earnings | | | | |
|---|---|---|---|---|---|
| | Total Hours | Regular | Overtime | Total | |
| Ross, Geller S. | 48 | 600 | | 600 | 1 |
| Elorid, G. | 53 | 470 | 70 | 540 | 2 |
| David, Jose C. | 48 | 1,008 | | 1,008 | 3 |
| McGram, Hill | 50 | 1,632 | 122 | 1,754 | 4 |
| ⋮ | ⋮ | ⋮ | ⋮ | ⋮ | ⋮ |
| Adam, Lee. | 48 | 576 | | 576 | 25 |
| Abram, Lincon . | 48 | 720 | | 720 | 26 |
| Total | | 15,993 | 688 | 16,681 | 27 |
| | | | | | 28 |

**Recording Employees' Earnings**

The column totals of the payroll register support the journal entry for payroll. The entry based on the payroll register in Exhibit 11-10 as follows, and Exhibit 11-11 is the conclusion.

Exhibit 11-10 The entry for payroll based on the payroll register

| Date | | Description | Debit | Credit |
|---|---|---|---|---|
| Dec. | 27 | Sales Salaries Expense | 13,346 | |
| | | Office Salaries Expense | 3,336 | |
| | | Social Security Tax Payable | | 771 |
| | | Medicare Tax Payable | | 250 |
| | | Employees Federal Income Tax Payable | | 3,998 |
| | | Retirement Savings Deductions Payable | | 816 |
| | | United Fund Deductions Payable | | 564 |
| | | Accounts Receivable—Fred G. Elrod (emp.) | | 60 |
| | | Salaries Payable | | 10,222 |
| | | Payroll for week ended December 27 | | |

**Recording and Paying Payroll Taxes**

The employer's payroll taxes become liabilities when the related payroll is paid to employees. In addition, employers are required to compute and report payroll taxes on a calendar-year basis, even if a different fiscal year is used for financial reporting and income tax purposes.

Assume that Everson Company's fiscal year ends on April 30. Also, assume that Everson Company owes its employees \$31,200 of wages on December 31. The following portions of the \$31,200 of wages are subject to payroll taxes on December 31, the calculation is shown in Exhibit 11-12.

**Exhibit 11-11 Concluded**

| Deductions | | | | | | Paid | | Accounts Debited | |
|---|---|---|---|---|---|---|---|---|---|
| Social Security Tax | Medicare Tax | Federal Income Tax | Retirement Savings | Misc. | Total | Net Amount | Check No. | Sales Salaries Expense | Office Salaries Expense |
| 36 | 9 | 88 | 24 | UF 12 | 169 | 430 | 6857 | 600 | |
| 32 | 8 | 74 | | AR 60 | 174 | 365 | 6858 | | 540 |
| 60 | 15 | 157 | 30 | UF 12 | 274 | 733 | 6859 | 1,008 | |
| 69 | 26 | 327 | 24 | UF 6 | 453 | 1,301 | 6860 | 1,754 | |
| ⋮ | ⋮ | ⋮ | ⋮ | ⋮ | ⋮ | ⋮ | ⋮ | ⋮ | ⋮ |
| 34 | 8 | 82 | 12 | | 138 | 438 | 6880 | 576 | |
| 43 | 10 | 94 | 6 | UF 2 | 157 | 562 | 6881 | | 720 |
| 771 | 250 | 3,998 | 816 | UF 564<br>AR 60 | 6,460 | 10,222 | | 13,346 | 3,336 |

Misc. Deductions: UF—United Fund; AR—Accounts Receivable.

**Exhibit 11-12 Earnings subject to payroll taxes**

| | |
|---|---|
| Social security ta x (6.0%) | 1,872($31,200×6.0%) |
| Medicare ta x (1.5%) | 468($31,200×1.5%) |
| State unemployment compensation ta x (5.4%) | 1,684.8($31,200×5.4%) |
| Federal unemployment compensation ta x (0.8%) | 249.6($31,200×0.8%) |

If the payroll is paid on December 31, the payroll taxes will be based on the preceding amounts. If the payroll is paid on January 2, however, the entire $31,200 will be subject to all payroll taxes. This is because the maximum earnings limitation for determining social security and unemployment taxes will not be exceeded at the beginning of the calendar year.

The payroll register for McDermott Supply Co. in Exhibit 11-13 indicates that the amount of social security tax withheld is $771.68 and Medicare tax withheld is $250.24. Since the employer must match the employees' FICA contributions, the employer's social security payroll tax will also be $771.68, and the Medicare tax will be $250.24. Further, assume that the earnings subject to state and federal unemployment compensation taxes are $3,252. Multiplying this amount by the state (5.4%) and federal (0.8%) rates yields the unemployment compensation taxes shown in the payroll tax computation, as shown in Exhibit 11-13.

**Exhibit 11-13 The unemployment compensation taxes**

| | |
|---|---|
| Social security tax | 771.68 |
| Medicare tax | 250.24 |
| State unemployment compensation tax (5.4% × $3,252) | 175.61 |
| Federal unemployment compensation tax (0.8% × $3,252) | 26.02 |
| Total payroll tax expense | 1,223.55 |

The entry to journalize the payroll tax expense for the week and the liability for the taxes accrued is shown in Exhibit 11-14.

**Exhibit 11-14 The entry to journalize the payroll tax expense**

| Date | | Description | Debit | Credit |
|---|---|---|---|---|
| Dec. | 27 | Payroll Tax Expense | 1,223.55 | |
| | | Social Security Tax Payable | | 771.68 |
| | | Medicare Tax Payable | | 250.24 |
| | | State Unemployment Tax Payable | | 175.61 |
| | | Federal Unemployment Tax Payable | | 26.02 |
| | | Payroll taxes for week ended December 27 | | |

## EMPLOYEE'S EARNINGS RECORD

The amount of each employee's earnings to date must be available at the end of each payroll period. This cumulative amount is required in order to compute each employee's social security and Medicare tax withholding and the employer's payroll taxes. It is essential, therefore, that a detailed payroll record be maintained for each employee. This record is called an employee's earnings record.

In addition to spaces for recording data for each payroll period and the cumulative total of earnings, the employee's earnings record has spaces for quarterly totals and the yearly total. These totals are used in various reports for tax, insurance, and other purposes. One such report is the Wage and Tax Statement, commonly called a Form W-2. You may recall receiving a W-2 form for use in preparing your individual tax return. This form must be provided annually to each employee as well as to the Social Security Administration.

## PAYROLL CHECKS

At the end of each pay period, payroll checks are prepared. Each check includes a detach able statement showing the details of how the net pay was computed. Many businesses pay their employees electronically with direct deposits to employee checking accounts, rather than preparing payroll checks. In this case, the employee will still. receive a statement summarizing the details of how the pay was computed.

The amount paid to employees is normally recorded as a single amount, regardless of the number of employees. There is no need to record each payroll check separately in the journal, since all of the details are available in the payroll register.

For paying their payroll, most employers use payroll checks drawn on a special bank account. After the data for the payroll period have been recorded in the payroll register, a single check for the total amount to be paid is written on the firm's regular bank account. This check is then deposited in the special payroll bank account. Individual payroll checks are written from the payroll account, and the numbers of the payroll checks are inserted in the payroll register.

An advantage of using a separate payroll bank account is that the task of reconciling the bank statements is simplified. In addition, a payroll bank account establishes control over payroll checks by preventing the theft or misuse of uncashed payroll checks.

## PAYROLL SYSTEM DIAGRAM

The diagram indicates the relationships among the primary components of the payroll system we described in this chapter. Our focus in the preceding discussion has been on the outputs of a payroll system: the payroll register, payroll checks, the employees' earnings records, and tax and other reports. The inputs into a payroll system may be classified as either constants or variables.

Constants are data that remain unchanged in payroll and thus do not need to be entered into the system each pay period. Examples of constants include such data as each employee's name and social security number, marital status, number of income tax withholding allowances, rate of pay, payroll category (office, sales, etc.), and department where employed. The FICA tax rates and various tax tables are also constants that apply to all employees. In a computerized accounting system, constants are stored within a payroll file.

Variables are data that change in payroll and thus must be entered into the system each pay period. Examples of variables include such data as the number of hours or days worked for each employee during the payroll period, days of sick leave with pay, vacation credits, and cumulative earnings and taxes withheld. If salespersons are paid commissions, the amount of their sales would also vary from period to period.

Most companies use computerized payroll systems that maintain an electronic payroll register and employee earnings record, similar to those discussed in this section. Payroll system outputs, such as employee checks and tax records, are automatically produced by the software.

## INTERNAL CONTROLS FOR PAYROLL SYSTEMS

Payroll processing requires the input of a large amount of data, along with numerous and sometimes complex computations. These factors, combined with the large dollar amounts involved, require controls to ensure that payroll payments are timely and accurate. In addition, the system must also provide adequate safeguards against theft or other misuse of funds.

The cash payment controls also apply to payrolls. Thus, it is normally desirable to use a system that includes procedures for proper authorization and approval of payroll. When a check-signing machine is used, it is important that blank payroll checks and access to the machine be carefully controlled to prevent the theft or misuse of payroll funds.

It is especially important to authorize and approve in writing employee additions and deletions and changes in pay rates. For example, numerous payroll frauds have involved a supervisor adding fictitious employees to the payroll. The supervisor then cashes the fictitious employees' checks. Similar frauds have occurred where employees have been fired but the Payroll Department is not notified.

As a result, payroll checks to the fired employees are prepared and cashed by a supervisor.

To prevent or detect frauds, employees' attendance records should be controlled. For example, employee arrival and departure times for computing pay are often determined from a time clock stamp or from the scan of an employee identification card or badge. A Payroll Department employee may be stationed near the time clock or scanning device to verify that authorized employees are "clocking in" only once and only for themselves. When payroll checks are distributed, employee identification cards may be used to deter one employee from picking up another's check.

Other controls include verifying and approving all payroll rate changes. In addition, in a computerized system, all program changes should be properly approved and tested by employees who are independent of the payroll system. The use of a special payroll bank account, as we discussed earlier in this chapter, also enhances control over payroll.

## 4. Employees' Fringe Benefits

Fringe benefits includes vacations, medical, and postretirement benefits, such as pension plans. The U. S. Chamber of Commerce has estimated that fringe benefits, excluding FICA, average approximately 33% of gross wages.

When the employer pays part or all of the cost of the fringe benefits, these costs must be recognized as expenses. To properly match revenues and expenses, the estimated cost of these benefits should be recorded as an expense during the period in which the employee earns the benefit, as we will illustrate in the next section for vacation pay.

### VACATION PAY

Most employers grant vacation rights, sometimes called compensated absences, to their employees. Such rights give rise to a liability. The liability for employees' vacation pay should be accrued as a liability as the vacation rights are earned. The entry to accrue vacation pay may be recorded in total at the end of each fiscal year, or it may be recorded at the end of each pay period. To illustrate this latter case, assume that employees earn one day of vacation for each month worked during the year. Assume also that the estimated vacation pay for the payroll period ending May 5 is $ 2,000. The entry to record the accrued vacation pay for this pay period is shown in Exhibit 11-15.

**Exhibit 11-15 Record the accrued vacation pay**

| Date | | Description | Debit | Credit |
|---|---|---|---|---|
| May | 5 | Vacation Pay Expense | 2,000 | |
| | | Vacation Pay Payable | | 2,000 |
| | | Vacation pay for week ended May 5 | | |

If employees are required to take all their vacation time within one year, the vacation pay payable is reported on the balance sheet as a current liability. If employees are allowed to accumulate their vacation time, the estimated vacation pay liability that is applicable to time that will not be taken within one year is a long-term liability.

When payroll is prepared for the period in which employees have taken vacations, the vacation pay payable is reduced. The entry debits Vacation Pay Payable and credits Salaries Payable and the other related accounts for taxes and withholdings.

## PENSIONS

A pension represents a cash payment to retired employees. Rights to pension payments are earned by employees during their working years, based on the pension plan established by the employer. One of the fundamental characteristics of such a plan is whether it is a defined contribution plan or a defined benefit plan.

### Defined Contribution Plan

In a defined contribution plan, a fixed amount of money is invested on the employee's behalf during the employee's working years. It is common for the employee and employer to make contributions. There is no promise of future pension benefit payments. The amount of the final pension depends on the total contributions and investment returns earned on those contributions over the employee's working years. The employee bears the investment risk under defined contribution plans.

Under defined contribution plans—401k plan[㊀], employees may contribute a limited part of their income to investments, such as mutual funds. A 401k plan offers employees two advantages: ① The contribution is deducted, before taxes, from current period income. ② The contributions and future investment earnings are tax deferred until withdrawn at retirement. In addition, in 90% of the 401k plans, the employer matches some portion of the employee's contribution. These advantages are why nearly 70% of eligible employees elect to enroll in a 401k.

The employer's cost of a defined contribution plan is debited to Pension Expense. To illustrate, assume that the pension plan of Heaven Scent Perfumes Company requires an employer contribution of 10% of employee monthly salaries, paid at the end of the month to the employee's plan administrator. The journal entry to record the transaction, assuming $600,000 of monthly salaries, is as shown in Exhibit 11-16.

**Exhibit 11-16 Pay the pension at the end of the month**

| Date | | Description | Debit | Credit |
|---|---|---|---|---|
| Dec. | 31 | Pension Expense | 60,000 | |
| | | Cash | | 60,000 |
| | | Contributed 10% of monthly salaries to pension plan | | |

㊀ A defined contribution plan offered by a corporation to its employees, which allows employees to set aside tax-deferred income for retirement purposes, and in some cases employers will match their contribution dellar-for-dollar. Taking a distribution of the funds before a certain specified age will trigger a penalty tax. The name 401 k comes forom the IRS section describing the program.

**Defined Benefit Plan**

Employers may choose to promise employees a fixed annual pension benefit at retirement, based on years of service and compensation levels. An example would be a promise to pay an annual pension based on a formula, such as the following:

Annual Pension = 1.5% × Years of Service × Average Salary for Most Recent 3 Years Prior to Retirement

Pension benefits based on a formula are termed a defined benefit plan. Unlike a defined contribution plan, the employer bears the investment risk in funding a future retirement income benefit. As a result, many companies are replacing their defined benefit plans with defined contribution plans.

The accounting for defined benefit plans is usually very complex due to the uncertainties of projecting future pension obligations. These obligations depend upon such factors as employee life expectancies, employee turnover, expected employee compensation levels, and investment income on pension contributions.

The pension cost of a defined benefit plan is debited to Pension Expense. The amount funded is credited to Cash. Any unfunded amount is credited to Unfunded Pension Liability. For example, assume that the pension plan of Hinkle Co. requires an annual pension cost of $80,000, based on an estimate of the future benefit obligation. Further assume that Hinkle Co. pays $60,000 to the pension fund. The entry to record this transaction is shown in Exhibit 11-17.

**Exhibit 11-17 Record annual pension cost and contribution to pension plan**

| Date | | Description | Debit | Credit |
|---|---|---|---|---|
| Dec. | 31 | Pension Expense | 80,000 | |
| | | Cash | | 60,000 |
| | | Unfunded Pension Liability | | 20,000 |
| | | To record annual pension cost and contribution to pension plan | | |

If the unfunded pension liability is to be paid within one year, it will be classified as a current liability. That portion of the liability to be paid beyond one year is a longterm liability.

## POSTRETIREMENT BENEFITS OTHER THAN PENSIONS

Employees may earn rights to other postretirement benefits from their employer. Such benefits may include dental care, eye care, medical care, life insurance, tuition assistance, tax services, and legal services for employees or their dependents. The amount of the annual benefits expense is based upon health statistics of the workforce. This amount is recorded by debiting Postretirement Benefits Expense. Cash is credited for the same amount if the benefits are fully funded. If the benefits are not fully funded, a postretirement benefits plan liability account is credited. Thus, the accounting for postretirement health benefits is very similar to that of defined benefit pension plans.

A business' financial statements should fully disclose the nature of its postretirement benefit obligations. These disclosures are usually included as notes to the financial statements. The complex nature of accounting for postretirement benefits is described in more advanced accounting courses.

# 5. Contingent Liabilities

Some past transactions will result in liabilities if certain events occur in the future. These potential obligations are called contingent liabilities. For example, Ford Motor Company would have a contingent liability for the estimated costs associated with warranty work on new car sales. The obligation is contingent upon a future event, namely, a customer requiring warranty work on a vehicle. The obligation is the result of a past transaction, which is the original sale of the vehicle.

If a contingent liability is probable and the amount of the liability can be reasonably estimated, it should be recorded in the accounts. Ford Motor Company's vehicle warranty costs are an example of a recordable contingent liability. The warranty costs are probable because it is known that warranty repairs will be required on some vehicles. In addition, the costs can be estimated from past warranty experience.

Assume that during June a company sells a product for $70,000 on which there is a 36-month warranty for repairing defects. Past experience indicates that the average cost to repair defects is 6% of the sales price over the warranty period. The entry to record the estimated product warranty expense for June is as shown in Exhibit 11-18.

**Exhibit 11-18 Record the estimated product warranty expenses**

| Date | | Description | Debit | Credit |
|---|---|---|---|---|
| June | 30 | Product Warranty Expense | 4,200 | |
| | | Product Warranty Payable | | 4,200 |
| | | Warranty expense for June, 6% × 70,000 | | |

This transaction matches revenues and expenses properly by recording warranty costs in the same period in which the sale is recorded. When the defective product is repaired, the repair costs are recorded by debiting Product Warranty Payable and crediting Cash, Supplies, Wages Payable, or other appropriate accounts. Thus, if a customer required a $300 part replacement on August 16, the entry would be as shown in Exhibit 11-19.

**Exhibit 11-19 Replace defective part under warranty**

| Date | | Description | Debit | Credit |
|---|---|---|---|---|
| Aug. | 16 | Product Warranty Payable | 300 | |
| | | Supplies | | 300 |
| | | Replaced defective part under warranty | | |

If a contingent liability is probable but cannot be reasonably estimated or is only possible, then the nature of the contingent liability should be disclosed in the notes to the financial statements. Professional judgment is required in distinguishing between contingent liabilities that are probable versus those that are only possible.

Common contingent liabilities disclosed in notes to the financial statements are litigation, environmental matters, guarantees, and contingencies from the sale of receivables. The following is an example of a contingency disclosure related to litigation from a recent annual report of Google Inc., the popular Internet search engine provider.

The accounting treatment of contingent liabilities is summarized in Exhibit 11-20.

**Exhibit 11-20 Accounting treatment of contingent liabilities**

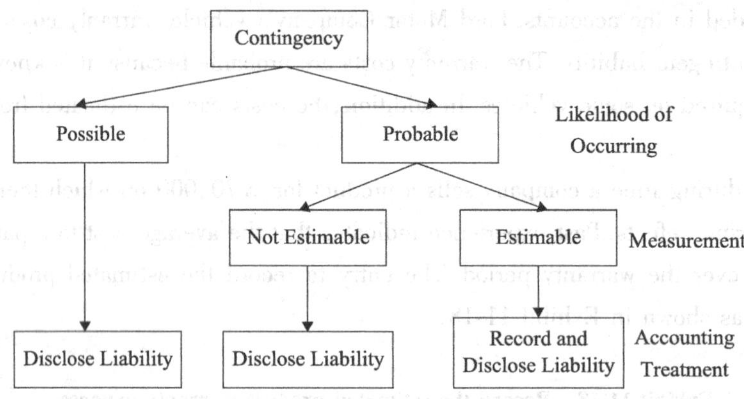


**TERMINOLOGY:**

Current Liabilities:流动负债
Accounts Payable:应付账款
Short-term Notes Payable:短期应付票据
Payroll:工薪总额
Payroll Taxes:工资税
Income Taxes:所得税
Payroll Register:工资表
Payroll Checks:工资支票
Salary and Wages:薪金及工资
Vacation Pay:假期工资
Pensions:退休金
OtherPostretirement Benefits:其他退休后福利
Contingent Liabilities:或有负债
Product Warranty Payable:应付产品保证金
Defined Contribution Plan:养老金固定缴款计划
Defined Benefit Plan:养老金固定收益计划

Federal Unemployment Compensation Tax:联邦失业保险税
FICA Tax:联邦社会保险税

## QUESTIONS:

**1. Describe and illustrate current liabilities.**

Current liabilities are obligations that are to be paid out of current assets and are due within a short time, usually within one year. The three primary types of current liabilities are accounts payable, notes payable, and current portion of long-term debt.

**2. List the factors that determine employer liabilities for payroll.**

An employer's liability for payroll is determined from employee total earnings, including overtime pay. From this amount, employee deductions are subtracted to arrive at the net pay to be paid to each employee. Most employers also incur liabilities for payroll taxes, such as social security tax, medicare tax, federal unemployment compensation tax, and state unemployment compensation tax.

**3. Describe payroll accounting systems that use a payroll register.**

The payroll register is used in assembling and summarizing the data needed for each payroll period. The payroll register is supported by a detailed payroll record for each employee called an employee's earnings record.

## PROBLEM:

Rags-to-Riches, a clothing resale store, employs one salesperson, Dee Hunter. Hunter's straight-time salary is $400 per week, with time-and - a-half pay for hours above 40. Rags-to-Riches withholds income tax(10%) and Federal Insurance Contributions Act(FICA) tax(8%) and state and federal unemployment tax(5.4% and 0.8%, respectively). In addition, Rags-to-Riches contributes 6% of Hunter's gross pay into her retirement plan.

During the week ended December 26, Hunter worked 50 hours. Prior to this week, she had earned $22,000.

**Requirements**(Round all amounts to the nearest dollar)

1. Compute Hunter's gross pay and net pay for the week.
2. Record the following payroll entries that Rags-to-Riches would make.

a. Hunter's gross pay, including overtime.

b. Expense for employee benefits.

c. Employer payroll taxes.

d. Payment of employee salary.

e. Payment for employee benefits.

f. Payment of all payroll taxes.

3. How much was Rags-to-Riches' total payroll expense for the week?

**Solution**

Requirement 1. The Exhibit 11-21 shows the calculation of Hunter's gross pay and net pay.

**Exhibit 11-21 Compute Hunter's gross pay and net pay**

| | | | |
|---|---|---|---|
| Gross pay: | Straight-time pay for 40 hours | | 400 |
| | Overtime pay: | | |
| | Rate per hour( $400/40hours ×1.5) | 15 | |
| | Hours(50 hours -40 hours) | 10 | 150 |
| | Gross pay | | 550 |
| Net pay: | Gross pay | | 550 |
| | Less: Withheld income tax( $550 ×0.10) | 55 | |
| | Withheld FICA tax( $550 ×0.08) | 44 | 99 |
| | Net pay | | 451 |

Requirement 2. The Exhibit 11-22 records the payroll entries.

**Exhibit 11-22 Record the payroll entries**

| | | | |
|---|---|---|---|
| a | Sales Salary Expense | 550 | |
| | Employee Income Tax Payable | | 55 |
| | FICA Tax Payable | | 44 |
| | Salary Payable | | 451 |
| | | | |
| b | Retirement-Plan Expense( $550 ×0.06) | 33 | |
| | Employee Benefits Payable | | 33 |
| c | Payroll Tax Expense | 78 | |
| | FICA Tax Payable( $550 ×0.08) | | 44 |
| | State Unemployment Tax Payable( $550 ×0.054) | | 30 |
| | Federal Unemployment Tax Payable( $550 ×0.008) | | 4 |
| d | Salary Payable | 451 | |
| | Cash | | 451 |
| | | | |
| e | Employee Benefits Payable | 33 | |
| | Cash | | 33 |
| f | Employee IncomeTax Payable | 55 | |
| | FICA Tax Payable( $44 ×2) | 88 | |
| | State Unemployment Tax Payable | 30 | |
| | Federal Unemployment Tax Payable | 4 | |
| | Cash | | 177 |

Requirement 3. Rags-to-Riches incurred total payroll expense of $661 (gross pay of $550 + payroll taxes of $78 + benefits of $33). See entries a through c.

# Chapter 12

## Stock Transactions, and Dividends

**Objectives**

1. **Describe the nature of the corporate form of organization.**
2. **Describe the two main sources of stockholders' equity.**
3. **Describe the classes of stock, and entries for issuing stock.**
4. **Journalize the entries for cash dividends and stock dividends.**
5. **Journalize the entries for treasury stock transactions.**
6. **Describe the reporting of stockholders' equity.**
7. **Describe the effect of stock splits on corporate financial statements.**

# 1. Nature of a Corporation

## WHAT'S THE BEST WAY TO ORGANIZE A BUSINESS?

Anyone starting a business must decide how to organize the company. Corporations differ from-proprietorships and partnerships in several ways.

**Separate Legal Entity**

A corporation is a business entity formed under state law. It is a distinct entity, an artificial person thatexists apart from its owners, the stockholders, or shareholders. The corporation has many of the rights that a person has. For example, a corporation may buy, own, and sell property. Assets and liabilities in the business belong to the corporation and not to its owners. The corporation may enter into contracts, sue, and be sued.

Nearly all large companies, such as IHOP, Toyota, and Wal-Mart, are corporations. Their full names may include Corporation or Incorporated (abbreviated Corp. and Inc.) to indicate that they are corporations, for example, IHOP Corp. and Pier 1 Imports, Inc. Corporations can also use the word Company, such as Ford Motor Company.

**Continuous Life and Transferability of Ownership**

Corporations have continuous lives regardless of changes in their ownership. The stockholders of a corporation may buy more of the stock, sell the stock to another person, give it away, or bequeath it in a will. The transfer of the stock from one person to another does not affect the continuity of the corporation. In contrast, proprietorships and partnerships terminate when their ownership changes.

**Limited Liability**

Stockholders have limited liability for the corporation's debts. They have no personal obligation for corporate liabilities. The most that a stockholder can lose on an investment in a corporation's stock is the cost of the investment. Limited liability is one of the most attractive features of the corporate form of organization. It enables corporations to raise more capital from a wider group of investors than proprietorships and partnerships can. By contrast, proprietors and partners are personally liable for all the debts of their businesses.

**Separation of Ownership and Management**

Stockholders own the corporation, but the board of directors—elected by the stockholders—appoints officers to manage the business. Thus, stockholders may invest \$1,000 or \$1 million in the corporation without having to manage it.

Management's goal is to maximize the firm's value for the stockholders. But the separation between owners and managers may create problems. Corporate officers may run the business for their own benefit and not for the stockholders. For example, the CEO of Tyco Corporation was accused of looting Tyco of \$600 million. The CFO of Enron Corporation set up outside partnerships and paid himself millions to manage the partnerships—unknown to Enron stockholders. Both men went to prison.

**Corporate Taxation**

Corporations are separate taxable entities. They pay several taxes not borne byproprietorships or partnerships, including an annual franchise tax levied by the state. The franchise tax keeps the corporate charter in force. Corporations also pay federal and state income taxes. Corporate earnings are subject to double taxation on their income.

First, corporations pay income taxes on their corporate income.

Then stockholders pay personal income tax on the cash dividends received from corporations. Proprietorships and partnerships pay no business income tax. Instead, the business's tax falls solely on the owners.

**Government Regulation**

Because stockholders have only limited liability for corporation debts, outsiders doing business with the corporation can look no further than the corporation if it fails to pay. To protect a corporation's creditors and stockholders, both federal and state governments monitor corporations. The regulations mainly ensure that corporations disclose the information that investors and creditors need to make informed decisions. Accounting provides much of this information.

Exhibit 12-1 summarizes the advantages and disadvantages of the corporate form of business organization.

**Exhibit 12-1 Advantages and disadvantages of a corporation**

| Advantages | Disadvantages |
|---|---|
| 1. Can raise more capital than a proprietorship or partnership can | 1. Separation of ownership and management |
| 2. Continuous life | 2. Corporate taxation |
| 3. Ease of transferring ownership | 3. Government regulation |
| 4. Limited liability of stockholders | |

## FORMING A CORPORATION

The creation of a corporation begins when its organizers, called theincorporators, obtain a charter from the state. The charter includes the authorization for the corporation to issue a certain number of shares of stock. A share of stock is the basic unit of ownership for a corporation. The incorporators pay fees, sign the charter, file documents with the state, agree to a set of bylaws, which act as the constitution for governing the company. The corporation then comes into existence.

Ultimate control of the corporation rests with the stockholders who elect a board of directors that sets company policy and appoints officers. The board elects a chairperson, who usually is the most powerful person in the organization. The chairperson of the board of directors has the title chief executive officer (CEO). The board also designates the president, who is the chief operating officer (COO) in charge of day-to-day operations. Most corporations also have vice presidents in charge of sales, manufacturing, accounting and finance (the chief financial officer, or CFO), and other key areas.

## 2. Stockholders' Equity

As we saw in Chapter 1, stockholders' equity represents the stockholders' ownership interest in the assets of a corporation. Stockholders' equity is divided into 2 main parts.

(1) Paid-in capital, also called contributed capital. This is the amount of stockholders' equity the stockholders have contributed to the corporation. Paid-in capital includes the stock accounts and any additional paid-in capital.

(2) Retained earnings. This is the amount of stockholders' equity the corporation has earned through profitable operations and has not used for dividends.

Companies report stockholders' equity by source. They report paid-in capital separately from retained earnings because most states prohibit the declaration of cash dividends from paid-in capital. Thus, cash dividends are declared from retained earnings.

The owners' equity of a corporation is divided into shares of stock. A corporation issues stock certificates to its owners when the company receives their investment in the business—usually cash. Because stock represents the corporation's capital, it is often called capital stock. The basic unit of capital stock is 1 share. A corporation may issue a stock certificate for any number of shares—1, 100, or any other number—but the total number of authorized shares is limited by charter.

Stock in the hands of a stockholder is said to be outstanding. The total number of shares of stock outstanding at any time represents 100% ownership of the corporation.

## 3. Paid-In Capital from Issuing Stock

The two main sources of stockholders' equity are paid-in capital (or contributed capital) and retained earnings. The main source of paid-in capital is from issuing stock. In the following paragraphs, we discuss the characteristics of stock, the classes of stock, and entries for recording the issuance of stock.

### CLASSES OF STOCK

When only one class of stock is issued, it is called common stock. In this case, each share of common stock has equal rights. To appeal to a broader investment market, a corporation may issue one or more classes of stock with various preference rights. A common example of such a right is the preference to dividends. Such a stock is generally called a preferred stock.

The dividend rights of preferred stock are usually stated in monetary terms or as a percent of par. For example, $4 preferred stock has a right to an annual $4 per share dividend. If the par value of the preferred stock were \$50, the same right to dividends could be stated as 8% ( \$4/ \$50) preferred stock.

The board of directors of a corporation has the sole authority to distribute dividends to the stockholders. When such action is taken, the directors are said to declare a dividend. Since dividends are normally based on earnings, a corporation cannot guarantee dividends even to preferred stockholders. However, because they have first rights to any dividends, the preferred stockholders have a greater chance of receiving regular dividends than do the common stockholders.

Assume that a corporation has 1,000 shares of \$4 preferred stock and 4,000 shares of common stock outstanding. Also assume that the net income, amount of earnings retained, and the amount of earnings distributed by the board of directors for the first three years of operations are as shown in Exhibit 12-2.

**Exhibit 12-2 Retained and distributed retained**

| | 2006 | 2007 | 2008 |
|---|---|---|---|
| Net income | 20,000 | 9,000 | 62,000 |
| Amount retained | 10,000 | 6,000 | 40,000 |
| Amount distributed | 10,000 | 3,000 | 22,000 |

Exhibit 12-3 shows the earnings distributed each year to the preferred stock and the common stock. The preferred stockholders received dividends of \$4, \$3, and \$4 per share. In contrast, common stockholders received dividends of \$1.50 per share in 2006, no dividends in 2007, and \$4.50 per share in 2008. You should note that although preferred stockholders have a greater chance of receiving a regular dividend, common stockholders have a greater chance of receiving larger dividends than do the preferred stockholders.

**Exhibit 12-3 Dividends to preferred and common stock**

| | 2006 | 2007 | 2008 |
|---|---|---|---|
| Amount distributed | 10,000 | 3,000 | 22,000 |
| Preferred dividend (1,000 shares) | 4,000 | 3,000 | 4,000 |
| Common dividend (4,000 shares) | 6,000 | 0 | 18,000 |
| Dividends per share: | | | |
| Preferred stock | 4.00 | 3.00 | 4.00 |
| Common stock | 1.50 | none | 4.50 |

In addition to dividend preference, preferred stock may be given preferences to assets if the corporation goes out of business and is liquidated. However, claims of creditors must be satisfied first. Preferred stockholders are next in line to receive any remaining assets, followed by the common stockholders.

## ISSUING STOCK

A separate account is used for recording the amount of each class of stock issued to investors in a corporation. For example, assume that a corporation is authorized to issue 12,000 shares of $150 par preferred stock and 120,000 shares of $20 par common stock. One-half of each class of authorized shares is issued at par for cash. The corporation's entry to record the stock issue is shown in Exhibit 12-4.

**Exhibit 12-4 Entry to record the stock issue**

| Date | Description | Debit | Credit |
|---|---|---|---|
| | Cash | 2,100,000 | |
| | Preferred Stock | | 900,000 |
| | Common Stock | | 1,200,000 |
| | Issued preferred stock and common stock at par for cash | | |

Stock is often issued by a corporation at a price other than its par. This is because the par value of a stock is simply its legal capital. The price at which stock can be sold by acorporation depends on a variety of factors, such as follows.

(1) The financial condition, earnings record, and dividend record of the corporation.

(2) Investor expectations of the corporation's potential earning power.

(3) General business and economic conditions and prospects.

The stock has sold at a premium when stock is issued for a price that is more than its par. When stock is issued for a price that is less than its par, the stock has sold at a discount. Thus, if stock with a par of $40 is issued for a price of $50, the stock has sold at a premium of $10. If the same stock is issued for a price of $35, the stock has sold at a discount of $5. Many states do not permit stock to be issued at a discount. In others, it may be done only under unusual conditions. Since issuing stock at a discount is rare, we will not illustrate it.

A corporation issuing stock must maintain records of the stockholders in order to issue dividend checks and distribute financial statements and other reports. Large public corporations normally use a financial institution, such as a bank, for this purpose. In such cases, the financial institution is referred to as a transfer agent or registrar. For example, the transfer agent and registrar for The Coca-Cola Company is First Chicago Trust Company of New York.

## VALUATION OF STOCK

Generally accepted accounting principles require a company to record its stock at the fair market value of whatever the corporation receives in exchange for the stock. When the corporation receives cash, there is clear evidence of the value of the stock because cash is worth its face amount. But when the corporation receives an asset other than cash, the value of the asset can create an ethical challenge. A computer whiz may start a new company by investing computer software. The software may be market-tested or it may be new. The software may be worth millions or worthless. The corporation must record the asset received and the stock given with a journal entry such as shown in Exhibit 12-5.

**Exhibit 12-5 Buy asset by giving stock**

| Date | Description | Debit | Credit |
|---|---|---|---|
| | Software | 500,000 | |
| | Common Stock | | 500,000 |
| | The asset received and the stock given | | |

If the software is really worth $500,000,the accounting records are okay. But if the software is new and untested,the assets and equity may be overstated.

Companies like to report large asset and equity amounts on their balance sheets. That makes them look prosperous and creditworthy. Gee-Whiz looks debt free and appears to have a valuable asset. Will you invest in this new business? Here are 2 take away lessons.

(1) Some accounting values are more solid than others.

(2) Not all financial statements mean exactly what they say—unless they are audited by independent CPAs.

## NO-PAR STOCK

Both preferred and common stock may be issued without a par value. When no-par stock is issued,the entire proceeds are credited to the stock account. This is true even though the issue price varies from time to time. For example,assume that a corporation issues 10,000 shares of no-par common stock at $40 a share and at a later date issues 1,000 additional shares at $36. The entries to record the no-par stock are as shown in Exhibit 12-6.

**Exhibit 12-6 Record the no-par stock**

| Description | Debit | Credit |
|---|---|---|
| Cash | 400,000 | |
| Common Stock | | 400,000 |
| Issued 10,000 shares of no-par common at $40 | | |
| | | |
| Cash | 36,000 | |
| Common Stock | | 36,000 |
| Issued 1,000 shares of no-par common at $36 | | |

The entire proceeds from the issue of no-par stock could be recorded as legal capital. In this case,the preceding entries would be proper. In other states,no-par stock may be assigned a stated value per share. The stated value is recorded like a par value, and the excess of the proceeds over the stated value. To illustrate, assume that in the preceding example the no-par common stock is assigned a stated value of $25. The issuance of the stock would be recorded as shown in 12-7.

**Exhibit 12-7 Record the issuance of the stock**

| Description | Debit | Credit |
|---|---|---|
| Cash | 400,000 | |
| Common Stock | | 250,000 |
| Paid-In Capital in Excess of Stated Value | | 150,000 |
| Issued 10,000 shares of no-par common at $40; stated value, $25 | | |
| Cash | 36,000 | |
| Common Stock | | 25,000 |
| Paid-In Capital in Excess of Stated Value | | 11,000 |
| Issued 1,000 shares of no-par common at $36; stated value, $25 | | |

# 4. Accounting for Dividends

When a board of directors declares a cash dividend, it authorizes the distribution of a portion of the corporation's cash to stockholders. When a board of directors declares a stock dividend, it authorizes the distribution of a portion of its stock. In both cases, the declaration of a dividend reduces the retained earnings of the corporation.

## CASH DIVIDENDS

Most dividends are cash dividends. Finance courses discuss how a company decides on its dividend policy. Accounting tells a company if it can pay a dividend. To do so, a company must have both enough retained earnings to declare the dividend and enough cash to pay the dividend.

A corporation declares a dividend before paying it. Only the board of directors has the authority to declare a dividend. The corporation has no obligation to pay a dividend until the board declares one, but once declared, the dividend becomes a legal liability of the corporation. There are 3 relevant dates for dividends (using assumed amounts).

(1) Declaration date, June 19. On the declaration date, the board of directors announces the dividend. Declaration of the dividend creates a liability for the corporation. Declaration is recorded by debiting Retained Earnings and crediting Dividends Payable. Assume a $50,000 dividend. Exhibit 12-8 records the declaration of dividends.

**Exhibit 12-8 Record the dividend**

| Date | Description | Debit | Credit |
|---|---|---|---|
| June 19 | Retained Earnings | 50,000 | |
| | Dividends Payable | | 50,000 |

Liabilities increase, and equity goes down.

| Assets | = | Liabilities | + | Stockholders' Equity |
|---|---|---|---|---|
| 0 | = | + $50,000 | | - $50,000 |

(2) Date of record, July 1. As part of the declaration, the corporation announces the record date, which follows the declaration date by a few weeks. The stockholders on the record date will receive the dividend. There is no journal entry for the date of record.

(3) Payment date, July 10. Payment of the dividend usually follows the record date by a week or 2. Payment is recorded by debiting Dividends Payable and Crediting Cash. This entry is shown in Exhibit 12-9.

**Exhibit 12-9 Record the payment of the dividend**

| Date | Description | Debit | Credit |
|---|---|---|---|
| July 10 | Dividends Payable | 50,000 | |
| | Cash | | 50,000 |

Both assets and liabilities decrease. The corporation shrinks.

| Assets | = | Liabilities | + | Stockholders' Equity |
|---|---|---|---|---|
| - $50,000 | = | - $50,000 | | |

## STOCK DIVIDENDS

A stock dividend is a proportional distribution by a corporation of its own stock to its stockholders. Stock dividends increase the stock account and decrease Retained Earnings. Total equity is unchanged, and no asset or liability is affected.

The corporation distributes stock dividends to stockholders in proportion to the number of shares they already own. If you own 300 shares of IHOP common stock and IHOP distributes a 10% common stock dividend, you get 30 (300 shares × 0.10) additional shares. You would then own 330 shares of the stock. All other IHOP stockholders would also receive 10% more shares, leaving all stockholders' ownership unchanged. Currently the book value of IHOP's common stock is $0.01 per share.

In distributing a stock dividend, the corporation gives up no assets. Why, then, do companies issue stock dividends? A corporation may choose to distribute stock dividends for these reasons:

(1) To continue dividends but conserve cash. A company may need to conserve cash and yet wish to continue dividends in some form. So the corporation may distribute a stock dividend. Stockholders pay no income tax on stock dividends.

(2) To reduce the per-share market price of its stock. Distribution of a stock dividend usually causes the stock's market price to fall because of the increased supply of the stock. The objective is to make the stock less expensive and therefore attractive to more investors.

Generally Accepted Accounting Principles (GAAP) label a stock dividend of 25% or less as small and suggest that the dividend be recorded at the market value of the shares distributed. Suppose IHOP declared a 10% stock dividend in 2008. At the time, assume IHOP had 20,000,000 shares of common stock outstanding, and IHOP's stock is trading for $60 per share. IHOP would record this stock dividend as shown in Exhibit 12-10.

**Exhibit 12-10 Distribute dividend at the market value of the shares**

| Date | Description | Debit | Credit |
|---|---|---|---|
| May 19 | Retained Earnings (20,000,000shares ×0.10 × $60) | 120,000,000 | |
| | Common Stock (20,000,000shares ×0.10 × $0.01) | | 20,000 |
| | Paid-in Capital in Excess of Par-Common | | 119,980,000 |
| | Distributed a 10% stock dividend | | |

The accounting equation clearly shows that a stock dividend has no effect on total assets, liabilities, or equity. The increases in equity offset the decreases, and the net effect is zero.

| Assets | = | Liabilities | + | Stockholders' Equity |
|---|---|---|---|---|
| 0 | = | 0 | | - $120,000,000 |
| | | | | + $20,000 |
| | | | | + $119,980,000 |

GAAP identifies stock dividends above 25% as large and permits large stock dividends to be recorded at par value. For a large stock dividend, IHOP would debit Retained Earnings and creditCommon Stock for the par value of the shares distributed in the dividend.

## 5. Treasury Stock Transactions

A corporation may buy its own stock to provide shares for resale to employees, for reissuing as a bonus to employees, or for supporting the market price of the stock. For example, General Motors Corporation bought back its common stock and stated that two primary uses of this stock would be for incentive compensation plans and employee savings plans. Such stock that a corporation has once issued and reacquired is called treasury stock.

A method of accounting for the purchase and resale of treasury stock is the cost method. When the stock is purchased by the corporation, paid-in capital is reduced by debiting Treasury Stock for its cost (the price paid for it). The par value and the price at which the stock was originally issued are ignored. In addition, no dividends are paid on stock held as treasury stock. To do so would place the corporation in the position of earning income through dealing with itself.

When the stock is resold, Treasury Stock is credited for its cost, and any difference between the cost and the selling price is normally debited or credited to Paid-In Capital from Sale of Treasury Stock.

To illustrate, assume that the paid-in capital of a corporation is as follows:

| | | |
|---|---|---|
| Common stock, $30 par (25,000 shares authorized and issued) | $750,000 | |
| Excess of issue price over par | $100,000 | $850,000 |

The purchase and sale of the treasury stock are recorded as in Exhibit 12-11.

**Exhibit 12-11 Record the purchase and sale of treasury stock**

| Description | Debit | Credit |
|---|---|---|
| Treasury Stock | 46,000 | |
| Cash | | 46,000 |
| Purchased 1,000 shares of treasury stock at $46 | | |
| | | |
| Cash | 15,000 | |
| Treasury Stock | | 13,800 |
| Paid-In Capital from Sale of Treasury Stock | | 1,200 |
| Sold 300 shares of treasury stock at $50 | | |
| | | |
| Cash | 12,600 | |
| Paid-In Capital from Sale of Treasury Stock | 1,200 | |
| Treasury Stock | | 13,800 |
| Sold 300 shares of treasury stock at $42 | | |

As shown above, a sale of treasury stock may result in a decrease in paid-in capital. To the extent that Paid-In Capital from Sale of Treasury Stock has a credit balance, it should be debited for any decrease. Any remaining decrease should then be debited to the retained earnings account.

## 6. Reporting Stockholders' Equity

As with other sections of the balance sheet, alternative terms and formats may be used in reporting stockholders' equity. In addition, the significant changes in the sources of stockholders' equity—retained earnings and paid-in capital—may be reported in separate statements or notes that support the balance sheet.

## STOCKHOLDERS' EQUITY IN THE BALANCE SHEET

Businesses may report stockholders' equity in a way that differs from our examples. We use a detailed format in this book to help you learn all the components of stockholders' equity.

One of the most important skills you will take from this course is the ability to understand the financial statements of real companies. Exhibit 12-12 presents a side-by-side comparison of our general teaching format and the format you are likely to encounter in real-world balance sheets, such as IHOP's. All amounts are assumed for this illustration.

**Exhibit 12-12 Stockholders' equity section of a balance sheet**

| General Teaching Format | | Real-World Format | |
|---|---|---|---|
| Stockholders' Equity | | Stockholders' Equity | |
| Paid-in capital: | | Preferred stock, 8%, $10par, 30,000, shares authorized and issued | 330,000 |
| Preferred stock, 8%, $10par, 30,000, shares authorized and issued | 300,000 | Common stock, $1 par, 100,000 shares (Authorized, 60,000 shares issued) | 60,000 |
| Paid-in capital in excess of Par-preferred | 30,000 | Additional paid-in capital | 2,150,000 |
| Common stock, $1 par, 100,000 shares (Authorized, 60,000 shares issued) | 60,000 | Retained earnings | 1,500,000 |
| Paid-in capital in excess of Par-common | 2,100,000 | Less treasury stock, common (1,400 shares at cost) | 40,000 |
| Paid-in capital from treasury stock transactions, common | 20,000 | Total stockholders'equity | 4,000,000 |
| Paid-in capital from retirement of Preferred stock | 30,000 | | |
| Total paid-in capital | 2,540,000 | | |
| Retained earnings | 1,500,000 | | |
| Subtotal | 4,040,000 | | |
| Less treasury stock, common (1,400 shares at cost) | (40,000) | | |
| Total stockholders' equity | 4,000,000 | | |

In general, Preferred Stock comes first and is usually reported as a single amount. Common Stock lists par value per share, the number of shares authorized and the number of shares issued. The balance of the Common Stock account is determined as follows.

$$\text{Common stock} = \text{Number of shares issued} \times \text{Par value per share}$$

Additional paid-in capital combines Paid-in Capital in Excess of Par plus Paid-in Capital from Treasury Stock Transactions plus Paid-in Capital from Retirement of Preferred Stock. Additional paid-in capital belongs to the common stockholders. Outstanding stock equals issued stock minus treasury stock. Retained Earnings comes after the paid-in capital accounts.

Treasury Stock can come last, as a subtraction in arriving at total stockholders' equity.

## REPORTING RETAINED EARNINGS

A corporation may report changes in retained earnings by preparing a separate retained earnings statement, a combined income and retained earnings statement, or a statement of stockholders' equity.

When a separate retained earnings statement is prepared, the beginning balance of retained earnings is reported. The net income is then added (or net loss is subtracted) and any dividends are subtracted to arrive at the ending retained earnings for the period. An example of a statement for Telex Inc. is shown in Exhibit 12-13.

**Exhibit 12-13 Retained earnings statement**

| Telex Inc.<br>Retained Earnings Statement<br>For the Year Ended December 31, 2008 | | | |
|---|---|---|---|
| Retained earnings, January 1, 2008 | | | 255,000 |
| Net income | | 290,000 | |
| Less dividends: | | | |
| Preferred stock | 12,000 | | |
| Common stock | 68,000 | 80,000 | |
| Increase in retained earnings | | | 210,000 |
| Retained earnings, December 31, 2008 | | | 465,000 |

An advantage of the combined format is that itemphasizes net income as the connecting link between the income statement and the retained earnings portion of stockholders' equity. Since the combined form is not often used, we do not illustrate it.

### Restrictions

The retained earnings available for use as dividends may be limited by action of a corporation's board of directors. These amounts, called restrictions or appropriations, remain part of the retained earnings. However, they must be disclosed, usually in the notes to the financial statements.

Restrictions may be classified as either legal, contractual, or discretionary. The board of directors may be legally required to restrict retained earnings because of state laws. For example, some state laws require that retained earnings be restricted by the amount of treasury stock purchased, so that legal capital will not be used for dividends. The board may also be required to restrict retained earnings because of contractual requirements. Finally, the board may restrict retained earnings voluntarily. For example, the board may limit dividend distributions so that more money is available for expanding the business.

### Prior Period Adjustments

Material errors in a prior period's net income may arise from mathematical mistakes and from mistakes in applying accounting principles. The effect of material errors that are not discovered within the same fiscal period in which they occurred should not be included in determining net income for the current period. Instead, corrections of such errors, called prior period adjustments, are reported in the retained earnings statement. These adjustments are reported as an adjustment to the retained earnings balance at the beginning of the period in which the error is discovered and corrected.

## 7. Stock Splits

A stock split is an increase in the number of shares of stock authorized, issued, and outstanding, coupled with a proportionate reduction in the stock's par value. For example, if the company splits its stock 2 for 1, the number of outstanding shares is doubled and each share's par value is halved. A stock split, like a large stock dividend, decreases the market price of the stock—with the intention of making the stock more attractive in the market. Most leading companies in the United States—including IBM, PepsiCo, and Best Buy—have split their stock.

The market price of a share of Best Buy common stock has beenapproximately $50. Assume that Best Buy wishes to decrease the market price to approximately $25 per share. Best Buy can split its common stock 2 for 1, and the stock price will fall to around $25. A 2-for-1 stock split means that the company will have twice as many shares of stock authorized, issued, and outstanding after the split as it had before. Each share's par value will be cut in half. Before the split, Best Buy had approximately 500 million shares of $0.10 (10 cents) par common stock issued and outstanding. Compare Best Buy's stockholders' equity before and after a 2-for-1 stock split.

All account balances are the same after the stock split as before. Only 3 Best Buy items are affected.

(1) Par value per share drops from 10 cents to 5 cents.

(2) Shares authorized double from 1,000 million to 2,000 million shares.

(3) Shares issued double from 500 million to 1,000 million shares.

Total equity doesn't change, nor do any assets or liabilities.

**TERMINOLOGY:**

Separate Legal Entity:独立法人

Limited Liability:有限责任

Stockholders'Equity:股东权益

Common Stock:普通股

No-par Stock:无面值股票

Cash Dividends:现金股利

Stock Dividends:股票股利

Treasury Stock:库存股

Retained Earnings Statement:留存收益表

Stock Splits:股票分割

## QUESTIONS:

**1. Describe the nature of the corporate form of organization.**

Corporations have a separate legal existence, transferable units of stock, and limited stockholders' liability. Corporations may be either public or private corporations, and they are subject to federal income taxes.

The documents included in forming a corporation include an application of incorporation, articles of incorporation, and bylaws. Costs often incurred in organizing a corporation include legal fees, taxes, state incorporation fees, and promotional costs. Such costs are debited to an expense account entitled Organizational Expenses.

**2. List the major sources of paid-in capital, including the various classes of stock.**

The main source of paid-in capital is from issuing stock. The two primary classes of stock are common stock and preferred stock. Preferred stock is normally nonparticipating and may be cumulative or noncumulative. In addition to the issuance of stock, paid-in capital may arise from treasury stock transactions.

**3. State the effect of stock splits on corporate financial statements.**

When a corporation reduces the par or stated value of its common stock and issues a proportionate number of additional shares, a stock split has occurred. There are no changes in the balances of any corporation accounts, and no entry is required for a stock split.

**4. Describe and illustrate the reporting of stockholders' equity.**

Significant changes in the sources of stockholders' equity—paid-in capital and retained earnings—may be reported in separate statements or notes that support the balance sheet presentation. Changes in retained earnings may be reported by preparing a separate retained earnings statement, a combined income and retained earnings statement, or a statement of stockholders' equity. Restrictions to retained earnings must be disclosed, usually in the notes to the financial statements. Material errors in a prior period's net income, called prior-period adjustments, are reported in the retained earnings statement.

## PROBLEM:

The financial information of Fiesta, Inc. was list in Exhibit 12-14 as at September 30, 2007.

**Exhibit 12-14 Some accounts and related balance**

| | | | |
|---|---|---|---|
| Common stock, \$1 par, 50,000 shares authorized, 20,000 shares issued | 20,000 | Long-term note payable | 70,000 |
| Salary payable | 3,000 | Inventory | 85,000 |
| Cash | 15,000 | Property, plant, and equipment | 205,000 |
| Accounts payable | 20,000 | Accounts receivable, net | 25,000 |

(Continued)

| | | | |
|---|---|---|---|
| Retained earnings | 80,000 | Preferred stock, $2.50, no-par, 10,000 shares authorized, 2,000 shares issued | 50,000 |
| Paid-in capital in excess of par-common | 75,000 | Income tax payable | 12,000 |

**Requirements:**

1. Use the accounts and related balances in Exhibit 12-14, to prepare the classified balance sheet of Fiesta, Inc., at September 30, 2007. Use the account format of the balance sheet.

2. Compute the book value per share of Fiesta's common stock. No preferred dividends are in arrears, and Fiesta has not declared the current-year dividend.

**1. Solution**

Requirement. Exhibit 12-15 shows the classified balance sheet.

**Exhibit 12-15 The classified balance sheet**

| Fiesta, inc. Balance Sheet<br>September 30, 2007 | | | | |
|---|---|---|---|---|
| Assets | | Liabilities | | |
| Current: | | Current: | | |
| Cash | 15,000 | Accounts payable | | 20,000 |
| Accounts receivable, net | 25,000 | Salary payable | | 3,000 |
| Inventory | 85,000 | Income tax payable | | 12,000 |
| Total current assets | 125,000 | Total current liabilities | | 35,000 |
| Property, plant, and equipment | 205,000 | Long-term note payable | | 70,000 |
| Total assets | 330,000 | Total liabilities | | 105,000 |
| | | Stockholders' Equity | | |
| | | Preferred stock, $2.50, no-par, 10,000 shares authorizd 2,000 shares issued | 50,000 | |
| | | Commonstock, $1 par, 50,000 shares authorized, 20,000 shares issued | 20,000 | |
| | | Paid-in capital in excess of par-common | 75,000 | |
| | | Total paid-in capital | 145,000 | |
| | | Retained earnings | 80,000 | |
| | | Total stockholders' equity | | 225,000 |
| | | Total liabilities and stockholders' equity | | 330,000 |

Requirement 2. Exhibit 12-16 shows the computation of the book value per share.

**Exhibit 12-16 Computation of the book value per share**

| | |
|---|---|
| Preferred equity: | |
| Carrying value | 50,000 |
| Cumulative dividend for the current year(2,000 shares × $2.50) | 5,000 |
| Preferred equity | 55,000 |
| Common: | |
| Total stockholder's equity | 225,000 |
| Less preferred equity | 55,000 |
| Common equity | 170,000 |
| Book value share of common( $170,000/20,000 shares) | 8.50 |

# Chapter 13

## Bonds Payable and Investments in Bonds

**Objectives**

1. Compute the impact of long-term borrowing on earnings per share.
2. Describe the characteristics and pricing of bonds payable.
3. Journalize entries for bonds payable.
4. Describe the payment and redemption of bonds payable.
5. Journalize entries for the purchase, interest, discount and premium amortization, and sale of bond investments.
6. Prepare a corporation balance sheet.

# 1. Financing Corporations

Corporations often finance their operations by purchasing on credit and issuing notes or bonds. We have discussed accounts payable and notes payable in earlier chapters. A bond is simply a form of an interest-bearing note. Like a note, a bond requires periodic interest payments, and the face amount must be repaid at the maturity date. Bondholders are creditors of the issuing corporation, and their claims on the assets of the corporation rank ahead of stockholders.

One of the many factors that influence the decision to issue debt or equity is the effect of each alternative on earnings per share. To illustrate the possible effects, assume that a corporation's board of directors is considering the following alternative plans for financing a $4,000,000 company, the plans are shown in Exhibit 13-1.

**Exhibit 13-1 Alternative financing plans**

| | Plan 1 | Plan 2 | Plan 3 |
|---|---|---|---|
| Issue 10% bonds | — | — | 1,000,000 |
| Issue 9% preferred stock, $50 par value | — | 3,000,000 | 2,000,000 |
| Issue common stock, $10 par value | 4,000,000 | 1,000,000 | 1,000,000 |
| | 4,000,000 | 4,000,000 | 4,000,000 |

In each case, we assume that the stocks or bonds are issued at their par or face amount. The corporation is expecting to earn $900,000 annually, before deducting interest on the bonds and income taxes estimated at 40% of income. Exhibit 13-2 shows the effect of the three plans on the income of the corporation and the earnings per share on common stock.

**Exhibit 13-2 Effect of alternative financing plans— $900,000 earnings**

| | Plan 1 | Plan 2 | Plan 3 |
|---|---|---|---|
| 10% bonds | — | — | 1,000,000 |
| Preferred 9% stock, $50 par | — | 3,000,000 | 2,000,000 |
| Common stock, $10 par | 4,000,000 | 1,000,000 | 1,000,000 |
| Total | 4,000,000 | 4,000,000 | 4,000,000 |
| Earnings before interest and income tax | 900,000 | 900,000 | 900,000 |
| Deduct interest on bonds | — | — | 100,000 |
| Income before income tax | 900,000 | 900,000 | 800,000 |
| Deduct income tax | 360,000 | 360,000 | 320,000 |
| Net income | 540,000 | 540,000 | 480,000 |
| Dividends on preferred stock | — | 270,000 | 180,000 |
| Available for dividends on common stock | 540,000 | 270,000 | 300,000 |
| Shares of common stock outstanding | 400,000 | 100,000 | 100,000 |
| Earnings per share on common stock | 1.35 | 2.70 | 3.00 |

Exhibit 13-2 indicates that Plan 3 yields the highest earnings per share on common stock and is thus the most attractive for common stockholders. If the estimated earnings are more than \$900,000, the difference between the earnings per share to common stockholders under Plan 1 and Plan 3 is even greater. However, if smaller earnings occur, Plans 2 and 3 become less attractive to common stockholders. To illustrate, the effect of earnings of \$480,000 rather than \$900,000 is shown in Exhibit 13-3.

**Exhibit 13-3 Effect of alternative financing plans— \$480,000 earnings**

| | Plan 1 | Plan 2 | Plan 3 |
|---|---|---|---|
| 10% bonds | — | — | 1,000,000 |
| Preferred 9% stock, \$50 par | — | 3,000,000 | 2,000,000 |
| Common stock, \$10 par | 4,000,000 | 1,000,000 | 1,000,000 |
| Total | 4,000,000 | 4,000,000 | 4,000,000 |
| Earnings before interest and income tax | 480,000 | 480,000 | 480,000 |
| Deduct interest on bonds | — | | 100,000 |
| Income before income tax | 480,000 | 480,000 | 380,000 |
| Deduct income tax | 192,000 | 192,000 | 152,000 |
| Net income | 288,000 | 288,000 | 228,000 |
| Dividends on preferred stock | — | 270,000 | 180,000 |
| Available for dividends on common stock | 288,000 | 18,000 | 48,000 |
| Shares of common stock outstanding | 400,000 | 100,000 | 100,000 |
| Earnings per share on common stock | 0.72 | 0.18 | 0.48 |

In addition to the effect on earnings per share, the board of directors should consider other factors in deciding whether to issue debt or equity. For example, once bonds are issued, periodic interest payments and repayment of the face value of the bonds are beyond the control of the corporation. That is, if these payments are not made, the bondholders could seek court action and force the company into bankruptcy. In contrast, a corporation is not legally obligated to pay dividends.

## 2. Characteristics and Pricing of Bonds Payable

In addition to their face values, interest rates, interest payment dates, and maturity dates, bonds may differ in a variety of ways. In this section, we describe the common characteristics of bonds and how bonds may differ from one another. In doing so, we introduce common terms used to describe types of bonds. In addition, we describe and illustrate how the price investors are willing to pay for a bond is determined.

### BOND CHARACTERISTICS

A corporation that issues bonds enters into a contract, called a bond indenture or trust indenture, with the bondholders. A bond issue is normally divided into a number of individual bonds. Usually, the face value of each bond, called the principal, is $1,000 or a multiple of $1,000. The interest on bonds may be payable annually, semiannually, or quarterly. Most bonds pay interest semiannually.

The prices of bonds are quoted as a percentage of the bonds' face value. Thus, investors could purchase or sell Wal-Mart bonds quoted at 125.63% for $1,256.30. Likewise, bonds quoted at 118% could be purchased or sold for $1,180.

When all bonds of an issue mature at the same time, they are called term bonds. If the maturities are spread over several dates, they are called serial bonds. For example, one-tenth of an issue of $2,500,000 bonds, or $250,000, may mature 14 years from the issue date, another $250,000 in the 15th year, and so on, until the final $250,000 matures in the 27th year.

Bonds that may be exchanged for other securities, such as common stock, are called convertible bonds. Bonds that a corporation reserves the right to redeem before their maturity are called callable bonds. Bonds issued on the basis of the general credit of the corporation are called debenture bonds.

## PRICING OF BONDS PAYABLE

When a corporation issues bonds, the price that buyers are willing to pay for the bonds depends upon the following three factors.

(1) The face amount of the bonds, which is the amount due at the maturity date.
(2) The periodic interest to be paid on the bonds.
(3) The market rate of interest.

The face amount and the periodic interest to be paid on the bonds are identified in the bond indenture. The periodic interest is expressed as a percentage of the face amount of the bond. This percentage or rate of interest is called the contract rate or coupon rate.

The market or effective rate of interest is determined by transactions between buyers and sellers of similar bonds. The market rate of interest is affected by a variety of factors, including, investor's assessment of current economic conditions as well as future expectations.

The bonds will sell at their face amount if the contract rate of interest equals the market rate of interest. If the market rate is higher than the contract rate, the bonds will sell at a discount, or less than their face amount. Why is this the case? Buyers are not willing to pay the face amount for bonds whose contract rate is lower than the market rate. The discount, in effect, represents the amount necessary to make up for the difference in the market and the contract interest rates. In contrast, if the market rate is lower than the contract rate, the bonds will sell at a premium, or more than their face amount. In this case, buyers are willing to pay more than the face amount for bonds whose contract rate is higher than the market rate.

The face amount of the bonds and the periodic interest on the bonds represents cash to be received by the buyer in the future. The buyer determines how much to pay for the bonds by computing the present value of these future cash receipts, using the market rate of interest. The concept of present value is based on the time value of money.

The time value of money concept recognizes that an amount of cash to be received today is worth more than the same amount of cash to be received in the future. For example, what would you rather have $100 today or $100 one year from now? You would rather have the $100 today because it could be invested to earn income. For example, if the $100 could be invested to earn 10% per year, the $100 will accumulate to $110 ($100 plus $10 earnings) in one year. In this sense, you can think of the $100 in hand today as the present value of $110 to be received a year from today. This present value is illustrated in the following time line, Exhibit 13-4 shows the present value of bond.

**Exhibit 13-4 The present value of bond**

Present value of $110 to be received one year from today

Face value of bond

$100

$110

Interest rate of 10%

TODAY

One Year From TODAY

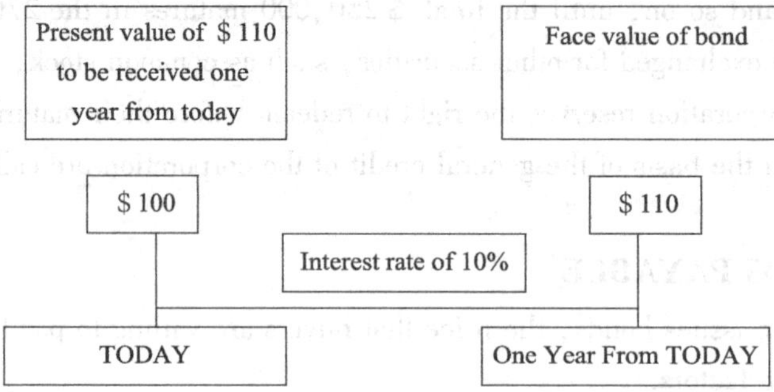

A related concept to present value is future value. In the preceding illustration, the $110 to be received a year from today is the future value of $100 today, assuming an interest rate of 10%.

## PRESENT VALUE OF THE FACE AMOUNT OF BONDS

The present value of the face amount of bonds is the value today of the amount to be received at a future maturity date. For example, assume that you are to receive the face value of a $2,000 bond in one year. If the market rate of interest is 10%, the present value of the face value of the $2,000 bond is $1,818.18 ($2,000/1.10). This present value is illustrated in the following time line in Exhibit 13-5.

**Exhibit 13-5 Present value of the face amount of bonds** (1 year)

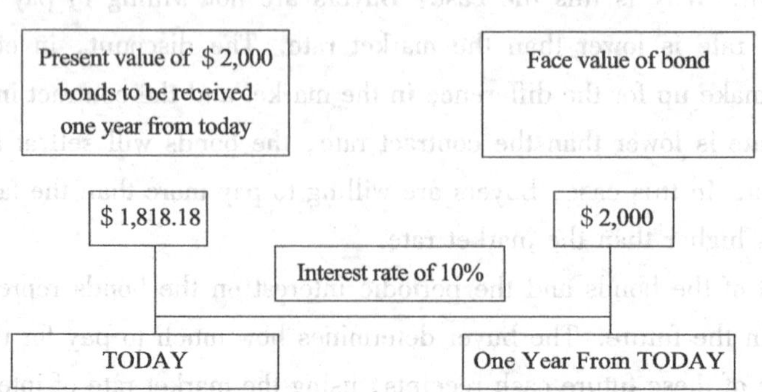

If you are to receive the face value of a $2,000 bond in two years, with interest of 10% compounded at the end of the first year, the present value is $1,652.90 ($1,818.18/1.10). We illustrate this present value in the following time line in Exhibit 13-6.

**Exhibit 13-6 Present value of the face amount of bonds** (2 year)

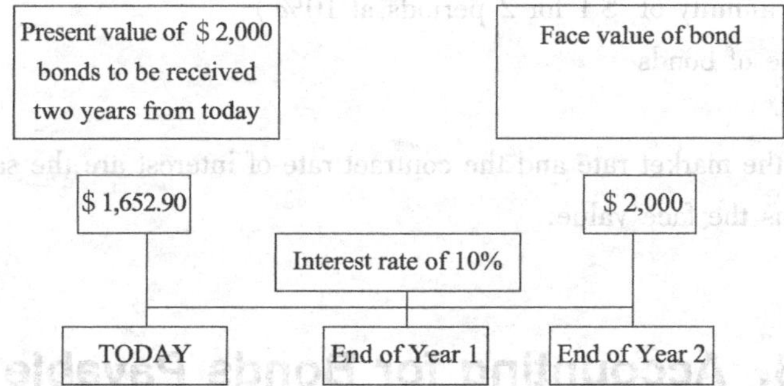


You can determine the present value of the face amount of bonds to be received in the future by a time line and a series of divisions. In practice, however, it is easier to use a table of present values. The present value of $1 table can be used to find the present value factor for $1 to be received after a number of periods in the future. The face amount of the bonds is then multiplied by this factor to determine its present value.

## PRESENT VALUE OF THE PERIODIC BOND INTEREST PAYMENTS

The present value of the periodic bond interest payments is the value today of the amount of interest to be received at the end of each interest period. Such a series of equal cash payments at fixed intervals is called an annuity.

The present value of an annuity is the sum of the present values of each cash flow. To illustrate, assume that the $2,000 bond in the preceding example pays interest of 10% annually and that the market rate of interest is 10%. In addition, assume that the bond matures at the end of two years. The present value of the two interest payments of $200 ($2,000 × 10%) is $347.10. It can be determined by using the present value table.

Instead of using present value of amount tables, separate present value tables are normally used for annuities. The table of the present value of an annuity of $1 at compound interest shows the present value of $1 to be received at the end of each period for various compound rates of interest. For example, the present value of $200 to be received at the end of each of the next two years at 10% compound interest per period is $347.10 ($200 × 1.735,5). This amount is the same amount that we computed previously.

As we stated earlier, the amount buyers are willing to pay for a bond is the sum of the present value of the face value and the periodic interest payments, calculated by using the market rate of interest. In our example, this calculation is as follows:

Present value due in 2 years, at 10% compounded annually: $ 2,000 ×0.826,45
(present value factor of $ 1 for 2 periods at 10%) $ 1,652.90
Present value of 2 annual interest payments of $ 200, at 10% compounded annually:
$ 200 ×1.735,5
(present value of annuity of $ 1 for 2 periods at 10%) $ 347.10
Total present value of bonds $ 2,000.00

In this example, the market rate and the contract rate of interest are the same. Thus, the present value is the same as the face value.

## 3. Accounting for Bonds Payable

In this section, we describe and illustrate how corporations record the issuance of bonds and the payment of bond interest.

### BONDS ISSUED AT FACE AMOUNT

To illustrate the journal entries for issuing bonds, assume that on January 1, 2008, a corporation issues for cash $ 100,000 of 10%, five-year bonds, with interest of $ 5,000 payable semiannually. The market rate of interest at the time the bonds are issued is 10%. Since the contract rate and the market rate of interest are the same, the bonds will sell at their face amount. This amount is the sum of the present value of the face amount of $ 100,000 to be repaid in five years and the present value of 10 semiannual interest payments of $ 5,000 each. This computation are shown below.

Present value of face amount of $ 100,000 due in 5 years, at 10% compounded semiannually:
$ 100,000 ×0.61391
(present value of $ 1 for 10 periods at 5%) $ 61,391
Present value of 10 semiannual interest payments of $ 5,000, at 10% compounded semiannually: $ 5,000 ×7.72174
(present value of annuity of $ 1 for10 periods at 5%) $ 38,609
Total present value of bonds $ 100,000

The entry records the issuing of the $ 100,000 bonds at their face amount, as shown in Exhibit 13-7.

**Exhibit 13-7 Journal entry of issuing bonds at their face amount**

| Date | | Description | Debit | Credit |
|---|---|---|---|---|
| 2008 Jan. | 1 | Cash | 100,000 | |
| | | Bonds Payable | | 100,000 |
| | | Issued $100,000 bonds payable at face amount | | |

Every six months after the bonds have been issued, interest payments of $5,000 are made. The first interest payment is recorded as shown in Exhibit 13-8.

**Exhibit 13-8 Journal entry of interest payments**

| Date | | Description | Debit | Credit |
|---|---|---|---|---|
| June | 30 | Interest Expense | 5,000 | |
| | | Cash | | 5,000 |
| | | Paid six months' interest on bonds | | |

At the maturity date, the payment of the principal of $100,000 is recorded in Exhibit 13-9.

**Exhibit 13-9 Journal entry to pay bond principal at maturity date**

| Date | | Description | Debit | Credit |
|---|---|---|---|---|
| 2012Dec. | 31 | Bonds Payable | 100,000 | |
| | | Cash | | 100,000 |
| | | Paid bond principal at maturity date | | |

## BONDS ISSUED AT A DISCOUNT

What if the market rate of interest is higher than the contract rate of interest? If the market rate of interest is 13% and the contract rate is 10% on the five-year, $100,000 bonds, the bonds will sell at a discount. The present value of these bonds is calculated as follows.

Present value of face amount of $100,000 due in 5 years, at 13% compounded semiannually:

$100,000 × 0.53273

(present value of $1 for 10 periods at 6.5%) $53,273

Present value of 10 semiannual interest payments of $5,000, at 13% compounded semiannually: $5,000 × 7.18883

(present value of annuity of $1 for 10 periods at 6.5%) $35,944

Total present value of bonds $89,217

The two present values that make up the total are both less than the related amounts in the preceding example. This is because the market rate of interest was 10% in the first example, while the market rate of interest is 13% in this example. The present value of a future amount becomes less and less as the interest rate used to compute the present value increases.

The entry to record the issuing of the $100,000 bonds at a discount is shown in Exhibit 13-10.

**Exhibit 13-10 Journal entry of issuing bonds at discount**

| Date | | Description | Debit | Credit |
|---|---|---|---|---|
| 2008 Jan. | 1 | Cash | 89,217 | |
| | | Discount on Bonds Payable | 10,783 | |
| | | Bonds Payable | | 100,000 |
| | | Issued $100,000 bonds at discount | | |

The $10,783 discount may be viewed as the amount that is needed to entice investors to accept a contract rate of interest that is below the market rate. You may think of the discount as the market's way of adjusting a bond's contract rate of interest to the higher market rate of interest. Using this logic, generally accepted accounting principles require that bond discounts be amortized as interest expense over the life of the bond.

## AMORTIZING A BOND DISCOUNT

There are two methods of amortizing a bond discount: ①The straight-line method. ② The effective interest rate method, often called the interest method. Both methods amortize the same total amount of discount over the life of the bonds. The interest method is required by generally accepted accounting principles. However, the straight-line method is acceptable if the results obtained do not materially differ from the results that would be obtained by using the interest method. Because the straight-line method illustrates the basic concept of amortizing discounts and is simpler, we will use it in this chapter. We will illustrate the interest method in this chapter later.

The straight-line method of amortizing a bond discount provides for amortization in equal periodic amounts. Applying this method to the preceding example yields amortization of 1/10 of $10,783, or $1,078.30, each half year. The amount of the interest expense on the bonds is the same, $6,078.30 ($5,000 + $1,078.30), for each half year. The entry to record the first interest payment and the amortization of the related discount in Exhibit 13-11.

**Exhibit 13-11 Journal entry to record the interest payment and amortization of discount**

| Date | | Description | Debit | Credit |
|---|---|---|---|---|
| June | 30 | Interest Expense | 6,078.30 | |
| | | Discount on Bonds Payable | | 1,078.30 |
| | | Cash | | 5,000 |
| | | Paid semiannual interest and amortized 1/10 bonds discount | | |

## BONDS ISSUED AT A PREMIUM

If the market rate of interest is 10% and the contract rate is 12% on the five-year, $100,000 bonds, the bonds will sell at a premium. The present value of these bonds is computed as shown below.

Present value of face amount of $ 100,000 due in 5 years, at 10% compounded semiannually:

$ 100,000 × 0.61391

(present value of $ 1 for 10 periods at 5%) $ 61,391

Present value of 10 semiannual interest payments of $ 6,000, at 10% compounded semiannually:

$ 6,000 × 7.72174

(present value of annuity of $ 1 for10 periods at 5%) $ 46,330

Total present value of bonds $ 107,721

The entry to record the issuing of the bonds is in Exhibit 13-12.

**Exhibit 13-12 Journal entry of issuing bonds at a premium**

| Date | | Description | Debit | Credit |
|---|---|---|---|---|
| 2008 Jan. | 1 | Cash | 107,721 | |
| | | Bonds Payable | | 100,000 |
| | | Premium on Bonds Payable | | 7,721 |
| | | Issued $ 100,000 bonds at a premium | | |

## AMORTIZING A BOND PREMIUM

The amortization of bond premiums is basically the same as that for bond discounts, except that interest expense is decreased, in the above example, the straight-line method yields amortization of 1/10 of $ 7,721, or $ 772.10, each half year. The entry to record the first interest payment and the amortization of the related premium is in Exhibit 13-13.

**Exhibit 13-13 Journal entry to record the interest payment and amortization of premium**

| Date | | Description | Debit | Credit |
|---|---|---|---|---|
| June. | 30 | Interest Expense | 5,227.90 | |
| | | Premium on Bonds Payable | 772.10 | |
| | | Cash | | 6,000 |
| | | Paid semiannual interest and amortized 1/10 bonds premium | | |

## ZERO-COUPON BONDS

Some bonds provide for only the payment of the face amount at the maturity date. Such bonds are called zero-coupon bonds. Because they do not provide for interest payments, these bonds sell at a large discount. For example, Merrill Lynch & Co. Inc.'s zero-coupon bonds maturing in 2028 were selling for \$21.50.

The issuing price of zero-coupon bonds is the present value of their face amount. To illustrate, if the market rate of interest is 13%, the present value of \$100,000 zero- coupon, five-year bonds is calculated as follows.

Present value of \$100,000 due in 5 years, at 13% compounded semiannually:

\$100,000 × 0.53273

(present value of \$1 for 10 periods at 6.5%) \$53,273

The accounting for zero-coupon bonds is similar to that for interest-bearing bonds that have been sold at a discount. The discount is amortized as interest expense over the life of the bonds. The entry to record the issuing of the bonds is in Exhibit 13-14.

**Exhibit 13-14 Journal entry of issuing zero-coupon bonds**

| Date | | Description | Debit | Credit |
|---|---|---|---|---|
| 2008 Jan. | 1 | Cash | 53,273 | |
| | | Discount on Bonds Payable | 46,727 | |
| | | Bonds Payable | | 100,000 |
| | | Issued \$100,000 zero-coupon bonds | | |

## 4. Payment and Redemption of Bonds Payable

The face value of bonds payable should be paid at the maturity date of the bonds. The entry to record the payment of bonds at their maturity date is a debit to Bonds Payable and a credit to Cash.

The bond indenture may require that funds for the payment of the face value of the bonds at maturity be set aside over the life of the bond issue. A bond indenture may restrict dividend payments to stockholders as a means of increasing the likelihood that the bonds will be paid at maturity. Finally, the bond indenture may allow for the early payment or redemption of the bond issue.

### BOND SINKING FUNDS

A bond indenture may require that cash be periodically transferred into a special cash fund over the life of the bond issue. Doing so ensures that an adequate amount of cash will be available at the maturity date for the payment of the face amount of the bonds. This special type of cash fund is called a sinking fund.

When cash is transferred to the sinking fund, it is recorded in an account called Sinking Fund Cash. When investments are purchased with the sinking fund cash, they are recorded in an account called Sinking Fund Investments. As income (interest or dividends) is received, it is recorded in an account called Sinking Fund Revenue.

Sinking fund revenue represents earnings of the corporation and is reported in the income statement as other income. The cash and the securities making up the sinking fund are reported in the balance sheet as investments, immediately below the Current Assets section.

A bond indenture may restrict dividend payments to stockholders as a means of increasing the likelihood that the bonds will be paid at maturity. In addition to or instead of this restriction, the bond indenture may require that funds for the payment of the face value of the bonds at maturity be set aside over the life of the bond issue. The amounts set aside are kept separate from other assets in the sinking fund.

## BOND REDEMPTION

A corporation may call or redeem bonds before they mature. This is often done if the market rate of interest declines significantly after the bonds have been issued. In this situation, the corporation may sell new bonds at a lower interest rate and use the funds to redeem the original bond issue. The corporation can thus save on future interest expenses.

A corporation often issues callable bonds to protect itself against significant declines in future interest rates. However, callable bonds are more risky for investors, who may not be able to replace the called bonds with investments paying an equal amount of interest.

A corporation usually redeems its bonds at a price different from that of the carrying amount (or book value) of the bonds. The carrying amount of bonds payable is the balance of the bonds payable account (face amount of the bonds) less any unamortized discount or plus any unamortized premium. If the price paid for redemption is below the bond carrying amount, the difference in these two amounts is recorded as a gain. If the price paid for the redemption is above the carrying amount, a loss is recorded. Gains and losses on the redemption of bonds are reported in the Other Income and Expense section of the income statement.

Assume that on June 30, 2007 a corporation has a bond issue of $200,000 outstanding, on which there is an unamortized premium of $8,000. Assuming that the corporation purchases one-fourth ($50,000) of the bonds for $48,000 on June 30, the entry to record the redemption is in Exhibit 13-15.

**Exhibit 13-15 Journal entry to record the redemption and the gain**

| Date | | Description | Debit | Credit |
|---|---|---|---|---|
| 2007 June | 30 | Bonds Payable | 50,000 | |
| | | Premium on Bonds Payable | 2,000 | |
| | | Cash | | 48,000 |
| | | Gain on Redemption of Bonds | | 4,000 |
| | | Redeemed $50,000 bonds for $48,000 | | |

In the preceding entry, only a portion of the premium relating to the redeemed bonds is written off. The difference between the carrying amount of the bonds purchased, $52,000 ($50,000 +

$ 2,000), and the price paid for the redemption, $ 48,000, is recorded as a gain.

If the corporation calls the entire bond issue for $ 210,000 on June 30, the entry to record the redemption is in Exhibit 13-16.

**Exhibit 13-16 Journal entry to record the redemption and the loss**

| Date | | Description | Debit | Credit |
|---|---|---|---|---|
| 2007 June | 30 | Bonds Payable | 200,000 | |
| . | | Premium on Bonds Payable | 8,000 | |
| | | Loss on Redemption of Bonds | 2,000 | |
| | | Cash | | 210,000 |
| | | Redeemed $ 200,000 bonds for $ 210,000 | | |

# 5. Investment in Bonds

In this section, we discuss the accounting for bonds from the point of view of investors, and assume that the investor uses the cost principle to account for these investments.

## ACCOUNTING FOR BOND INVESTMENTS—PURCHASE, INTEREST, AND AMORTIZATION

Bonds may be purchased either directly from the issuing corporation or through an organized bond exchange. Bond exchanges publish daily bond quotations. These quotations normally include the bond interest rate, maturity date, volume of sales, and the high, low, and closing prices for each corporation's bonds traded during the day. Prices for bonds are quoted as a percentage of the face amount. Thus, the price of a $ 1,000 bond quoted at 99.5% would be $ 995, while the price of a bond quoted at 104.25% would be $ 1,042.50.

As with other assets, the cost of a bond investment includes all costs related to the purchase. For example, for bonds purchased through an exchange, the amount paid as a broker's commission should be included as part of the cost of the investment.

When bonds are purchased between interest dates, the buyer normally pays the seller the interest accrued from the last interest payment date to the date of purchase. The amount of the interest paid is normally debited to Interest Revenue, since it is an offset against the amount that will be received at the next interest date.

Assume that an investor purchases a $ 1,000 bond at 102% plus a broker- age fee of $ 5.30 and accrued interest of $ 10.20. The investor records the transaction as shown in Exhibit 13-17.

**Exhibit 13-17 Journal entry to record the investment in bond**

| Date | | Description | Debit | Credit |
|---|---|---|---|---|
| 2007 Apr. | 2 | Investment in Bonds | 1,025.30 | |
| | | Interest Revenue | 10.20 | |
| | | Cash | | 1,035.50 |

The cost of the bond is recorded in a single investment account. The face amount of the bond and the premium (or discount) are normally not recorded in separate accounts. This is different from the accounting for bonds payable. Separate premium and discount accounts are usually not used by investors, because they usually do not hold bond investments until the bonds mature.

If bonds held as long-term investments are purchased at a price other than the face amount, the premium or discount should be amortized over the remaining life of the bonds. The amortization of premiums and discounts affects the investment and interest accounts as shown below.

Premium Amortization:

| | | |
|---|---|---|
| Dr. Investment Revenue | XXX | |
| Cr. Investment in Bonds | | XXX |

Discount Amortization:

| | | |
|---|---|---|
| Dr. Investment in Bonds | XXX | |
| Cr. Investment Revenue | | XXX |

The amount of the amortization can be determined by using either the straight-line or interest methods. Unlike bonds payable, the amortization of premiums and discounts on bond investments is usually recorded at the end of the period, rather than when interest is received.

To illustrate the accounting for bond investments, assume that on July 1, 2007, Crenshaw Inc. purchases $50,000 of 8% bonds of Deitz Corporation, due in 8.75years. Crenshaw Inc. purchases the bonds directly from Deitz Corporation to yield an effective interest rate of 11%. The purchase price is $41,706 plus interest of $1,000 ($50,000 × 8% × 3/12) accrued from April 1, 2007, the date of the last semiannual interest payment. Entries in the accounts of Crenshaw Inc. at the time of purchase and for the remainder of the fiscal period ending December 31, 2007, as shown in Exhibit 13-18.

**Exhibit 13-18 Journal entry to record the investment in bond**

| Date | | Description | Debit | Credit |
|---|---|---|---|---|
| 2007 July | 1 | Investment in Detiz Corporation Bonds | 41,706 | |
| | | Interest Revenue | 1,000 | |
| | | Cash | | 42,706 |
| | | Purchased investment in bonds, plus accrued interest | | |
| | | | | |
| 2007 Oct | 1 | Cash | 2,000 | |
| | | Interest Revenue | | 2,000 |
| | | Received semiannual interest for April 1 to October 1 | | |
| | | | | |

(Continued)

| Date | | Description | Debit | Credit |
|---|---|---|---|---|
| 2007 Dec | 31 | Interest Receivable | 1,000 | |
| | | Interest Revenue | | 1,000 |
| | | Accrued interest from October 1 to December 31 | | |
| | 31 | Investment in Deitz Corporation Bonds | 474 | |
| | | Interest Revenue | | 474 |
| | | Amortization of discount from July 1 to December 31 (( $50,000 - $41,706)/105 ×6 = $474) | | |

The effect of these entries on the interest revenue account is shown in Exhibit 13-19.

**Exhibit 13-19 The effect of entries on the interest revenue account**

| July 1 | 1,000 | Oct. 1 | 2,000 |
|---|---|---|---|
| | | Dec. 31 Adj | 1,000 |
| | | 31 Adj | 474 |
| | | Adj. Bal. | 2,474 |

## ACCOUNTING FOR BOND INVESTMENTS—SALE

When many long-term investments in bonds are sold before their maturity date, the seller receives the sales price (less commissions and other selling costs) plus any accrued interest since the last interest payment date. Before recording the cash proceeds, the seller should amortize any discount or premium for the current period up to the date of sale. Any gain or loss on the sale is then recorded when the cash proceeds are recorded. Such gains and losses are normally reported in the Other Income and Expense section of the income statement.

To illustrate, assume that the Deitz Corporation bonds in the preceding example are sold for $47,350 plus accrued interest on June 30, 2014. The carrying amount of the bonds (cost plus amortized discount) as of January 1, 2014 (78 months after their purchase) is $47,868 ($41,706 + ($79 per month ×78 months)). The entries to amortize the discount for the current year and to record the sale of the bonds are shown in Exhibit 13-20.

**Exhibit 13-20 Journal entry to record the amortization and the sale of bond**

| Date | | Description | Debit | Credit |
|---|---|---|---|---|
| 2014 June | 30 | Investment in Deitz Corporation Bonds | 474 | |
| | | Interest Revenue | | 474 |
| | | Amortized discount for current year | | |
| | | | | |

(Continued)

| Date | | Description | Debit | Credit |
|---|---|---|---|---|
| | 30 | Cash | 48,350 | |
| | | Loss on Sale of Investment | 992 | |
| | | Interest Revenue | | 1,000 |
| | | Investment in Deitz Corporation Bonds | | 48,342 |
| | | Received interest and proceeds from sale of bonds | | |
| | | Interest for April 1 to June 31 = \$50,000 × 8% × 3/12 = \$1,000 | | |

# 6. Corporation Balance Sheet

In previous chapters, we illustrated the income statement and retained earnings statement for a corporation. The consolidated balance sheet in Exhibit 13-21 illustrates the presentation of many of the items discussed in this and preceding chapters. These items include bond sinking funds, investments in bonds, goodwill, deferred income taxes, and bonds payable and unamortized discount.

**Exhibit 13-21 Balance sheet of a corporation**

**Escoe Corporation and Subsidiaries**
**Consolidated Balance Sheet**
**December 31, 2008**

| Assets | | | | |
|---|---|---|---|---|
| Current assets: | | | | |
| Cash and cash equivalents | | | 423,500 | |
| Accounts and notes receivable | | 734,000 | | |
| Less allowance for doubtful receivables | | 40,000 | 694,000 | |
| Inventories, at low of cost (first-in, first-out) or market | | | 887,500 | |
| Prepaid expense | | | 67,000 | |
| Total current assets | | | | 2,072,000 |
| Investments: | | | | |
| Bond sinking fund (market value, \$473,000) | | | 456,500 | |
| Investment in bonds of Dalton (market value, \$231,000) | | | 250,000 | |

(Continued)

| Assets | | | | |
|---|---|---|---|---|
| Total investments | | | | 706,500 |
| | Cost | Accumulated Depreciation | Book Value | |
| Property, Plant, and equipment (depreciated by the straight-line method): | | | | |
| Land | 254,000 | — | 254,000 | |
| Buildings | 945,000 | 343,235 | 601,765 | |
| Machinery and equipment | 2,657,400 | 785,200 | 1,872,200 | |
| Total property, plant, and equipment | 3,856,400 | 1,128,435 | | 2,727,965 |
| Intangible assets: | | | | |
| Goodwill | | | | 365,000 |
| Total assets | | | | 5,871,465 |
| **Liabilities** | | | | |
| Current liabilities: | | | | |
| Account payable | | | 634,150 | |
| Income tax payable | | | 110,500 | |
| Dividends payable | | | 95,300 | |
| Accrued liabilities | | | 80,400 | |
| Deferred income tax payable | | | 12,000 | |
| Total current liabilities | | | | 932,350 |
| Long-term liabilities: | | | | |
| Debenture 8% bonds payable, due December 31, 2026 (market value, $950,000) | | | 1,000,000 | |
| Less unamortized discount | | | 60,000 | |
| Total long-term liabilities | | | | 940,000 |
| Deferred credits: | | | | |
| Deferred income tax payable | | | | 84,500 |
| Total liabilities | | | | 1,956,850 |
| **Stockholders' Equity** | | | | |
| Paid-in capital: | | | | |
| Common stock, $23 par (250,000 shares authorized, 100,000 shares issued) | | 2,300,000 | | |
| Excess of issue price over par | | 340,000 | | |
| Total paid-in capital | | | 2,640,000 | |
| Retained earnings | | | 1,274,615 | |
| Total stockholders' equity | | | | 3,914,615 |
| Total liabilities and stockholders' equity | | | | 5,871,465 |

### BALANCE SHEET PRESENTATION OF BONDS PAYABLE

In Exhibit 13-21, Escoe Corporation's bonds payable are reported as long-term liabilities. If there were two or more bond issues, the details of each would be reported on the balance sheet or in a supporting schedule or note. Separate accounts are normally maintained for each bond issue.

If the balance sheet date is within one year of the maturity date of the bonds, the bonds may be classified as a current liability. This would be the case if the bonds are to be paid out of current assets. If the bonds are to be paid from a sinking fund or if they are to be refinanced with another bond issue, they should remain in the non-current category. In this case, the details of the retirement of the bonds are normally disclosed in a note to the financial statements.

The balance in Escoe's discount on bonds payable account is reported as a deduction from the bonds payable. Conversely, the balance in a bond premium account would be reported as an addition to the related bonds payable. Either on the face of the financial statements or in accompanying notes, a description of the bonds (terms, due date, and effective interest rate) and other relevant information such as sinking fund requirements should be disclosed. Finally, the market (fair) value of the bonds payable should also be disclosed.

### BALANCE SHEET PRESENTATION OF BONDS INVESTMENT

Investments in bonds or other debt securities that management intends to hold to their maturity are called held-to-maturity securities. Such securities are classified as long-term investments under the caption Investments. These investments are reported at their cost less any amortized premium or plus any amortized discount. In addition, the market (fair) value of the bond investments should be disclosed, either on the face of the balance sheet or in an accompanying note.

## 7. Effective Interest Rate Method of Amortization

The effective interest rate method of amortizing discounts and premiums provides for a constant rate of interest on the carrying amount of the bonds at the beginning of each period. This is in contrast to the straight-line method, which provides for a constant amount of interest expense.

The interest rate used in the interest method of amortization is the market rate on the date the bonds are issued. The carrying amount of the bonds to which the interest rate is applied is the face amount of the bonds minus any unamortized discount or plus any unamortized premium. Under the interest method, the interest expense to be reported on the income statement is computed by multiplying the effective interest rate by the carrying amount of the bonds. The difference between the interest expense computed in this way and the periodic interest payment is the amount of discount or premium to be amortized for the period.

## AMORTIZATION OF DISCOUNT BY THE INTEREST METHOD

To illustrate the interest method for amortizing bond discounts, we assume the following data from the chapter illustration of issuing $100,000 bonds at a discount:

| | |
|---|---|
| Face value of 10%, 5-year bonds, interest compounded semiannually: | $100,000 |
| Present value of bonds at effective (market) rate of interest of 13%: | $89,217 |
| Discount on bonds payable: | $10,783 |

Applying the interest method to these data yields the amortization table in Exhibit 13-22. You should note the following items in this table.

(1) The interest paid (Column A) remains constant at 5% of $100,000, the face amount of the bonds.

(2) The interest expense (Column B) is computed at 6.5% of the bond carrying amount at the beginning of each period. This results in an increasing interest expense each period.

(3) The excess of the interest expense over the interest payment of $5,000 is the amount of discount to be amortized (Column C).

(4) The unamortized discount (Column D) decreases from the initial balance, $10,783, to a zero balance at the maturity date of the bonds.

(5) The carrying amount (Column E) increases from $89,217, the amount received for the bonds, to $100,000 at maturity.

**Exhibit 13-22 Amortization of discount on bonds payable**

| | A | B | C | D | E |
|---|---|---|---|---|---|
| Interest Payment | Interest Paid (5% of Face Amount) | Interest Expense (6.5% of Bond Carrying Amount) | Discount Amortization (B-A) | Unamortized Discount (D-C) | Bond Carrying Amount ($100,000-D) |
| | | | | 10,783 | 89,217 |
| 1 | 5,000 | 5,799 (6.5% of 89,217) | 799 | 9,984 | 90,016 |
| 2 | 5,000 | 5,851 (6.5% of 90,016) | 851 | 9,133 | 90,867 |
| 3 | 5,000 | 5,906 (6.5% of 90,867) | 906 | 8,227 | 91,773 |
| 4 | 5,000 | 5,965 (6.5% of 91,773) | 965 | 7,262 | 92,738 |
| 5 | 5,000 | 6,028 (6.5% of 92,738) | 1,028 | 6,234 | 93,766 |
| 6 | 5,000 | 6,095 (6.5% of 93,766) | 1,095 | 5,139 | 94,861 |
| 7 | 5,000 | 6,166 (6.5% of 94,861) | 1,166 | 3,973 | 96,027 |
| 8 | 5,000 | 6,242 (6.5% of 96,027) | 1,242 | 2,731 | 97,269 |
| 9 | 5,000 | 6,322 (6.5% of 97,269) | 1,322 | 1,409 | 98,591 |
| 10 | 5,000 | 6,408 (6.5% of 98,591) | 1,409 | — | 100,000 |

The entry to record the first interest payment on June 30, 2008, and the related discount amortization is shown in Exhibit 13-23.

**Exhibit 13-23 Journal entry to record interest payment and discount amortization**

| Date | | Description | Debit | Credit |
|---|---|---|---|---|
| 2008 June | 30 | Interest Expense | 5,799 | |
| | | Discount on Bonds Payable | | 799 |
| | | Cash | | 5,000 |
| | | Paid semiannual interest and amortized bond discount for 1/2 year | | |

If the amortization is recorded only at the end of the year, the amount of the discount amortized on December 31 would be $1,650. This is the sum of the first two semiannual amortization amounts ($799 and $851) from Exhibit 13-22.

## AMORTIZATION OF PREMIUM BY THE INTEREST METHOD

To illustrate the interest method for amortizing bond premiums, we assume the following data from the chapter illustration of issuing $100,000 bonds at a premium:

| | |
|---|---|
| Present value of bonds at effective (market) rate of interest of 10%: | $107,721 |
| Face value of 12%, 5-year bonds, interest compounded semiannually: | $100,000 |
| Premium on bonds payable: | $7,721 |

Using the interest method to amortize the above premium yields the amortization table in Exhibit 13-24. You should note the following items in this table.

(1) The interest paid (Column A) remains constant at 6% of $100,000, the face amount of the bonds.

(2) The interest expense (Column B) is computed at 5% of the bond carrying amount at the beginning of each period. This results in a decreasing interest expense each period.

(3) The excess of the periodic interest payment of $6,000 over the interest expense is the amount of premium to be amortized (Column C).

(4) The unamortized premium (Column D) decreases from the initial balance, $7,721, to a zero balance at the maturity date of the bonds.

**Exhibit 13-24 Amortization of premium on bonds payable**

| | A | B | C | D | E |
|---|---|---|---|---|---|
| Interest Payment | Interest Paid (6% of Face Amount) | Interest Expense (5% of Bond Carrying Amount) | Discount Amortization (A-B) | Unamortized Discount (D-C) | Bond Carrying Amount ($100,000 + D) |
| | | | | 7,721 | 107,721 |
| 1 | 6,000 | 5,386(5% of 107,721) | 614 | 7,107 | 107,107 |

(Continued)

| Interest Payment | A<br>Interest Paid (6% of Face Amount) | B<br>Interest Expense (5% of Bond Carrying Amount) | C<br>Discount Amortization (A-B) | D<br>Unamortized Discount (D-C) | E<br>Bond Carrying Amount ($100,000 + D) |
|---|---|---|---|---|---|
| 2 | 6,000 | 5,355(5% of 107,107) | 645 | 6,462 | 106,462 |
| 3 | 6,000 | 5,323(5% of 106,462) | 677 | 5,785 | 105,785 |
| 4 | 6,000 | 5,289(5% of 105,785) | 711 | 5,074 | 105,074 |
| 5 | 6,000 | 5,254(5% of 105,074) | 746 | 4,328 | 104,328 |
| 6 | 6,000 | 5,216(5% of 104,328) | 784 | 3,544 | 103,544 |
| 7 | 6,000 | 5,177(5% of 103,544) | 823 | 2,721 | 102,721 |
| 8 | 6,000 | 5,136(5% of 102,721) | 864 | 1,857 | 101,857 |
| 9 | 6,000 | 5,093(5% of 101,857) | 907 | 950 | 100,950 |
| 10 | 6,000 | 5,048(5% of 100,950) | 950 | — | 100,000 |

The entry to record the first interest payment on June 30, 2008, and the related premium amortization is shown in Exhibit 13-25.

**Exhibit 13-25 Entry to record interest payment and premium amortization**

| Date | | Description | Debit | Credit |
|---|---|---|---|---|
| 2008 June | 30 | Interest Expense | 5,386 | |
| | | Premium on Bonds Payable | 614 | |
| | | Cash | | 6,000 |
| | | Paid semiannual interest and amortized bond premium for 1/2 year | | |

If the amortization is recorded only at the end of the year, the amount of the premium amortized on December 31,2008, would be $1,259. This is the sum of the first two semiannual amortization amounts ($614 and $645) from Exhibit 13-24.

## TERMINOLOGY:

Annuity:年金
Premium:溢价

## QUESTION:

Describe the potential impact of long-term borrowing on the earnings per share of a corporation?

Three alternative plans for financing a corporation are issuing common stock, preferred stock, or bond. The effects of alternative financing on the earnings per share vary significantly, depending upon the level of earnings.

**PROBLEM:**

Trademarks, Inc., has outstanding a $100,000 issue of 6% convertible bonds payable that mature in 2026. Suppose the bonds were dated April 1, 2006, and pay interest each April 1 and October 1.

**Requirement**

Record the following transactions for Trademarks.

(1) Issuance of the bonds at 104.8% on April 1, 2006.

(2) Payment of interest and amortization of premium on October 1, 2006.

(3) Accrual of interest and amortization of premium on December 31, 2006.

(4) Payment of interest and amortization of premium on April 1, 2007.

(5) Conversion of one-half of the bonds payables into no-par common stock on April 1, 2007.

(6) Retirement of one-half of the bonds payable on April 1, 2007. Purchase price to retire the bonds was 102%.

**Solution**

(1) April 1, 2006:

| | | |
|---|---|---|
| Dr. Cash ($100,000 × 1.048) | 104,800 | |
| Cr. Bonds Payable | | 100,000 |
| Premium on Bonds Payable | | 4,800 |

Issued bonds at a premium

(2) Oct. 1, 2006:

| | | |
|---|---|---|
| Dr. Interest Expense | 2,880 | |
| Premium on bonds Payable ($4,800/40) | 120 | |
| Cr. Cash ($100,000 × 0.06 × 6/12) | | 3,000 |

Paid interest and amortized premium

(3) Dec. 31, 2006:

| | | |
|---|---|---|
| Dr. Interest Expense | 1,440 | |
| Premium on bonds Payables ($4,800/40 × 1/2) | 60 | |
| Cr. Interest Payable ($100,000 × 0.06 × 3/12) | | 1,500 |

Accrued interest and amortized premium

(4) April 1, 2007:

| | | |
|---|---|---|
| Dr. Interest Payable (from Dec. 31) | 1,500 | |
| Interest Expense | 1,440 | |
| Premium on Bonds Payable ($4,800/40 × 1/2) | 60 | |
| Cr. Cash ($100,000 × 0.06 × 6/12) | | 3,000 |

Paid interest and amortized premium

(5) April 1, 2007:

| | | |
|---|---|---|
| Dr. Bonds Payable ($100,000 × 1/2) | 50,000 | |
| Premium on bonds Payable ($4,800 - $120 - $60 - $60) × 1/2 | 2,280 | |

Cr. Common Stock 52,280

Recorded conversion of bonds payable

(6) April 1, 2007:

Dr. Bonds Payable ( $ 100,000 × 1/2) 50,000

Premium on bonds Payable ( $4,800- $120- $60- $60) × 1/2 2,280

Cr. Cash ( $ 50,000 × 1.02) 51,000

Gain on Retirement of Bonds Payable 1,280

Retired bonds payable

# Chapter 14

## Income Taxes, Unusual Income Items, and Investments in Stocks

**Objectives**

1. Journalize for corporate income taxes, including deferred income taxes.
2. Describe the reporting of unusual items on the income statement.
3. Prepare an income statement reporting earnings per share data.
4. Describe the reporting of comprehensive income.
5. Describe the accounting for investments in stocks.

# 1. Corporations Income Taxes

Corporations are taxable entities that must pay federal income taxes. Depending upon where it is located, a corporation may also be required to pay state and local income taxes. Although we limit our discussion to federal income taxes, the basic concepts also apply to other income taxes.

## PAYMENT OF INCOME TAXES

Most corporations are required to pay estimated federal income taxes in four installments throughout the year. For example, assume that a corporation with a calendar-year accounting period estimates its income tax expense for the year as $96,000. The entry to record the first of the four estimated tax payments of $24,000 (1/4 of $96,000) is as follows: Dr. Income Tax Expense, $24,000; Cr. Cash, $24,000.

At year-end, the actual taxable income and the related tax are determined. If additional taxes are owed, the additional liability is recorded. If the total estimated tax payments are greater than the tax liability based on actual taxable income, the overpayment should be debited to a receivable account and credited to Income Tax Expense.

Income taxes are normally disclosed as a deduction at the bottom of the income statement in determining net income, as shown in Exhibit 14-1, in an excerpt from an income statement for Procter & Gamble.

**Exhibit 14-1 Income statement for Procter & Gamble** (amounts in millions)

| **Year Ended June 30, 2005** | |
|---|---|
| Net sales | 45,634 |
| Cost of products sold | 16,228 |
| Marketing, research, and administrative expenses | 9,313 |
| Income from operations | 20,093 |
| Interest expense | 922 |
| Other income, net | 355 |
| Fixed asset impairment | 100 |
| Restructuring charge | 100 |
| Earnings from continuing operations | 19,326 |
| Income taxes | 2,000 |
| Net earnings from continuing operations | 17,326 |
| Cost of discontinued operations | 326 |
| Net earning | 17,000 |

The ratio of reported income tax expense to earnings before taxes is shown for selected industries, as shown in Exhibit 14-2.

**Exhibit 14-2 Income tax range of different industries**

| Industry | Percent of Reported Income Tax Expense to Earnings before Taxes |
|---|---|
| Automobiles | 33% |
| Banking | 35% |
| Computers | 23% |
| Food | 35% |
| Integrated oil | 39% |
| Pharmaceuticals | 30% |
| Retail | 39% |
| Telecommunication | 37% |
| Transportation | 38% |

The reported income tax expense is normally between 30% ~ 40% of earnings before tax. Therefore, taxes are a significant expense for most companies and must be considered when analyzing a company. Differences in tax rates between industries can be due to tax regulations unique to certain industries.

## ALLOCATING INCOME TAXES

The taxable income of a corporation is determined according to the tax laws and is reported to taxing authorities on the corporation's tax return. It is often different from the income before income taxes reported in the income statement according to generally accepted accounting principles. As a result, the income tax based on taxable income usually differs from the income tax based on income before taxes. This difference may need to be allocated between various financial statement periods, depending on the nature of the items causing the differences.

Some differences between taxable income and income before income taxes are created because items are recognized in one period for tax purposes and in another period for income statement purposes. Such differences, called temporary differences, reverse or turn around in later years. Some examples of items that create temporary differences are listed below.

(1) Revenues or gains are taxed after they are reported in the income statement. Example: In some cases, companies that make sales under an installment plan recognize revenue for financial reporting purposes when a sale is made but defer recognizing revenue for tax purposes until cash is collected.

(2) Expenses or losses are deducted in determining taxable income after they are reported in the income statement. Example: Product warranty expense estimated and reported in the year of the sale for financial statement reporting is deducted for tax reporting when paid.

(3) Revenues or gains are taxed before they are reported in the income statement. Example:

Cash received in advance for magazine subscriptions is included in taxable income when received but included in the income statement only when earned in a future period.

(4) Expenses or losses are deducted in determining taxable income before they are reported in the income statement. Example: Modified Accelerated Cost-Recovery System (MACRS) depreciation is used for tax purposes, and the straight-line method is used for financial reporting purposes.

As temporary differences reverse in later years, they do not change or reduce the total amount of taxable income over the life of a business. Exhibit 14-3 illustrates the reversing nature of temporary differences in which a business uses MACRS depreciation for tax purposes and straight-line depreciation for financial statement purposes. Exhibit 14-3 assumes that MACRS recognizes more depreciation in the early years and less depreciation in the later years. The total depreciation expense is the same for both methods over the life of the asset.

**Exhibit 14-3 Temporary differences**

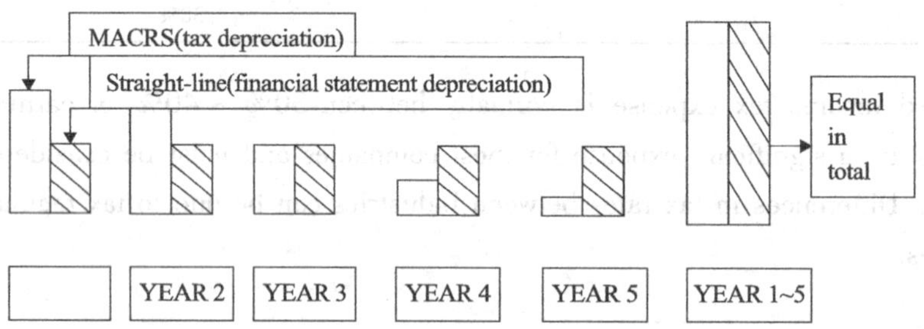


As Exhibit 14-3 illustrates, temporary differences affect only the timing of when revenues and expenses are recognized for tax purposes. As a result, the total amount of taxes paid does not change. Only the timing of the payment of taxes is affected. As shown in Exhibit 14-3, most managers use tax-planning techniques so that temporary difference delay or defer the payment of taxes to later years. As a result, at the end of each year the amount of the current tax liability and the postponed (deferred) liability must be recorded.

To illustrate, assume that at the end of the first year of operations a corporation reports $350,000 income before income taxes on its income statement. If we assume an income tax rate of 40%, the income tax expense reported on the income statement is $140,000 ($350,000 × 40%). However, to reduce the amount owed for current income taxes, the corporation uses tax planning to reduce the taxable income to $160,000. Thus, the income tax actually due for the year is only $64,000 ($160,000 × 40%). The $76,000 ($140,000 − $64,000) difference between the two tax amounts is created by temporary differences in recognizing revenue. This amount is deferred to future years. The example is summarized below.

| | |
|---|---|
| Income tax expense based on $350,000 reported income at 40%: | $140,000 |
| Income tax payable based on $160,000 taxable income at 40%: | $64,000 |
| Income tax deferred to future years: | $76,000 |

To match the current year's expenses (including income tax) against the current year's revenue on the income statement, income tax is allocated between periods, using the following journal entry: Dr. Income Tax Expense, $140,000; Cr. Income Tax Payable, $64,000, Deferred Income Tax Payable, $76,000.

The income tax expense reported on the income statement is the total tax, $140,000, expected to be paid on the income for the year. In future years, the $76,000 in Deferred Income Tax Payable will be transferred to Income Tax Payable as the temporary differences reverse and the taxes become due. For example, if $45,000 of the deferred tax reverses and becomes due in the second year, the following journal entry would be made in the second year: Dr. Deferred Income Tax Payable, $45,000; Cr. Income Tax Payable, $45,000.

### REPORTING AND ANALYZING TAXES

The balance of Deferred Income Tax Payable at the end of a year is reported as a liability. The amount due within one year is classified as a current liability. The remainder is classified as a long-term liability or reported in a Deferred Credits section following the Long-Term Liabilities section.

Differences between taxable income and income (before taxes) reported on the in- come statement may also arise because certain revenues are exempt from tax and certain expenses are not deductible in determining taxable income. Such differences, which will not reverse with the passage of time, are sometimes called permanent differences. For example, interest income on municipal bonds may be exempt from taxation. Such differences create no special financial reporting problems, since the amount of income tax determined according to the tax laws is the same amount reported on the income statement.

## 2. Reporting Unusual Items on the Income Statement

Certain unusual items should be reported separately on the current or prior period's income statement. These items can be classified into items affecting the current period income statement and those affecting prior period income statement as shown below.

Unusual Items Affecting the Current Period's Income Statement:

(1) Fixed asset impairments.

(2) Restructuring charges.

(3) Discontinued operations.

(4) Extraordinary item.

Unusual Items Affecting the Prior Period's Income Statement:

(1) Errors.

(2) Change in accounting principles.

The first category of unusual items affects the current period's income statement. However, the location of the disclosure on the income statement is different between these items. Fixed asset impairment and restructuring charges are reported above income from continuing operations as shown in Exhibit 14-1. That is, fixed asset impairment and restructuring charges are subtracted in arriving at income from continuing operations. Although discontinued operations and extraordinary items affect net income, they are reported below income from continuing operations as shown in Exhibit 14-1.

In the following paragraphs, we first describe and illustrate unusual items affecting the current period's income statement. We then discuss unusual items affecting prior period income statements.

## UNUSUAL ITEMS AFFECTING THE CURRENT PERIOD'S INCOME STATEMENT

Unusual items affecting the current period's income statement include fixed asset impairments, restructuring charges, discontinued operations, and extraordinary items. Fixed asset impairments and restructuring charges, sometimes termed special charges when combined, will be discussed first. Following these, we will discuss discontinued operations and extraordinary items. Exhibit 14-4 shows the unusual items should record on the income statement.

**Exhibit 14-4 Reporting of unusual items on the income statement**

| | |
|---|---|
| Unusual items subtracted from continuing operations | Restructuring charges |
| | Fixed asset impairments |
| Unusual items that adjust income from continuing operations in determining net income | Discontinued operations |
| | Extraordinary items |

### Fixed Asset Impairments

A fixed asset impairment occurs when the fair value of a fixed asset falls below its book value (cost less accumulated depreciation) and is not expected to recover. Examples of events that might cause an asset impairment are decreases in the market price of fixed assets, significant changes in the business or regulations related to fixed assets, adverse conditions affecting the use of fixed assets, or expected cash flow losses from using fixed assets. For example, on March 1, assume that Jones Corporation consolidates operations by closing a factory. As a result of the closing, plant and equipment are impaired by $720,000. The journal entry to record the impairment is as follows: Dr. Loss on Fixed Asset Impairment, $720,000; Cr. Equipment, $ 720,000.

The loss on fixed asset impairment is reported as a separate expense item deducted from gross profit in determining income from continuing operations, as illustrated for Jones Corporation in Exhibit 14-5. In addition, note disclosure should describe the nature of the asset impaired and the cause of the impairment.

The loss reduces the book value of the fixed asset and thus reduces the depreciation expense for future periods. If the asset is later sold, the gain or loss on the sale would be based on the lower book value. Thus, asset impairment accounting recognizes the loss when it is first identified, rather than when the asset is later sold.

**Exhibit 14-5 Income statement of Jones Corporation**

Jones Corporation
Income statement
For the Year Ended December 31, 2008

| | | |
|---|---|---|
| Net sales | | 13,540,000 |
| Cost of merchandise sold | | 6,300,000 |
| Gross profit | | 7,240,000 |
| Selling and administrative expenses | 3,520,000 | |
| Loss from asset impairment | 720,000 | |
| Restructuring charge | 1,050,000 | 5,290,000 |
| Income from continuing operations before income tax | | 1,950,000 |
| Income tax expense | | 940,000 |
| Income from continuing operations | | 1,010,000 |
| Loss on discontinued operations (net of applicable income tax benefit of $50,000) | | 100,000 |
| Income before extraordinary items | | 910,000 |
| Extraordinary item: | | |
| Gain on condemnation of land (net of applicable income tax of $65,000) | | 150,000 |
| Net income | | 1,060,000 |

## Restructuring Charges

Restructuring charges are costs incurred with actions such as canceling contracts, laying off or relocating employees, and combining operations. Often, these events incur initial one-time costs in order to obtain long-term savings. For example, terminated employees often receive a one-time termination or severance benefit at the time of their dismissal. Employee termination benefits are normally the most significant restructuring charges; thus, they will be the focus of this section.

Employee termination benefits arise when a plan specifying the number of terminated employees, the benefit, and the benefit timing has been authorized by senior management and communicated to the employees. To illustrate, assume that the management of Jones Corporation communicates a plan to terminate 210 employees from the closed manufacturing plant on March 1. The plan calls for a termination benefit of $5,000 per employee. Once the plan is communicated to employees, they have the legal right to work for 60 days but may elect to leave the firm earlier. That is, employees may be paid severance at the end of 60 days or at any time in between.

The expense and liability to provide employee benefits should be recognized at fair value on the plan communication date. The fair value of this plan would be $1,050,000 (210 employees × $5,000), which is the aggregate expected cost of terminating the employees. Thus, the $1,050,000 restructuring charge would be recorded as follows: Dr. Restructuring Charge, $1,050,000; Cr. Employee Termination Obligation, $1,050,000.

The restructuring charge is reported as a separate expense deducted from gross profit in determining income from continuing operations, as shown in Exhibit 14-5. The employee termination obligation would be shown as a current liability. If the plan called for expected severance payments beyond one year, then a long-term liability would be recognized. In addition, a note should disclose the nature and cause of the restructuring event and the costs associated with the type of restructuring event.

The actual benefits paid to terminated employees should be debited liabilities as employees leave the firm. For example, assume that 23 employees find other employment and leave the company on March 23. The entry to record the severance payment to these employees would be as follows: Dr. Employee Termination Obligation, $ 115,000; Cr. Cash, $ 115,000.

**Discontinued Operations**

A gain or loss from disposing of a business segment or component of an entity is reported on the income statement as a gain or loss from discontinued operations. The term business segment refers to a major line of business for a company, such as a division, department, or certain class of customer. A component of an entity is the lowest level at which the operations and cash flows can be clearly distinguished, operationally and for financial reporting purposes, from the rest of the entity. Examples would be a store for a retailer, a territory for a sales organization, or a product category for a consumer products company.

Assume that Jones Corporation has separate divisions that produce electrical products, hardware supplies, and lawn equipment. Jones sells its electrical products division at a loss. As shown in Exhibit 14-5, this loss is deducted from Jones's income from continuing operations (income from its hardware and lawn equipment divisions). In addition, a note should disclose the identity of the segment sold the disposal date, a description of the segment's assets and liabilities, and the manner of disposal.

**Extraordinary Items**

An extraordinary item results from events and transactions that are significantly different (unusual) from the typical or the normal operating activities of thebusiness and occur infrequently. The gains and losses resulting from natural disasters that occur infrequently, such as floods, earthquakes, and fires, are extraordinary items. Gains or losses from condemning land or buildings for public use are also extraordinary. Such gains and losses, other than those from disposing of a business segment, should be reported in the income statement as extraordinary items, as shown in Exhibit 14-5.

Extraordinary items may result in unusual financial results. For example, Delta Air Lines once reported an extraordinary gain of over $ 5.5 million as the result of the crash of one of its 727s. The plane that crashed was insured for $ 6.5 million, but its book value in Delta's accounting records was $ 962,000. Gains and losses on the disposal of fixed assets are not extraordinary items. This is because they are not unusual and they recur from time to time in the normal operations of a business. Likewise, gains and losses from the sale of investments are usual and recurring for most businesses.

## UNUSUAL ITEMS AFFECTING THE PRIOR PERIOD'S INCOME STATEMENT

In addition to unusual items impacting the income statement, there are two major items that require a retroactive restatement of prior period earnings. These two items are:

(1) Errors in the recognition, measurement, presentation, or disclosure of financial statements.

(2) Changes from one generally accepted accounting principle to another generally accepted accounting principle.

A retroactive restatement requires previously issued financial statements to be adjusted for the impact of errors and changes in accounting principle. If an error is discovered that impacts a prior period financial statement, the prior period statement, and all following statements, should be restated to reflect the correction. If there is a change from one generally accepted accounting principle to another generally accepted accounting principle, then the change is applied to prior period financial statements. That is, the prior period financial statements are restated as if the new accounting principle had always been used. Thus, in both cases, these changes do not impact current period earnings, but will impact the earnings reported in past periods. As a result, the present Retained Earnings and other balance sheet accounts will be restated to reflect these prior period changes. Illustrations of these types of adjustments are provided in advanced accounting courses.

## 3. Earnings per Common Share

Net income by itself is difficult to use in comparing companies of different sizes. Also, trends in net income may be difficult to evaluate, using only net income, if there have been significant changes in a company's stockholders' equity. Thus, the profitability of companies is often expressed as earnings per share. Earnings per common share (EPS), sometimes called basic earnings per share, are the net income per share of common stock outstanding during a period.

Because of its importance, earnings per share are reported in the financial press and by various investor services, such as Moody's and Standard & Poor's. Changes in earnings per share can lead to significant changes in the price of a corporation's stock in the marketplace. For example, the stock of eBay Inc. fell by over 19% to $83 per share after the company announced earnings per share of 33 ¢ as compared to Wall Street analysts' estimate of 34 ¢ per share.

Corporations whose stock is traded in a public market must report earnings per common share on their income statements. If no preferred stock is outstanding, the earnings per common share are calculated as follows:

Earnings per Common Share = Net Income/Number of Common Shares Outstanding

When the number of common shares outstanding has changed during the period, a weighted average number of shares outstanding is used. If a company has preferred stock outstanding, the net income must be reduced by the amount of any preferred dividends, as shown below.

Earnings per Common Stock = (Net Income—Preferred Stock Dividends)/Number of Common Shares Outstanding

Comparing the earnings per share of two or more years, based on only the net in- comes of those years, could be misleading. For example, assume that Jones Corporation, whose partial income statement was presented in Exhibit 14-5, reported $1,000,000 net income for 2007. Also assume that no extraordinary or other unusual items were reported in 2007. Jones has no preferred stock outstanding and has 250,000 common shares outstanding in 2007 and 2008. The earnings per common share is $4.00 ($1,000,000/250,000 shares) for 2007 and $4.24 ($1,060,000/250,000 shares) for 2008. Comparing the two earnings per share amounts suggests that operations have improved. However, the 2008 earnings per share comparable to the $4.00 is $4.04, which is the income from continuing operations of $1,010,000 divided by 250,000 shares. The latter amount indicates a slight downturn in normal earnings.

When unusual items reported below income from continuing operations exist, earnings per common share should be reported for those items. To illustrate, a partial income statement for Jones Corporation, showing earnings per common share, is shown in Exhibit 14-6. In this income statement, Jones reports all the earnings per common share amounts on the face of the income statement. However, only earnings per share amounts for income from continuing operations and net income are required to be presented on the face of the statement. The other per share amounts may be presented in the notes to the financial statements.

**Exhibit 14-6 Income statement with earnings per share**

Jones Corporation
Income Statement
For the Year Ended December 31, 2008

| | |
|---|---|
| Earnings per common share: | |
| Income from continuing operations | 4.04 |
| Loss on discontinued operations, net of 50,000 tax benefit | 0.40 |
| Income before extraordinary items | 3.64 |
| Extraordinary item | |
| Gain on condemnation of land, net of applicable income tax of 65,000 | 0.60 |
| Net income | 4.24 |

In the preceding paragraphs, we have assumed a simple capital structure with only common stock or common stock and preferred stock outstanding. Often, however, corporations have complex capital structures with various types of securities outstanding, such as convertible preferred stock, options, warrants, and contingently issuable shares. In such cases, the possible effects of converting such securities to common stock must be calculated and reported as earnings per common share assuming dilution or diluted earnings per share. This topic is discussed further in advanced accounting texts.

## 4. Comprehensive Income

Comprehensive income is defined as all changes in stockholders' equity during a period, except those resulting from dividends and stockholders' investments. Companies must report traditional net income plus or minus other comprehensive income items to arrive at comprehensive income.

Other comprehensive income items include foreign currency items, pension liability adjustments, and unrealized gains and losses on investments. Generally accepted accounting principles (GAAP) require these items to be disclosed separately from earnings. To the extent that other comprehensive income items give rise to tax effects, the taxes should be allocated to these items similar to that illustrated in Exhibit 14-5 for extraordinary items. The cumulative effects of other comprehensive income items must be reported separately from retained earnings and paid-in capital, on the balance sheet, as accumulated other comprehensive income. When other comprehensive income items are not present, the income statement and balance sheet formats are similar to those we have illustrated in this and preceding chapters.

Companies may report comprehensive income on the income statement, in a separate statement of comprehensive income, or in the statement of stockholder's equity. In addition, companies may use terms other than comprehensive income, such as "total non-owner changes in equity".

Assume that Triple-A Enterprises Inc, reported comprehensive income on a separate statement, called the statement of comprehensive income, as shown in Exhibit 14-7.

**Exhibit 14-7 The statement of comprehensive income**

Triple-A Enterprises Inc.
Statement of Comprehensive Income
For the Year Ended December 31, 2008

| | |
|---|---|
| Net income | 730,000 |
| Other comprehensive income, net of tax | 6,000 |
| Total comprehensive income | 736,000 |

The Stockholders' Equity section of the balance sheet for Triple-A Enterprises Inc. as shown in Exhibit 14-8.

Accumulated other comprehensive income is the cumulative effect of other comprehensive income items. Thus, the additional other comprehensive income of $60 for 2008 is added to the accumulated other comprehensive income on December 31, 2007, to yield the December 31, 2008, balance of $1,160.

Comprehensive income does not affect net income or retained earnings. In the next section, we will illustrate the determination of other comprehensive income, using unrealized gains and losses on investments.

**Exhibit 14-8 The stockholders' equity section of balance sheet for Triple-A Enterprise Inc.**

Triple-A Enterprises Inc.
Stockholders' Equity
December 31

| | 2008 | 2007 |
|---|---|---|
| Stockholders' equity: | | |
| Common stock | 23,000 | 23,000 |
| Paid-in capital in excess of par | 34,000 | 34,000 |
| Retained earnings | 147,500 | 133,000 |
| Accumulated other comprehensive | 1,160 | 1,100 |
| Total stockholders' equity | 205,660 | 191,100 |

# 5. Accounting for Investment in Stocks

Like individuals, businesses have a variety of reasons for investing in stocks, called equity securities. A business may purchase stocks as a means of earning a return (income) on excess cash that it does not need for its normal operations. Such investments are usually for a short period of time. In other cases, a business may purchase the stock of another company as a long-term investment. Such investments can be as a means of developing or maintaining business relationships with another company. Sometimes, a business will purchase most, if not all, of the common stock of another company for purposes of owning and controlling another entity. This is termed a business combination. In this section, we will discuss short-term investments in equity securities, long-term investments in equity securities, sales of investments, and business combinations. First, however, we will introduce two major equity security classifications according to generally accepted accounting principles.

The equity securities in which a business invests may be classified as trading securities or available-for-sale securities. Trading securities are securities that management intends to actively trade for profit. Businesses holding trading securities are those whose normal operations involve buying and selling securities. Examples of such businesses include banks and insurance companies. Available-for-sale securities are securities that management expects to sell in the future but which are not actively traded for profit. For example, Warren Buffett, one of the wealthiest men in the world, invests through a public company called Berkshire Hathaway Inc. In a recent annual report, Berkshire Hathaway Inc. reported over $35 billion of equity investment holdings listed on its balance sheet as available-for-sale securities. Some of these investments include The Coca-Cola Company, McDonald's, and American Express Company. In this section, we describe and illustrate the accounting for available-for-sale equity securities. The accounting for trading securities is described and illustrated in advanced accounting texts.

## SHORT-TERM INVESTMENTS IN STOCKS

Available-for-sale securities are classified as temporary investments or marketable securities. Although such investments may be retained for several years, they continue to be classified as temporary, provided they meet two conditions. First, the securities are readily marketable and can be sold for cash at any time. Second, management intends to sell the securities when the business needs cash for operations.

Temporary investments in available-for-sale securities are recorded in a current asset account, Marketable Securities, at their cost. This cost includes all amounts spent to acquire the securities, such as broker's commissions. Any dividends received on the investment are recorded as a debit to Cash and a credit to Dividend Revenue.

To illustrate, assume that on June 1 Crabtree Co. purchased 2,200 shares of Inis

Corporation common stock at $88.25 per share plus a brokerage fee of $450. On October 1, Inis Corporation declared a $0.85 per share cash dividend payable on November 30. Crabtree Co.'s entries to record the stock purchase and the receipt of the dividend are as shown in Exhibit 14-9.

**Exhibit 14-9 Entries for stock purchase and receipt of dividend**

| Date | | Description | Debit | Credit |
|---|---|---|---|---|
| June | 1 | Marketable Securities | 194,600 | |
| | | Cash | | 194,600 |
| | | Purchased 2,200 shares of Inis Corporation common stock (($ 88.25 ×2,200 shares) + $450) | | |
| Nov. | 30 | Cash | 1,870 | |
| | | Dividend Revenue | | 1,870 |
| | | Received dividend on Inis Corporation common stock (2,200 shares × $0.85) | | |

On the balance sheet, temporary investments are reported at their fair market value. Market values are normally available from stock quotations in financial newspapers, such as The Wall Street Journal. Any difference between the fair market values of the securities and their cost is an unrealized holding gain or loss. This gain or loss is termed "unrealized" because a transaction (the sale of the securities) is necessary before a gain or loss becomes real (realized).

Assume that Crabtree Co.'s portfolio of temporary investments was purchased during 2008 and has the fair market values and unrealized gains and losses on December 31, 2008 as shown in Exhibit 14-10.

**Exhibit 14-10 Fair market values and unrealized gains or losses**

| Common Stock | Cost | Market | Unrealized Gain (Loss) |
|---|---|---|---|
| Edwards Inc. | 150,000 | 190,000 | 40,000 |
| SWS Corp. | 200,000 | 200,000 | — |
| Inis Corporation | 180,000 | 210,000 | 30,000 |
| Bass Co. | 160,000 | 150,000 | (10,000) |
| Total | 690,000 | 750,000 | 60,000 |

If income taxes of $18,000 are allocated to the unrealized gain, Crabtree Co.'s temporary investments should be reported at their total cost of $690,000, plus the unrealized gain (net of applicable income tax) of $42,000 ($60,000 − $18,000), as shown in Exhibit 14-11.

**Exhibit 14-11 Temporary investments on the balance sheet**

Crabtree Co.
Balance sheet (selected items)
December 31, 2008

| **Assets:** | | |
|---|---|---|
| Current assets: | | |
| Cash | | 119,500 |
| Temporary investments in marketable securities at cost | 690,000 | |
| Unrealized gain (net of applicable income tax of $18,000) | 42,000 | 732,000 |
| **Stockholders' Equity:** | | |
| Accumulated other comprehensive income | | 42,000 |

The unrealized gain (net of applicable taxes) of $42,000 should also be reported as another comprehensive income item, as we mentioned in the preceding section. For example, assume that Crabtree Co. has net income of $720,000 for the year ended December 31, 2008. Crabtree Co. elects to report comprehensive income in the statement of comprehensive income, as shown in Exhibit 14-12. In addition, the accumulated other comprehensive income on the balance sheet would also be $42,000, representing the beginning balance of zero plus other comprehensive income of $42,000, as shown in Exhibit 14-11.

**Exhibit 14-12 Statement of comprehensive income**

Crabtree Co.
Statement of Comprehensive Income
For the Year Ended December 31, 2008

| Net income | 720,000 |
|---|---|
| Other comprehensive income: | |
| Unrealized gain on temporary investments in marketable securities (net of applicable income tax of $18,000) | 42,000 |
| Comprehensive income | 762,000 |

Unrealized losses are reported in a similar manner. Unrealized gains and losses are reported as other comprehensive income items until the related securities are sold. When temporary securities are sold, the unrealized gains or losses become realized and are included in determining net income.

## LONG-TERM INVESTMENTS IN STOCKS

Long-term investments in stocks are not intended as a source of cash in the normal operations of the business. Rather, such investments are often held for their income, long-term gain potential, or influence over another business entity. They are reported in the balance sheet under the caption Investments, which usually follows the Current Assets section.

Long-term investments in stock are treated as available-for-sale securities. Thus, a long-term in vestment treated as an available-for-sale security is recorded at cost and reported at fair market value net of any applicable income tax effects. In addition, any unrealized gains and losses are reported as part of the comprehensive income. For example, Delta Air Lines disclosed investments in Priceline. com preferred stock as noncurrent investment at the appraised fair market value.

However, if the investor (the buyer of the stock) has significant influence over the operating and financing activities of the investee (company whose stock is owned), the equity method is used. When the equity method is used, a stock purchase is recorded at cost, as shown previously. Evidence of significant influence includes the percentage of ownership, the existence of intercompany transactions, and the interchange of managerial personnel. Generally, if the investor owns 20% or more of the voting stock of investee, it is assumed that the investor has significant influence over the investee.

Under the equity method, the investment is not subsequently adjusted to fair value. Rather, the book value of the investment is adjusted as follows.

(1) The investor's share of the periodic net income of the investee is recorded as an increase in the investment account and as income for the period. Likewise, the investor's share of an investee's net loss is recorded as a decrease in the investment account and as a loss for the period.

(2) The investor's share of cash dividends from the investee is recorded as an increase in the cash account and a decrease in the investment account.

Assume that on January 1, Hally Inc. pays cash of $450,000 for 40% of the common stock and net assets of Brock Corporation. Assume also that, for the year ending December 31, Brock Corporation reports net income of $125,000 and declares and pays $60,000 in dividends. Using the equity method, Hally Inc. (the investor) records these transactions as shown in Exhibit 14-13.

**Exhibit 14-13 The transactions in Hally Inc.**

| Date | | Description | Debit | Credit |
|---|---|---|---|---|
| Jan. | 2 | Investment in Brock Corporation Stock | 450,000 | |
| | | Cash | | 450,000 |
| | | Purchased 40% of Brock Corporation Stock | | |
| Dec. | 31 | Investment in Brock Corporation Stock | 50,000 | |
| | | Income of Brock Corporation | | 50,000 |
| | | Recorded 40% share of Brock Corporation | | |
| | | | | |

(Continued)

| Date | | Description | Debit | Credit |
|---|---|---|---|---|
| Dec. | 31 | Cash | 24,000 | |
| | | Investment in Brock Corporation Stock | | 24,000 |
| | | Recorded 40% share of Brock Corporation | | |

The combined effect of recording 40% of Brock Corporation's net income and dividends is to increase Hally Inc.'s interest in the net assets of Brock Corporation by \$26,000 (\$50,000 − \$24,000), as shown in Exhibit 14-14.

**Exhibit 14-14 Combined effect of investment**

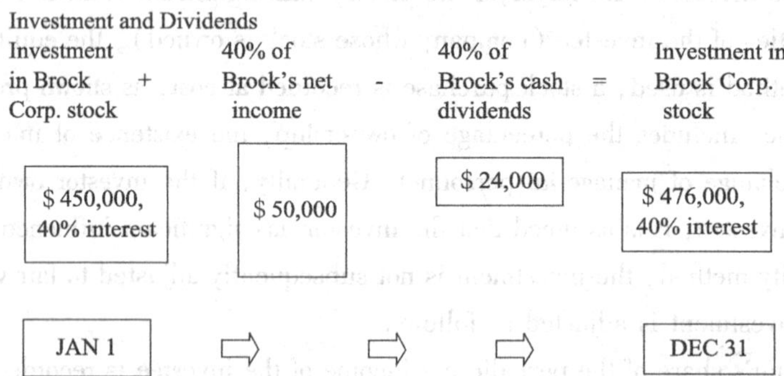


The equity method causes the investment account to mirror the proportional changes in the book value of the investee. Thus, Brock Corporation's book value increased by \$65,000 (\$125,000 − \$60,000), while the investment in Brock Corporation stock account increased by Hally Inc.'s proportional share of that increase, or \$26,000 (\$65,000 × 40%). Thus, both the book value of Brock Corporation and Hally Inc.'s investment in Brock Corporation increased at the same rate from the original cost.

## SALE OF INVESTMENTS IN STOCKS

Accounting for the sale of stock is the same for both short-term and long-term investments. When shares of stock are sold, the investment account is credited for the carrying amount (book value) of the shares sold. The cash or receivables account is debited for the proceeds (sales price less commission and other selling costs). Any difference between the proceeds and the carrying amount is recorded as a gain or loss on the sale and is included in determining net income.

Assume that an investment in Drey Inc. stock has a carrying amount of \$16,700 when it is sold on March 1. If the proceeds from the sale of the stock are \$18,500, the entry to record the transaction is as shown in Exhibit 14-15.

**Exhibit 14-15 Entry for sale of stock investment**

| Date | | Description | Debit | Credit |
|---|---|---|---|---|
| Mar. | 1 | Cash | 18,500 | |
| | | Investment in Drey Inc. Stock | | 16,700 |
| | | Gain on Sale of Investments | | 1,800 |

## BUSINESS COMBINATIONS

A business may make an investment in another business by acquiring a controlling share, often greater than 50%, of the outstanding voting stock of another corporation by paying cash or exchanging stock. This is termed a business combination. Businesses may combine in order to produce more efficiently, diversify product lines, expand geographically, or acquire know-how.

A corporation owning all or a majority of the voting stock of another corporation is called a parent company. The corporation that is controlled is called the subsidiary company. For example, PayPal became a subsidiary of eBay Inc. when eBay exchanged eBay common stock for all the outstanding common stock of PayPal. Although parent and subsidiary corporations may operate as a single economic unit, they continue to maintain separate accounting records and prepare their own periodic financial statements.

At the end of the year, the financial statements of the parent and subsidiary are combined and reported as a single company. These combined financial statements are called consolidated financial statements. Such statements are usually identified by adding "and subsidiary (ies)" to the name of the parent corporation or by adding "consolidated" to the statement title. For example, eBay's income statement is titled, "Consolidated Statement of Income." To the stockholders of the parent company, consolidated financial statements are more meaningful than separate statements for each corporation. This is because the parent and its subsidiaries are separate entities. Accounting for business combinations and preparing consolidated financial statements are discussed in greater detail in advanced accounting courses.

## TERMINOLOGY:

Accumulated Other Comprehensive Income：累积非经营性综合收入
Available-for-sale Securities：可供出售证券
Business Combination：商业合并
Comprehensive Income：综合性收入
Consolidated Financial Statements：合并财务报表
Discontinued Operations：不连续经营
Earnings per Common Share (EPS)：每股盈余
Equity Method：权益法
Equity Securities：权益证券
Extraordinary Item：异常项目

Fixed Asset Impairment：固定资产减值
Investment：投资
Other Comprehensive Income：非经营性综合收入
Parent Company：母公司
Permanent Differences：永久性差异
Restructuring Charge：重组成本
Subsidiary Company：子公司
Taxable Income：应税收入
Temporary Differences：暂时性差异
Temporary Investment：短期投资
Trading Securities：交易性证券
Unrealized Holding Gain or Loss：未实现持有损益

## QUESTIONS：

**1. Describe an income statement reporting the following unusual items：fixed asset impairments，restructuring charges，discontinued operations，extraordinary items，and cumulative changes in accounting principles.**

Fixed asset impairments occur when the fair value of a fixed asset falls below its book value and is not expected to recover. The asset is written down and a loss is recognized. The loss is deducted from gross profit on the income statement.

Restructuring charges are costs associated with involuntarily terminating employees，terminating contracts，consolidating facilities，or relocating employees. The accrued expenses associated with such a plan are recognized in the period that senior executives approve and communicate the plan. The expense is deducted from gross profit on the income statement.

A gain or loss resulting from the disposal of a business segment，net of related tax，should be added to or deducted from income from continuing operations on the income statement.

Gains and losses may result from events and transactions that are unusual and occur infrequently. Such extraordinary items，net of related income tax，should be added to or deducted from income from continuing operations on the income statement.

A change in an accounting principle results from the adoption of a generally accepted accounting principle different from the one used previously for reporting purposes. The effect of the change in principle on net income in the current period，as well as the cumulative effect on income of prior periods，should be disclosed in the financial statements，net of tax，below income from continuing operations.

**2. Describe the accounting for investments in stocks.**

A business may purchase stocks as a means of earning a return (income) on excess cash that it does not need for its normal operations. Such investments are recorded in a marketable securities account. Their cost includes all amounts spent to acquire the securities. Any dividends received on an investment are recorded as a debit to Cash and a credit to Dividend Revenue. On the balance sheet， temporary investments are reported as available-for-sale securities at their fair market values. Any difference between the fair market values of the securities and their cost is an unrealized holding gain or loss (net of applicable taxes) that is reported as an other comprehensive income item.

Long-term investments in stocks are not intended as a source of cash in the normal operations of the business. They are reported in the balance sheet either as available-for-sale securities, and disclosed at fair value, or reported under the equity method.

The accounting for the sale of stock is the same for both short-term and long-term investments. The investment account is credited for the carrying amount (book value) of the shares sold, the cash or receivables account is debited for the proceeds, and any difference between the proceeds and the carrying amount is recorded as a gain or loss on the sale.

**3. Describe alternative methods of combining businesses and how consolidated financial statements are prepared.**

Businesses may combine in a merger or a consolidation. Business combinations may also occur when one corporation acquires a controlling share of the outstanding voting stock of another corporation. In this case, a parent-subsidiary relationship exists, and the companies are called affiliated companies.

Although the corporations that make up a parent-subsidiary affiliation may operate as a single economic unit, they usually continue to maintain separate accounting records and prepare their own periodic financial statements. The financial statements prepared by combining the parent and subsidiary statements are called consolidated financial statements.

When a parent corporation purchases less than 100% of the subsidiary's stock, the remaining stockholders' equity is identified as minority interest. The minority interest is reported on the consolidated balance sheet, usually following the total liabilities.

In preparing consolidated income statements for a parent and its subsidiary, all amounts from intercompany transactions, such as intercompany sales of merchandise and cost of merchandise sold, are eliminated.

## PROBLEM:

The following information in Exhibit 14-16 was taken from the ledger of Calenergy Corporation at Dec. 31, 2008.

**Exhibit 14-16 Financial information of Calenergy Corporation at Dec. 31, 2008**

| | | | |
|---|---|---|---|
| Common stock, no-par, 45,000 shares issued | 180,000 | Discontinued operations income | 20,000 |
| Sales revenue | 620,000 | Prior-period adjustment-credit to Retained Earnings | 5,000 |
| Extraordinary gain | 26,000 | Gain on sale of plant assets | 21,000 |
| Loss due to lawsuit | 11,000 | Income tax expense (saving): | |
| General expenses | 62,000 | Continuing operations | 32,000 |

(Continued)

| | | | |
|---|---|---|---|
| Preferred stock 8% | 50,000 | Discontinued operations | 8,000 |
| Selling expenses | 108,000 | Extraordinary gain | 10,000 |
| Retained earnings, beginning, as originally reported | 103,000 | Treasury stock, common (5,000 shares) | 25,000 |
| Dividends | 14,000 | | |
| Cost of goods sold | 380,000 | | |

**Requirement**

Prepare a single-step income statement and a statement of retained earnings for Calenergy Corporation for the year ended Dec. 31, 2008. Include the EPS presentation and show your computations. Calenergy Corporation had no changes in its stock accounts during the year.

**Solution**

Exhibit 14-17presents the income statement of Calenergy Corporation.

**Exhibit 14-17 Income statement of Calenergy Corporation at Dec. 31, 2008**

Calenergy Corporation
Income Statement
Year Ended December 31, 2008

| | | |
|---|---|---|
| Revenue and gains | | |
| Sales revenue | 620,000 | |
| Cost of goods sold | 380,000 | |
| Gross Profit | | 240,000 |
| Operation Expenses: | | |
| Selling expenses | 108,000 | |
| General expenses | 62,000 | 170,000 |
| Other Gains and Losses: | | |
| Loss due to lawsuit | 11,000 | |
| Gain on sale of plant assets | 21,000 | 10,000 |
| Net Operation Profit | | 80,000 |
| Income tax expense | 32,000 | |
| Income from continuing operations | | 48,000 |
| Discontinued operations ,income of $20,000 less income tax of $8,000 | | 12,000 |
| Income before extraordinary item | | 60,000 |
| Extraordinary gain, $26,000, less income tax, $10,000 | | 16,000 |
| Net Comprehensive Income | | 76,000 |
| | | |
| Earnings per share: | | |
| Income from continuing operations(($48,000 − $4,000)/40,000shares) | | 1.10 |
| Income from discontinued operations($12,000/40,000shares) | | 0.30 |
| Income from before extraordinary item(($60,000 − $4,000)/40,000shares) | | 1.4 |
| Extraordinary gain($16,000/40,000shares) | | 0.40 |
| Net income(($76,000 − $4,000)/40,000shares) | | 1.80 |

Exhibit 14-18 presents the statement of retained earnings of calenergy corporation.

**Exhibit 14-18 Statement of retained earnings of Calenergy Corporation**

Calenergy Corporation
Statement of Retained Earnings
Year Ended December 31,2008

| | |
|---|---|
| Retained earnings balance, beginning, as originally reported | 103,000 |
| Prior-period adjustment-credit | 5,000 |
| Retained earnings balance, beginning, as adjusted | 108,000 |
| Net income | 76,000 |
| | 184,000 |
| Dividends | 14,000 |
| Retained earnings balance, ending | 170,000 |

**Computations:**

$$EPS = \frac{\text{Income} - \text{Preferred dividends}}{\text{Common shares outs tan ding}} = \frac{\$76,000 - \$4,000}{40,000\text{shares}} = \$1.80$$

Preferred dividends: $\$50,000 \times 0.08 = \$4,000$

Common shares outstanding:

45,000 shares issued − 5,000 treasury shares = 40,000 shares outstanding

# Chapter 15

## Statement of Cash Flows

**Objectives**

1. Summarize the cash flow activities reported in the statement of cash flows.
2. Prepare a statement of cash flows, using the indirect method.
3. Prepare a statement of cash flows, using the direct method.

# 1. Reporting Cash Flows

The balance sheet reports financial position, and balance sheets from two periods show whether cash increased or decreased. But that doesn't tell why the cash balance changed. The income statement reports net income and offers clues about cash, but the income statement doesn't tell why cash increased or decreased. We need a third financial statement.

The statement of cash flows reports cash flows—cash receipts and cash payments—in other words, where cash came from (receipts) and how it was spent (payments). The statement covers a span of time and therefore is dated "Year Ended December 31, 2008" or "Month Ended June 30, 2009". Exhibit 15-1 illustrates the relative timing of the 4 basic statements.

**Exhibit 15-1 Timing of the financial statements**

| December 31,20□8<br>(a point in time) | For Year Ended December 31,20□9<br>(a period of time) | December 31,20□9<br>(a point in time) |
|---|---|---|
| | Income Statement | |
| Balance Sheet ——→ | ——Statement of Stockholders□ Equity—— | ——→Balance Sheet |
| | Statement of Cash Flows | |

The statement of cash flows serves these purposes:

(1) Predicts future cash flows. Past cash receipts and payments are reasonably good predictors of future cash flows.

(2) Evaluates management decisions. Businesses that make wise decisions prosper, and those that make unwise decisions suffer losses. The statement of cash flows reports how managers got cash and how they used cash to run the business.

(3) Determines ability to pay dividends and interest. Stockholders want dividends on their investments. Creditors demand interest and principal on their loans. The statement of cash flows reports on the ability to make these payments.

(4) Shows the relationship of net income to cash flows. Usually, high net income leads to an increase in cash, and vice versa. But cash flow can suffer even when net income is high.

On a statement of cash flows, cash means more than just cash in the bank. It includes cash equivalents, which are highly liquid short-term investments that can be converted into cash immediately. Examples include money-market accounts and investments in U. S. Government securities. Throughout this chapter, the term cash refers to cash and cash equivalents.

We have not discussed the statement of cash flows since introducing the statement in Chapter 1. We did this because a more complete understanding of operating, investing, and financing activities is helpful prior to developing and interpreting this statement. Previous chapters have introduced and described these activities so that you now have a foundation for the discussion that follows.

The cash flows from operating activities are normally presented first, followed by the cash flows from investing activities and financing activities. The total of the net cash flow from these activities is the net increase or decrease in cash for the period. The cash balance at the beginning of the period is added to the net increase or decrease in cash, resulting in the cash balance at the end of the period. The ending cash balance on the statement of cash flows equals the cash reported on the balance sheet. Exhibit 15-2 illustrates a simple statement of cash flows for Darming.

**Exhibit 15-2 Statement of cash flows—Darming**

Darming
Statement of Cash Flows
For the Month Ended November 30,2009

| | | |
|---|---|---|
| Cash flows from operating activities: | | |
| Cash received from customers | 7,500 | |
| Deduct cash payments for expenses and payments to creditors | 4,600 | |
| Net cash flow from operating activities | | 2,900 |
| Cash flows from investing activities: | | |
| Cash payments for purchase of land | | (20,000) |
| Cash flows from financing activities: | | |
| Cash received as owner's investment | 25,000 | |
| Deduct cash withdrawal by owner | 2,000 | |
| Net cash flow provided by financing activities | | 23,000 |
| Net cash flow and November 30, 2009, cash balance | | 5,900 |

A source of cash causes the cash flow to increase, also called a cash inflow. For example, in Exhibit 15-2, the $25,000 cash received as owner's investment from John is a financing activity that is a source of cash. A use of cash causes cash flow to decrease, also called a cash outflow. In Exhibit 15-2,Darming's $20,000 cash payment for purchase of land is a use of cash. By reporting cash flows by operating, investing, and financing activities, significant relationships within and among the activities can be evaluated. For example, the cash receipts from issuing bonds can be related to repayments of borrowings when both are reported as financing activities. Also, the impact of each of the three activities (operating, investing, and financing) on cash flows can be identified. This allows investors and creditors to evaluate the effects of a firm's profits on cash flows and its ability to generate cash flows for dividends and for paying debts.

## CASH FLOWS FROM OPERATING ACTIVITIES

Operating activities create revenues, expenses, gains, and losses—net income, which is a product of accrual-basis accounting. The statement of cash flows reports on operating activities. Operating activities are the most important of the 3 categories because they reflect the core of the organization. A successful business must generate most of its cash from operating activities.

There are 2 ways to format operating activities on the statement of cash flows:

(1) Indirect method, which reconciles from net income to net cash provided by operating activities.

(2) Direct method, which reports all cash receipts and cash payments from operating activities.

The direct method reports the sources of operating cash and the uses of operating cash. The major source of operating cash is cash received from customers. The major uses of operating cash include cash paid to suppliers for merchandise and services and cash paid to employees for wages. The difference between these operating cash receipts and cash payments is the net cash flow from operating activities. The direct method is illustrated in Exhibit 15-2 for Darming. The 2 methods use different computations, but they produce the same figure for cash from operating activities. The 2 methods do not affect investing or financing activities. Exhibit 15-3 summarizes the differences between the 2 approaches.

**Exhibit 15-3 The difference between direct and indirect methods**

| Direct Method | | Indirect Method | |
|---|---|---|---|
| Collection from Customers | 2,000 | Net income | 600 |
| Deduction | | Adjustments | |
| Payments to suppliers, etc. | (1,100) | Depreciation, etc. | 300 |
| Net cash provided by operating activities | 900 | Net cash provided by operating activities | 900 |

same

## CASH FLOWS FROM INVESTING ACTIVITIES

Investing activities increase and decrease long-term assets, such as computers, land, buildings, equipment, and investments in other companies. Purchases and sales of these assets are investing activities. Investing activities are important, but they are less critical than operating activities.

Cash flows from investing activities are reported on the statement of cash flows by first listing the cash inflows. The cash outflows are then presented. If the inflows are greater than the outflows, net cash flow provided by investing activities is reported. If the inflows are less than the outflows, net cash flow used for investing activities is reported.

The cash flows from investing activities section in the statement of cash flows for Darming from Exhibit 15-2 is shown below.

Cash flows from investing activities:

Cash payments for purchase of land ($20,000)

## CASH FLOWS FROM FINANCING ACTIVITIES

Financing activities obtain cash from investors and creditors. Issuing stock, borrowing money, buying and selling treasury stock, and paying cash dividends are financing activities. Paying off a loan is another example. Financing cash flows relate to long-term liabilities and owners' equity. They are the least important of the 3 categories of cash flows, and that's why they come last. Exhibit 15-4 shows how operating, investing, and financing activities relate to the various parts of the balance sheet.

**Exhibit 15-4 How operating, investing, and financing cash flows affect the balance sheet**

| | | | |
|---|---|---|---|
| Operating Cash Flows → | Current Assets | Current Liabilities | ← Operating Cash Flows |
| Investing Cash Flows → | Long-term Assets | Long-term Liabilities | Financing Cash Flows |
| | | Owner's Equity | |

Cash flows from financing activities are reported on the statement of cash flows by first listing the cash inflows. The cash outflows are then presented. If the inflows are greater than the outflows, net cash flow provided by financing activities is reported. If the inflows are less than the outflows, net cash flow used for financing activities is reported.

The cash flows from financing activities section in the statement of cash flows for Darming from Exhibit 15-2 is shown below.

Cash flows from financing activities:

| | |
|---|---|
| Cash received as owner's investment | $25,000 |
| Deduct cash withdrawal by owner | $2,000 |
| Net cash flow provided by financing activities | $23,000 |

## NONCASH INVESTING AND FINANCING ACTIVITIES

Companies make investments that do not require cash. They also obtain financing other than cash. Our examples have included none of these transactions. Now suppose The Roadster Factory issued common stock valued at $500,000 to acquire a warehouse.

This transaction would not be reported as a cash payment because The Roadster Factory paid no cash. But the investment in the warehouse and the issuance of stock are important.

These noncash investing and financing activities can be reported in a separate schedule under the statement of cash flows. Exhibit 15-5 illustrates noncash investing and financing activities (all amounts are assumed).

**Exhibit 15-5 Noncash investing and financing activities** (all amounts are assumed)

| Noncash Investing and Financing Activities: | |
|---|---|
| Acquisition of building by issuing common stock | 300,000 |
| Acquisition of land by Issuing note payable | 70,000 |
| Payment of long-term debt by issuing common stock | 100,000 |
| Total noncash investing and financing activities | 470,000 |

### NONCASH FLOW PER SHARE

The term cash flow per share is sometimes reported in the financial press. Often, the term is used to mean "cash flow from operations per share". Such reporting may be misleading to users of the financial statements. For example, users might interpret cash flow per share as the amount available for dividends. This would not be the case if most of the cash generated by operations is required for repaying loans or for reinvesting in the business. Users might also think that cash flow per share is equivalent or perhaps superior to earnings per share. For these reasons, the financial statements, including the statement of cash flows, should not report cash flow per share.

## 2. Statement of Cash Flows—The Indirect Method

The indirect method of reporting cash flows from operating activities is normally less costly and more efficient than the direct method. In addition, when the direct method is used, the indirect method must also be used in preparing a supplemental reconciliation of net income with cash flows from operations. The 2005 edition of *Accounting Trends & Techniques* [⊖] reported that 99% of the companies surveyed used the indirect method. For these reasons, we will first discuss the indirect method of preparing the statement of cash flows.

To collect the data for the statement of cash flows, all the cash receipts and cash payments for a period could be analyzed. However, this procedure is expensive and time consuming. A more efficient approach is to analyze the changes in the noncash balance sheet accounts. The logic of this approach is that a change in any balance sheet account (including cash) can be analyzed in terms of changes in the other balance sheet accounts. To illustrate, the accounting equation is rewritten below to focus on the cash account.

$$\text{Assets} = \text{Liabilities} + \text{Stockholders' Equity}$$

$$\text{Cash} + \text{Noncash Assets} = \text{Liabilities} + \text{Stockholders' Equity}$$

$$\text{Cash} = \text{Liabilities} + \text{Stockholders' Equity} - \text{Noncash Assets}$$

⊖ A publication that is published annually by the American Institute of Certified Public accountants for the purpose of updating accounting professionals on current practices of financial reporting.

Any change in the cash account results in a change in one or morenoncash balance sheet accounts. That is, if the cash account changes, then a liability, stockholders' equity, or noncash asset account must also change.

Additional data are also obtained by analyzing the income statement accounts and supporting records. For example, since the net income or net loss for the period is closed to Retained Earnings, a change in the retained earnings account can be partially explained by the net income or net loss reported on the income statement.

To illustrate the statement of cash flows, we use The Roadster Factory Inc., a dealer in auto parts for sports cars. The income statement and comparative balance sheet for The Roadster Factory Inc. on December 31, 2009 and 2008, is used to illustrate the indirect method. This balance sheet is shown in Exhibit 15-6. Selected ledger accounts and other data are presented as needed.

**Exhibit 15-6 Comparative balance sheet and income statement**

The Roadster Factory Inc. Comparative Balance Sheet
December 31, 2009 and 2008

| | 2009 | 2008 | Increase (Decrease) |
|---|---|---|---|
| **Assets** | | | |
| Current | | | |
| Cash | 34,000 | 42,000 | (8,000) |
| Accounts receivable | 96,000 | 81,000 | 15,000 |
| Inventory | 35,000 | 38,000 | (3,000) |
| Prepaid expenses | 8,000 | 7,000 | 1,000 |
| Notes receivable | 21,000 | — | 21,000 |
| Plant assets, net of depreciation | 343,000 | 219,000 | 124,000 |
| Total | 537,000 | 387,000 | 150,000 |
| **Liabilities** | | | |
| Current | | | |
| Accounts payable | 91,000 | 57,000 | 34,000 |
| Salary and wage payable | 4,000 | 6,000 | (2,000) |
| Accrued liabilities | 1,000 | 3,000 | (2,000) |
| Long-term debt | 160,000 | 77,000 | 83,000 |
| **Stockholders' Equity** | | | |
| Common stock | 162,000 | 158,000 | 4,000 |
| Retained earnings | 119,000 | 86,000 | 33,000 |
| Total | 537,000 | 387,000 | 150,000 |

The Roadster Factory Inc.
Income Statement
For the Year Ended December 31, 2009

| | | |
|---|---|---|
| Revenues and gains: | | |
| Sales revenue | 303,000 | |
| Interest revenue | 2,000 | |
| Gain on sale of plant assets | 8,000 | |
| Total revenues and gains | | 313,000 |
| Expenses: | | |
| Cost of goods sold | 150,000 | |
| Salary and wage expense | 56,000 | |
| Depreciation expense | 18,000 | |
| Other operating expense | 17,000 | |
| Income tax expense | 15,000 | |
| Interest expense | 7,000 | |
| Total expenses | | 263,000 |
| Net income | | 50,000 |

## RETAINED EARNINGS

The comparative balance sheet for The Roadster Factory Inc. shows that retained earnings increased $33,000 during the year. Analyzing the entries posted to the retained earnings account indicates how this change occurred.

The retained earnings account must be carefully analyzed because some of the entries to retained earnings may not affect cash. For example, a decrease in retained earnings resulting from issuing a stock dividend does not affect cash. Such transactions are not reported on the statement of cash flows.

## CASH FLOWS FROM OPERATING ACTIVITIES—INDIRECT METHOD

In practice, the list of adjustments often begins with expenses that do not affect cash. Common examples are depreciation of fixed assets and amortization of intangible assets. Thus, in Exhibit 15-7, these two items are added to net income in determining cash flows from operating activities.

Typically, the next adjustments to net income are for gains and losses from disposal of assets. These adjustments arise because cash flows from operating activities should not include investing or financing transactions. For example, assume that land costing $50,000 was sold for $90,000 (a gain of $40,000). The sale should be reported as an investing activity: "Cash receipts from the sale of land, $90,000." However, the $40,000 gain on the disposal of the land is included in net income on the income statement. Thus, the $40,000 gain is deducted from net income in determining cash flows from operations to avoid "double counting" the cash flow from the gain. Likewise, losses from the disposal of fixed assets are added to net income in determining cash flows from operations.

Net income is also adjusted for changes in noncash current assets and current liabilities that support operations. Under the indirect method, these items are often listed last as "changes in current operating assets and liabilities". Under this heading, current assets are listed first, followed by current liabilities. Changes in noncash current assets and current liabilities are the result of revenue or expense transactions that may or may not affect cash flow. For example, a sale of \$10,000 on account increases accounts receivable by \$10,000. However, cash is not affected. Thus, the increase in accounts receivable of \$10,000 between two balance sheet dates is deducted from net income in arriving at cash flows from operating activities. In contrast, a decrease in accounts receivable indicates the collection of cash that may have been reported as revenues in a prior period. Thus, a decrease in accounts receivable is added to net income in arriving at cash flows from operating activities.

Similar adjustments to net income are required for the changes in the other current asset and liability accounts supporting operations, such as inventory, prepaid expenses, accounts payable, and other accrued expenses. The direction of the adjustment is shown at the bottom of Exhibit 15-7. For example, an increase in accounts payable from the beginning to the end of the period would be added to net income in determining cash flows from operating activities.

The effect of dividends payable, though a current liability, is not included in the operating activity section of the statement of cash flows. Dividends payable is omitted from Exhibit 15-7 because dividends are not an operating activity that affects net income. Later in the chapter, we will discuss how dividends are reported in the statement of cash flows as a part of financing activities. In the following paragraphs, we will discuss each of the adjustments that convert The Roadster Factory Inc.'s net income to "Cash flows from operating activities".

Depreciation has no effect on cash. But depreciation, like all other expenses, decreases net income. Therefore, to convert net income to cash flows, we add depreciation back to net income. The add-back cancels the earlier deduction.

For example: Suppose you had only 2 transactions, a \$1,000 cash sale and depreciation expense of \$300. Cash flow from operations is \$1,000, and net income is \$700 (\$1,000 - \$300). To go from net income (\$700) to cash flow (\$1,000), we add back the depreciation (\$300). amortization are treated like depreciation.

**Gain on Sale of Plant Assets**

Sales of long-term assets are investing activities and there's often a gain or loss on the sale. On the statement of cash flows, the gain or loss is an adjustment to net income. During 2009, The Roadster Factory sold equipment for \$62,000. The book value was \$54,000, so there was a gain of \$8,000. The \$62,000 cash received from the sale is an investing activity, and the \$62,000 includes the \$8,000 gain. Net income also includes the gain, so we must subtract the gain from net cash provided by operations, as shown in the statement of cash flows (we explain investing activities in the next section).

**Exhibit 15-7 Adjustments to net income (loss) using the indirect method**

Net income (loss)

Adjustments to reconcile net income to net cash flow operating activities:

Depreciation of fixed assets

Amortization of intangible assets

Losses on disposal of assets

Gain on disposal of assets

Changes in current operating assets and liabilities

Increase in noncash current operating assets

Decrease in noncash current operating assets

Increase in current operating liabilities

Decrease in current operating liabilities

Net cash flow from operating activities

| Subtract | Add |
|---|---|
| Increase in accounts receivable | Decrease in accounts receivable |
| Increase in inventory | Decrease in inventory |
| Increase in prepaid expenses | Decrease in prepaid expenses |
| Decrease in accounts payable | Increase in accounts payable |
| Decrease in accrued expenses payable | Increase in accrued expense payable |

**Depreciation**

Depreciation is added back to net income to convert net income to cash flow. Let's see why.
Depreciation is recorded as follows.

| Depreciation Expenses | | Accumulated Depreciation | |
|---|---|---|---|
| $18,000 | | | $18,000 |

A loss on the sale of plant assets also creates an adjustment in the operating section. Losses are added back to net income to compute cash flow from operations.

**Changes in Current Operating Assets and Liabilities**

Most current assets and current liabilities result from operating activities. For example, accounts receivable result from sales, inventory relates to cost of goods sold, and so on. Changes in the current accounts are adjustments to net income on the cash flow statement. The reasoning follows:

(1) An increase in another current asset decreases cash. It takes cash to acquire assets. Suppose you make a sale on account. Accounts receivable are increased, but cash isn't affected yet. Exhibit 15-6 reports that during 2009, The Roadster Factory's Accounts Receivable increased by $ 15,000. To compute cash flow from operations, we must subtract the $ 15,000 increase in Accounts Receivable, as shown in Exhibit 15-7. The reason is this: We have not collected this $ 15,000 in cash. The same logic applies to all the other current assets. If they increase, cash de-

creases.

(2) A decrease in another current asset increases cash. Suppose The Roadster Factory's Accounts Receivable balance decreased by $4,000. Cash receipts caused Accounts Receivable to decrease, so we add decreases in Accounts Receivable and the other current assets to net income.

(3) A decrease in a current liability decreases cash. Payment of a current liability decreases both cash and the liability, so we subtract decreases in current liabilities from net income. In Exhibit 15-6, the $2,000 decrease in Accrued Liabilities is subtracted to compute net cash provided by operations.

(4) An increase in a current liability increases cash. The Roadster Factory's Accounts Payable increased. That can occur only if cash was not spent to pay this debt. Cash payments are therefore less than expenses and The Roadster Factory has more cash on hand. Thus, increases in current liabilities increase cash.

**Reporting Cash Flows from Operating Activities**

We have now presented all the necessary adjustments to convert the net income to cash flows from operating activities for The Roadster Factory Inc. These adjustments are summarized in Exhibit 15-8 for the statement of cash flows.

**Exhibit 15-8 Cash flows from operating activities—indirect method**

| | | |
|---|---|---|
| Cash flows from operating activities | | |
| Net income (loss) | | 50,000 |
| Adjustments to reconcile net income to net cash provided by operating activities: | | |
| Depreciation | 18,000 | |
| Gain on sale of plant assets | (8,000) | |
| Changes in current operating assets and liabilities: | | |
| Increase in accounts receivable | (15,000) | |
| Decrease in inventory | 3,000 | |
| Increase in prepaid expenses | (1,000) | |
| Increase in accounts payable | 34,000 | |
| Decrease in salary and wage payable | (2,000) | |
| Decrease in accrued liabilities | (2,000) | 27,000 |
| Net cash provided by operating activities | | 77,000 |

## CASH FLOWS USED FOR PAYMENT OF DIVIDENDS

If dividend payments are not given elsewhere, they can be computed. The Roadster Factory's dividend payments are computed in Exhibit 15-9.

**Exhibit 15-9 Roadster Factory's dividend payments**

| Retained Earnings | | | | |
|---|---|---|---|---|
| Beginning balance | + Net income | – Dividend declarations and payments | = | Ending balance |
| 86,000 | + 50,000 | – $X$ | = | 119,000 |
| | | – $X$ | = | 119,000 - 86,000 - 50,000 |
| | | $X$ | = | 17,000 |

Exhibit 15-10also show the dividend computation.

**Exhibit 15-10 Roadster Factory's dividend payments**

| Retained Earnings | | |
|---|---|---|
| Dividend declarations and payments | Beginning balance | 86,000 |
| | Net income | 50,000 |
| 17,000 | Ending balance | 119,000 |

## COMMON STOCK

This cash flow can be determined from the stock accounts. For example, cash received from issuing common stock is computed from Common Stock and Capital in Excess of Par. We use a single summary Common Stock account as we do for plant assets. The Roadster Factory data are:

| Common Stock | | | | |
|---|---|---|---|---|
| Beginning Balance | + | Issuance of new stock | = | Ending Balance |
| $ 158,000 | + | $ 4,000 | = | $ 162,000 |

| Common Stock | | |
|---|---|---|
| | Beginning balance | $ 158,000 |
| | Issuance of new stock | $ 4,000 |
| | Ending balance | $ 162,000 |

## ISSUANCES AND PAYMENTS OF LONG-TERM DEBTS

The beginning and ending balances of Long-Term Debt, Notes Payable, or Bonds Payable come from the balance sheet. If either new issuances or payments are known, the other amount can be computed. The Roadster Factory's new debt issuances total $ 94,000, as shown in Exhibit 15-11.

**Exhibit 15-11 Roadster Factory's long-term debt**

| Long-term Debt (Notes Payable, Bonds Payable) | | | | | | |
|---|---|---|---|---|---|---|
| Beginning balance | + | Issuance of new debt | – Payments of debt | = | Ending balance |
| 77,000 | + | 94,000 | – $X$ | = | 160,000 |
| | | | – $X$ | = | 160,000 – 77,000 – 94,000 |
| | | | $X$ | = | 11,000 |

| Long-term Debt | | |
|---|---|---|
| | Beginning balance | 77,000 |
| Payments11,000 | Issuance of new debt | 94,000 |
| | Ending balance | 160,000 |

## PURCHASES AND SALES OF PLANT ASSETS

Companies keep a separate account for each plant asset. But for computing cash flows, it is helpful to combine all the plant assets into a single summary account. Also, we subtract accumulated depreciation and use the net figure. It's easier to work with a single plant asset account.

To illustrate, observe that:

(1) The Roadster Factory's Balance sheet reports beginning plant assets, net of accumulated depreciation, of $219,000. The ending balance is $343,000.

(2) Income statement shows depreciation expense of $18,000 and an $8,000 gain on sale of plant assets.

The Roadster Factory's purchases of plant assets total $196,000. How much, then, are the proceeds from the sale of plant assets? First, we must determine the book value of the plant assets sold, as shown in Exhibit 15-12.

**Exhibit 15-12 Calculation of the book value of the plant assets sold**

| Plant Asset, Net | | | | |
|---|---|---|---|---|
| Beginning balance | + Acquisitions | − Depreciation | − Book value of assets sold | = Ending balance |
| 219,000 | +196,000 | −18,000 | − *X* | = 343,000 |
| | | | −*X* | = 343,000 − 219,000 − 196,000 + 18,000 |
| | | | *X* | = 54,000 |

The sale proceeds are $62,000, determined as follows.

| Sale proceeds | = | Book value of assets sold | + Gain − Loss |
|---|---|---|---|
| *X* | = | $54,000 | + $8,000 − $0 |
| *X* | = | $62,000 | |

Trace the sale proceeds of $62,000 to the statement of cash flows. The Plant Assets T-account provides another look at the computation of the book value of the assets sold, as shown in Exhibit 15-13.

**Exhibit 15-13 Calculation of the book value of the plant assets sold in T-account**

| Plant Assets, Net | | | |
|---|---|---|---|
| Beginning balance | 219,000 | Depreciation | 18,000 |
| Acquisition | 196,000 | Book value of assets sold | 54,000 |
| Ending balance | 343,000 | | |

If the sale resulted in a loss of $3,000, the sale proceeds would be $51,000 ($54,000 − $3,000), and the statement of cash flows would report $51,000 as a cash receipt from this investing activity.

## PREPARING THE STATEMENT OF CASH FLOWS

Let's step back and evaluate The Roadster Factory's operating cash flows during 2009. The Roadster Factory's operations provided net cash flow of $77,000. This amount exceeds net income, and it should because of the add-back of depreciation. Now let's examine The Roadster Factory's investing and financing activities, as reported in Exhibit 15-14.

**Exhibit 15-14 Statement of cash flows—indirect method**

The Roadster Factory Inc.
Statement of Cash Flows
For the Year Ended December 31,2009

| | | |
|---|---|---|
| Cash flows from operating activities: | | |
| Net income | | 50,000 |
| Depreciation | 18,000 | |
| Gain on sale of plant assets | (8,000) | |
| Increase in accounts receivable | (15,000) | |
| Decrease in inventory | 3,000 | |
| Increase in prepaid expenses | (1,000) | |
| Increase in accounts payable | 34,000 | |
| Decrease in salary and wage payable | (2,000) | |
| Decrease in accrued liabilities | (2,000) | 27,000 |
| Net cash provided by operating activities | | 77,000 |
| Cash flows from investing activities: | | |
| Acquisition of plant assets | (196,000) | |
| Loan to another company | (21,000) | |
| Proceeds from sale of plant assets | 62,000 | |
| Net cash used for investing activities | | (155,000) |
| Cash flows from financing activities: | | |
| Proceeds from issuance of long-term debt | 94,000 | |
| Proceeds from issuance of common stock | 4,000 | |
| Payment of long-term debt | (11,000) | |
| Payment of dividends | (17,000) | |
| Net cash provided by financing activities | | 70,000 |
| Net Increase (Decrease) in cash | | (8,000) |
| Cash balance, December 31, 2008 | | 42,000 |
| Cash balance, December 31, 2009 | | 34,000 |

## 3. Statement of Cash Flows—The Direct Method

The Financial Accounting Standards Board (FASB) prefers the direct method of reporting operating cash flows because it provides clearer information about the sources and uses of cash. But only about 1% of companies use this method because it takes more computations than the indirect method. Investing and financing cash flows are unaffected by the operating cash flows.

To illustrate the statement of cash flows, we use The Roadster Factory, Inc., a dealer in auto parts for sports cars. To prepare the statement of cash flows by the direct method, proceed as follows.

**Step 1**: Lay out the template of the statement of cash flows by the direct method, as shown in Exhibit 15-15.

**Step 2**: Use the balance sheet to determine the increase or decrease in cash during the period. The change in cash is the "check figure" for the statement of cash flows. The Roadster Factory's comparative balance sheet shows that cash decreased by \$8,000 during 2009. Why did cash fall during 2009? The statement of cash flows explains.

**Step 3**: Use the available data to prepare the statement of cash flows. The Roadster Factory's transaction data appear in Exhibit 15-16. These transactions affected both the income statement and the statement of cash flows. Some transactions affect one statement and some affect the other. For example, sales are reported on the income statement. Cash collections go on the statement of cash flows. Other transactions, such as interest expense and payments affect both statements. The statement of cash flows reports only those transactions with cash effects.

**Exhibit 15-15 Template of the statement of cash flows—direct method**

The Roadster Factory Inc.
Statement of Cash Flows
Year Ended December 31, 2009

| | | |
|---|---|---|
| Cash flows from operating activities: | | |
| Receipts: | | |
| Collections from customers | | |
| Interest received on notes receivable | | |
| Total cash receipts | | |
| Payments: | | |
| To suppliers | | |
| To employees | | |
| For interest | | |

(Continued)

| |
|---|
| For income tax |
| Total cash payments |
| Net cash provided by (used for) operating activities |
| Cash flows from investing activities |
| ⋮ |
| Cash flows from financing activities |
| ⋮ |
| Net increase (decrease) in cash during the year |
| + Cash balance at December 31, 2008 |
| = Cash balance at December 31, 2009 |

**Exhibit 15-16 Summary of the Roadster Factory's 2009 transactions**

| |
|---|
| Operating Activities |
| 1. Sales on credit, 303,000 |
| 2. Collections from customers, 288,000 |
| 3. Interest revenue and receipts, 2,000 |
| 4. Cost of goods sold, 150,000 |
| 5. Purchase of inventory on credit, 147,000 |
| 6. Payments to suppliers, 133,000 |
| 7. Salary and wage expense, 56,000 |
| 8. Payments of salary and wages, 58,000 |
| 9. Depreciation expense, 18,000 |
| 10. Other operating expense, 17,000 |
| 11. Income tax expense and payments, 15,000 |
| 12. Interest expense and payments, 7,000 |
| Investing Activities |
| 13. Cash payments to acquire plant assets, 196,000 |
| 14. Loan to another company, 21,000 |
| 15. Proceeds from sale of plant assets, 62,000, including 8,000 gain |
| Financing Activities |
| 16. Proceeds from issuance of long-term debts, 94,000 |
| 17. Proceeds from issuance of common stock, 4,000 |
| 18. Payment of long-term debt, 11,000 |
| 19. Declaration and payment of cash dividends, 17,000 |

## CASH RECEIVED FROM CUSTOMERS

Both cash sales and collections of accounts receivable are reported on the statement of cash flows as "Cash received from customers, $288,000".

Cash received from customers (cash collections) start with sales revenue (an accrual-basis amount). The Roadster Factory's income statement (Exhibit 15-6) reports sales of $303,000. Accounts receivable increased from $81,000 at the beginning of the year to $96,000 at year end, a $15,000 increase (Exhibit 15-6). Based on those amounts, Cash Collections equal $288,000, as shown in Exhibit 15-17.

**Exhibit 15-17 Calculation of the cash received from customers**

| Accounts Receivable | | | | |
|---|---|---|---|---|
| Beginning balance | + | Sales | – Collections | = Ending balance |
| 81,000 | + | 303,000 | – *X* | = 96,000 |
| | | | – *X* | = 96,000-81,000-303,000 |
| | | | *X* | = 288,000 |

T-account for Accounts Receivable provides another view of same computation, as shown in Exhibit 15-18.

**Exhibit 15-18 Calculation of the cash received from customers in T-account**

| Accounts Receivable | | | |
|---|---|---|---|
| Beginning balance<br>Sales | 81,000<br>303,000 | Collections | 288,000 |
| Ending balance | 96,000 | | |

## CASH PAYMENTS FOR INVENTORY

Payments for inventory are computed by converting cost of goods sold to cash basis. We use Cost of Goods Sold, Inventory, and Accounts Payable. The calculation of cash payment is shown in Exhibit 15-19.

**Exhibit 15-19 Calculation of cash payment**

| Cost of Goods Sold | | | | | |
|---|---|---|---|---|---|
| Beginning inventory | + | Purchases | – | Ending inventory | = Cost of goods sold |
| 38,000 | +*X* | | – | 35,000 | = 150,000 |
| | *X* | | | | = 150,000 – 38,000 + 35,000 |
| | *X* | | | | = 147,000 |
| **Accounts Payable** | | | | | |
| Beginning balance | + | Purchases | – | Payments for inventory | = Ending balance |
| 57,000 | + | 147,000 | – | *Y* | = 91,000 |
| | | | – | *Y* | =91,000-147,000 -57,000 |
| | | | | *Y* | = 113,000 |

The T-accounts show where the data come from. Start with Cost of Goods Sold, as shown in Exhibit 15-20.

**Exhibit 15-20 Calculation of cash payment in T-account**

| Cost of Goods Sold | |
|---|---|
| Beg. inventory 38,000 | End. Inventory 35,000 |
| Purchases 147,000 | |
| Cost of goods sold 150,000 | |

| Accounts Payable | |
|---|---|
| Payment for Inventory 113,000 | Beg. bal 57,000 |
| | Purchases 147,000 |
| | End. bal 91,000 |

Accounts Payable increased, so payments for inventory are less than purchases.

## CASH PAYMENTS FOR OPERATION EXPENSES

Payments for operating expenses other than interest and income tax are computed from accounts: Prepaid Expenses, Accrued Liabilities, Other Operating Expenses. The process of calculation is shown in Exhibit 15-21.

**Exhibit 15-21 Calculation of cash payments for operating expenses**

Prepaid Expenses

| Beginning balance | + | Payments | − | Expiration of prepaid expense (assumed) | = | Ending Balance |
|---|---|---|---|---|---|---|
| 7,000 | + | X | | −7,000 | = | 8,000 |
| | | X | | | = | 8,000 − 7,000 + 7,000 |
| | | X | | | = | 8,000 |

Accrued Liabilities

| Beginning balance | + | Accrual of expenses at year end (assumed) | − | Payments | = | Ending balance |
|---|---|---|---|---|---|---|
| 3,000 | + | 1,000 | − | X | = | 1,000 |
| | | | − | X | = | 1,000 − 3,000 − 1,000 |
| | | | | X | = | 3,000 |

Other Operating Expenses

| Accrual of expense at year end | + | Expiration of prepaid expense | + | Payments | = | Ending balance |
|---|---|---|---|---|---|---|
| 1,000 | + | 7,000 | + | X | = | 17,000 |
| | | | | X | = | 17,000 − 1,000 − 7,000 |
| | | | | X | = | 9,000 |

Total payments for operating expenses = 8,000 + 3,000 + 9,000 = 20,000

The T-accounts give another picture of the same data, as shown in Exhibit 15-22.

**Exhibit 15-22 Calculation of cash payments for operating expenses in T-account**

| Prepaid Expenses | |
|---|---|
| Beg. bal. 7,000 | Expiration of prepaid |
| Payments 8,000 | expense 7,000 |
| End. bal. 8,000 | |

| Accrued Liabilities | |
|---|---|
| | Beg. bal. 3,000 |
| Payments 3,000 | Accrual of espense |
| | at year end 1,000 |
| | End. bal. 1,000 |

| Other Operating Expenses |
|---|
| Accrual of expense at |
| Year end 1,000 |
| Expiration of prepaid |
| expense 7,000 |
| Payments 9,000 |
| End. bal. 17,000 |

Payments to suppliers include all expenditures for inventory and operating expenses except employee pay, interest, and income taxes. Suppliers are those entities that provide inventory and essential services. For example, a clothing store's suppliers may include Tommy Hilfiger, Adidas, and Ralph Lauren. Other suppliers provide advertising, utilities, and office supplies. So, the payments to suppliers are $133,000($113,000 + $20,000)

## PAYMENTS TO EMPLOYEES

This category includes salaries, wages, and other forms of employee pay. Accrued amounts are excluded because they have not yet been paid. The statement of cash flows reports only the cash payments ( $58,000).

It is convenient to combine all payments to employees into 1 account, Salary and Wage Expense. We then adjust the expense for the change in Salary and Wage Payable, as shown in Exhibit 15-23.

**Exhibit 15-23 Calculation of cash payments to employees**

| Salary and Wage Payable | | | | | |
|---|---|---|---|---|---|
| Beginning balance | + | Salary and wage expense | − | Payments | = Ending balance |
| 6,000 | + | 56,000 | − | $X$ | = 4,000 |
| | | | − | $X$ | = 4,000 − 6,000 − 56,000 |
| | | | | $X$ | = 58,000 |

| Salary and Wage Payable | |
|---|---|
| Payments to employees 58,000 | Beginning balance 6,000<br>Salary and wage expense 56,000 |
| | Ending balance 4,000 |

## INTEREST EXPENSE AND INCOME TAXES

Interest and income tax payments are reported separately. The Roadster Factory paid cash for all its interest and income taxes. Therefore, the same amount goes on the income statement and the statement of cash flows. These payments are operating cash flows because the interest and income tax are expenses.

The Roadster Factory's expense and payment amounts are the same for interest and income tax, so no analysis is required. If the expense and the payment differ, the payment can be computed as above.

## REPORTING CASH FLOWS FROM OPERATING ACTIVITIES—DIRECT METHOD

Exhibit 15-24 is a complete statement of cash flows for The Roadster Factory, Inc. , using the direct method for reporting cash flows from operating activities.

**Exhibit 15-24 Statement of cash flows—direct method**

The Roadster Factory Inc.
Statement of Cash Flows
For the Year Ended December 31, 2009

| | | |
|---|---|---|
| Cash flows from operating activities: | | |
| Receipts: | | |
| Collections from customers | 288,000 | |
| Interest received | 2,000 | |
| Total cash receipts | | 290,000 |
| Payments: | | |
| To suppliers | (133,000) | |
| To employees | (58,000) | |
| For income tax | (15,000) | |
| For interest | (7,000) | |
| Total cash payments | | (213,000) |
| Net cash flow from operating activities | | 77,000 |
| Cash flows from investing activities: | | |
| Acquisition of plant assets | (196,000) | |
| Loans to another company | (21,000) | |
| Proceeds from sale of plant assets | 62,000 | |
| Net cash flow used for investing activities | | (155,000) |
| Cash flows from financing activities: | | |
| Proceeds from issuance of long-term debt | 94,000 | |
| Proceeds from issuance of common stock | 4,000 | |
| Payment of long-term debt | (11,000) | |

(Continued)

| | | |
|---|---|---|
| Payment of dividends | (17,000) | |
| Net cash provided by financing activities | | 70,000 |
| Net Increase(decrease) in cash | | (8,000) |
| Cash balance, December 31, 2008 | | 42,000 |
| Cash balance, December 31, 2009 | | 34,000 |

**TERMINOLOGY:**

Cash Flow per Share: 每股现金流

Cash Flows from Financing Activities:筹资活动产生的现金流量

Cash Flows from Investing Activities:投资活动产生的现金流量

Cash Flows from Operating Activities:经营活动产生的现金流量

Direct Method:直接法

Indirect Method:间接法

Statement of Cash Flows:现金流量表

**QUESTIONS:**

**1. Classify transactions that either provide or use cash into either operating, investing, or financing activities.**

The statement of cash flows reports cash receipts and cash payments by three types of activities: operating activities, investing activities, and financing activities. Investing and financing for a business may be affected by transactions that do not involve cash. The effect of such transactions should be reported in a separate schedule accompanying the statement of cash flows.

**2. Adjust net income for noncash expenses and gains and losses from asset disposals under the indirect method.**

The changes in the noncash balance sheet accounts are used to develop the statement of cash flows, beginning with the cash flows from operating activities.

Determine the cash flows from operating activities using the indirect method by adjusting net income for expenses that do not require cash and for gains and losses from disposal of fixed assets.

**3. Prepare the cash flows from operating activities and the remainder of the statement of cash flows under the direct method.**

The direct method reports cash flows from operating activities by major classes of operating cash receipts and cash payments. The difference between the major classes of total operating cash receipts and total operating cash payments is the net cash flow from operating activities. The investing and financing activities sections of the statement are the same as under the indirect method.

**PROBLEM:**

Bigwood, a public company, is a high street retailer that sells clothing and food. The managing is very disappointed with the current year's results. The company is operations and commissioned a famous designer to restyle its clothing products. This has led to increased sales in both retail lines, yet overall profits are down. Details of the financial statement for the two years to 30 September 2004 are shown in Exhibit 15-25.

**Exhibit 15-25 Details of the financial statement**

| **Income statements:** | **year to 30 September 2004** | | **year to 30 September 2003** | |
|---|---|---|---|---|
| Revenue—clothing | 16,000,000 | | 15,600,000 | |
| —food | 7,000,000 | 23,000,000 | 4,000,000 | 19,600,000 |
| Cost of sales—clothing | 14,500,000 | | 12,700,000 | |
| —food | 4,750,000 | 19,250,000 | 3,000,000 | 15,700,000 |
| Gross profit | | 3,750,000 | | 3,900,000 |
| Other operating expenses | | 2,750,000 | | 1,900,000 |
| Operating profit | | 1,000,000 | | 2,000,000 |
| Interest expense | | 300,000 | | 80,000 |
| Profit before tax | | 700,000 | | 1,920,000 |
| Income tax expense | | 250,000 | | 520,000 |
| Profit for the period | | 450,000 | | 1,400,000 |
| **Summarised Changes in Equity:** | **year to 30 September 2004** | | **year to 30 September 2003** | |
| Retained profit bring forward(b/f) | | 1,900,000 | | 1,100,000 |
| Profit for the period | | 450,000 | | 1,400,000 |
| Dividends paid | | 600,000 | | 600,000 |
| Retained profit carry forward(c/f) | | 1750,000 | | 1,900,000 |
| **Balance sheets as at:** | **30 September 2004** | | **30 September 2003** | |
| Property, plant and equipment at cost | | 17,000,000 | | 9,500,000 |
| Accumulated depreciation | | 5,000,000 | | 3,000,000 |
| | | 12,000,000 | | 6,500,000 |
| Current Assets | | | | |
| Inventory—clothing | 2,700,000 | | 1,360,000 | |
| —food | 200,000 | | 140,000 | |
| Trade receivables | 100,000 | | 50,000 | |
| Bank | 0 | 3,000,000 | 450,000 | 2,000,000 |
| Total assets | | 15,000,000 | | 8,500,000 |

(Continued)

| Balance sheets as at: | 30 September 2004 | | 30 September 2003 | |
|---|---|---|---|---|
| Equity and liabilities | | | | |
| Issued ordinary capital ($1 shares) | | 5,000,000 | | 3,000,000 |
| Share premium | | 1,000,000 | | 0 |
| Retained profits | | 1,750,000 | | 1,900,000 |
| | | 7,750,000 | | 4,900,000 |
| Non-current liabilities | | | | |
| Long-term loans | | 3,000,000 | | 1,000,000 |
| Current liabilities | | | | |
| Bank overdraft | 930,000 | | 0 | |
| Trade payables | 3,100,000 | | 2,150,000 | |
| Current tax payable | 220,000 | 4,250,000 | 450,000 | 2,600,000 |
| | | 15,000,000 | | 8,500,000 |

**Note:** The directors have signaled their intention to maintain annual dividends at $600,000 for the foreseeable future.

**The follow information is relevant:**

(1) The increase in property, plant and equipment was due to the acquisition of five new stores and the refurbishment of someexisting stores during the year. The carrying value of fixtures scrapped at the refurbished stores was $1,200,000; they had originally cost $3,000,000. Bigwood received no scrap proceeds from the fixtures, but did incur costs of $50,000 to remove and dispose of them. The losses on the refurbishment have been charged to operating expenses. Depreciation is charged to cost of sales apportioned in relation to floor area (see below).

| The floor sales areas (in square metres) were: | 30-Sep-2004 | 30-Sep-2003 |
|---|---|---|
| Clothing | 48,000 | 35,000 |
| Food | 6,000 | 5,000 |
| | 54,000 | 40,000 |

(2) The share price of Bigwood averaged $6.00 during the year to 30 September 2003, but was only $3.00 at 30 September 2004.

**Requirement**

Prepare, using the indirect method, a cash flow statement for Bigwood for the year to 30 September 2004.

**Solution**

Cash flow statement for Bigwood for the year to 30 September 2004 is shown in Exhibit 15 – 26.

**Exhibit 15-26 Bigwood-cash flow statement for the year to 30 September 2004**

| | | |
|---|---|---|
| Net profit before tax | | 700,000 |
| Adjustments for: | | |
| Depreciation-non-current assets(1) | 3,800,000 | |
| Loss on disposal of fixtures(1) | 1,250,000 | |
| Interest expense | 300,000 | 5,350,000 |
| Operating profit before working capital changes | | 6,050,000 |
| Increase in inventory( $2,900,000 – $1,500,000) | | (1,400,000) |
| Increase in trade receivables( $100,000- $50,000) | | (50,000) |
| Increase in trade payables( $3,100,000- $2,150,000) | | 950,000 |
| Cash generated from operations | | 5,550,000 |
| Interest paid | | (300,000) |
| Income tax paid(2) | | (480,000) |
| Net cash from operating activities | | 4,770,000 |
| Cash generated from investing activities | | |
| Purchase of Property, plant and equipment(1) | (10,500,000) | |
| Disposal costs of fixtures(1) | (50,000) | (10,550,000) |
| | | (5,780,000) |
| Cash flows from financing activities | | |
| Issue of ordinary shares( $2,000,000 + $1,000,000) | 3,000,000 | |
| Long term loans( $3,000,000 – $1,000,000) | 2,000,000 | |
| Equity dividend paid | (600,000) | 4,400,000 |
| | | (1,380,000) |
| Net decrease in cash and cash equivalents | | 450,000 |
| Cash and Cash equivalents at end period | | (930,000) |

| | | |
|---|---|---|
| Workings: | | |
| (1)Property, plant and equipment-cost | | |
| Balance b/f | | 9,500,000 |
| Disposal | | (3,000,000) |
| Balance c/f | | (17,000,000) |
| Difference cash purchase | | 10,500,000 |
| | | |
| Depreciation | | |
| Balance b/f | | (3,000,000) |

(Continued)

| | | |
|---|---|---|
| Disposal( $3,000,000 - $1,200,000) | | 1,800,000 |
| Balance c/f | | 5,000,000 |
| Difference charge for year | | 3,800,000 |
| | | |
| Disposal | | |
| Cost | | 3,000,000 |
| Depreciation | | (1,800,000) |
| Net book value | | 1,200,000 |
| Cost of disposal | | 50,000 |
| Total loss on disposal | | (1,250,000) |
| | | |
| (2) Income tax paid: | | |
| Provision b/f | | (450,000) |
| Income statement tax charge | | (250,000) |
| Provision c/f | | 220,000 |
| Difference cash paid | | (480,000) |

# References

[1] Wild J J, Shaw K W, Chiappetta B, et al. Principles of Accounting [M] 20th ed. New York: McGraw-Hill, 2010.

[2] Harrison, Horngren, Financial Accounting [M] 7th ed. Beijing: Tsinghua University Press, 2008.

[3] Black G, Introduction to Accounting and Finance [M]. Englewood Cliffs, N. J.: Prentice Hall, 2005.

[4] Warren, Reeve, Fess, Accounting [M]. 23th ed. Beijing: China Machine Press, 2011.

[5] Kieso D E, Weygandt J J, Intermediate Accounting [M]. 12th ed. Beijing: China Renmin University Press, 2007.